WORK, SOCIETY AND POLITICS

The culture of the factory in later Victorian England

WORK, SOCIETY AND POLITICS

The culture of the factory
in later Victorian England

PATRICK JOYCE

Lecturer in History,
University of Manchester

THE HARVESTER PRESS

First published in Great Britain in 1980 by
THE HARVESTER PRESS LIMITED

Publishers : John Spiers and Margaret A. Boden
16 Ship Street, Brighton, Sussex

© Patrick J. Joyce, 1980

British Library Cataloguing in Publication Data

Joyce, Patrick
  Work, society and politics.
  1. England—Industries—History
  1. Title
  301. 2′ 43′ 09427   HC255

  ISBN 0-85527-680-0

Photosetting by Thomson Press (India) Limited, New Delhi
Printed in Great Britain by Redwood Burn Limited, Trowbridge & Esher

CONTENTS

v

Contents

TABLES, MAPS, FIGURES AND PHOTOGRAPHS

Figures

Photographs

Between pages 134 and 135

A note on sources: guidance to the documents used is provided in the apparatus of notes. Place of publication is London unless otherwise stated. Chapter summaries are printed at the end of each chapter and the epilogue.

ACKNOWLEDGEMENTS

THIS book was long in the making, and it would be difficult to express my debt to all who contributed to its completion. To those not mentioned by name I can only plead the limitation of the present written convention. From the earliest days the advice and encouragement of Dr Brian Harrison and Professor John Vincent have been a special source of support. The generosity of historians with whose work one takes issue is a special source of pleasure in the writing of history, and I acknowledge with gratitude the criticism and interest shown by Dr John Foster and Dr Peter Clarke. Mrs Dorothy Thompson, Mr Raphael Samuel, Dr John Marshall and the late Professor H.J. Dyos have also been generous with their time and their historical insight. Of those who read parts of the manuscript of this book, the advice of Dr Gareth Stedman Jones, Mr E.P. Thompson and Lord Asa Briggs has been especially helpful. I would also like to express my thanks to Mr Philip Waller, Professor E.J. Hobsbawm and Professor A.G. Dickens. To none of those mentioned, or un-mentioned, can be attributed any errors of fact or judgement that the book contains.

The librarians and staff of the Lancashire and Yorkshire public and university libraries, and of the Lancashire Record Office, eased the labour of research greatly. I remember with particular gratitude the interest and expertise of the local history departments in Manchester and Bradford Central Libraries, and in the Public Libraries of Blackburn and Ashton-under-Lyne. To the many who accorded me hospitality and guidance in the industrial North – publicans and clergymen, political clubmen, the officers of trade unions and employers' associations – I extend my warmest thanks. I should also like to thank Janice and Tom Cleary for help in the preparation of the manuscript, and Mr John Spiers for his encouragement along the road to its publication. My debt to my wife can only be expressed in the dedication of this work.

My thanks are due to Manchester University Library and Liverpool Central Library for making the Kay-Shuttleworth and Derby papers available to me, also to Paul Thompson and Thea Vigne for permission to quote from the oral history archive at Essex University. Parts of chapters five and six originally appeared as 'The factory politics of Lancashire in the later nineteenth century', in *The Historical Journal*, 18, 3 (1975). The photographs came from the Manchester Polytechnic Cotton Industry Records Project, and my special thanks are due to Jill Liddington, Manchester Studies Unit, Manchester Polytechnic. The research and writing of the book were made possible by a Social Science Research Council postdoctoral research fellowship, and its typing by an award from the Twenty-Seven Foundation at the University of London. My debt to the Institute of Historical Research over the years has been very considerable.

P.J.J.

To Rosaleen and Séan

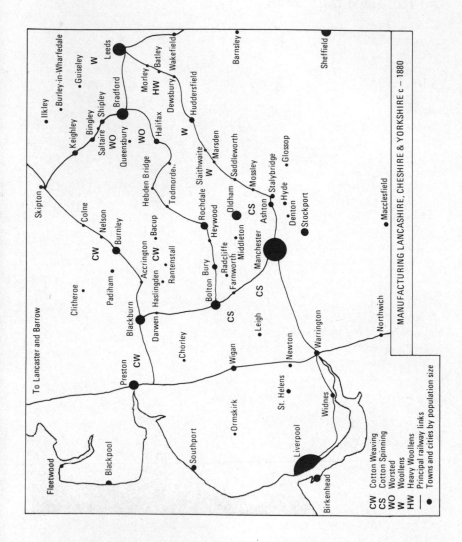

MANUFACTURING LANCASHIRE, CHESHIRE & YORKSHIRE c – 1880

CW   Cotton Weaving
CS   Cotton Spinning
WO   Worsted
W   Woollens
HW   Heavy Woollens
——   Principal railway links
●   Towns and cities by population size

INTRODUCTION

THIS work had its inception in an attempt to write the history of popular politics in the period between the decline of Chartism and the rise of independent Labour politics towards the end of the nineteenth century. What had been questions about politics very quickly resolved themselves into questions about class, and it became apparent that the answer to most of these questions was to be found in the world of work. The history of politics was in the end indistinguishable from the history of work and its cultures. Probably the central theme in such a history must be the rise of factory production and the creation of a factory proletariat. The manufacturing districts of Lancashire and the West Riding of Yorkshire were the cradle of factory production, and it is to them that posterity has looked in seeking to discern the nature of the class structure to which the new system of manufacture gave rise.

If the factory system was perhaps the most characteristic expression of modernity in nineteenth-century economic organisation, it was not the only such mark nor the sole means of industrial production to which attention must be directed. Thus this book makes no claim to a comprehensive understanding of nineteenth-century British society, and is primarily about the social system to which factory production gave rise in the North after about 1850. In being primarily about the northern factory, and most of all about the textile factory, it has, nonetheless, much to say by implication not only about factory industry in Britain and elsewhere, but also about the wider relationship of work and social outlook.

The force of that relationship is urged with some insistence in this work. No single area of experience defined all of experience, but when the business of reconstructing the society of the northern factory had been entered upon it became clear that so much of what had seemed to lie outside the purview of work was in truth an expression of the experience of work. The now unsmoking chimneys of the factory towns had dominated not only the physical but the mental landscape of these years to an extent that is difficult now to realise. What a contemporary called 'the rule of the tall chimneys' had entered into the workpeople's lives to a degree that made their acceptance of the social regime of capitalist industry a matter of inward emotion as much as of outward calculation. It is the intimacy of the link between work and mentality, so profusely revealed in the evidence, that justifies the degree of attention given the cultures of work in what follows. A recognition that the social relations of employer and worker amounted to more than a matter of coercion and resignation alone, and involved the internalisation of an entire social reality, in turn suggested forcibly that the history which had brought such a situation about should be looked at again.

Thus it is to the course of the industrial revolution itself that attention has to be redirected. Contrary to received opinion, it was not until the years around mid-century that mechanised factory production was consolidated in the North; and, contrary to the simplified version of class formation arising from the prevailing version of industrial change, the human consequences of factory industry were vastly more subtle and elusive than is so often thought. In tracing the character of these consequences the application of the 'labour aristocracy' notion to the factory worker does not seem especially productive.[1] A concentration on what is taken to be an élite in the working class not only diverts attention from the majority, but fails also to discern that what working people had in common is more important for an understanding of class relationships than that which is held to have divided them in work and in the life beyond work.

The injunction to study the mass of the working class and not its minorities, the cultures of everyday life and not the institutional arrangements of organised labour and organised politics, is one that has been followed with great energy in recent years. This is of the utmost value, but so often it is the moments of conflict only that are culled from the life of the people. It is with an awareness of this imbalance in the record that much attention will be given here to what can be termed the mechanics of social stability and class domination, and to the emergence of feelings sufficiently deep-rooted to be called deference. An appreciation of the attenuation rather than the augmentation of class consciousness has been greatly retarded by the tendency, implicit in the 'labour aristocracy' notion as well, to conceive of class as an idealized, platonic category; in Edward Thompson's words, as a 'thing' and not a 'relationship'.[2]

The idealist notion of class prejudges the central problems concerning the formation of class consciousness. In the context of the labour aristocracy argument, when the evidence is considered there are no grounds for imagining that the revolutionary, class-conscious potential of the majority was choked back by a reformist labour aristocracy.[3] On the contrary, when the reductionist implications of the structuralist conception of class are rejected, and the formation of class consciousness is seen as the product of concrete, problematic historical process, it is clear that the labour aristocracy notion explains a problem that exists rather less in nineteenth-century history than in twentieth-century historiography. Reformism was not the product of a mid-nineteenth-century labour aristocracy but evolved in all its qualifications and ambiguities out of the working-class radical tradition. Far from being the 'moderates', the labour aristocrats were in the forefront of radical politics in this period. It is in this light that the politics of labour will be considered in our last chapter. The politics of labour, however, were only vestigially the politics of the factory workforces. Such politics were chiefly the concern of those outside the cultural environment of the factory, and especially the craft and skilled sectors in the working class. If these were a labour aristocracy then it was independence rather than reformist 'collaboration' that was their political legacy.

More recent exponents of the labour aristocracy notion than John Foster, in particular Robert Gray and Geoffery Crossick, have combined the traditional argument with a more flexible working of the idea of 'ideological hegemony'.[4] Whatever the merits of this work on the 'traditional' labour aristocracy – the workshop trades in which the factory system was but little advanced – it is to be doubted if this concentration on a common stock of ideas in mediating the social relations of the classes can take us very far when it comes to the experience of the factory proletariat. The kind of social attitudes held to have been represented by the 'negotiated' acceptance of ruling-class values among the craft workers were of an altogether different nature from those found among factory workers. The operation of 'ideological hegemony' does not begin to explain the inwardness that characterised the accommodation of so many of the northern factory workers in the social system of modern, factory production. This accommodation occurred not so much at the level of ideas and values, but at the centre of people's daily concerns, in terms of their sense of personal and communal identity. This was so because work got under the skin of life.

When the labour aristocracy idea is set to one side, an array of possibilities present themselves as explanations for the more accommodative, quiescent popular attitudes seen after mid-century. What is argued here is that in the factory North it was the social effect of the capitalist workplace that mattered most. This was the case because so many of these other aspects – education, religion, leisure, the family, and so on – were not in fact discrete areas of experience but had their most profound effect on class relations in so far as they were aspects of the culture of the factory. The degree to which the late nineteenth-century factory dominated the world of the operative can hardly be exaggerated.

It is in urging the peculiar force of this influence that most of the difficulties of interpretation lie. What is so significant about work is that it was the source of defensive forms of class solidarity *and* of a culture of subordination. In saying that the seemingly conflicting could in the concrete historical situation be quite compatible one is saying something perhaps not often enough said. In maintaining that deference existed, and that it had an inwardness, one is not disputing the centrality of class consciousness in industrial society. About this there should be no confusion: deference was an aspect of the class relationship of employers and workpeople with sufficient power at the time greatly to erode the consciousness of conflict but never to displace it, to change the form in which conflict was perceived but not to obliterate its perception.

The institutions of working-class self-help, from the trade union to the co-op, represented a cultural autonomy and class identification that were in tension with the world of the factory. Similarly, the world of the factory was itself shot through by ambiguity and contradiction. No form of class hegemony is reducible to mere social control. Rather than the unilateral imposition of cultural uniformity from above, such situations always involve mutual constraints, boundaries beyond which neither side can trespass if the social relationship in question is to remain viable; and the hegemony the northern employer class exerted in the second half of the century was no exception. A sense of this complexity informs this work as a whole, and is given special emphasis in the discussion of trade unionism in chapter 2, of deference in chapter 3, and of class cultures and political cultures in chapter 8.

That for some readers this sense may not be argued with sufficient insistence is a consequence of the attempt made here to comprehend the implications of the enormous influence of the factory at the time. The danger of any insistence that deference represented only the conscious 'negotiation' of class relationships is that the reality of the internalisation of the paternalist ethos is lost sight of, and its significance evaded. If it is granted that such an internalisation did take place (and to deny it would seem to contradict the weight of the evidence to hand), then the fact that it did so in nineteenth-century English industrial society is really of the first importance.[5] For it is class consciousness and conflict that have traditionally been associated with the nineteenth-century factory system. This is why, in the following, more attention is directed to the rootedness of deference than to the qualifications that hedged it about. The widespread reluctance of British labour historians to explore the reverse of the coin of independence has equally contributed to the degree of attention given here to deference and dependence.

The reason for this concentration on the moral legitimation of class domination lies not only in the fact of internalisation but even more in its mechanics. For it is these that remind us how complex was the social articulation of class consciousness. The desire for a more subtle and responsive understanding of class formation has been a primary motive in the writing of this book. A distinction between the 'ideological' and the communal or social will already be apparent: notions of 'ideological hegemony', in their concentration on the nexus of ideas defined by the terms 'respectability' and 'self-improvement', fail to comprehend that it was at the deeper level of family and community that the workpeople's accommodation in the social system of the factory was enacted.

In attacking the 'structural reductionism' of the idealist notion of class, Edward Thompson has been pre-eminent in stressing that whatever mediates the social relations of one class with another grows out of the soil of the means of production and is not imposed from without as 'superstructure'.[6] In Thompson's (and subsequent) hands, 'hegemony' has rightly been seen as carrying with it the freight of independence. It is, however, the truth of the obverse of this that in the present state of historical scholarship demands attention: the *success* of employer hegemony in the North is what really stands in need of detailed explanation. And, in Thompson's own terms, that success grew out of the centre of people's lives and was not something imposed from without. At the time it was work that was at the centre of people's lives, and it was ideological values that were external. Such values were at most merely subsidiary to the quotidian life of the factory and its neighbourhood, and in all likelihood bore no comparison to the real nature of working-class culture. Without wishing to proceed further into the swampy terrain of current Marxology, the distinction between the 'ideological' and 'social' will be maintained and explored throughout the course of this work. The subordination of the factory proletariat was both more profound and less profound than has been supposed: the middle-class gospel of 'improvement' made few inroads in working-class life, but that life was deeply marked by the social régime of the factory.

In order to appreciate the depth of this influence the nature of industrial change in the mid-nineteenth-century years has to be understood anew. Recent work on the coming of factory production outside Britain has very rightly suggested that the ascription of class consciousness and political action solely to factory mechanisation and the changed society it brought about is a simplistic reading of the historical process.[7] Rather than 'rational' factory production producing class awareness, the links with pre-factory modes of production and the network of life inside and outside the factory have to be considered. This is so, but only a part of the story. For the pre-factory link and the 'artisan' tradition have to be understood in a rather more complex way than this. Especially in Lancashire, they could be powerful sources of integration in the system of authority to which factory production gave rise. Just as the legacy brought into the factory was of multiform social effect, so too was the experience of factory mechanisation itself.

The Lancashire textile industry represented the first, and in the mid-century years the most completely developed, example of factory production in the world. It attained this peak of development much later than is often realised. It was not until the two decades following the mid-1830s that mechanisation reached anything like its full nineteenth-century extent, and, most important of all, not until then that the mechanisation of adult male labour was completed with any thoroughness. This altered perspective on the course of industrial change in turn demands a revised conception of the social transformation such change brought about. Lancashire was the first: elsewhere the outcome of the transition to mechanised factory production would not thereafter be in doubt. In Lancashire it was, and the realisation of the permanence of industrial capitalism was of profound psychological effect. This awareness, however, was only one facet of a whole range of social changes that the consolidation of factory production was ushering in. Marx's panoptic vision of the power inherent in what he termed 'Modern Industry' is as good a guide as any to what many of these changes amounted to.[8] Unlike many who have followed in his stead, he knew how deeply the experience of authority and dependence was felt among a factory proletariat subject to the full brunt of mechanisation. In chapter 3 these consequences will be given the emphasis they warrant. However much the attitudes emerging in the factory North after 1850 have to be interpreted in terms of consent, consent was always inseparable from the experience of work authority and economic dependence. This experience was common to workers new to the textile industry and to those with experience of the industry before the consolidation of the factory system around mid-century.

With regard to the latter, it is the Marxian emphasis on control over the labour process that is so suggestive when the consequences of dependence come to be more fully explored. In chapter 2 it will be argued that what makes this period of such strategic importance in the history of industrialisation was the passage of control over the labour process from the worker to the employer. The distinction between 'real' and 'formal' control of the work process has recently been interpreted by Gareth Stedman Jones in the light of the historical experience of Lancashire, and it is to this revealing essay that a debt must be acknowledged here.[9] In the identification of this central development the fully complex social effect of the legacy brought into the mid-nineteenth-century factory begins to manifest itself.

In both factory and domestic production, early nineteenth-century industry retained very powerful elements of craft practice and craft-mindedness. What seems to have been happening around mid-century was that the substance of these long-persisting elements of craft autonomy and control was being replaced by debased and purely formal distinctions of status.[10] Under the pressure of fully-fledged mechanisation, the retention of these status distinctions appears to have been a chief means whereby the factory worker was brought within the pale of the new disposition of authority in the factory towns. This loss of purchase on the labour process, and the transformation of status that accompanied it, were most advanced where mechanisation was most advanced: in the cotton industry of Lancashire. As will be seen in chapter 2, this basic change is to be regarded as having occurred not in terms of the creation of a labour aristocracy and the fragmentation of working-class culture, but in terms of pressures upon the division of authority and status within the operative family.

Though the evidence is by no means conclusive, it warrants the argument that it was in large part to the resolution of these pressures that can be ascribed the cotton community's acceptance of the wider social order of capitalist industry. When the situation is interpreted in terms of the retention of traditional, paternal authority, then the kinds of attitudes that were to develop later begin to make historical sense. For these attitudes bore all the hallmarks of communal cohesion and identification. With the family as the connecting link between the individual and society, and attitudes to work mutually reinforcing attitudes in the life beyond work, the legitimation of social inequality can be seen to have taken place in terms of the whole community and not a part of it, and to have involved people's own sense of their standing and purpose rather than the exertion of an extraneous ideological domination. The re-stabilisation of the family economy of the operatives is thus to be understood as carrying with it a wider acceptance of the relationship of master and operative the dimensions of which have to be sought in the workings of neighbourhood life and in the sense of community itself. The problematic nature of the legacy of pre-mechanisation days will be apparent.

Concentration on the family, however, provides only one key to an understanding of the work-dominated culture that was to characterise the factory North. The somewhat abstract argument seen in chapter 2 gives way in chapters 3 to 6 to the historical reconstruction of factory society. This exploration, especially as carried forward in chapter 5, must serve to justify the suggestiveness of the theoretical opening. There were many aspects to the emergence of deference: though control and influence could be exerted by all manner of employers, it was the paternalist employer who most successfully translated dependence into deference. In chapter 4 the renewed paternalism of the mid-century years will be examined. The paternalism of the family firm was vastly more important than is generally recognised. In the changed technological and cultural environment after mid-century this piecemeal, unsung paternalism cut more deeply into operative life than had the paternalism of the early founders of industry. It provided the fiction of community that consolidated the communitarian aspects inherent in the new attitudes to authority emerging at the time. Though the reassertion of employer paternalism from the 1840s was sufficiently far-reaching to deserve the adjective 'new', continuities in styles of industrial ownership also marked the transition to fully developed factory production and consolidated the social effect of the workplace: again, the Janus-faced legacy of the past reveals itself.

The degree of paternalism practised depended in large measure on the history of the individual trade and industry. It is here that the comparative, regional aspect to this work comes into play. In this as in so many respects, the textile industries of the West Riding of Yorkshire are a touchstone by which the changes occurring in Lancashire cotton may be understood. Aside from the regional context, the situation in engineering and the coal industry also provides a perspective on the transformation taking place in textiles. As a consequence of later and less complete mechanisation in West Riding textiles, together with the attendant delay in urban growth, the economic organisation of industry across the Pennines was far less favourable to the emergence of industrial paternalism. As a consequence of the relative primitiveness of West Riding industry, the lack of paternalism that resulted from a more exploitative factory system was only one of a range of regional differences that illuminate the links between labour process and social outlook.

The modernity of Lancashire was also reflected in a high degree of trade unionism in cotton, and the most elaborate institutionalisation of labour relations seen anywhere in the kingdom. It was in the most stable economic environments that paternalism thrived best, and the stability and harmony of labour relations in Lancashire contributed much to the success with which paternalism elicited an affirmative response. In the West Riding also, the element of craft autonomy in industry was more resistant than in Lancashire, and the role of the family in the new social climate was only partly effective. Though the regional contrast was by no means absolute – certain trades and certain areas sharing much in common with Lancashire industry – independence rather more than deference was the key-note of class relations in much of the West Riding.

The relationship between labour process and mentality is inexplicable without an understanding of urban change. The fiction of paternalist community was effective to the extent that it accorded with the facts of neighbourhood community. The implications of the discussion of industry and community in chapter 3 are developed in the course of the long chapter 5. The social effect of paternalism is comprehensible only when the nature of population movement, and the changing ecological patterns of the factory town, are related to the characteristics of the factory workforce. What made paternalism so effective was the employers' capacity for defining and thus delimiting the social outlook of the workforce. This capability was facilitated by the development of the later nineteenth-century factory town in such a way that the evolution of the sense of neighbourhood community was permeated by the presence of the workplace. This claim that the sense of community itself was involved in the consolidation of deference will be an argumentative one. Yet it seems to be true that if the attitudes developing out of the culture of the factory are to be properly evaluated then such a formulation is the only one that will suffice. Needless to say, community did not make deference, but deference is inexplicable without a sense of its imbrication in community.

In chapter 6 the politics of the factory districts are interpreted as the logical cultural extension of the wider relationship of employers and workpeople. A recognition that this was so in turn prompts a reappraisal of the later nineteenth-century political system. If social history with the politics left out is a kind of vulgarism, so is politics without the social history. The final part of this book opens outwards beyond the factory work-forces to the political system of the North as a whole. A concern that political and cultural events should be given their due independence but that this independence should always be seen as conditional informs this part of the book as well as the early chapters. The reappraisal of the orthodoxies of political history is begun in the sub-section of chapter 6, where the implications of the factory politics of the North are allowed to illuminate both the political and industrial systems of the other regions.

Given the state of research, this can only be provisional and suggestive. The real work of interpretation is begun in chapter 8, where the cultures of the factory and of religion explicate the political culture of the North. Chapter 7 involves a close look at the impact of religion on life and on politics. This impact, it is suggested, is more comprehensible when seen in social or cultural terms rather than in the terms of belief and practice. The social penumbra of religious affiliation, and the interaction of ethnic feeling and denominational allegiance, compounded a politics that had little to do with politics and religion as commonly understood. The kind of communal, clan-like loyalties revealed in the treatment of religion are seen to be of a piece with the loyalties bred in the work situation. It is in the light of these kinds of loyalty that later Victorian political history bears rewriting. The working-class Tory plays a prominent part in the account of politics given here. This is because he/she is still the most shadowy of figures. Popular Conservatism was undoubtedly of more importance everywhere in the nation than is often allowed, and this was especially so in Lancashire. The 'Tory in clogs' turns out to be a somewhat different phenomenon from that subject to the blinkered scrutiny of twentieth-century sociologists.

The working-class radical tradition is given its due weight in the final chapter on the politics of labour. If these politics were not broadcast widely in society they were sown deeply, and, contrary to the earlier emphasis of this work, this independence is seen to have been powerful and persistent among the restricted circle of working men that was their prime constituency. These men mainly came from outside the factory workforces, and this chapter will take up the political implications of the occupational cultures of these workers previously discussed in the third section of chapter 8.

The history of the factory workforces cannot be understood without the history of the factory owners. The book opens therefore with an extended discussion of the society and politics of the employers. The book as a whole concerns the relations of employer and worker, and from this first chapter develop many of the themes later treated in detail. The history of élite formation, and of the social and political links of industry and land, is a history that remains for the most part related in the generalisations of events at the national level. Chapter 1 is an attempt to redress this imbalance. The employers are studied in and for themselves, as well as in relation to the other elements in the ruling class. The dominant themes are two: the persistence of landed-industrial conflict, the fragmentation of employer society itself, and the role of religion in this diversity; and the growth of a ruling class in which politics, religion and styles of life at last come to match class interest.

Something should finally be said about the approach taken to the writing of this book. It seemed that an inter-regional approach was the best way forward. In determining the nature of a region it was an area's culture rather than its administrative boundaries that was allowed the choice: this is a study of the factory districts in which little will be heard of economically various Liverpool and Leeds. The choice of minute local reconstruction made early in the growth of this work presented certain difficulties: the region revealed the illusion of the nation, the town that of the region, and the locale that of the town. Whatever the difficulties of determining the representative, the town seemed as good a place as any to begin, and the choice of Ashton, Stalybridge and Blackburn does provide a valuable span of industrial and political diversity. However, as the town dissolved into its parts, the necessity of analysis at street and neighbourhood level whenever possible strongly asserted itself.

The reason for the choice of detail at these levels was in part a matter of the demands the chosen past makes on its historian: so much of nineteenth-century social experience was formed at the level of the concrete, the familiar and the immediate. The patterns so hopefully discerned at the national and regional levels disintegrate when the immediate social context is explored. Rather than a counsel of despair, however, it is to be maintained that only when analysis develops out of this context will the deeper and more profound regularities in society be known. The choice of approach was also dictated by the choice of theme: the history of work in its full cultural plentitude. In order to encompass this theme a synthesis of social theory and the fullness of the historical process had to be arrived at. In the present state of sociology and social history this synthesis is likely to be an unsatisfactory one: until the theory of society is subject not merely to the qualification of the historical example but to the wholesale re-ordering of the force of historical change the way ahead will not be easy. Nonetheless, this work is a step along that road: it is to be hoped that something of the necessary tension between structure and event has been maintained in what follows, and that the concrete particular has been given its due eminence in patterning the flow of events with that which is durable.

This is not to be done without a sense for the connectedness of things. The themes of this work and the treatment given them in turn grew out of a desire to reconstruct the totality of the historical experience, and view society in the fullest possible sense of interdependent possibility. However elusive may be the goal of 'totality' in the writing of history, it remains a prize of inestimable value, and the historian's hard-won attempt to grasp it one of his proudest boasts. Within the discipline and the limits of the themes chosen here, if the society of the factory North in the second half of the nineteenth century can be rendered with something approaching the roundedness that its identity as a unique civilisation warrants, then the effort will have been rewarded.

Notes

1. J. Foster, *Class Struggle and the Industrial Revolution* (1974), esp. chp. 7.
2. E.P. Thompson, *The Making of the English Working Class* (1963), Preface.
3. For a useful discussion see H.F. Moorhouse, 'The Marxist theory of the labour aristocracy', *Social History*, *3*, no. 1, Jan. 1976.
4. R.Q. Gray, *The Labour Aristocracy in Victorian Edinburgh* (Oxford 1976); G. Crossick, 'The labour aristocracy and its values: a study of mid-Victorian Kentish London', *Victorian Studies*, *19*, no. 3, March 1976; see also T. Tholfsen, *Working Class Radicalism in Mid-Victorian Britain* (1976).

5. A parallel may be drawn with the work of Eugene Genovese on a very different kind of paternalism and society from those of the factory North. Genovese employs the dialectics of culture and authority to great effect in showing how the Southern slaves' acceptance of a paternalist ethos that involved *reciprocal* rights and obligations not only legitimised class rule but equally developed the slaves' most powerful defence against the dehumanization of slavery. But if, in seeking to rescue the Southern slave from the 'condescension of posterity', Genovese justly concentrates on the elements of dignity and independence, it can be argued that in the generically different environment of nineteenth-century English industrial society it is the element of class subordination rather than autonomy that requires our most urgent attention; cf. E.D. Genovese, *Roll, Jordan, Roll—the world the slaves made* (1975), also 'Rebelliousness and docility in the Negro slave: a critique of the Elkins thesis', in *In Red and Black: Marxian explorations in Southern and Afro-American history* (1971). For a much less satisfactory treatment of the problem of paternalism and deference see H.G. Gutman, *The Family in Slavery and Freedom, 1750–1925* (Oxford 1976), esp. pp. 309–18.
6. E.P. Thompson, *Whigs and Hunters; the origins of the Black Acts* (1975), pp. 258–69.
7. See for example, D.H. Bell, 'Worker culture and worker politics: the experience of an Italian town, 1880–1915', *Social History*, 3, no. 1, Jan. 1978; H.G. Gutman, *Work, Culture and Society in Industrializing America*. (Oxford 1977).
8. K. Marx, *Capital* (Chicago 1915), Vol. 1, pt IV, esp. chp. XV.
9. G. Stedman Jones, 'England's first proletariat: "Class struggle and the Industrial Revolution"', *New Left Review*, 90, Mar.—Apr. 1975.
10. K. Marx, *op. cit.* p. 461.

I
THE ELITES: CLASS, STATUS AND POWER

> At the beginning of this century the nobles were
> rich, the people poor. Circumstances – manu-
> facture and commerce – have made many pleb-
> eians rich. They should stay with the people.
> Alas! many have joined the nobles.
>
> (Isaac Holden, Notebook, 1892)[1]

THERE was truth as well as idealisation in this verdict on his
century by one of the greatest of the Bradford worsted masters.
Much of the truth was in fact to lie in the idealisation: many
among the industrial bourgeosie were to hold firmly to a vision
of themselves as the custodians of a unique industrial civilisation,
the urban character of which they long asserted against the power
and prestige of the landed classes. While the sturdiness of an
historical vision reaching back to the seventeenth century is not
to be gainsaid, the truth of the matter was somewhat different
from the mythology of the matter.

In the account of élite society that follows it will be apparent
that not only did the industrial rich not spring from the 'plebeians',
but they often came out of landed society itself. In Lancashire
especially, there was a substantial urban, industrial Torysim that
often owed much to the landed pedigree, and which continued
a close social and political commerce with landed society. Whether
of landed stock or not, this native, employer Toryism, already
generations old by 1850, is of a significance that has gone largely
unremarked by historians. Anglicanism was the sheet-anchor of
this Toryism, and Anglicanism was the religion of the territorial
gentry and aristocracy: economic origins, and social and religious
life, went far to blur the line between industry and land in parts
of the North. Not only this, however, for landed families who
retained their estates and standing also had close and often
active links with town industry. Beside the industrial connection,
the commercial and social links of land and town were often
strong, receiving expression in the long-continuing influence of
landed wealth in town life.

The social formation of urban Toryism serves to remind us
how long a common class interest had supervened in the general

process of British élite formation. Common economic interests
found expression in an economic ideology the parentage of which
is to be sought as much in the corn belt of agricultural capitalism
as in the manufacturing regions of industrial capitalism.[2] This
conflation of ideological interests was a commonplace in the later
nineteenth-century industrial North. John Wilson-Patten for
instance, among the foremost of the greater Lancashire gentry,
was in the 1850s the parliamentary mouthpiece of the National
Association of Factory Occupiers, the textile employers' anti-
Factory Acts pressure group.[3] In 1860 Wilson-Patten, along
with the aristocratic Tory Egertons and Leghs and the Liberal
Devonshires, was to be numbered among the Council of the
Manchester Cotton Supply Association.[4] Ten years later, Tory
country gentlemen were as active as Liberal employers in support
of the Manchester Free Labour Society.[5]

Yet the interpenetration of land and industry in some sectors
of the employer class, and the direct industrial and commercial
involvement of some landed families, is only one theme in the
complex narrative of class. If political economy could serve
as a bridge between the agrarian and industrial interests it was a
bridge that both sides were often unwilling to cross: 1846 was a
real conflict and a real victory for the industrialists. If, in the
second half of the century, economic conflict gave way to the
conflict over political power, and just as much to the conflict
between styles of life, these conflicts were no less bitter and
protracted for that. It is as mistaken to minimise the persistence
of this conflict as to exaggerate the initial degree of polarisation
between land and industry.

It is the former of these undue emphases that has become
something of the fashion in recent years, both in Marxist and
anti-Marxist circles. Perry Anderson has discerned in the nineteenth-century aristocracy the somewhat unlikely form of 'the
vanguard of the bourgeoisie', successfully imposing its political
power and the ethos of its civilisation upon its more-than-willing
partners in 'the ruling bloc', the industrial bourgeoisie.[6] On the
other side of the divide, the work of Harold Perkin, [7] and more
recently W.D. Rubinstein,[8] has contributed to a similar understanding of the Northern industrial bourgeoisie as the poor
relations among modern British élites, lacking in status, influence
and power when compared with their landed and City-commercial
counterparts, buffeted by the counter 'ideals' of the landed and
professional classes, and increasingly subject to the depredations
of state power.[9]

What follows in this chapter is restricted in terms of both

period and geography. Nevertheless, a limitation to concretely reconstructed local and regional *milieux* can offer commentary on 'theoretical' formulations that are often poorly articulated in terms of what really went on in history. What this study will suggest most forcibly is the complexity of the landed–industrial relation, and the difficulty of providing any easy answer to the question 'who did what to whom' after 1832. To encompass the full amplitude of the historical situation the treatment that follows will be marked by thematic tensions: the first of these was that existing between the continuity of the landed–industrial relation and the slowness of the social and political integration between the two classes. While the disadvantages of not looking from the centre to the localities must be admitted, the advantages of looking outwards from the regions are not inconsiderable.

Looking outwards upon his world in the mid-century years, the Northern industrialist had every cause for self-satisfaction and little cause to consider himself a poor relation. The mid-century years had a strategic importance the nature of which is not always appreciated. If the first quarter of the century saw the making of the English working class, the second quarter may fairly be judged to have seen the making of the northern employer class. After mid-century the industrial bourgeoisie was to leave its iron days behind and enter on its inheritance of power and prestige. Central to this change was the completion of the mechanisation of factory production, for it was only in the two decades before the mid-1850s that this most profound transition was successfully consolidated, confirming the historical inevitability of industrial capitalism in the mind of the employer as much as in the mind of the operative. As will be seen,[10] with the passing of the economic and political crises of the 1840s, the buoyancy of the economic expansion that followed was reflected in the overwhelming confidence implicit in the employers' notions of Progress and Duty. When the mentality of the industrial bourgeoisie in these years is correctly understood, there is cause for looking again at the national scene through the eyes of Marx, and seeing England as the most bourgeois of nations, the industrial bourgeoisie going from strength to strength and consolidating its economic power in political terms despite the aristocratic appearances of national government.[11]

The consolidation of power and the search for status were to coincide with the growth of the factory town and the expansion of its civic and cultural life. In seeking the impact of the industrial bourgeoisie on the life of the nation the special importance of the local must not be lost to view. When the distribution of power in the urban localities is considered,[12] the employers and merchants (jointly termed the employers here) enjoyed a near-absolute sway in parliamentary politics, as well as in the whole range of municipal affairs, from the town council to the school board.[13] Beyond the overtly political, juridical power was theirs too: by mid-century the struggle for control of the borough magistracies had ended in favour of industry,[14] the conflict that continued being in political and personal rather than in social terms.[15] Beyond these spheres, in turn, employer power was expressed through the whole range of town institutional life. The distinction between this local entrenchment and the more qualified picture that has to be drawn at the national level can be a misleading one: the limitations on centralised state power in the nineteenth century were considerable, what state power there was in any case being filtered through the apparatus of local power and influence.

This account of the Northern employer class will dwell as much on the relations within that class as on its relations with the other classes. Again, the substance of men and events can only be rendered by allowing the material to express the conflict and ambiguity that marked the internal life of a class, as well as its dealings with the landed class. In the first section the importance of bourgeois class unity will be stressed, and in the second an account will be given of class fragmentation. Such is the nature of the approach the evidence demands, that the themes of unity and fragmentation will be interwoven in both sections. The basic source of cultural opposition within the employer class was religion. Though denominational conflict had its own history and was not solely a reflection of the land–industry opposition, at the time it signified most as an expression of this basic social cleavage. Thus the tensions within the social relations of the employer class reflected and reinforced the tensions existing between the classes.

Considered at the level of class interest, the coherence of the urban élites will be examined in two senses; which may be termed the functional and the ideological. The second half of the century saw the adaptation of the employer class to the demands of caste preservation and perpetuation. Dynasticism was as much the mark of northern English as of European capitalism in these years.[16] Just as employers of various persuasions shared the problems of survival, so too did they share the need to moralise and to control the working classes. Political Reform and the anti-Corn Law struggle similarly divulged underlying unity and cemented a common class allegiance. Yet even at the hour of unity disharmony was apparent. Somewhat paradoxically, the victories of 1832 and 1846 once secured allowed for the increased expression of internal conflict.

The old, unresolved difficulties in politics and religion were scored with a new emphasis as denominational conflict took a central place on the political stage from the 1850s. This was particularly so in Lancashire, where the Anglicanism of native employer Toryism was at its most virulent, and the 'religious difficulty' at its most intractable.[17] Political and religious differences, however, were not mere matters of opinion: they represented divided and distinguished worlds among the employer class, which in turn reflected different notions of what the social relations of land and industry should be. The extent to which sectarian differences had a deep cultural root is suggested by the position of a number of West Riding employers on the Factory Acts question. Among these men, the strength of the Anglican-Tory cultural tradition was great enough to rupture the unity of a class and incline them to Protectionism in their detestation of *laissez-faire* economics.

The chief source of cultural disunion among the employers, however, lay mainly though not exclusively in the camp of the Nonconformists. An elusive and ambiguous movement was at work among this class as a whole: on the one hand, urban Toryism and 'landed' industry and commerce were something like familiar strangers in industrialist society, offering a constant enticement to a common cultural style and outlook. This organic connection with landed society, together with the fact that for many employers the prizes of 1832 and 1846 were sufficient to cool radical ardour, set in train that drift to the cultural and political 'Right' which characterised employer society from early in the century. While landed society and its representation in urban Toryism beckoned covertly, the high-handedness of these interests and their embodiment of Privilege in the urban *milieu* repelled overtly. It cannot be too much emphasised that this consciousness of Privilege, excited by the virulence of sectarian politics, was of profound and long-lasting effect in the North. Industry long continued to exert its own identity, the urban identification serving as a rallying cry for the forces of anti-Privilege. And it is clear that it was the dissent of Dissent that was the soul of what was most distinctive in the mental universe of industrial capitalism.

Thus two currents worked powerfully against each other in the status structure of the business élites. Though class union was probably delayed longer in the industrial North than elsewhere, the erosion of diversity and disunion, and the development of a dominant, unitary cultural style and a common politics in the

Conservative party, was in the end the conclusive movement. It
is this movement, often slow and tortured, that will concern us
at the conclusion of this account.

The formation of the élites: the dispositions, origins and coherence of power

The correspondence of economic power and political influence
was sufficiently close to make possible a description of the disposition of both in the same breath. At the head of the landed influence
were the great aristocratic families.[18] The house of Stanley stood
above all others, its influence conjoining national, regional
and local. The family's enormous Lancashire reputation was
based on large landholdings, mostly within the Liverpool –
Preston – Bury triangle. The future 15th Earl, visiting Bury in
1857, confided to his journal: 'Although the town has 40,000
inhabitants, with an immense trade, I found remaining an almost
feudal respect for our family, which has not been only cultivated.'[19]

What limited Liberal influence there was in Lancashire was
organised by the Cavendish family, and the Seftons in the south-
west. There was no equal to the Lancashire heads of the Tory
aristocracy in the West Riding, though the Earls of Dartmouth
held influence in the heavy woollen districts and the Colne
Valley, and the Wood family, ennobled as Viscounts Halifax,
retained a considerable influence in the politics of Halifax
borough.[20]

The charmed aristocratic circle was completed by intermarriage, and occasional judicious recruitment among the
greater genty.[21] Only the slightest indication of the dense undergrowth of marriage connections can be given. Whether Tory
or Whig, county politics and urban influence were underpinned
by the understandings of the blood tie. The Tory Egertons were
so linked with the Stanleys, the Bootle-Wilbrahams (Earls of
Lathom), the Lindsays (Earls of Crawford and Balcarres), the
Leghs (Lords Newton), but also across the political divide with
the Cavendish family (the Earls of Devonshire). The aristocratic
marriage paid little heed to the Whig–Tory political difference,
the Halifax Woods for instance, Whigs, joining with the Tory
Earls of Crawford (Wigan) and the politically mixed 'squires'
of Bingley, the Busfields. However, the most subtle ramifications
were the Lancashire Tory ones, the greater gentry being con-
scripted in the form of the Blackburnes of Hale (to the Leghs)
and the Townley-Parkers (to the Egertons). The latter were an
amalgam of two powerful Burnley area families, and of considerable political weight in their own right in Preston.[22]

The only area in the region where a lively political opposition existed between the gentry was the north-east of Lancashire. At the centre of the Liberal influence, overseen by the Devonshires, were the Kay-Shuttleworths of Gawthorpe Hall. The Shuttleworths, prosperous local landowners in the fifteenth century, had built a considerable influence for the dynasty through patronage and charity, not only in the county but also in Burnley and the smaller weaving towns.[23] James and Ughtred Kay-Shuttleworth worked their inheritance manfully, representing Clitheroe and the North-East in Parliament (Kay family members also stood in Clitheroe and Salford). The Kays were a professional family, originally from Bury, who married into the Shuttleworths in 1842. The family papers illustrate well the continuing influence of the gentry in town life and politics, the joint political management of gentry and aristocracy, and the pervasive presence of the family in northern politics.[24]

In 1873 the ailing head of one dynasty, Sir James Kay-Shuttleworth, worked with the head of another, the 7th Duke of Devonshire, in bringing out Lord Edward Cavendish for the county seat. The job was carried forward with all the expertise of the practised wire-puller, above all the harmonising of the gentry and employer political efforts.[25] Father, sons and daughters worked strenuously to make Gawthorpe the centre of the whole Liberal effort. It was to Gawthorpe that Liberalism went in search of unity: 'The elements of division in our party are many. These Gawthorpe reunions instituted by you seem to be the only bond of cohesion that keeps the sections together.'[26]

The family's local standing was thus used to attempt the necessary marriage of the town's Nonconformist Radicalism and the county's Anglican Whiggism; on the one side, gentry and gentry ex-manufacturing families like the Rochdale Fentons, the Clitheroe Forts, the Lomaxes, and on the other, the Blackburn, Darwen and Padiham cotton masters. Ughtred wrote to James in 1873; 'The Nonconformists will want to be managed with care. They will treat Lord Edward Cavendish as a "Whig", when his name is proposed by and by; and will only accept him, and another moderate Liberal and Churchman, if most delicately handled.'[27]

If such was the measure of landed influence on the refractory Liberal side, how much more was the Tory gentry an integral part of the social and political influence of wealth. Against the Liberal gentry in the north-east was arrayed the greater galaxy of Tory country gentlemen, in far less need of a *generalissimo* like Sir James Kay-Shuttleworth, mixing in regular social contact (at one of the 'great feeds' at the Starkies of Huntroyde that Sir James mentions), and united in Anglicanism and hereditary domination of the land. Families like the Asshetons of Clitheroe and those of the Burnley area Tory halls led the urban élites in county politics, and, by virtue of their prestige, had a considerable say in urban, Tory politics.

The influence of these notables was reinforced if some connection with 'trade' could be shown. The Lancashire aristocracy were the most heavily involved, the Egertons having active coal interests in the Worsley area (the Bridgewater estates), and the Lindsays being directly involved in the giant Wigan Coal and Iron Company. A despairing local Liberal described the Lindsay influence towards the end of this period; ' . . . the dutiful old town is but an appendage of the House of Haigh.'[28] The Devonshire involvement in the development of Barrow-in-Furness provided some Liberal answer to this Tory domination.

Below the level of the aristocratic coalowners a number of families, either long-established in land or acquiring landed status by around the turn of the eighteenth century, provided a more highly developed Tory access to urban life. In Burnley the intermarried Thursbys and Hargreaves owned and ran large collieries in the area, and led Burnley Conservatism alongside the Parkers, Townleys and Chamberlayne Starkies. The Rev. William Thursby and Canon Townley-Parker were leading town clerics and Tory leaders. These families were the pinnacles of status in late-developing, boom Burnley. But in early factory towns like Oldham the same situation obtained, the old landed coalowning families in the town by mid-century being long a part of the Anglican–Tory world of county society.[29] The Bolton Hultons and the Blundels of Ince, both long-established in land, completed further west one vital strand from which organised Conservatism was later to be woven.

Gentry penetration of town life was especially important in parts of the south and east of Lancashire where Tory industrial-commercial leadership was thinner on the ground than elsewhere. In Rochdale the ex-manufacturing landed Royds and the landed Entwistles dominated Tory politics for much of the century.[30] The Royds' banking and railway interests further tied them into town life, in a similar fashion to the leading Burnley families whose interests were wider than the coal one alone. In such situations the leadership of hereditary parsons ('squarsons') was important. To the Burnley figures can be added the Rochdale Molesworths and the Rev. Greenaway in Darwen, a vigorous opponent of the Liberalism of local Nonconformist industry.

In an area of Tory strength, the landed Bridgeman family (the Earls of Bradford) provided clerical and political leadership that was of the first importance in Bolton and Wigan.

Across the Pennines, the influence of the gentry, mainly Whig, was considerably less potent than in Lancashire. Huddersfield, largely owned and developed by the Ramsden family, was an important exception. Elsewhere West Riding 'squarsons' mobilised against predominating Liberalism as in parts of Lancashire, the intermarried Busfields and Ferrands of Bradford and Bingley providing Tory leadership after the Busfields had put aside their earlier Whig ways.

The amphibian nature of much of the landed interest was duplicated in terms of the economic formation of a good deal of urban, industrial Toryism. Not only was there a substantial industrialist Toryism – a statement that can still elicit surprise – but in its main centres of Preston, Bolton, Blackburn, and to a lesser extent Bradford, it was often rooted in local life long before the arrival of *parvenu* Radicals and Nonconformists. Anglican to a fault, it was integrated in landed society not least because it often evolved out of a landed background. Its differences with Nonconformist Liberalism were often sunk in the common struggle before 1850, but after then the earlier intermarriage of these landed-industrial dynasties, and their unions with unsullied landed families, served to integrate urban and county Conservatism, providing a familial network upon which Conservatism was later to build its considerable Lancashire success. Just as much of south Lancashire Liberal politics rested on the foundations of first Unitarian,[31] and then Congregational marriage (the Liberal lack of a regional dimension was always a disadvantage), so too was Tory politics supported by Anglican intermarriage.

Only the centre of the Lancashire bond can be considered here,[32] the old-established, intermarried and landed Hornbys and Birleys of Kirkham. Branches of the Birleys were by mid-century major employers and political leaders in Preston and Manchester. The Blackburn Hornbys had a similar eminence, and were married into the Feildens, thus strengthening the Tory hold in the north of the region. Hornby and Feilden family lines were dispersed throughout the area. The Kirkham Hornbys were related to the Assheton Cross family of Red Scarr, Preston (the same family as that of the Conservative Home Secretary), as well as to a prominent Preston commercial and political family, the Peddars. In their turn the Feildens had married with the Peddars and the Asshetons of Clitheroe.

The Bolton connection worked through the Rev. John Shepherd Birley of Kirkham who had married into the Bolton Cross (Mortfield) family, which had extensive industrial, commercial and political links with the town. The union produced H. Shepherd-Cross, a leading cotton master and Bolton's M.P. Landed influence was further strengthened by the coal interests of the Hultons and Fletchers. The extent to which Radicalism saw local society divided along these lines of background and status is indicated by the opinion of the *Blackburn Times*, a very representative Liberal organ of the time.[33] Despite an involvement in town life every bit as intense as any Radical Nonconformist employer, the Hornbys were regarded as industrialists having adopted the creed of the territorial gentry, the Feildens as the epitome of that creed (although then a family member was only a few years out of the Blackburn cotton trade), and the Congregationalist, cotton Pilkingtons as the essence of a mercantile class enshrining Liberal principles.

In a West Riding dominated by Liberal and Nonconformist employers Bradford was the nearest equivalent to the Lancashire situation. There the foremost leaders of old-style Toryism were the Hardy family, who owned and ran the massive Low Moor ironworks, and, together with a group of partners almost exclusively Anglican and either Whig or Tory, had important interests in the Bowling and Bierley ironworks as well. The Hardys, and H.W. Wickham their managing partner, sprang from substantial eighteenth-century landed stock, with considerable clerical connections. The Hardys were married with the landed Ferrands (members of both families sharing the experience of Bingley Grammar School as well), and further welded disparate influences by their union with John Wood, one of the first Bradford worsted masters and a foremost Tory-Radical advocate of factory reform.

Matthew Thompson was as prominent among the early Bradford employers as Wood, though the family also had considerable landed and clerical connections. His son, M.W. Thompson the brewer, was to lead the mild Liberals of Bradford into modern Conservatism, as was the silkmaster S.C. Lister, from the 1860s one of the foremost Bradford employers. Lister's pedigree was as pure as many a *parvenu* lordling. As in Lancashire, this small group of Anglican employers provided the nub around which later Toryism was to revolve.[34]

Turning to the more significant urban leadership proper, Manchester and Bradford, as the chief commercial and political capitals, had much in common. The Tory revival in both, and the emergence of modern, business Conservatism, were based on solid cores of early support, mobilised as the unity of the Radical alliance dissolved after the decline of the Anti-Corn Law League.[35] Nevertheless, Liberalism continued for most of the second half of the century to be the political faith of the majority of big business, and the opposition of Anglican and Nonconformist Protestantism continued to rupture the united front of property. The character of the Conservative leadership in the Manchester and Salford of the third quarter of the century illustrates well the imbalance of wealth and social prestige between the parties.[36] The conversion of major employers, like W.H. Houldsworth and W. Romaine Callendar from the political faith of their fathers, and in Callendar's case the religious and ideological faith as well, was at this time the exception rather than the rule, though the topmost layer of the party leadership involved some of the biggest employers in Manchester.

In Bradford the landed clerical leadership of industrialist Conservatism, and of that moderate Liberalism that can best be described as Liberal Conservatism, was supplemented by a vocal minority of worsted masters, Anglican to a man and considerably more committed to the Factory Acts cause than most of their Manchester counterparts. The foremost of these, William and John Rand, William Rouse, John Hollings, John Wood and William Walker, indicate the extreme tension in a local situation dominated by militant Nonconformity: they split fairly evenly over the question of Protectionism versus Free Trade. As their influence declined in the 1850s and 60s employers like the Anglican Ripleys, early established in the dyeing trade, were to complement the efforts of other Liberal Conservatives, such as M.W. Thompson, in merging elements of the Liberal right and Toryism in modern, Disraelian Conservatism. Below this level however, influence in Bradford Toryism itself, until probably the 1870s, was mostly made up of the small fry of Bradford business together with the more energetic of the Anglican clergy.[37]

Despite the disharmonies within Manchester Liberalism it would be wrong to underestimate the strength of the Liberal revival in the third quarter of the century. Many of the dynasties that had created Liberal Manchester regenerated themselves in the era of mass politics,[38] the unity that shared denominational allegiances brought doing much to further this revival. The leading families were closely bound by the ties of marriage and religion, and formed a kind of south-east Lancashire Liberal aristocracy. Though Unitarianism still connected many leading

manufacturing and merchant families in the area, Congregationalism, as Figure 1 makes clear, formed the backbone of the
interest. (Again, only a sample of the dense undergrowth of
connection is given).

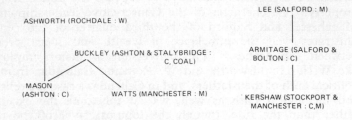

(a) CONGREGATIONALISTS

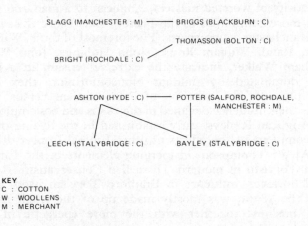

(b) OTHER NONCONFORMISTS

KEY
C : COTTON
W : WOOLLENS
M : MERCHANT

FIGURE 1. Marriage links of Liberal
nonconformist families, politically active
1850–1900. South-east Lancashire

In Bradford the tie of denomination was every bit as firm,
expressing itself in both marriage and business links. The
Manchester disposition of power was paralleled in much of the
south-east, though Bolton, as will be seen, was rather exceptional,
and in Oldham the Liberal Anglican complement was larger

than was common in the area. Liberalism and Nonconformity (especially Congregationalism) predominated in an area for which the towns of Ashton and Stalybridge can stand as paradigms. The mills and chapels of such families as the Reyners, Leeches, Masons and Buckleys were the unofficial headquarters of Liberalism throughout the period.[39] The minority Conservative element in local cotton was, however, long established in the town by the 1850s, and secure in its unvarying Anglicanism.[40] Professional and lower middle-class elements invaded the Conservative party structure as in Manchester. The scant respect of the Liberal employer leadership for those they considered their inferiors meant that politics and religion provided the focus for an often bitter status conflict, those of the professional class who were not already Anglican and Tory often adopting the persuasion that best expressed their desire for the revenge a little brief authority could bring.[41]

In northern weaving Lancashire Conservatism was very much more powerful among the employer class, especially in its ancient citadels of Preston and Blackburn. In Preston, a prime example of a long-established Tory employer class enjoying links of birth and society with the gentry,[42] the giant firm of Horrocks translated prestige into political influence throughout the century. The north-east of Burnely and the smaller weaving towns and villages was an exception to this Tory dominance, the area being in many ways an extension of the West Riding pattern of employer allegiance. In Burnley, late-arriving Liberal cotton confronted the Tory landed and coalworking interest. In the west the influence of Tory Liverpool radiated outwards to combine with the predominant Toryism of the Wigan coal-owners, though large parts of the south-west coalbelt were under the Liberal influence of the very large firm of Andrew Knowles and Sons. Nonconformity confronted Anglicanism directly in Warrington, in the form of the brewing Greenalls and the Radical soap-making Crosfields and wireworking Rylands. St Helens, then as now, lay under the shadow of the influence of the great glassworking Pilkington concern.

In the West Riding the Bradford pattern predominated, the Tory presence being much less weighty than in Lancashire. The exceptions, families like the Huddersfield Croslands and the Brookes of Armitage Bridge, were often of respectable, established local stock; the Brookes enjoying close links with the Anglican Establishment. The Liberalism that predominated was fired by the endemic Nonconformity of the region, though Liberal Conservatism was to be increasingly important, the Halifax

Akroyds being an important case in point. Analysis of the
employer class in a number of northern towns will now enable
us to pursue some of the themes of this section in a little more
detail.

Bury may briefly be considered first, providing one mark
of reference in the range of variation. Smaller and more
technologically stable than a number of factory towns it offers
perhaps the most striking example of a tightly-knit ruling élite.[42]
At the centre of the principal grouping were the Tory and
Anglican loyalties that made of Bury another example of in-
digenous, early-established, business Toryism. Thomas Openshaw, who died in the 1870s, was the last survivor of twenty-one
brothers and sisters. The ramifications of the Openshaw pedigree
in Bury life were correspondingly many and subtle, combining
the fortunes of another clan, the Walkers, as well as the Oram
and Pilkington families. The Walkers were in turn married to the
Anglican and Tory cotton Hutchinsons. Between them these
five families controlled the major part of the industry of the town,
as well as the Conservative party. If the political complexion
of the five clans, though predominantly Conservative, was in
some cases mixed, its religious character was not, being steadfastly
Anglican. Comparison with Blackburn again indicates the social
importance of the denominational line of division, but also shows
the great importance of status distinctions between old and new
employers in a borough with a less leisurely industrial history
than Bury.

With the expansion of the town's weaving trade in the 1850s
and 60s new men flocked into the employer ranks. Though not a
textile employer, and Smith and Blackburn were extremes of
rudeness, the story of one 'Jack' Smith reveals the uncouthness
of much of local society, and the great contemporary awareness of
manners and the lack of them. The dignity of Blackburn rested
with John Smith during the mayoral years of 1867–69. 'Jack',
'horny handed' and with 'gestures uncouth', was 'a Blackburn
man bred, whose place of nativity was attested by his manners,
his speech, and everything about him'.[44] Having risen from
poverty and obscurity he returned to them prior to his death in
1892, but not before building up a quarrying business and practis-
ing the most unashamed kind of political opportunism. Representing the town 'abroad' Smith made even Blackburn wince;
supping wine with a lord in Barrow for instance – 'Eh lad; ow
con sup beer wi' onybody; but aw soon fun eawt aw cudn't sup
wine wi' a lord'.[45] Jack's words of welcome to a visiting dignitary
in 1869 sum up many of the Blackburn graces; 'Th'art welcome;

but wod will ta have to sup?/Theer's some stunnin' "Owd'Ben" if th'all co at Bull.'[46]

Though the accounts of the superior and cosmopolitan Manchester *Free Lance* were somewhat exaggerated,[47] they tell us much about the roughness of the town and the role of political activity in the scramble for status. The Liberal journal proclaimed in 1867:[48]

There is scarcely a manufacturer, a doctor, or a lawyer, the tone of whose voice and whose accent and phraseology, and an indescribable something in the sit of their clothes, do not manifest a certain provincial vulgarity. Gentlemen in the high and true sense many of them are ... but you would not be surprised if you heard that they were bricksetters or joiners.

It went on, 'There is no material for magistrates, D.L.s, and all the various compliments'; and described one 'only unlike a tackler in that he wore broadcloth every day and not once a week on Sunday', who had been recommended to the Liberal government for a Deputy Lieutenancy in the Blackburn Hundred.

A number of the more important employer leaders in the 1860s were indeed of immediately low origin, and the Protestant lecturer William Murphy spared no pains in attacking them for their pretensions.[49] James Thompson's father was a self-made stonemason and Joseph Harrison had built up a large ironworks after starting as an illiterate blacksmith. Henry Ward of Brookhouse was once a barber, his mill at one time being known as the 'lather box'.[50] The names popularly given to mills indicate not only the backgrounds of their owners but also the operatives' keen awareness of pretension – 'Apostles Twelve', 'Butter Tubs Two', 'Holy Brush' and 'Noggin Pinch'.[51] However, the Thompsons were already in their third generation of political stalwarts by the 1860s and went on to build a considerable cotton empire,[52] and the polished Robert Hopwood Hutchinson succeeded the lowly Robert Hopwood in the same decade. These are but two indications of the extent to which the once lowly had established themselves in the economic and social life of the town by the 1860s and 70s. Contrary to popular mythology, the path from rags to riches was in fact not the usual one for the major northern employers.

As an intervening layer between the pinnacles of Blackburn society and the rough hordes of aspiring tacklers making good, most of the big employers, Liberal and Tory, had secured positions of leadership in the industry and life of the town before the boom of the 1850s. Many of them came from respectable business backgrounds: William Coddington (later the town's

M.P.), who moved to Blackburn in 1842, was the son of a Manchester cotton merchant, and the Quaker Richard Shackleton, a
rich corn miller who came to the town in 1839, was from a Leeds
business family. Eli Heyworth's father, like his son a Congregationalist, was a Chorley cotton manufacturer. By the 1880s a
number of the new men of the 1850s and 60s had made it to the
top of the Blackburn tree. The social gulf between them and the
old industrialist families was considerable. As figure 2 shows,
families of lowly origin like the Kays, Hamers and Liveseys were
separated by both caste and religious denomination from the
world of the Hornbys, Feildens and Jacksons.

A landed background and long industrial association with the
borough meant that the Hornbys and Feildens led local society
by divine right of precedence. The Anglican 'Whig', Robert
Raynsford Jackson, one of the largest millowners in the town
and of impeccable military stock, also moved in this high society.
Jackson's partnership with M.J. Feilden was severed only in the
1860s. By dint of respectable background (their father was a
Blackburn cotton merchant early in the century) and of decidedly
moderate politics, these were joined by the foremost Liberal
leaders, the Congregational Pilkington brothers. W.H. Hornby,
Jackson and James Pilkington frequently travelled in the same
train compartment to the Manchester Exchange,[53] and all three
shared in the patronage of a wide range of town institutions. The
comparison between the superiority of the old families and the
vulgarity of the new was one often made in the town.[54]

Behind the Pilkington standard, however, much of Blackburn
Liberalism issued from the Congregational chapels, and denomination (itself of course often an index of status) rather than the
status of pedigree or of long association, moulded the choice of
marriage and business partner. Figure 2 makes plain the various
shaping pressures on the status structure of the big employers,
pointing to the special importance of denomination, Nonconformist and Anglican. A somewhat different situation obtained
in the case of mid-century Oldham that John Foster so expertly
analyses.[55] There the borders of demarcation ran rather more
along the lines of economic formation and function, geographical location, and social prestige than was elsewhere the case,
at least in the second half of the century. It is necessary to insist
on the widespread representativeness and special force of religious
affiliation in shaping the social lives of the employer class. Indeed,
it seems probable that in the two or three decades after 1850
religious adherence was a more potent force for social division
than at any time in the century.

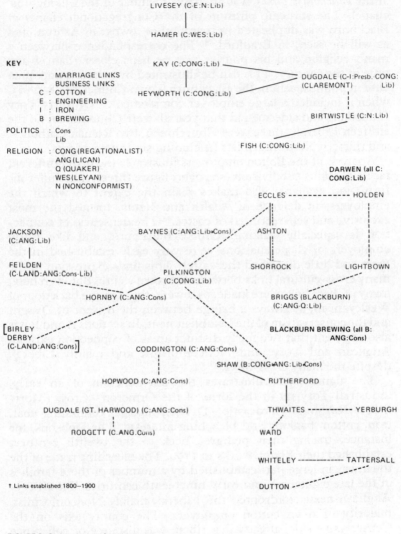

FIGURE 2. Social cohesion of employer
class, Blackburn & Darwen 1850–1900.
Principal marriage & business connections †

In Blackburn the Pilkington's Park Road chapel, and the less
eminent James Street one, were the means by which the Liberal
leadership, lower-middle-class rank and file, and the Liberal
press were concerted in the political cause. W.A. Abram, editor

of the *Blackburn Times*, was an active member of the Pilkingtons'
chapel. The strategic position of the Congregational chapel in
Blackburn was duplicated in many other towns; in Ashton, and
as will be seen, in Bradford.[56] The correspondence between a
man's religion and his politics was perhaps closer than at any
time in the century. This can be illustrated by a description of an
élite in political action, the Blackburn Town Council of 1862–63,
when it included a large employer complement.[57] Of thirty Tory
councillors and aldermen in that year all were Churchmen. Of the
eithteen Liberals, three were Churchmen, two Roman Catholics,
and thirteen Nonconformists (including six Independents).

Analysis of the Bolton employers illustrates the many different
facets of status subdivision (see over, figure three). The fuller information available also makes plain the extent to which the
employers, in defence of wealth and status, formed the most
exclusive and self-recruited of castes.[58] The denseness of connection is especially striking. Unlike Blackburn, and like Bury,
employers of all persuasions were very early established in the
town and little disturbed thereafter. This finds expression in the
many cross-cultural links between the town's élite. But even here,
many of these links were made, as it were, through the back door of
Wesleyanism, as always a bridge between the dissent of Dissent
and the conservatism of the Establishment. In sections A and B it is
also apparent that two fairly distinct areas of connection existed,
Anglican and Tory, and Nonconformist and mainly Liberal,
despite the many cross-links.

The figure again illustrates the phenomenon of an early,
industrial Toryism in the form of the Ormerod – Cross (Mortfield) – Rushton – Hardcastle – Dobson linkage, combining coal,
iron, cotton, banking and bleaching interests. The Dobsons, for
instance, tracing their pedigree back to the twelfth century,
established their Bolton works in 1790. The bleaching trade of the
town was in large part established by a number of these families
in the late eighteenth and early nineteenth centuries. This Tory-
Anglican nexus confronted the Liberal, mainly Nonconformist,
majority of town cotton employers. The county axis on the
Conservative side, already described, was a source of coherence
to this grouping as well.

The information on the origins of the major employers already
assembled suggests very strongly the advisability of locating
the notion of the rise from humble origins within the mythology
rather than the reality of industrial capitalism. As seen, those who
did rise from manual backgrounds before 1850 were building up
decades of local attachment in the third quarter of the century,

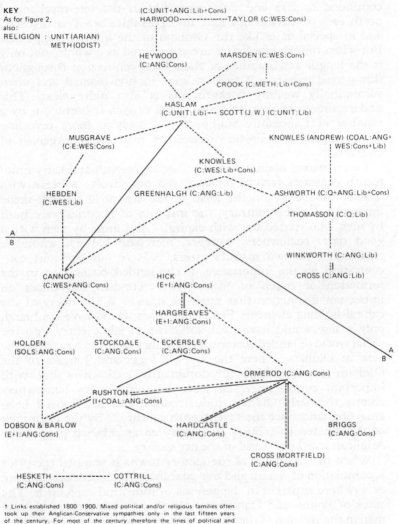

KEY
As for figure 2,
also:
RELIGION : UNIT(ARIAN)
                METH(ODIST)

HARWOOD---------------TAYLOR (C:WES:Cons)
(C:UNIT+ANG:Lib+Cons)

HEYWOOD   MARSDEN (C:WES:Cons)
(C:ANG:Cons)

CROOK (C:METH:Lib+Cons)

HASLAM
(C:UNIT:Lib)--- SCOTT (J. W.) (C:UNIT:Lib)

MUSGRAVE   KNOWLES (ANDREW) (COAL:ANG+
(C-E:WES:Cons)   WES:Cons+Lib)

KNOWLES
(C:WES:Lib+Cons)

HEBDEN   GREENHALGH (C:ANG:Lib)   ASHWORTH (C:Q+ANG:Lib+Cons)
(C:WES:Lib)

THOMASSON (C:Q:Lib)

A
B

WINKWORTH (C:ANG:Lib)

CROSS (C:ANG:Lib)

CANNON   HICK
(C:WES+ANG:Cons) (E+I:ANG:Cons)

HARGREAVES
(E+I:ANG:Cons)

HOLDEN   STOCKDALE   ECKERSLEY
(SOLS:ANG:Cons) (C:ANG:Cons) (C:ANG:Cons)

A
B

ORMEROD (C:ANG:Cons)

RUSHTON
(I+COAL:ANG:Cons)

DOBSON & BARLOW   HARDCASTLE   BRIGGS
(E+I:ANG:Cons)   (C:ANG:Cons)   (C:ANG:Cons)

CROSS (MORTFIELD)
(C:ANG:Cons)

HESKETH ------------ COTTRILL
(C:ANG:Cons)   (C:ANG:Cons)

† Links established 1800–1900. Mixed political and/or religious families often
took up their Anglican-Conservative sympathies only in the last fifteen years
of the century. For most of the century therefore the lines of political and
denominational allegiance were firmer than the diagram suggests.

FIGURE 3. Social cohesion of employer
class, Bolton 1850–1900. Principal
marriage & business connections †

and establishing the inheritance of accumulated wealth very
firmly in the mentality of the employers. Of course, employers

continued to rise and fall, especially in the late-mechanised north-east of Lancashire and the Yorkshire woollen districts, and in special cases like the Oldham of the limited companies. But when the big employers are considered as a whole, not only is the length and stability of their local connection throughout this period apparent,[59] their origins in non-manual and often substantially wealthy backgrounds is also quite clear. This understanding of economic and social origins is borne out by a number of Lancashire studies.[60] No study is more revealing in this regard than Foster's dissection of the big bourgeoisie of Oldham.[61]

Foster makes plain how in the late eighteenth and early nineteenth centuries factory building did not involve a break with 'traditional society' in the form of the arrival of the self-made innovator. On the contrary, the majority of factories were built by men who started out with capital: 'And most by men with a good deal: coalowners, bankers, merchant hatters, wholesale tradesmen, yeomen manufacturers.'[62] Here our previous concentration on the importance of the landed connection in the formation of much of industrialist Toryism introduces an important distinction that must be drawn. While many of the capital-holding elements Foster describes would have held land, only a few would have held sufficient to allow entry into the social world of landed society. This in fact seems to have been the case in Oldham, where the Lees, Cleggs and Joneses of the Oldham out-townships (predominantly coalowners but with important cotton interests) were the only major landowners among the early Oldham industrialists, and had indeed been amassing land since the seventeenth century.[63] By the beginning of the nineteenth century they were an established part of the Anglican and Tory world of county society.

When the full range of the factory towns is scanned the prior accumulation of wealth and the established social background are everywhere apparent in the genesis of industrial capitalism. The cases of Bolton and Darwen emphasise the importance of local men in the creation of the factory system, and above all men with a long history in outwork manufacturing.[64] In both towns the leading employer families of the 1870s, who had often risen to prominence in the late eighteenth- and early nineteenth-century transition to factory industry, frequently came from substantial outwork manufacturing or farming backgrounds, where wealth and expertise had long been accumulated. The prominence of the outworking textile tradition was especially marked in the Yorkshire woollen districts.[65] Even when the rise appeared to be from manual labour and poverty, and especially when it was dramatised in the rhetoric of Improvement, as in the cases of Joseph Wilson of Bradford and James Ickringill of Keighley, a close attention to the success story often reveals the multi-generational rise from obscurity.[66]

In the boom Bradford of the 1850s, when the worsted trade was inundated by 'Jews, Germans and cigar smoking puppies', the cream of merchant and manufacturer society stood apart, its standing guaranteed by respectable antecedents and sanctified by wealth. The manufacturer W.E. Forster's father was a Quaker minister, the merchant J.V. Godwin's a Baptist one. Titus Salt's father was a Bradford wool-stapler and farmer, and John Smith the worsted manufacturer similarly came from established textile stock. Jonas Foster, founder of the Queensbury dynasty, was a farmer and colliery owner.[67] The Quaker Priestmans (old Bradford corn millers), the manufacturing Peels, and the merchant Kell brothers (Unitarians) also came from anything but proletarian stock.

The pedigree of 'Illingworth, Kell and Company' and the other Nonconformist dynasties that made Bradford an English capital of religious Radicalism was not, however, quite the match of that of the leading Anglican families. There was a decidedly lowly infusion in the form of the Scottish merchant brotherhood, Robert Milligan being typical of a number in starting as a travelling draper. The great worsted master, the Methodist Scot Isaac Holden (the family were doubly married into the Baptist Illingworths), was the son of a poor farmer and pitman. Bradford always attracted 'incomers' like these, and was in this respect something of an exception to the general rule of local origins in the factory towns. The Scottish brotherhood, combined and recombined in merchant partnerships, illuminate a principal strand in the social life of industrial and commercial wealth: the intimate connection between the helping hand in business (a partnership, a managership, or even the bookkeeping position), the fraternity of religion (especially of the chapel), and political activism and leadership.

While the Scots were never averse to the adoption of an Englishman – Joseph Farrar, one of the Anti-Corn Law League activists in Bradford, was helped out of his drapery business by Milligan[68] – the English for their part were quite as adept as the Scots in proffering the helping hand to men of fellow-feeling. Though there was always a great deal of commerce between Nonconformist sects (including Wesleyanism), the most elaborate nexus was the Congregational one. The centre of the web seems to have been Horton Lane chapel. The connections of its members made up a good deal of the underlying structure of Nonconformist Radicalism and business life in the town.

Titus Salt and Robert Milligan were only the most eminent of the many manufacturers and merchants patronising the chapel at different times. John Arthur Clapham, who insured many of the big Bradford mills, attended the chapel and worked manfully in the Liberal cause. He was at one time in partnership with the Priestleys, a prominent millowning Congregational family. Building naturally complemented insurance: Alderman William Moulson, who built many of the big Bradford factories, much of Saltaire, a number of Nonconformist and Board schools, as well as the chapel itself, was a Horton Lane man, and the town's mayor in 1888. The Byles family supplied a chaplain and a deacon for Horton Lane. As so often, the link between chapel and press was close: deacon W.G. Byles and his son owned and ran the *Bradford Observer*. The connection spread from chapel to chapel. Elias Thomas, one of the most important Liberal Nonconformist organisers in Bradford (in the party, the Liberation Society and the Sunday School Union), was connected with the chapel of Edward Miall's brother, J.G. Miall. He was also a buyer in the firm of Milligan, Forbes.[69]

Though the marriage connections of the industrial bourgeoisie served both to express and intensify the lines of social cleavage within that class, the frequent examples of union across the religious and political divide indicate the fundamental importance of the needs of class preservation and perpetuation. Analysis of the Bolton employers in particular has shown the degree to which the survival instinct made of the big employers the most exclusive of castes. Having made much play of cultural diversity and disunion among the employers it is necessary now to show, in terms of marriage, economic interests and residence, how at the basic level of class interest the coherence of the big bourgeoisie was ensured.

The trials of many a master when shopping in the marriage market are expressed thus by one Keighley man remembering the late nineteenth century; 'Shoes won't come and clogs daren't.'[70] The assiduity and success with which matchmaking parents overcame these trails is suggested by the very denseness of the marriage links of the employers within and between the factory towns. The Thompson and Vigne oral historical material indicates the extent to which the people of Keighley, though aware of political and religious differences, saw the town's employers as a group apart. Locked within their own social and family relations,

they were aloof, in the popular conception 'gentry' or 'aristocracy'.[71] They often behaved with appropriate *hauteur*: one almost
dare not look at the Haggas family house in the town, and preserved
silence when one of the family went by. John Clough, another
worsted master, put a ban on all washing that spoiled the view from
this residence.[72] The employers' social life was understood as a
charmed and mysterious circle, the upper ten of Shipley, for instance, bowling in their own gentlemen's club protected by the
armoury of freemasonry.[73] Popular understanding reflected
present realities exactly. The large worsted masters that emerged
in the Keighley of the 1840s, including the Haggases and Cloughs,
shared holidays and leisure, as did the families that made up
"Illingworth, Kell and Co."[74]

This judicious preservation of dynasticism, in which it should
be stressed no distinctions were made between commercial wealth
and industrial wealth, had of course the widest significance for
the stability of industrial society in the period. The marriage
and business links that preserved the authority and status of the
élites in the interbred factory towns were, as we have seen,
duplicated on the regional and sub-regional levels. The networks
within networks of power and influence that these connections
represented extended into the whole economic and cultural life
of the North. The framework of this life was thus built on the
institution which was central to the maintenance of the form of
capitalism that typified the economic organisation, not only of the
North, but of large parts of England, Europe, and the U.S.A.
in this era as well. This form was dynastic industrialism, to
which the institution of marriage was integral. Something of
the local and regional coherence of a class has been shown here.
When the history of relations between the industrial bourgeoisie
and the state comes to be written these underlying structures
will surely form one vital point of departure in any analysis.
The economic and cultural transformations involved in the
progression from a local to a regional and thence to a 'national'
bourgeoisie will, in large measure, be understood in terms of the
burgeoning growth of these industrial clans, and this is so in
England no less than with such as the Protestant and Jewish
banking clans of Europe.[75]

'The employer saw himself as son and grandson to an estate
and judged himself within this familial (still almost peasant)
perspective.'[76] In such terms does John Foster describe the
'puritan', out-township employer in Oldham. Such a characterisation, however, applied not merely to this singular and increasingly outmoded example of the capitalist, and describes without

exaggeration the typical large-scale northern employer for most of this period. The management function of the family was directly geared to the preservation of the estate. In fully urbanised Bolton for example, the family head retained control while the other family members ran the sometimes scattered mills: the firm of Musgraves though exceptional in having eight mills, was representative in seeing the management structure staffed by as many sons or family members as possible. Thus from early on the family was immersed in factory life, family managers in Bolton enjoying a good deal of managerial autonomy.[77] As will be seen, a common way of starting a son in business life, and one not at all excluding a public school or Oxbridge education, was to 'put him through the mill' as an apprentice or even a 'half-timer'. The Bolton Heskeths, Harwoods and Haslams were not unusual in starting sons in the cardrooms of their spinning mills.

The management division of the firm thus made the marriage settlement an occasion for the unity and perpetuation of the dynasty and not for family conflict. The Lancashire and West Riding stress on the continuity of the firm as a single-family concern was in fact more marked than in the case of their European counterparts. Though dynasticism was still the central theme, in France, especially among textile employers, the patrimonial emphasis was displaced by the desire to expand and strengthen the dynasty: the hyphenated firm name, the husband and wife jointly running the factory, and the compulsory *fest* of the weekly family dinner were absent from the English scene.[78]

Though the inviolate family firm signified the continuity of the English dynasty, as we have seen, there were many business links among the élite. This was especially the case in the economically buoyant years after 1850, which witnessed a considerable diversification of capital within but especially beyond the textile industry, as well as a marked accentuation of the concentration of capital resources in the hands of the big employers.[79] Much of this would have taken place irrespective of cultural differences, and would in turn have fused the social life of those sharing business interests. Investment in railways was specially important, in Blackburn for instance, combining the economic and social fortunes of the two leading political families of the town, the Hornbys and the Pilkingtons. The Bolton Junction Railway Company was a typical case in point, involving the whole spectrum of Bolton employers, as well as many Chorley ones. Some of the Bolton employers also bought into the early limiteds of the 1870s and 80s, as well as the Indian textile industry, though this was rather exceptional.[80] More typical was joint involvement in insurance, especially boiler and fire insurance. The Bolton Cotton Trade Mutual Fire Insurance Ltd was formed in 1873 with £500,000 capital, in part provided by the leading cotton spinners of the town. Local banking, in the absence of a centralised system, was another vital economic link.

Rather more important in eroding cultural differences than shared business interests alone, was the social mixing involved in shared membership of local, regional and national institutions dedicated to the economic preservation of industry. In Blackburn, and aside from the Town Council and the bench, which were themselves in many senses economic institutions, local employers would have cemented socially the bond of shared ideology in such as the Blackburn Chamber of Commerce, the North East Lancashire Employers' Association, and the Blackburn and District Textile Employers' Association. The Chamber of Commerce was in fact founded by two arch-political rivals, Henry Harrison and Eli Heyworth. The Manchester Cotton Supply Association, the Bradford Chamber of Commerce, and the National Federation of Associated Employers of Labour represented the regional and national extensions of this local organisation.

Cases of religious and political opposition taking economic form were rare. Such seems to have been the case in the Bradford of 1854 when Liberal employers, in bitter conflict with Tory ones, aided ironworkers locked out by Tory masters.[81] 1879 in Burnley saw the mostly cotton and Nonconformist Town Council take away the coal contract from the Hargreaves company, for reasons that seem to have had much to do with the specially sharp conflict of Establishment–industrial and urban-industrial interests in the town.[82] Much more common was the way in which the middle class of Blackburn regarded the town's cotton employer M.P.s as the true representatives of the spirit of Blackburn, irrespective of party colours. In 1874 the election of the Liberal cotton master William Briggs was greeted with delight in the gentlemen's clubs of the town.[83]

The employer's place of residence also reflected an underlying social unity, but this community of residence did not mean an emotional separation from town life, and it is most important that this point should be stressed. The pattern established in the cities by mid-century – rigid zonal segregation by class and the flight to the remote countryside – was not repeated in the factory towns. As in so many respects, they story of Leeds, Liverpool and Manchester was a separate and different one. The smaller size of the factory town, and its still considerable isolation, meant that urban residential enclaves and easily accessible rural residences were developed that allowed of a considerable access to popular urban life. Development in Oldham, where the biggest employers had moved their permanent residences far beyond the town, and indeed the county, by the 1860s, do not seem to have been representative of the general situation.[84]

Bradford is perhaps the best place to consider developments first, being the largest of the factory towns rather than the smallest of the industrial cities. If class segregation and impersonality were restricted here, how much more was this so in the more representative towns. The move of the big employers from the town centre seems to have been completed by mid-century. In the third quarter of the century individual and estate residences developed rapidly on the outskirts of the town and in the surrounding Pennine valleys. However, as implacable a foe of the Bradford employers as the Socialist Fred Jowett could remark on how close to the working class the employers lived until the very end of the century, when the inexorable expansion of town industry finally pushed the Illingworths and Holdens into the 'County Family Class of the present generation' (he wrote in the 1940s).[85] This proximity and local association owed much to a considerable township consciousness, typical of the other factory towns as well. Until very late in the century the factory town was in fact more a congeries of settlements than an entity in its own right.[86] The life of many of the leading Bradford employers was led within the confines of Thornton, Great Horton, or Manningham, residential continuity being reflected in an intensive and personal involvement in the life of the township.[87]

Manningham perhaps reflects developments best. In the early part of the century it was the most select residential area in the town. As Bradford grew after mid-century employers continued to move into Manningham in considerable numbers, also further west into the nearby semi-rural surrounds (the Illingworth and Holdens into Daisy Hill for example). Land and houses changed hands many times, as the Thompsons and Listers, early-century local squires and patrons, relinquished many of their local involvements. The final movement out of the high-walled houses and gardens of Manningham was not to occur until the end of the century. Until then, though the big employers' colonisation of the slopes of Wharfedale and retreats like Ilkley was to continue, there was a close connection with Bradford life. In 1889 two of the four directors of Lister's massive Manningham Mills lived in Manningham. The link was especially strong for Nonconformists like the Illingworths and Kells: in the 1870s they lived inside the town boundaries, Anglicans like the Thompsons and Ripleys outside.[88]

In the factory towns proper, and especially in a West Riding mechanised and urbanised later than elsewhere, residential propinquity was considerably more marked. As in Keighley, so in smaller settlements like the Fielden's Todmorden, the employer's residence could overawe the town. Nevertheless, Bradford set the pattern repeated somewhat later elsewhere. In late-urbanised Huddersfield, for example, it was not until well into the third quarter of the century that enclaves like the New North Road, 'the Kensington of Huddersfield', and villa suburbs in Lindley and Highfield came into prominence. The common pattern for the Lancashire factory towns was for the smaller employers to live in the neighbourhood of their works, the medium-sized but also many of the biggest employers in enclaves like Moor Park in Preston and the Preston New Road in Blackburn (on the exclusive high ground, within easy walk of the town-centre, and all rapidly developed in the 1850s and 60s), and for the very largest to build or buy country seats near the town, sometimes in conjunction with one or a range of far flung rural residences.[89] Even so, in the late 1860s some of the greatest employers, such as the Preston Swainsons and Edward Hermon, and the Hornbys in Blackburn, retained part-time town-centre residences.

Despite this, the more numerous rural residences of the big employers were sited sufficiently far from the town to prevent contamination by its Lancashire roughness. James Bryce, the contemporary social analyst of middle-class education, noted this desire for distance and gentility in the 1860s.[90] Though the social intercourse attendant on common areas of residence was always apparent, towards the end of the period a note of quickening change was sounded as a life in common gave way to an outlook in common. Something of the direction, and ambiguity, of this change can be understood in the case of the Blackburn Hornbys, among the grandest of employers. In the 1860s and 70s the family's Pool Hall residence, near Nantwich in Cheshire, seems to have become the permanent residence of most of W.H. Hornby's children. Nevertheless, E.K. and A.N. Hornby, Blackburn M.P. and renowned cricketer respectively, retained very close links with the town and enjoyed considerable local reputations. At the same time the Blackburn connection was fully kept up by another son, Sir 'Harry' Hornby, who continued to reside just outside the town and run the family business. Thus urban links were maintained, especially with the involved industrial stem of the family. In this regard, therefore, it is advisable to question the historical inevitability that so often invests accounts of entrepreneurial entry into great wealth and high status, as measured by country residences, and southern social connections and education.

As will become apparent, the 'haemorrhage of talent' – that loss of the urban-industrial connection once the heights of the Establishment had been scaled – was no simple story. If, as Rubinstein maintains,[91] the road from wealth to status, for the manufacturer as opposed to the commercial man, was a one-way street, then it was often a long and winding one. Two rather separate questions are involved: the loss of a distinctive entrepreneurial ideal and of Radical vigour, and the loss of entrepreneurial economic commitment (the latter what might be termed the decline of British entrepreneurship argument). In both respects considerable reservations have to be made. It was the competition of the Limiteds, rather more than the lures of the Establishment, that applied the *coup de grace* to the old order in Lancashire.

Though a determined rearguard action was put up, it would nevertheless be idle to maintain that a real change was not everywhere apparent from the 1870s. A distinct shift in the centre of gravity of employer family life in the North was taking place. The Fosters of Queensbury are perhaps a better example of this translation into the empyrean of the British Establishment than the Hornbys, who were already gentry-connected to begin with.[92] John Foster, who died in 1879, inherited considerable economic backing from his father, though only a modicum of social prestige. His fortune set him the usual problem of matching wealth and social standing. Congress with the landed and titled South of England was not to occur within a single generation. His horizons were limited to the very local, indeed very Bradford stock of substantial manufacturing, merchant and professional families. These alliances of the 1850s and 60s complemented the activities of his son William (1821–84), who remained steadfastly involved with the daily running of the Queensbury mills, like Harry Hornby in Blackburn. The father himself was in fact brought back from his Lancashire estates for burial in the family vault in Queensbury. William regularly gathered the whole family about him at Christmas, when the Black Dyke Mills Band serenaded them on Christmas morning. The firm is unusual in remaining in family hands to the present day.

The next generation after William was to reflect the shift of the centre of the family's interests and outlook from the North to the South, and the weakening of the structure of northern intermarriage that had done so much to ensure a distinctive style of life. The acquisition of Hornby Castle in 1862 (Lancashire) and the Whitby residence in 1869, was followed by the purchase of Cranwell Hall (Staffordshire) in 1872 and Moor Park (Oxfordshire) in 1873. As the family crept south the next generation, John Foster's grandchildren, were to secure the prize of inclusion among the titled acreocracy of the South and education in the forcing house of Oxbridge. This slow erosion of northern ways and gradual merger of a variety of employer cultural styles in a common, Establishment culture was to be representative of the North. The Fosters, as Anglicans, were in some ways in the van of events. It is this movement from diversity to uniformity, and the considerable resistance against it, that will now be considered.

Diversity to uniformity: education, social life and politics

The change in cultural emphasis was all the more profound when the starting-point of that change was the mingled pride and inferiority of excluded, embattled Nonconformity. For most of this period the religion of the employer was the surest guide to his politics.[93] In considering the status system of the employers, as expressed in the various nexus defined by marriage and business connections, something of the degree to which the denominational identification shaped separate and distinct social worlds has been seen. This was especially the case in Lancashire, where after mid-century the pugnacity of Nonconformity was matched by the aggressiveness of Anglican Protestantism. Education is the first area in which the reality of diversity and the growth of cultural and political uniformity will be explored.

Except for the better schools such as Preston, Lancaster and Leeds, by the late 1860s the grammar schools were no longer a principal source of education for the large employers. It was then that James Bryce drew his pertinent but still somewhat exaggerated contrast between the presentday, wealthy trustees of the Schools, born between 1800 and 1830, and the presentday sons of the rich. The former were educated in the grammar schools beside the tradesman class, while the latter were increasingly turning to the newly developing public schools of the South, boarding schools of the North, and an Oxbridge now thrown open to all denominations.[94] In these polish could be applied, accents and cousins lost, and cricket (rather than classics) learned in the attempt to dull the hard edge of Lancashire roughness.

Under Anglican domination, the old regime of the grammar

schools was often bitterly sectarian. Indeed, in many schools well after 1850, the ethos was distinctly Anglican-Tory. Blackburn and Rochadale were two somewhat notorious examples,[95] and the Schools Inquiry Commission of 1867–8 mentioned many more, especially schools like the Burnley one, where in areas not then fully urbanished the landed gentury had taken control thirty or forty years before and continued to exclude commercial men from the governing bodies.[96] What was even in the 1860s a source of real disquiet,[97] after the schools had of late adopted a more inclusive and liberal definition of their purpose, was earlier on a source of real division among the élite. At least nineteen out of twenty-five of the leading cotton employer families of post-1850 Bolton sent one or more son to either Bolton Grammar School or the Bolton Church Institute.[98] Though by the 1860s dogma was no longer enforced in the latter, the former was still a source of considerable Roman Catholic and Nonconformist bitterness. The West Riding grammar schools before the 60s had much of the coterie Tory about them too. The Old Grammar School, Bingley, was the common lot of Low Moor's John Hardy and H.W. Wickham, as well as the Radical-Tory squire W.B. Ferrand. The experience of the fathers of the 1860s was substantially different from that of the sons.

If not always a matter of a Tory inflexion, then the denominational division of education meant that men of like mind were made like in private schools that seem to have recruited almost exclusively along denominational lines. The Anglican Liberal-Conservative Fosters, Akroyds of Halifax and Bradford Ripleys grew up together at the Brookhouse School, Ovenden. Joseph Hinchcliffe's Horton House Academy in Bradford, in which some of the wealthiest men in Bradford were educated, seems likewise to have been almost exclusively the choice of Anglican parents (though Hinchcliffe was a Moravian).[99] While old-established Anglican families like the Thompsons and Listers had the choice of Oxbridge, the soul of Nonconformity gestated in such as the Wesley College, Sheffield (the Holden boys, the girls attending the Moravian School, Gomersal) and the Huddersfield College (the Illingworths).

Elite education in the West Riding was always denominationally more divided than in Lancashire, and for long after mid-century. The bitterness that surrounded the conflict between Huddersfield College (mainly Nonconformist) and the Anglican Huddersfield Collegiate School smouldered on in the 1860s after the conflagration of the 1840s.[100] Huddersfield College was founded in 1838 as a counter to the Anglican domination of local education.

The major proprietary schools were exclusively sectarian, expressing the strength of West Riding Nonconformity. Besides the Wesley College, Sheffield, the Unitarians, Quakers, Congregationalists and the other sects all provided a Nonconformist education, the Primitive Methodists, the last in the field, supplying for their rich members 'a liberal education without sending them beyond the reach of those religious influences to which they attach the greatest value'.[101]

Thus the range of employer educational provision in the third quarter of the century spanned a considerable variety of institutions, many of them still decidedly partisan. Bryce's characterisation of developments in the 1860s pointed more to future change than present practice: the South of England public school was the experience of only a minority of even the largest employers. The most important institutions, taking the employer class as a whole, were the large number of small, very localised private schools, and the increasingly important proprietary boarding schools below the level of the better-known public schools. These were usually the basic, and often the only education of employers of all sizes. The former, especially, provided an often spirited introduction to religious controversy. John Morley recollected that Hoole's Academy in Blackburn 'abounded in the unadulterated milk of the Independent word, and perhaps accounted for the nonconformist affinities ... of days to come'.[102] Though important for all employers, the private schools were especially the preserve of those below the ranks of the greatest, situated as they were between the mediocre grammar schools and the sparse and expensive proprietary schools, such as Wesley College.[103] Indeed, the Schools Inquiry Commission noted that a number of employers but recently risen from obscurity hungered not at all for gentility, and were often content with National or British Schools, just as they were later to be with the Board Schools.[104]

If by the 1860s 'the demon of gentility' was abroad in the land, it was not to find its full social expression until at least a generation in the future. For most employers until well into the third quarter of the century education was home-spun and denominationally inflected. The historian of Blackburn Grammar School noted in 1892 that as late as the 1850s and 60s the boys of the 'best families' were not so often sent away for their education as in his own day.[105] Though the biggest employers increasingly sent their children to boarding schools from the 1850s, the extent to which this involved the better public schools and Oxbridge can be exaggerated. Very few went to the select South:

in Blackburn only the Hornbys (Harrow and Oxford), William Briggs (Rugby and Oxford), the Bayneses (Rugby and Oxford), the Jacksons (Harrow), and the brewer Sir John Rutherford seem to have had this background in the 1860s. Significantly, in the cases of Briggs and Rutherford the southern experience entailed a later conversion from Radical to Conservative politics. The kind of boarding schools involved in this change were often the West Riding religious proprietary ones (to which Lancashire employers sometimes sent their sons) or the boarding schools of Liverpool, Manchester and Cheshire, especially 'the two great public schools' of Liverpool, the College and the Royal Institution.[106]

Nevertheless, a definite shift had taken place,[107] and one ante-dated by the public school history of some of the biggest Non-conformist industrialist families in the 1830s and 40s, even though the Scottish and European educational experience of such as the Unitarians and Quakers was still of importance at mid-century. Exclusiveness was to be had near home as well as far away: in whatever grammar schools the rich still attended, segregation between dayboys and boarders preserved caste, and boarders in the West Riding were able to buy themselves out of the religious difficulty. Liverpool College was typical in being segregated by money and social background.[108] These changes, however, ought not lead us to over-estimate the degree of severance from urban, industrial life.

Attention to the reformation of local education involved an élite in the creation of the skills necessary for its own continued maintenance in power and prosperity. The movement for National Education, set in train by the Manchester Liberal élite after its Corn Law victory, was represented in a local context by the successful attempt, realised in 1849, to provide a commercial education in Manchester Grammar School.[109] Such an education not only served the needs of Manchester's growing army of clerks and managers, but also provided for many a small merchant and manufacturer, alive to the evils of 'too much' education and not at all averse to putting a commercially educated son to work in the family warehouse at the age of fifteen or so.[110] The foundation of Owens College, Manchester in 1851 (it was not given its independence until 1880)[111], and Victoria College in Leeds, expanding in the 1880s, was part of the same process, though local pride and self-advertisement played its part as well.

The old, unreformed Bradford Grammar School was replaced in the 1870s by Bradford High School, founded by rich Bradford men to combine the influence of home life and public school, as well as the best of the English and German educational traditions (Jacob Behrens, the emigré German merchant, was instrumental in its foundation).[112] Run by the wealthy, but also patronised by them, the school is one example of the strength of the pull of a local, industrial culture at this date.[113] It indicates too how the end of a culturally divided élite was not always to be resolved in term of the outlook of southern acres and southern manners.

While neither the Manchester and Leeds university colleges, nor the top northern public schools like Rossall were especially heavily subscribed by the employers, at the same time a southern education led to no inevitable loss of commitment to the factory and the factory town. The vigorous attention of the Bolton masters to the factory tour of duty as part of a son's education was not at all incompatible with the experience of Oxbridge. An established family like the Ormerods provide one example, and John Clough of Keighley worked as a mill apprentice before Cambridge, returning immediately afterwards to take up his predestined responsibilities.[114]

This sense of commitment to the means of production was especially marked in the case of the Radical Nonconformists, for whom the town was the touchstone of their sense of themselves. This was expressed in their education. Samuel Morley represented on the national stage the experience of many of the northern employers. After boarding school, like his brothers, he started work in the 'school of experience' of the family firm.[115] The Baptist Alfred Illingworth of Bradford was similarly at work in the family mills at the age of sixteen, after his time at Huddersfield College. Nor was it solely a matter of Nonconformists. Many of the Low Moor Hardys, like J. Gathorne Hardy, drifted into southern life, but many also stayed on in early and close connection with the family works; and S.C. Lister showed a similar appetite for work in eschewing Oxbridge after his Clapham Common private school for the education of experience in a Liverpool merchant house, before going into business at the age of twenty-three. For employers more recently wealthy education in the factory was especially marked.[116]

This sense of a distinctive industrial identity was reflected in the public life of the employers, a life shaped and segregated by the experience of the community of church and chapel to an extent that is perhaps difficult to realise today. The daily life of the church and chapel, the day and Sunday school, as well as a whole range of denominational institutions like the Liberation Society, the Church Defence Association, the Nonconformist Association, and the National Education League and Union, engrossed a major part of the public attention of the employers throughout the period. Manchester Cathedral can serve as a microcosm of this life: most of the manufacturing Birleys, the merchant J.W. Maclure (at eighteen years a sidesman, his brother being Cathedral deacon), W.R. Callendar and W.T. Charley, the Salford M.P. – in short the Manchester Tory leadership – were all intimately involved for much of their lives with the running of Cathedral affairs.

This absorption was all the more emphatic in the factory towns, where the means of an organised social life for the élite were still undeveloped. The Ashton of W.H. Mills's youth in the 1880s and 90s was a chronically divided society: 'Our local Christendom was not united, did not want to be.'[117] Where a genteel life struggled for existence it was riddled by the consciousness of sect: in order to belong to the badminton club it was 'just as well' to be an Anglican. Of course the employers lived a life larger than the purely local, but it would be incorrect to undervalue the extent to which their sense of purpose was given strength and direction by the experience of the industrial locale. The factory, church and chapel were not only sources of economic and political power but of an imaginative life too, and one drawing on decades of the local connection.

Employers like the Ashton Masons, Reyners and Buckleys regarded their chapels as a life concern, something over which they exercised proprietorship. As leaders of the congregation they were involved in the plethora of 'committees, "general" "executive", or better still "sub"' that characterised chapel life, as well as in the world of treats, bazaars and outings to be organised and enjoyed.[118] In his Albion chapel Mason was both 'dictator' and 'tremendous citizen' to the congregation.[119] In the West Riding the rivalry of Leeds and Bradford was only the patriotic rivalry of each of the textile towns writ large.[120] The Holden–Illingworth letters testify to the all-pervading and time-consuming concern of the Bradford employers with chapel life.

The lives of Liberal Anglicans reveal the divisiveness the consciousness of schismbred, and suggest the extent to which this division was represented in social life far beyond the church and chapel. R.R. Jackson and the Oldham Platts, for instance, were on good terms with the local clergy and landed society, the Platts setting themselves up as part-time country gentlemen in North Wales at the beginning of this period. In Ashton, Oldham Whittaker and his son-in-law Alexander Rowley ('genial sportsman') were on good terms with the Earls of Stamford and Warrington and present at Court Leet meetings.

Rowley moved in the world of the Hunt and the Volunteers. Mason and his co-religionists shunned the Stamford influence and despised the Volunteers. The Volunteer movement is in fact a good means of exploring further the social distinctions religion produced.

Whatever element of riposte to the territorial gentry's monopoly of military prestige there may have been in the formation of the Volunteer movement in the post-Crimean years; it very quickly came under titled and gentry patronage, and showed every sign of aping rather than rivalling the upper crust. As the Volunteers became socially acceptable, a social whirl was created involving land and industry together in Officers' Associations such as the Manchester and District one, and in the great military gatherings at the Derby or Egerton family seats.[121] By 1881 the Honorary Colonelships involved figures like Le Gendre Starkie (2nd Blackburn Corps), the Earl of Stamford and Warrington (the 23rd Ashton), Lord Frederick Cavendish (2nd Bradford Artillery), Alfred Egerton (40th Manchester) and the Burnley Hargreaves.[122] The upper echelons of the officer ranks included other landed figures but were mainly made up of the large employers and more prominent professional families.

An irate Oldham workingman wrote to the press in 1859: 'Let anyone watch proceedings in this or any other town and places respecting the rifle volunteer movement, and he will soon be able to ascertain that all the parties promoting it are arrant Tories.'[123] Despite some exaggeration, he was not too wide of the mark, and was joined in his opposition by many of the leading Nonconformist employers of the area. Huddersfield and Rochdale, dominated by such employers, were centres of resistance to the movement, Rochdale in 1861 being the only town in the country still refusing to initiate a corps.[124] It was felt that the Volunteers would give power to the gentry and thus to Toryism. Certainly, Anglican clergymen and Tory employers were heavily involved in the formation of the local corps, though in Bradford for example, those moderate Anglican Liberals soon to be Conservatives in name, like M.W. Thompson and S.C. Lister, as well as some Nonconformist Liberals, pre-eminently Titus Salt, were all involved, to the outrage of 'Illingworth, Kell and Co.'[125]

This very limited Nonconformist enthusiasm was to be the thin end of the wedge. As the corps rooted themselves in local life, bringing the opportunity to play the military man, evince Nonconformist patriotism and confute the Peace Society, as well as mix with one's betters, the Volunteers increasingly attracted Nonconformist support. Yet this was to be a matter of the sons and grandsons of the Nonconformist employers, rather than the leaders of the 1860s and 70s themselves. What is particularly striking is the extent to which the Volunteers in the early 1880s was still mainly the preserve of Tories and Anglicans. The 1881 officer listings indicate an overwhelmingly Anglican employer interest that was especially Tory in such towns as Blackburn, Bolton, Bury, Preston and Warrington. In the West Riding more Nonconformists were involved, but the predominant character was one of moderate, Anglican Liberalism, like that of the Halifax Akroyds and the Fosters.[126]

The world of sport, and especially that of the horse and the turf, was predominantly Anglican. Its quintessentially Tory aspect was symbolised in the trinity of London clubs, the Carlton, the Cavalry, and Boodles. The Blackburn hunt, the Pendle Harriers, is a case in point: the pack was run by the landed Starkies of Huntroyde, honorary colonels of the local Volunteers, and supported by the leading employer and professional families of the town, most of them Anglican and Tory. The ungodly world of equestrian sport was outside the experience of most Nonconformists, finding its true expression in the activities of such men as the intermarried Tory brewers of Blackburn.[127] These pursuits thus evince divided and distinguished worlds, but were to serve as blandishments for many a radical townsman.

The frontiers of these worlds were not so definite, nor the ascription of motive so simple as is often assumed. The semi-rural location of a good deal of industry, especially in the West Riding, meant that the hunt was second nature to many a Nonconformist employer. The Quaker Ashworths of Bolton and James Briggs of Blackburn, as well as Alfred Illingworth, were hunters and marksmen who retained many of their religious and political sympathies intact.[128] Patricipation in the hunt, or the building of neo-feudal castles in rural retreats, meant no necessary slavish adoption of the *mores* of county society. Both activities in fact shared much in common with town hall and public parks movement.

The public parks movement, a kind of surrogate *rus in urbe*, together with all these other activities, as well as the great provincial exhibitions, were at one and the same time pretexts for the most unashamed flunkeyism and emulation, and examples of a counter-version of an aristocracy, drawing its strength from a still powerful pride in the unique value of urban, industrial life. The attitudes revealed in events leading up to the choice of design for the Bradford Wool Exchange in 1864 convey much of this ambiguity.[129]

The choice of a modified gothic that rejected the critical implications of the designs of Ruskin and Manners, asserted an industrial identity yet expressed a desire for association with Establishment feeling, mirrors clearly the shape of employer doubts and certainties. Much of the meaning implicit in the choice of design was reflected in the choice of Palmerston to open the building. It is of the first interest that the choice of design, and of Palmerston, was mainly the work of Henry William Ripley; an Anglican, not a Nonconformist, a milk-and-water Liberal, not a Radical.

How late the attractions of rural life were scorned and how persistent was the stigma of trade is conveyed by the examples of two Nonconformist employers, John Clough of Keighley and Isaac Holden, whose lament of the 1890s opened this chapter. Born in 1893, Clough could still feel the condescension of those who felt they were a cut above the regal Cloughs. Secure in the knowledge that he was hardly self-made (rather, after six generations, 'self-inherited' as he says), the family 'talked another language' and knew nothing of country sports. A levelling sense that the family had more in common with the working class than the upper class was expressed in his father's injunction never to call the visiting Asquith 'Sir'.[130] Nevertheless by the 1890s things were changing rapidly: Holden was one of a fast-disappearing breed that, by their own lights, were to stay with the people. The developments that Holden mourned were not a little facilitated by the creation of a social life that unified rather than fragmented the worlds of employer social life.

Freemasonry is a striking example of this, the history of which remains to be written. While its aristocratic trappings and the integration of Masonic and Church ritual may have deterred Nonconformists early on, there are many examples of such membership from at least the 1870s.[131] The Order was a part of the increasing cohesion and organisation of town social life that in turn owed everything to the creation of a civic culture and a civic sense from the 1840s. Bradford is again representative of the factory towns. Jacob Behrens, who moved there in 1838 before the coming of the railway in 1846, described it well: no public buildings, no public control, no cabs, and 'the only thing approaching a club was a toddy-drinking Thursday evening meeting of manufacturers in the hired room of an inn'.[132]

The third quarter of the century witnessed the fundamental change, with the civic building and the creation of the representative institutions of northern middle-class civilisation that followed incorporation in 1847: the Chamber of Commerce

(1851), St George's Hall (started 1851), the new Infirmary (1866) and Exchange (1867), the Bradford Philosophical Society and its Subscription Concerts (1869) and the Town Hall (1873).[133] Along with these went a range of clubs that was to do much to weld the the activities and outlook of the employers, like the Union Club (1857) and the Bradford Club (1866). All the other towns did as Bradford in these decades, the Club in Huddersfield, the Union Club in Blackburn, the Field Club in Warrington, and the many political clubs alike testifying to a new permanence and stability in urban life after the iron days of economic uncertainty and social conflict had been left behind.[134]

For the majority of men of property denominational allegiance and conflict underlay political allegiance for most of the period. This work is at one in this respect with that of Peter Clarke in understanding the party politics of the time to be suffused in the ideas and imagery of religious thought and feeling.[135] The last political testament of that most 'progressive' of all Conservatives, W.R. Callendar, the friend of Labour, confidant of Disraeli, and exponent of middle-class business Conservatism, was of all things a blistering attack on the notion of a Liberal Churchman, entitled 'The Worthlessness of Mr Gladstone's Protestantism'.[136] Religious loyalty stood behind political loyalty, and was so fixed a part of personal identity because it carried with it a whole weight of distinctive social experience.

Disraeli's development of the Liberalism of Peel and Palmerston into modern business Conservatism represented one crucial stage in the movement of the urban, propertied classes into Toryism. The ever firmer hold of this creed on the Manchester business class was apparent from the 1860s, though there were substantial pools of such support in earlier years. It was this concern with the rights and privileges of property, rather than any democratic implication in Tory Democracy, that gave Conservatism its appeal to Manchester in the third quarter of the century.[137] The same can be said for Bradford where right-centre Liberalism was merging with Conservatism in the 1870s and 80s, a process hastened by the outright opposition of many Nonconformist Radicals to compromise over the education issue.[138]

It was not until Toryism had lost its old-fashioned air and raw Protestant and Factory Act edges that the conjunction with Bradford Liberal Conservatism could be made. The two decades after 1865 were perhaps crucial, as the leading Anglican families fused their influence with organised Toryism. Though Liberal unity was firmly re-established after 1874, the drift to the right

was to continue.[139] Perhaps facilitated by the growing worsted
depression of the 70s, 1886 seems to have bitten more deeply
into the ranks of West Riding than of Lancashire property.[140]
Even so, the hold of Liberalism on the Bradford employers,
especially the Nonconformists, was still considerable.

A number of Lancashire observers noted the somewhat slower
rightward movement of property in that county.[141] A bitter
John Morley assailed Manchester ('home of mean ambitions')
and the other factory towns as early as 1868,

For the new feudalism is just beginning to organise itself . . . the Lancashire towns are turning to what they consider the politer faith. . . . The
man who began life as a beggar and a Chartist softens down into a radical
when he has got credit enough for a weaving shed; a factory of his own
mollifies him into what is called a strong Liberal; and by the time he owns
a mansion and a piece of land he has a feeling as of blue blood tingling in
his veins, and thinks of a pedigree and a motto in old French.[142]

Morley and the others anticipated events considerably,
however, noting what were in fact only the beginnings of a slow
change. Manchester was as always in the van of change, and within
Manchester merchant rather than industrial wealth was the more
receptive.[143] The history of two fairly representative families
conveys best the gradualness of change. The two leading Warrington Liberal families were the Crosfields and the Rylands. John
Rylands senior represented the 1840s heyday of Liberal Nonconformity. His son Peter, in his youth Radical and Independent,
turned Anglican just before the 1868 election, and Liberal
Unionist in 1886. Peter's son William Peter (b. 1868) was an
ardent Warrington Churchman and Tory in the 1890s; he was
also Cambridge educated, and trained as a barrister. On the other
hand, Arthur H. Crosfield, one of John Crosfield II's three sons,
was a foremost Liberal leader in turn-of-the-century Warrington.
By this time the Quaker dynasty was in its third generation
of close, political involvement.[144]

The Home Rule split was to reinforce the class perspective of
party politics, again especially in Manchester.[145] In Lancashire
at large a number of the disaffected were later to return to the fold,
and 1886 was if anything to accentuate the importance of Nonconformity in the party, thus perpetuating the old politics.
Baxendale's work on Liberal parliamentary candidates after 1886
suggests it was the commercial and not the industrial sector in
Liberalism that was to diminish.[146] The losses in the larger
factory towns, such as Bolton, Blackburn, Ashton and Stalybridge,

seem to have been far less considerable than in smaller towns like St Helens, Bury and Darwen.

Thus the period was to see a slow seepage rather than any dramatic loss to Conservatism. But of the reality of the change by 1900 there seems little doubt.[147] By the turn of the century the religious sectarianism which had so much divided the élites was in rapid political decline.[148] This was to coincide with the new political articulateness of labour, at first in the West Riding of the 1880s and 90s, and then rather later in Lancashire. As the old barriers fell the threat of labour increasingly drove the employers into the ranks of the upper classes and of the Conservative party. By the coming of the new century Privilege had been shared among the privileged classes, though not in the proportions Cobden might have thought just, and the signs of cultural differences eroded and cultural homogeneity in the making were everywhere apparent. By then culture and politics were well on the way to matching class interest, presaging the disposition of power in the twentieth century.

Summary

The society and politics of the northern employers and merchants are explored here in relation to the place of the monied and propertied elites in the English class structure. In the introduction general questions of class formation are raised which are treated at greater length in the bulk of the chapter. The role of land in the origin of the employers, the involvement of landed society in industrial and urban life, and the amalgamation of both interests in a common Anglican religion and Tory politics all indicate the fluidity and complexity of the class structure. At the level of class interest, in terms of economic interests and ideology, and in relation to the labouring classes, a substantial degree of unity existed between the two sectors. However, centred upon Nonconformity and a specific urban-industrial identity, the level of conflict between industry and land, and the degree of fragmentation within employer society itself, were in the second half of the century both considerable. If this conflict was largely one of cultural style and politics, it was none the less bitter for that. Rather than the industrial bourgeoisie being taken as the poor relation among the British elites, as a subordinate partner in the ruling class, there is cause to conceive of the period as one in which the outlook and power of this class were imposed on society and the state. The especially late persistence of conflict, but the eventual creation of a unitary culture among the dominant classes forms the final topic discussed.

These themes are interwoven in the two sections of the chapter, though many of the issues bearing upon the core of this work – the relations between the industrial bourgeoisie and the working class – are taken up for the first time in these sections too. Similarly, the nuances of employer society are treated at length and leisure. In the first section on elite formation the political-religious map of the North is drawn, and some of the characteristics of the landed-industrial relation are considered. The economic and social origins of the manufacturing class are explored, and related to the status structure of towns. The self-made man was all but an illusion in the factory North. Marriage patterns are used to elicit the significance of religion and politics in fragmenting employer society, though at another level they also point to the essential unity of class interest, and the ways in which a class once formed maintained itself in being. The mechanics of functional maintenance are seen in terms of marriage and dynasticism, the management function, economic interests and activities, and residence.

The second section traces the growth of uniformity (in Conservative politics and the religion of the Established Church especially), out of the diversity and disunion that characterised employer society for most of the period. Fragmentation is viewed in terms of education, the social life religion engendered, involvement in voluntary organisations, and the persistence of a resistant urban-industrial sense of identity. All these areas contained within themselves, however, the seeds of their own dissolution. The rise of a common culture among the elites is finally traced in political terms.

Notes

(Place of publication of books : London unless otherwise indicated)

1. E.H. Illingworth, ed., *The Holden-Illingworth Letters* (Bradford 1927), p. 593.
2. E.P. Thompson, 'The peculiarities of the English', *The Socialist Register*, 1965, pp. 318–19, 324–7.
3. B.L. Hutchins and A. Harrison, *A History of Factory Legislation* (1926).
4. *Manchester Cotton Supply Association, 3rd Annual Report of the Executive Committee, 1860* (Manchester Central Library).
5. *First Annual Report of the Manchester Free Labour Society, 1870* (M.C.L.).
6. P. Anderson, 'Origins of the present crisis', *New Left Review*, **23**, Jan.–Feb. 1964; also *New Left Review*, **35**, Jan.–Feb. 1966.
7. H. Perkin, *The Origins of Modern British Society* (1969).

8.   W.D. Rubinstein, 'Wealth, élites and the class structure of modern Britain', *Past and Present*, **76**, Aug. 1977.

9.   The following may also be consulted: R.S. Neale, *Class and Ideology in the Nineteenth Century* (1972); R. Gray, 'Bourgeois hegemony in Victorian Britain', in J. Bloomfield, ed., *Class, Hegemony and Party* (1977).

10. See below, p. 147.

11. Thompson, *loc. cit.* pp. 328–37.

12. See below, pp. 260–272.

13. See below, p. 169.

14. D. Foster, 'The changing social and political composition of the Lancashire magistracy 1821–1851' (Lancaster Univ. Ph.D. 1971), ch. 3.

15. J. Vincent, *The Formation of the Liberal Party 1857–1868* (1966), pp. 126–38.

16. See ch. 4 below, 'The New Paternalism'.

17. P.F. Clarke, *Lancashire and the New Liberalism* (Cambridge 1971), chs 3, 10.

18. For the chief figures and their areas of influence see H.J. Hanham, *Elections and Party Management* (1959), ch. 14, esp. pp. 287–8, and Clarke, *op. cit.* pp. 249–52.

19. 15th Earl Derby Papers, Liverpool Record Office, 920/DER, 43/3, p. 49, Stanley's notebook, 22 Nov. 1857.

20. J.A. Jowitt, 'Parliamentary politics in Halifax 1832–1847', *Northern History*, **12** (1976).

21. For the areas of influence of the greater gentry, some ennobled in the period, see Patrick Joyce, 'Popular Toryism in Lancashire 1860–1890' (Oxford Univ. D. Phil. 1975), pp. 12–13.

22. Basic source on intermarriage of all élite families, E.A. Walford, *The County Families of England*. For further biographical information see p. 48.

23. For the family see W. Bennett, *The History of Burnley* (Burnley 1951), Vol. 4, pp. 235–49; *passim* for other leading Burnley families.

24. Kay-Shuttleworth Family Papers, Manchester University Arts Library.

25. *Ibid.*, Duke of Devonshire/James Kay-Shuttleworth, 6 June 1873, 26 Dec. 1873; James Kay-Shuttleworth (J. K-S)/Blanche K-S, 30 Jan. 1874; and J. K-S/Janet K-S, 10 Feb. 1874.

26. Ughtred K-S/J. K-S, 22 Nov. 1873. See also U. K-S/J.K-S, 18 Nov. 1873.

27. 20 Nov. 1873; see also U. K-S/J. K-S, 22 Nov. 1873.

28. *Wigan Observer*, 10 Jan. 1891.

29. J. Foster, *Class Struggle and the Industrial Revolution* (1974), pp. 181–6, 196–8.

30. Vincent, *op. cit.* pp. 112–16.

31. V.A.C. Gatrell, 'The commercial middle class in Manchester, *c.* 1820–1857' (Cambridge Univ. Ph.D. 1972), tables 9a and 9b.

32. For further examples of Lancashire industrialists springing from

landed backgrounds, or acquiring landed status early in the century, also for the politically almost unbeatable borough combinations of land and industry on the Tory side see Joyce, *op. cit.* pp. 19–20. For information on a number of these industrialist families see R.O. Knapp, 'Social mobility in Lancashire society, with special reference to the origins of landowners in the "Modern Domesday" 1873–1876' (Lancaster Univ. Ph.D. 1970), ch. IV.

33. *Blackburn Times*, 8 June 1865 (leader).

34. For biographical sources see p. 48.

35. On this see Gatrell, *op. cit.*, Pt 2, ch. 7. See also P. Whitaker, 'The growth of Liberal organisation in Manchester from the 1860s to 1903' (Manchester Univ. Ph.D. 1956). On Bradford see the invaluable D.G. Wright, 'Politics and opinion in 19th-century Bradford, 1832–1880' (Leeds Univ. Ph.D. 1966).

36. For this, and for discussion and documentation of points raised in this paragraph see Joyce, *op. cit.* pp. 22–6. For the growing adherence of the Manchester business classes to Disraeli's development of Palmerstonian Liberalism into modern business Conservatism see also Clarke, *op. cit.* pp. 31–3, Hanham, *op. cit.*, ch. 14, esp. pp. 314–20; and P. Smith, *Disraelian Conservatism and Social Reform* (1967), E.J. Feuchtwanger, *Disraeli, Democracy and the Tory Party* (Oxford 1968).

37. Wright, *op. cit.*, *passim*. See also J.T. Ward, 'Some industrial reformers', and 'Two pioneers of industrial reform', *Bradford Textile Society Journal*, 1962–63; 1964.

38. Joyce, *op. cit.* pp. 28–9.

39. See W.H. Mills, *Grey Pastures* (1924) for a marvellously evocative description of Ashton Congregationalism in the period.

40. For a leading and old-established Conservative Anglican cotton family in Ashton life see H. Heginbottom, *Thomas Heginbottom, his life and times* (1913).

41. For a discussion of this see Joyce, *op. cit.*, pp. 31–6. For the character of this professional class Toryism see Henry Brierley, *Reminiscences of Rochdale* (Rochdale 1923), esp. pp. 1–45.

42. For information on the early textile masters I acknowledge the assistance of A.C. Howe, Oriel College, Oxford, whose Oxford D. Phil. thesis, 'The Lancashire textile masters *c.* 1820–1860', is in preparation at the time of writing.

43. There is a large amount of biographical information in Bury Public Library. For a very useful account of Bury families see B.T. Barton, *History of the Borough of Bury and Neighbourhood* (Bury 1874).

44. For Smith, W.A. Abram, *Blackburn Characters of a Past Generation* (Blackburn 1894), pp. 174–95, and *Blackburn Times*, 7 Jan. 1893.

45. Abram, *op. cit.* pp. 183–4. Smith was drunk into insensibility by the Lord.

46. See the Liberal satire, *Ye Blackburn Election Petition or Ye Last Crow of Ye Olde Game Cocke (Blackburn Times* Office 1868).

47.   *Free Lance*, 26 Oct. 1867.
48.   *Ibid.*, 12 Oct. 1867.
49.   *Blackburn Standard*, ˜23 Oct. 1867.
50.   *Ibid.*, 21 Nov. 1868 (Letters).
51.   See satire on Blackburn brewers for names, *Danyell or Shylock's Kinsman* (Blackburn n.d.).
52.   Cf. James Thompson's obituary, *Preston Guardian*, 29 June 1887.
53.   Abram, *op. cit.* pp. 302–3.
54.   *Blackburn Times*, 20 Jan. 1883; *Blackburn Standard*, 29 Dec. 1883.
55.   Foster, *op. cit.* pp. 177–86, 194–202.
56.   See below, pp. 21–2, 175, 177; also Joyce, *op. cit.* 31–2, 236–7.
57.   *The Chronicles of Blackburn during the Mayoralty of Robert Hopwood Hutchinson Esq. 1861–1862* (Blackburn 1863), pp. 3–4; also Joyce, p. 36.
58.   Bolton Public Library biographical files and folders, esp. runs of articles in *Bolton Journal and Guardian*, 1933, and *Bolton Evening News*, 1933. For useful compilations of biographical information see also G. Evans, 'Social leadership and social control, Bolton 1870–1898' (Lancaster Univ. M.A. 1974), and E. Thorpe, 'Industrial relations and the social structure: a case study of Bolton cotton mule spinners, 1884–1910' (Salford Univ. M.Sc. 1969).
59.   See below, pp. 159–60.
60.   Foster, *op. cit.* ('Lancashire Magistracy'), ch. 3, sec. 2; J.H. Fox, 'The Victorian entrepreneur in Lancashire', in S.P. Bell, ed., *Victorian Lancashire* (Newton Abbot 1974), pp. 103–27. The study of S.J. Chapman and F.J. Marquis has long led scholars into overestimating the degree of social mobility in the cotton industry, 'The recruitment of the employing classes from the ranks of the wageearners in the cotton industry', *Journal of the Royal Statistical Society*, Feb. 1912, pp. 293–306. For a useful critique see Thorpe, *op. cit.* ch. 5 and Appx.
61.   J. Foster, *op. cit.* pp. 9–13, 22–8, 177–86.
62.   *Ibid.* p. 9.
63.   *Ibid.* p. 12.
64.   Evans, *op. cit.* Appx A. ; M. Doyle, 'Social control in Over Darwen, 1839–1878' (Lancaster Univ. M.A. 1972), Appx 2.
65.   E. Lockwood, *Colne Valley Folks* (1936).
66.   J. Wilson, *Joseph Wilson, his life and work* (n.d., privately printed), 'Home life'; J. Ickringill, *Autobiography of James Ickringill* (Keighley 1919). Wilson, b. 1833, owed everything to his mother, a weaver and charwoman, who scrimped to set up her husband, a 'gentleman comber', in the woollen waste business. Ickringill owed a similar debt to his father, who had made the transition from hand woolcombing to engine tenting and mill overlooking.
67.   On Foster see E. Sigsworth, *Black Dyke Mills : a history* (Liverpool 1958).
68.   G.H. Farrar, *Autobiography of Joseph Farrar* (Bradford 1889).
69.   For these links see. J. Beckett, ed., *Bradford Portraits* (Bradford

1892), and William Cudworth, *Historical Notes on the Bradford Corporation* (Bradford 1887). See also biographical sources, p. 48.

70. P. Thompson and T. Vigne Oral History Interviews at Essex University (hereafter Thompson and Vigne); Int. 206 ('Community and Class', hereafter C/C).

71. *Ibid.*, Int. 162 (Work); see also Ints 132, 143, 147 (all C/C).

72. *Ibid*, Ints 162, 165, 181 (C/C).

73. *Ibid*, Int. 172 (C/C).

74. I. Dewhirst, *A History of Keighley* (Keighley 1974), p. 45; E.H. Illingworth, ed., *The Holden-Illingworth Letters* (Bradford 1927), pp. 475–6.

75. E.J. Hobsbawn, *The Age of Capital* (1975), pp. 240, *et seq.*

76. J. Foster, *op. cit.* p. 180.

77. Thorpe, *op. cit.* ch. 7 and Biographical Appx.

78. T. Zeldin, *France 1845–1845* (Oxford 1973), vol. 1, pp. 63–8.

79. For a discussion of these developments see below, p. 147.

80. The 'New companies' column in the journal of the National Federation of Associated Employers of Labour, *Capital and Labour*, is a useful, ready source of information on employer business interests; see for example, *ibid.*,9 June 1875.

81. Wright, *op. cit.* 598.

82. R.P. Cook 'Political élites and electoral politics in late 19th-century Burnley' (Lancaster Univ. M.A. 1974), ch. IV, sec. A.

83. *Blackburn Times*, Feb. 1874.

84. Foster, *op. cit.* p. 182.

85. F.W. Jowett, 'Bradford seventy years ago', in F. Brockway, *Socialism Over Sixty Years* (1946), p. 14.

86. See below, pp. 117–9.

87. See the many examples in Beckett, *op. cit.*

88. The works of William Cudworth provide an invaluable means of piecing together the lives of the Bradford employers, see W. Cudworth, *Manningham, Heaton and Allerton* (Bradford 1896), *History of Bolton and Bowling* (Bradford 1891), *Round About Bradford* (Bradford 1876), *Rambles Round Horton* (Bradford 1886), as well as work previously cited. See also J. Burnley, *Phases of Bradford Life* (Bradford 1889), *West Riding Sketches* (Bradford 1875).

89. Residence of all employers in Blackburn and Preston examined for 1868, with directories, pollbooks, census enumerators schedules.

90. Schools Inquiry Commission: General Reports of Asst. Commissioners :- Northern Counties, *Parliamentary Papers (P.P.)* 1867–68, XXVIII, Pt VIII, vol. IX (3966–viii), p. 753.

91. Rubinstein, *loc. cit.* pp. 115–17.

92. On the Fosters, Sigsworth, *op. cit.* ch. xi, esp. pp. 364–7.

93. See below, pp. 33–5.

94. *P.P.* 1867–68, XXVIII, Pt VIII, Vol. IX, pp. 498, 589, 719–20, 752–3.

95. J. Garstang, *History of Blackburn Grammar School* (Blackburn 1897), p. 143, and Brierley, *op. cit.* on Rochdale.

96.   *P.P.* 1867–68, XXVIII, etc., pp. 441–2. See also Schools Inquiry Commission, *P.P.* 1867–68, XXVIII, Pt XIV, Vol. XVII (3666–XVI), 'Special Report of Assistant Commissioners:- N.W. Division', on Lancashire Grammar Schools.

97.   *P.P.* 1867–68, XXVIII, Pt VIII, Vol. IX, pp. 185–8, 434–34, 509–21, 758.

98.   Evans, *op. cit.* Appx A.

99.   W. Scruton, 'Joseph Hinchcliffe, schoolmaster', *The Bradford Antiquary*, Pt IX, Vol. II, Jan. 1894.

100. D.F.E. Sykes, *The History of Huddersfield and its Vicinity* (Huddersfield 1897) p. 420; *P.P.* 1867–8, XXVIII, Pt VIII, Vol. IX, pp. 233–4.

101. *Ibid.* pp. 231–45.

102. J. Morley, *Recollections* (1917), Vol. I, p. 4. William Hoole was a leading local Liberal.

103. *P.P.* 1867–68, XXVIII, Vol. VIII, p. 255; for the importance of these private schools see the biographical information on a large number of West Riding businessmen in W.H. Scott, *The West Riding of Yorkshire at the Opening of the Twentieth Century* (Brighton 1902).

104. *P.P.* 1867–68, XXVIII, VIII, p. 751.

105. Garstang, *op. cit.* p. 142.

106. *P.P.* 1867–68, XXVIII, VIII, pp. 535–6.

107. *Ibid.* p. 498.

108. *Ibid.* pp. 185, 744–9, and reports on Lancashire grammar schools.

109. B.A. Phythian and J.A. Graham, *The Manchester Grammar School 1515–1965* (Manchester 1965), ch. 3.

110. *PP.* 1867–68, XXVIII, VIII, pp. 712–32.

111. A Briggs, *Victorian Cities* (Pelican 1968), pp. 135–6.

112. Jacob Behrens, *Sir Jacob Behrens 1806–1889* (1925?), trans. Harry Behrens, ch. IV. See also *P.P.* 1867–68, XXVIII, VIII, pp. 234–5; also reports on West Riding proprietary schools, *P.P.* 1867–68, Pt XV, Vol. XVII.

113. For a fascinating account of school life, G. Hurst, *Closed Chapters* (Manchester 1942), ch. I.

114. Thompson and Vigne, Int. 282 (Work).

115. E. Hodder, *The Life of Samuel Morley* (1887), pp. 12–14, 18–19, 32–7.

116. See, for example, the biographies of employer families in D.F.E. Sykes, *The History of the Colne Valley* (Slaithwaite 1906).

117. Mills, *Grey Pastures*, p. 28.

118. *Ibid*, pp. 37–8.

119. On Albion see J.G. Rogers, *An Autobiography* (1903), p. 109, also pp. 107–8.

120. Briggs, *op. cit.* pp. 150–1.

121. For the great Volunteer Review at Derby's Knowsley Hall see *Preston Chronicle*, i, 8 Sept. 1860.

122. J. Walter, *The Volunteer Movement* (1881).

123. *Oldham Illustrated Telegraph*, 3 Dec. 1859 (Letters: 'Workingman').

124. *Rochdale Pilot*, 23 Nov. 1861, 10 Dec. 1859, 14 Feb. 1861 and *Rochdale Observer*, 10 Dec. 1859. H. Cunningham, *The Volunteer Force 1859–1908* (1975), pp. 19–20.
125. Wright, *op. cit.* ch. 5, esp. p. 503.
126. Walter, *op. cit.*
127. See below, p. 288.
128. R. Boyson, *The Ashworth Cotton Enterprise; the rise and fall of a family firm* (Oxford 1970), pp. 249, 254–6.
129. I. Webb, 'The Bradford Wool Exchange: industrial capitalism and the popularity of Gothic', *Victorian Studies*, **20**, no. 1, 1976.
130. Thompson and Vigne, Int. 282 (C/C).
131. See biographies in W.H. Scott, *op. cit.*
132. Behrens, *op. cit.* ch III, IV, esp. p. 38. On the hardworking, puritan, isolated Bradford of the 1840s see also Hurst, *op. cit.* ch. 1.
133. Briggs, *op. cit.* chs 3 and 4; see also *Brear's Guide to Bradford and District* (Bradford 1873), and *The Handy Guide to Bradford, by 'One who knows the Town'* (Bradford 1873).
134. On Preston clubs see A. Hewitson, *A History of Preston* (Preston 1883). There are interesting histories of the Union Club and the East Lancs Cricket Club in Blackburn Public Library.
135. Clarke, *op. cit.* chs 3 and 10 and pp. 14–24.
136. Printed and published Manchester 1876.
137. See above, p. 10–11, and below, pp. 324–6.
138. M. Hurst, 'Liberal versus Liberal: the General Election of 1874 in Bradford and Sheffield', *Historical Journal*, **15**, 4 (1972) also the resulting exchange in *Historical Journal*, **16**, 3 (1973), **17**, 1 (1974), **18**, 3 (1975), **19**, 4 (1976).
For the political thoughts of a typical Liberal Conservative employer, Edward Akroyd of Halifax, see E. Akroyd, *The Present Attitude of the Political Parties* (1874).
139. Wright, *op. cit.* ch. 10.
140. Hurst, *op. cit.* p. 12.
141. W.A. Abram, 'Social conditions and political prospects of the Lancashire workman', *Fortnightly Review*, Oct. 1868, pp. 439–40; F. Harrison, 'The Conservative reaction', *Fortnightly Review*, Mar. 1874, p. 305.
142. J. Morley, 'The Chamber of Mediocrity', *Fortnightly Review*, Dec. 1868, p. 690.
143. W.H. Smith Papers (Brit. Mus.), PS/7 80, R.G.C. Mowbray to W.H. Smith, 10 Aug. 1881.
144. Biographies in *Warrington Guardian Yearbook*, 1892, 1901, 1911, 1914.
145. K.C. Chorley, *Manchester Made Them* (1950), pp. 234–45; A. Hopkinson, *Penultima* (1930), ch. VII.
146. On 1886 in the North-West see J.D. Baxendale, 'The development of the Liberal party in England with special reference to the North-West, 1886–1900' (Oxford Univ. D. Phil. 1971), ch. 1, and Appendices 2 and 3.

147. To postpone the conjunction of classes until 1919–25, as does Rubinstein, would seem therefore to over-dramatise events that had reached a significant stage by the first decade of the new century. The notion that the 1886–1922 period saw the movement of commercial but not industrial wealth into the Conservative party is similarly subject to the exaggeration of revisionism. See Rubinstein, *loc. cit.* pp. 123–6.
148. Clarke, *op. cit.* ch. 14.

BIOGRAPHICAL SOURCES

It is impossible to give full details here of the large range of local sources consulted in almost all the public libraries in the factory towns. There are particularly useful collections of press biographies in Manchester and Bradford Central Libraries, and Blackburn, Bolton and Oldham Public Libraries. These are all alphabetically arranged. The Manchester and Bradford collections cover the surrounding areas as well. Local chronologies and yearbooks may be consulted for dates of death, and obituaries followed up in the local press, though these are very uneven in the quality of information given. There is often no alternative to reading the local press unaided. There are useful indexes to the following in Manchester Central Library: *Manchester Guardian, Manchester Faces and Places, Manchester City News, Notes and Queries.* Aside from the footnote references to this chapter the following are particularly useful:

Collected biography
S. Horrocks, ed. *A Contribution Towards a Lancashire Bibliography, 3. Lancashire Business Histories* (Manchester 1971), and, *4. Lancashire Family Histories, Pedigrees, Heraldry* (Manchester 1972).
P. Hudson, *The West Riding Woollen Textile Industry* (Pasold 1975) (These items are invaluable.)
W.B. Tracy, *Manchester and Salford at the Close of the Nineteenth Century* (1898), and *Lancashire at the Opening of the Twentieth Century* (1898)
Lancashire Leaders Social and Political (2 vols, 1897)
Men of the Period, Lancashire, pt 1 (1895)
W.R Hall Caine, ed. *Lancashire Biographies, Rolls of Honour* (1917)
J. Croston, *County Families of Lancashire and Cheshire* (Manchester 1887)
Fortunes Made in Business (3 vols, 1884–87)
Men of the Period, Yorkshire (1897)
Industries of Yorkshire (2 vols, 1890)
Yorkshire Lives Social and Political (1899)
Yorkshire Leaders Social and Political (Leeds 1892, 1893)
The Century's Progress, Yorkshire (1893)
Yorkshire, Fifty Years of Progress (Leeds 1887)
Yorkshire Who's Who (1912)
A Descriptive Account of Halifax and District (Brighton 1895)

Local items
R.S. Crossley, *Accrington Captains of Industry* (Accrington 1930)

H. Heginbottom, *Stockport Ancient and Modern* (Stockport 1892)
A. Hewitson ('Atticus'), *Preston Town Council: or portraits of local legislators* (Preston 1870)
J. Hodgson, *Textile Manufacture and Other Industries in Keighley* (Keighley 1879)
A. Marcroft, *Landmarks of Local Liberalism* (Oldham 1913)
J. Middleton, *Oldham Past and Present* (Oldham 1903)
R.D.Mattley, *Annals of Rochdale* (Rochdale 1899)
G.C. Miller, *Blackburn Worthies of Yesterday* (Blackburn 1959)
W. Robertson, *Rochdale Past and Present* (Rochdale 1875), and cther publications
J.G. Shaw, *History and Traditions of Darwen and its People* (Blackburn 1889)

2
INDUSTRY AND THE ADVENT OF CLASS STABILITY

> I can look back to a time when the relationship
> that existed betwixt employer and employed was
> not such as we find it now. ... Fifty years ago the
> outlook was dark and uncertain. ... A gulf has
> been bridged over wide as the poet's dream of
> chaos; and the knitting together of units, that now
> form a strong brotherhood, has been one of the
> results ... the relationship of employers and
> employed is not merely a union of separate
> interests; but a recognition of the fact that both
> are identical.
>
> (Ben Brierley, inauguration of the operatives'
> *Cotton Factory Times*, 1885)[1]

Families and machines

THE years around 1850 were to witness perhaps the most profound
change in the temper of the nineteenth-century English working
class. Nowhere was the transition from popular protest and
disturbance to social stability more significant than in the textile
North of England, the home of the nation's and of the world's
first factory proletariat. It was only from the 1840s that the full
consequences of industrialism made themselves humanly felt.
This was so because it was only in these years that a modern
factory proletariat came into mature being. The consequences
of modern factory production were to be expressed in the first
evidences of that reformism which has since characterised English
working-class movements. More than this however, and much
less immediately apparent, this reformism was itself shaped and
delimited by what were for contemporaries more immediate
pressures making for the erosion of class feeling and the augmentation of class domination. The consolidation of mechanised,
factory industry in the second half of the nineteenth century was
the occasion of class harmony more than of class conflict.

The extent of our knowledge of the origins and experience of
the first few generations of factory workers is still minimal.
A recognition that this is so makes much of what follows both
tentative and provisional. Two works in particular stand out

50

as especially suggestive for an understanding of changes around mid-century, those of John Foster and N.J. Smelser.[2] While Foster see the central stabilising force as a newly created 'labour aristocracy' of the factory, Smelser views disturbance and stability in terms of, first, the rupture of work and home roles, and then their differentiation in the post-1840 reformist years. As will be seen, there are important truths in both views, any full understanding of these years having to encompass both transformations of status within labour, and transformations of the family division of labour.

In Foster's scheme the 'aristocrats' are considered to be the self-acting mule spinners in cotton, the skilled piecework gangs in engineering and ironworking, and the hewers and checkweighmen in the coal industry. The mode of division in the workplace was the pace-making, authority-enforcing function of these sectors (as distinct from the authority in supervision proper). Though it does seem clear that around mid-century the limited craft autonomy of skilled factory labour was drastically and irrevocably eroded, it is doubtful whether the new system of authority and status that replaced this autonomy can be understood quite in the terms of Foster's labour aristocracy. In this, technical change, guided by what seems to have been direct employer intervention, is seen to have brought about a situation in which alternative and opposed sub-cultures accreted around the two labour subgroups of the 'aristocrats', and the semi- and unskilled 'undermass' that bore the brunt of their authority.[3] Broadly speaking, these cultures involved the oppositions of the 'abstinent' (skilled) and the 'non-abstinent', and of pro- and anti-employer attitudes.[4]

The content of these arguments will first be more closely examined. The section of the adult male workforce that the spinner would have confronted in the exercise of his putative work authority was a limited one, and hardly sufficient to warrant the notion of sub-grouping. The other grades, mostly cardroom hands, would have experienced authority from orthodox, supervisory workers. The spinners' assistants, the piecers, were mainly boys and youths; some became spinners, many left the industry altogether, and only a few remained to bear the burden of whatever authority was exerted.[5] Overriding all other considerations, and subverting the whole notion of working-class status 'fragmentation', the spinner's family would have been deployed in the whole range of mill occupations, from male piecer to female cardroom hand.

There is a similar lack of concrete definition when the labour aristocracy notion is applied to the engineers and ironworkers. For these groups, the development of piecework, ultimately of the profit-sharing gang, is held to have paralleled the spinners' retention of work authority and status—in the manning of the self-actor – as the means by which technological change produced the *rapprochement* with industrial capitalism. When the evidence is considered,[6] however, it would seem that piecework most often degenerated into a crude 'butty' system, authority residing with the piecemaster alone, and the piecework system driving master and skilled man apart rather than concerting their interests. The piecework system was condemned, not praised, by the many unions involved. Outside textile machinery manufacture piecework was very rare.

In the case of the engineers and ironworkers, the transition from craft autonomy to the loss of control over the productive process attendant upon factory mass production was a long-drawn-out process lasting most of the century. If the engineering lock-out of the early 1850s was a considerable step on this road, dilution of skill and status were apparent from the 1830s, and can be said not to have reached epidemic proportions until the late nineteenth century.[7] Indeed, a union such as that of the foundry workers came out of the conflict of 1851–52 with its craft standing more cohesive than ever.[8]

In coal there was a strong hereditary influence in the hewers' subcontracting system, though recruitment to the hewer grade in an industry marked by constant labour turnover – due to age, migration and sickness – was uncontrolled by any effective traditional or trade union limitation.[9] The checkweighman system, constantly attacked by the employers and therefore hardly a means of binding the interests of the 'skilled' man and his employer, was introduced slowly; not until the 1870s in the Ashton area and as late as 1902 in north-east Lancashire. Unlike the cotton masters, the coalowners were the outright opponents of that most characteristic institution of the 'aristocrat', the trade union. It is difficult to imagine any great cultural divide within the ranks of the mineworkers: aside from the Temperance and Nonconformist leadership, the common lot of the collier was anything but an abstinent one.[10]

While there is much in the content of the labour aristocracy or status 'fragmentation' argument that seems seriously at fault, its emphasis may be ultimately even more misleading. Concentration on 'skilled' factory workers has drawn attention from the role of the less skilled elements of the workforce in the mid-century stabilisation of industrial society. Here the profound importance of textiles is clear, outside a few towns like Oldham the overwhelming source of factory employment, both female and male. By the 1850s the single most important group apart from the spinners were the powerloom weavers, weaving by then being mainly localised in the north of Lancashire. For both spinners and weavers it seems probable that it is in the larger implications of the family's division of labour, first ruptured by industrialisation and then partially reconstituted in the modern factory, rather than in the lesser implications of the labour aristocracy that we shall discern one central clue to the structural elements underlying the coming of stability.

The transmission of pre-mechanised forms of craft or 'artisan' status into the era of fully mechanised factory production, more properly the transformation and debasement of these forms leaving only formal distinctions intact, was of prime importance, but it is doubtful whether these changes can be interpreted in terms of social expressions of working-class status oppositions.[11] What seems more properly the case is that these changes are to be understood in the light of the family, the retention of status being enacted in terms of pressures on family roles. To the limited degree that they were of social effect, expressions of the labour aristocracy figuration can be considered as a sub-category of the renewed covergence of work and home life.

This, of course, is to stand the functionalist thesis on its head. Contrary to the claims of its most immediately relevant exponent N.J. Smelser, work and home do not seem to have been increasingly differentiated after the 1840s. In performing this disrespect to the functionalist corpus one joins one's voice with those of other historians of industrial society,[12] family labour in industry outside the United Kingdom, above all in textiles, being marked until well into the twentieth century. Whether the changes that will be outlined here were of more widespread significance than the English example remains to be known. What seems clear is that in the North of England the kind of 'deference' that will later be discussed (the term is used advisedly), had its roots in community life and was no moral or ideological construct of the 'aristocrats' floating on the unfathomable sea of a disaffected undermass.

What little is known of the orgins of factory labour in the third quarter of the century would suggest that many, and perhaps a majority, had come into the factory from backgrounds outside domestic industry, and in particular from the land.[13] A point too often missed is that in these decades migration to the town still continued at a considerable rate, especially in the weaving boom, in north Lancashire of the 1830s and 40s. What is of fundamental importance is the timing of mechanisation itself, an importance so often obscured by the concentration on the early-mechanised cotton spinners. Labouring processes in both Lanca-shire and West Riding textiles, especially in the Yorkshire woollen trades, were not comprehensively mechanised until the three and and even four decades after the 1830s. In this process adult male labour was the last to be mechanised, in cotton powerloom weaving especially women and children preceding men into the factories. These observations will be considered in more detail later. For the moment it is the role of the non-domestic factory immigrant that will be briefly considered.

These workers would have come into the factory throughout the second quarter of the century and beyond, often without the protection and resource of any artisan tradition whatsoever. As Michael Anderson so pertinently observes in his expert dissection of Smelser's work,[14] rather than coming from an undifferentiated to a differentiated set of economic and family roles in the factory, the reverse may well have been the case, or in many instances no substantial change would have occurred at all. For the rural immigrant in particular aspects of the transition to factory industry may have been a source not of disequilibrium but of coherence and stability. This constitution of the family in the factory would have been of special effect in the 1840s, when in cotton weaving especially men were joining their families in the factory with increased frequency. Thus one link with the timing of the decline of movements of social and political protest is suggested.

This is not to diminish the profound shock of factory life, but merely to say that the operation of the factory on people's lives may have been a good deal more mysterious than is commonly allowed. On the contrary, a consideration of dependence and authority, inseparable from the regime of modern factory industry, will be a major topic of concern in what follows. Rather than inter-generational continuity and adaptation, what so often happened was that men and women continuously came new to the factory and its ways in these years. What they met, and the years between 1840 and 1860 may have been crucial, was industry only recently developed to its extreme of mechanisation. As Marx saw, the force of fully developed mechanisation was well-nigh irresistible:

The advance of capitalist production, develops a working class, which by education, tradition, habit, looks upon the conditions of that mode of production as self-evident laws of nature. The organisation of the capitalist process of production, *once fully developed*, breaks down all resistance. . . .

The dull compulsion of economic relations completes the subjection of the labourer to the capitalist [my italics].[15]

The question of generational change around mid-century is important too. The sons and daughters of fathers who had known the violent and transforming power of mechanisation were often a *tabula rasa* on which the factory impressed its mighty stamp from childhood on. It is with some perspective on the vulnerability of so much factory labour around mid-century that we shall now return to a more detailed consideration of the cotton spinners.

Contrary to Smelser's definition of the position, the 1825–35 period does not seem to have seen the culmination of the erosion of the spinners' authority over their families in work, nor the beginning of any sharp differentiation of work and home roles.[16] Family employment, recruitment, and training of labour characterised most of the factory textile trades throughout the century.[17] Where direct patrimonial employment was not the case, these other family work functions meant that parental authority was often expressed in the individual factory. Aside from these workgroup and labour exchange aspects the cotton operative's family retained many other economic functions throughout the century.[18]

While the limited consequences of changes in factory legislation in the 1820s and 30s clear,[19] the real threat to the prevailing status and family position of the spinner seems to have come in the late 1830s and early 1840s. This lay in the introduction of the larger mule, and most of all in the introduction of the self-acting machine; it is in this context, rather than in that of the creation of 'aristocratic' work authority, that we should consider technological change. The self-actor threatened the whole tenure of the spinner's position; his economic well-being, his work authority, and above all the old kinship-based manning and training system. It seems possible that the 1820–40 period saw an increasing tendency for the master rather than the spinner to employ the piecer.[20]

The lifting of this threat occurred in the course of the 1840s, when the trend of investment in the cotton industry became increasingly labour-using rather than labour-saving, and the industry's organisation and technology took on the 'modern' form that was to survive almost unchanged until the Second World War.[21] The scarcity value of the element of skill in mule spinning was thereby preserved, and with it the superior status of the mule spinner. This change, in the 1840s and 50s, meshed fairly closely with the waning of social protest, though, as will be seen, changes in the family and status structure of labour cannot be simply or solely associated with such ideological currents.

It must at once be said that the fine spinning area may well have fallen outside these terms of reference. With Bolton at its centre, the fine spinning area did not see the extensive adoption of the self-actor until well into the 1850s and 60s, though the hand mule in operation was in fact semi-automatic and long a part of factory production.[22] It is possible that the threat to the coarse and medium spinner was felt by the fine spinner too, even though the technology of fine self-acting spinning had not developed in the 1840s. Quite clearly, it would be of the first importance to know whether the absence of technological threat in a town like Bolton meant that popular protest in general, and spinner involvement in particular, were less marked than in a town like Oldham.

In the more extensive coarse and medium spinning districts the resolution of the spinner's position meant that the spinning community at large was accommodated in the new order of mechanised industry. This was so not only because the spinner's authority over family members in the same factory was consolidated, but also because the spinner was the head of a household diversified in the whole range of cotton occupations. Distinctions of status would thus in large measure have been subsumed in and contained by the family dimension to work. While it may not be semantically improper to consider an 'aristocracy' as being created and controlled by the family and community,[23] it is a decidedly old situation when the plebeians are the rightful and recognised progeny of the aristocrats.

The work situation was thus symmetrical with the shape of family and social relations outside work.[24] The neighbourhood reflected and strengthened the new division of authority and status within the factory, just as in turn the family economy of work amplified the solidarity of place and community. If the family was of central significance in the social changes that led to the acceptance of the social order of mechanised factory industry, then, because of this symbiosis of work and community, so too was people's own sense of communal identity involved in that acceptance. Thus it was that family and community were themselves instrumental in mediating the class system of factory society, and securing the consolidation of the factory's domination over people's lives. It is only with this sense of the rootedness of the new dispensation in people's daily concerns, when communal feeling is seen to have been productive of the consolations of acceptance as well as of scepticism and resistance, that the real

nature of the society emerging in the factory North can be understood. The full import of these considerations will be taken up in
the following chapter.

A very similar situation obtained in the weaving districts, the
family economy being even more marked due to relatively low
individual earnings. The history of the transition from cotton
handloom to powerloom weaving is still a matter of some controversy. It seems that the demise of the handloom weaver was
neither so early nor so rapid, nor the introduction of the powerloom so triumphant, as the work of Bythell would suggest.[25] The
periods of most acute handloom weaver decline can be considered
as 1825–35 in the early-mechanised south of Lancashire, and
1835–45 in the north of the county, especially after 1842 and
the massive expansion and localisation of weaving in the north.

In textiles at large the mechanisation of adult male labour
outside the precocious spinning south of Lancashire, where
powerloom weaving was also first introduced, came rather later
and more slowly than is often supposed. The wholesale entry
of men into the factory can be considered as occurring as late as
the early 1840s in north Lancashire, and even then in Blackburn
and Preston before the smaller urban industry of the north-east.
It was not until long after 1840 that mechanisation was completed
in West Riding textiles, and adult male textile labour finally
became mechanised factory labour.

The mechanisation of male labour took place rather later than
the introduction of the cotton powerloom because women and
children preceded men in the operation of these looms.[26] To what
degree cotton handloom weavers made the transition to powerloom weaving is again unclear, though it seems reasonable to
suggest that many would have done so. Despite a considerable
aversion to factory work, many in the towns would have trans-
ferred, and in all areas the move would have been likely to occur
quite late, after the decay of domestic industry and the early
reliance on female and child labour in the factories.[27] The fact
that the form of trade union organisation adopted by the powerloom weavers owed much to the practice of handloom combination suggests a considerable degree of transference also.[28]
The parallel with the much more rapidly mechanised trade of
woolcombing in Bradford may be an instructive one: there by
1860 10,000 of the 22,000 hand woolcombers displaced by the
late 1840s and early 50s mechanisation had found work in machine
woolcombing, many of the remainder drifting away from the area
altogether.[29]

It thus seems probable that the decisive entry of adult males into the powerloom weaving of the main Lancashire centres occurred in the course of the 1840s. It was then that the family was reconstituted in the factory setting. In these years the labour-using emphasis in capital utilisation became uppermost, the north Lancashire industry expanded enormously, and employment was offered to the village and town handworker, men and women alike. In the course of the 1840s successive Factory Hours Acts took their effect, decreasing the proportion of child and youth labour in cotton and increasing that of adult labour, though this increase was to be more in terms of female than of male labour, contrary to the hopes of the Short-Time Committees.

Though operative employment of children in weaving existed before the 1840s it seems to have been limited in extent.[30] The convergence of work and home roles was crucially facilitated by technological improvements, which meant that the number of looms that could be worked by the single operative increased in the 1840s. It was in that decade that the use of weavers' assistants, paid directly by the weaver as the piecer was by the spinner, increased enormously to meet the increased work load.[31] The difference with the West Riding in this respect was a very important one: indirect wage payment and therefore direct kin employment were relatively uncommon across the Pennies.[32] Though there were other aspects to family involvement in work, the absence of this central element contributed much to the lack of community integration in the world of the factory, and hence to the comparative social instability of the West Riding.

These structural changes seem congruent with changes in the nature and degree of popular social and political protest around mid-century. More certainly, they describe crucial elements underlying the very different kinds of industrial society that were to characterise the two halves of the century. In putting forward the suggestive conjunction of ideological and structural change one does not wish too arbitrarily to marry what are often very ill-assorted partners. Anderson in particular has shown the dangers inherent in the insensitive relation of historical evidence to sociological 'models'.[33] Chartism was probably the most significant of these earlier strands of popular dissent because it most consistently and effectively articulated an alternative and independent view of what the social relations of the classes should be. Its decline, and the rise of ideologies of class harmony based on the entrenchment of mechanised capitalist industry, has to be understood in terms of the interaction of many diverse elements.

A new political adaptability and openness on the part of local employers and politicians was undoubtedly important. The shift of awareness on the local level preceded national events by at least a decade, the slogans and organisations of local Toryism and Liberalism increasingly accommodating working-class interests.[34]

Rather than an explicitly political adaptability, however, the mighty reassertion of employer paternalism after the 1840s probably did more to bring the mass of workers within the purview of the new industrial order. Underlying the response to these overtures was the operatives' knowledge that industrial capitalism was there to stay and had to be lived with in this knowledge: the light had failed and the radical prophecy was unfulfilled. The social vision of the factory worker after mid-century was to be radically different from the social vision of Chartism.

These influences worked in sequence with an economic re-covery in cotton, engineering and woollens that was to be sustained for at least two decades after 1850. The effects of this recovery should not be exaggerated: the life-cycle of poverty, and the recurring bad economic year, were still the lot of the factory worker.[35] But the relativity of the improvement was considerable and was what mattered: people had a clear notion of bad times gone and better times on the way. Along with econo-mic improvement went a whole range of social changes, symboli-sed by the passing of the Factory Acts and the increased leisure they afforded. The long-term effect of improved housing, diet, child and adult education, together with the granting of the vote, was perhaps as important as economic change.

Under the pressure of all these changes a concentration on trade union forms of action to the exclusion of political forms – at first by skilled workers and then by the mass of workers – was the characteristic mark of working-class organisation as the 1840s gave way to the 1850s. This concentration can be related to the pace and timing of the mechanisation of labour in textiles, especially adult male labour, but also to its nature and degree, the West Riding textile industries always being more primitive in the economic organisation of their finally mechanised forms than was the case in cotton. What seems generally to have been the case was that the later and the less complete was the mechanisation of adult male labour, the more was the political action of Chartism and the Chartist inheritance uppermost from the 1840s onwards, and the less was working-class protest contained and modified by trade union action. This was the prevailing West Riding pattern. In Lancashire, earlier and more complete mechanisation led to an earlier and more exclusive reliance on trade union action, which took the prime source of class antagonism – the workplace relations of master and operative – substantially out of the field of class feeling by giving it bureaucratic and ritual expression.

This is not to say that the trade union, and the pattern of labour relations which evolved, did not articulate the experience of opposed interests. Class relations after 1850 were always characterised by a real if limited element of conflict, though this was felt most directly, and most effectively expressed in political senses, by the activist trade union minority; a minority, it should be said, that has been the centre of historiographical attention for too long.[36] Least of all, for activist and rank-and-file alike, does one want to suggest that the creation of trade union organisation did not represent an advance secured, and the legitimation under popular pressure of an autonomous identity for labour in a class society. It must be emphasised however that not only were trade unionism and the kinds of 'deference' later described compatible,[37] but that in institutionalising class feeling in a particular way trade unionism actively facilitated the emergence of such feelings.

Exceptions to these predominating patterns again indicate the autonomy of political and class traditions, and the failure of structural explanations fully to comprehend their plurality. As was the case in the economic sphere, the legacy of Chartism involved advances in popular political awareness, as well as political concessions enforced by popular organisation. In Ashton and Stalybridge, two towns that will form a principal focus for discussion in what follows, much of this legacy of class feeling took the not unusual form of working-class Toryism, the presence of exceptional local leaders like Joseph Rayner Stephens doing much to keep old traditions alive in these two rather exceptional towns. While local circumstances may not be ignored, it is nevertheless clear that structural change was effective here as elsewhere, and the relationship between trade union and political action apparent: the element of continuing antagonism in these towns probably owed much to the retention of a sizeable weaving sector after the localisation of the industry in the later-mechanised north of the county. Unlike their counterparts in the north, local weavers failed to form a viable trade unionism until at least the 1870s.

The other principal exception to the Lancashire pattern of union-contained and politically unexpressed class tension was the north-east weaving area outside Blackburn. As was the case in the south-east towns, it should be emphasised that existing antagonisms were attenuated by all manner of circumstances and nothing like as forceful as in the years before mid-century. The north-east in fact indicates the validity of the Lancashire rule. The area was mechanised last of all, a town like Burnley, where weaving trade unionism was not properly established until well into the 1870s, approximating in most respects to the West Riding pattern of development. Burnley in particular seems to have been the centre of a lively popular radicalism throughout this period, and one giving way to a widespread acceptance of Socialism in the 1880s and 90s, unlike Lancashire at large.

In the pre-1850 period the dichotomy between trade union and political forms of action was nothing like as acute as it was later to be. As Gareth Stedman Jones has so revealingly suggested,[38] the nature of popular conflict in the North in the first half of the century turned on the struggle for control of the productive process. Understood as the destination of control over the labour process, the conflict can be said to have commenced in the latter part of the eighteenth century with the coming of the first factories, and only to have reached issue in the years around 1850. It was in these years that the full human consequences of the industrial revolution took shape. However complex the division of labour was, for most of this period the technical basis of manufacture retained significant handicraft elements, the work practices and attitudes of the craft 'artisan' standing as an obstacle to the full development of capitalist industry. In the years around mid-century the appearances of the 'formal' control of wage labour gave way to the substance of 'real' control, male labour becoming fully a part of mechanised factory production. Control over the labour process was lost as the craft, or quasi-craft, worker became the modern factory proletarian.

Such a process was gradual, cumulative, and diverse, events between 1840 and 1860 intensifying developments that had begun long before. As previously indicated, groups like the engineers and ironworkers would have retained many of the characteristics of craft practice and craft-mindedness. Craft autonomy, like trade union autonomy, was an important quali-fication to the post-1850 industrial settlement, though the engineers and ironworkers were nonetheless to play an important role in the maintenance of social calm and class harmony. Never-theless, for all factory workers it was in the years around 1850 that debased and purely formal distinctions of status took precedence over the reality of craft status and control. This was especially the case for the great mass of textile workers outside cotton spinning, and including West Riding textiles, whose labour status and control were in the process of disintegration long before this time, and for whom the factory represented a source of new equilibrium.[39] This transformation was to take place chiefly in terms of the family, a change which was to leave its indelible mark on the industrial society of the second half of the century.

The spinner and the engineer were for much of the first half of the century factory workers with the attitudes and aspirations of the craft worker and the manufacturing workshop. Their location at the centre of technological change which threatened their whole way of life suggested to them the mutuality of political and industrial protest and organisation.[40] Their struggle was, however, for control over the labour process rather than for the ownership of the means of production, and Stedman Jones is quite right to controvert Foster's ahistorical introduction of Lenin's distinction between industrial and political struggle, reformist and trade union 'consciousness' and revolutionary class consciousness, into the earlier period. Popularisations of that dichotomy that have issued from anywhere but the Left have also marred the writing of the history of Chartism. Chartism represented the unity of all modes of social protest.

This was in fact related to its ultimate ineffectiveness. Despite its radical and anti-capitalist components (and in this it was at one with the radical ideologies that preceded it), Chartism was the idelogy of the artisan outlook, its critique failing to comprehend the class relations of wage labour in modern industry.[41] In this it was as much the natural expression of the early nineteenth-century factory worker as of the artisan proper. For the factory worker, in so many ways an artisan in the factory, was engaged in a similar struggle; that for control rather than for ownership of the means of production. As a 'pre-mechanical' ideology in a newly mechanised industrial world Chartism signified the limits of early nineteenth-century protest.

With the coming of the new industrial system and the loss of control over production, there was a limitation of organisation and protest to narrower forms, chiefly trade union ones. For the skilled worker 'it was not so much their privileged position as the vulnerability of that position that changed their industrial outlook'.[42] All workers, skilled and unskilled, turned to a first though incomplete learning of the new 'rules of the game'.[43] The energies of the new industrial proletariat were given over to the maintenance and gradual improvement of an often perilous economic position. The wage bargain increasingly became the centre of concern, and the institutionalisation of that bargain in the attempt to work the laws of supply and demand the characteristic mark of industrial relations in the second half of the century. Men were congregated in factories in unprecedented numbers, the trade union solution of their concerns pressing itself with increasing force as the most logical and efficacious.

It does indeed seem to have been the case that in those areas where male labour was mechanised last of all the association of the handworkers and Chartism was very close. The politics of Chartism, and its infusion in the radical politics to come, characterised those areas where handworking traditions were last to fall.[44] In the West Riding, above all in Huddersfield and its Pennine valley hinterland, areas which were not fully mechanised until the 1860s and even 1870s, the fusion of Chartism and the protest and traditions of the handworkers was a commonplace in the popular memory, until the later coalescence with Socialism.

The Lancashire handworkers were a great force in the Chartism of the 1840s,[45] especially in the late-mechanised weaving northeast, and it is in such areas that Thompson's understanding of the movement most particularly applies: 'The fullest expression of the values of the weaving communities belongs to the history of the Chartist movement.'[46] Of course the influence of south-east Lancashire factory workers in the Chartism of the 1830s and early 40s was considerable, but the shift in Chartism's centre of gravity from Lancashire to the West Riding after 1842 was clearly of the first significance.[47] Chartism followed to where the condition of the handworker at the onset of mechanisation was at its most parlous, and thus where the Chartist social critique was at its most telling. In Lancashire Chartism lost its immediacy as the social consequences of technological change began to work themselves out in the creation of the factory proletarian.

In Halifax in the 1840s the handworkers embraced Chartism and the new factory workers stood aloof.[48] In Bradford too the soon-to-be mechanised handcombers were the soul of Chartism in the late 1840s. Often immigrants, both Irish and English, the handworkers were culturally distinct and self-sufficient, despite their appalling poverty. The combers and handweavers were the exponents of the kind of militant and insurrectionary Chartism that so often typified the handworkers.[49] In the outlying Bradford townships, such as Horton, where handworking was retained longest, the politics of the Chartist inheritance continued powerfully into the 1850s and 60s.[50]

Thus the shape of things to come was apparent in Lancashire by the early 1840s. In 1842 factory defences by groups of workers were made against the majority of their fellows in Oldham and Manchester.[51] In the West Riding too the 1842 and 1848 disturbances saw the mobilisation of the factory workforce; at the great works of the Keighley Marriners, the Halifax Akroyds, the Fosters of Queensbury, and also in Bradford[52]. It is to the role of industrial relations in preparing the way for the enormous multiplication of events of this order that we shall now turn, detecting in the different experiences of Lancashire and the West Riding an important source of difference in the nature of class relations.

The course of industrial relations

A central distinction between the two regions lay in the development in Lancashire of a modern system of industrial relations, consequent on earlier and more intensive mechanisation. Because of the inherent character of the woollen and worsted industries, as well as their later development, capital investment was not so intensive nor the division of labour so sophisticated as in Lancashire. A primitive system of industrial organisation, involving a considerable turnover of employers, small unit size, and great subdivision of productive processes, made for a primitive system of industrial relations, with all the consequences for class relations that this involved. The following discussion will explore the extent to which the climate of industrial relations in Lancashire was such as to contain and erode class feeling, and bolster notions of class harmony.

In Lancashire cotton the years between 1850 and the mid-1870s were in general ones of boom, increased wages and prosperity, and good labour relations. Increased foreign competition and technical stagnation induced depression thereafter, though this was always much more intense in West Riding textiles. The Blackburn and north-east weaving strike of 1878 was the most serious in north Lancashire for over a quarter of a century, and was followed by less serious stoppages in the early 1880s, though by then the centre of conflict had shifted to the south, and to Oldham in particular. Prolonged strikes in the south-east, culminating in the Stalybridge and Brooklands disputes of the early 1890s, prepared the way for the most thoroughgoing institutionalisation of labour relations seen nineteenth-century Britain, the Brooklands Agreement of 1893.[53]

Brooklands, however, was only the culmination and codification of the practice of industrial peace characteristic from the 1850s. Although there was no total transformation in the 1850s and 60s, by contrast with the 1840s, and especially after the bitter

Preston strike of 1853–54, the change in these decades was very considerable. While not unaccompanied by variations in militancy between a moderate leadership and the rank and file, the 1850s and 60s saw the very rapid development of the bureaucratisation and centralisation of union affairs that was to characterise the reminder of the century. This was especially the case with the weavers, driven to moderation and conciliation by the inherent weakness of their less skilled position. A conciliatory attitude, professing the identification of the interests of employer and operative, was the mark of all cotton trade unionism in these years, and one often considerably pre-dating the change in employer attitudes.[54]

In the following years the stress on co-operation was all the stronger, whether from the skilled, the unskilled, or the Trades Councils.[55] It took a widely representative form in the voice of Ben Bierley, the literary spokesman of so many of the operatives' feelings. The recognition of identical interests, reflected in the words of Brierley which opened this chapter, could receive the most explicit of expressions. Alfred Hill, who succeeded J.T. Fielding as General Secretary of the Bolton Spinners in 1895, in turn resigned from his post to become Secretary of the Bolton Employers' Association, and later a cotton spinning director in his own right. This upward progression, and the lack of rancour that accompanied it, was by no means uncommon.[56] Fielding was one of the formeost Lancashire advocates of the identity of interests. His impressive funeral in 1894 was attended by many employers, lavish in their praise of a great industrial peacemaker.[57] All the cotton unions giving evidence before the Royal Commission on Labour in the early 1890s were unanimous that the possibility of identifying their own interests with those of their employers, and the common sense displayed by both sides, were among the chief reasons for the contentment of the Lancashire cotton operatives.[58]

This sense of the identification of interests was understood in terms of a common commitment to the means of production as the source of a livelihood and a future. Though it entailed a widespread recognition of a mutuality of purpose and destiny, on the operatives' part this very infrequently extended to an acceptance of *laissez-faire* economic doctrine. If the spinners were receptive to cretain aspects of the wages fund theory,[59] for all textile labour the lesson of the capitalist marketplace was that of the unavoidable divergence of economic interests.[60] The cotton unions deserved their reputation for pragmatism: when in 1878 the Blackburn employers organised a series of popular lectures on Political Economy in the town, they were met with the eminently fair charge of the cotton unions that these were got up to swindle the working man.[61]

It was the weavers who first moved towards an institutionalised reconciliation with the employers, above all in the great northern centres; the minority weaving of the south found difficulty in organising its much smaller numbers, and encountered much employer opposition. Building on strong though informal and intermittent traditions, town and amalgamated organisation developed rapidly in the 1850s, the weavers' techniques being laggardly borrowed by the spinners thereafter.[62] These involved a centralised bureaucracy, the formalisation of wage negotiation and dispute procedure, and the active co-operation of master and man. Such techniques demanded union officials who were far more mathematical functionaries than radical firebrands. The foundation of all these efforts was the highly intricate system of wages 'Lists'.

The Webbs remarked of these, 'It is difficult to convey to the general reader any adequate idea of the important effect which these elaborate "lists" had upon the trade union movement in Lancashire.'[63] The Blackburn List of 1853, preceded from the late 1840s by local attempts at agreement on spinners' and weavers' wages,[64] spread throughout the weaving, and then, from the late 1850s, the spinning branches of the trade.

The spinners were always more highly unionised than the weavers, in the 1880s achieving almost complete unionisation. However, the majority of male weavers, especially in the chief northern centres, would probably have been unionised from the 1860s.[65] The distinction between union and non-union labour in weaving before the 1870s was never sharp, those who were not nominally members often receiving benefit and paying subscriptions.[66] Nevertheless, the great majority of women weavers were not unionised until the 1890s, and seem to have had little to do with union affairs. The revival of spinners' unionism occurred in the 1850s and 60s (Oldham was not thoroughly reorganised until 1868), though it was based on informal and tenacious traditions of organisation.[67] After the settlement of the crucially important question of manning on the self-actors there was little of major principle left to separate the spinner and his employer. The spinners were the Olympians of the factory; their organisation classically 'New Model' and 'closed', and dedicated to moderation and co-operation with the employers.[68]

The privileged position of the spinner was further reinforced from the mid-1870s, when the stress on labour utilisation was intensified by the onset of foreign competition and a slowdown in the rate of capital accumulation and technological innovation. The employers were thus obliged to ratify the spinners' position in the attempt to obviate the conflict predicted by reduced profit margins. By so further enforcing the strength of patrimony in the family economy of cotton, and thus the work and extra-work leadership role of the spinners, the whole of the cotton community was more deeply immured in the *status quo* of industrial society, despite the low wages and often poor conditions of those relatives of the spinner in the less-skilled grades.[69]

Cardroom and piecer organisation developed only in the 1880s and 90s when amalgamation was again the key to success. By 1903 the differential between cardroom and skilled workers had decreased considerably. The organisation of the other skilled grades developed in two waves, between 1850 and 1860, and again between 1877 and 1891, in large part stimulated by decreasing differentials with the unskilled.[70]

Local variations in the course of labour relations tell us much about the nature of society in the second half of the century. In limited company dominated Oldham between 1883 and 1893 there were 3,000 disputes, though the vast majority were minor ones (some perspective on this is provided when it is considered that there were around 300 mills in the town).[71] In the weaving Blackburn of the private company, on the other hand, the level of dispute was down to a few minor stoppages a month for long periods.[72]

Thus there was always a groundswell of local disputation that would have come between master and man. Mill and neighbourhood organisation during individual mill disputes would have occasioned solidarity and expressed anti-employer feeling. The impromptu organisation and solidarity of the unorganised worker in particular can be too easily minimised.[73] But such stoppages were also in a sense domestic and ceremonial matters: the employer knew that most often he must take back the same group of known and proficient operatives, who, in a well-ordered world, would anyway have stopped work over the breach of a generally recognised code ('bad spinning', or 'time cribbing'), rather than over any more irreconcilable difference.

Though most important strikes were long, big strikes were very rare. When they came, in both spinning and weaving, the great majority of organised labour was peaceful and resolute. The violent conduct of the great weaving strike of 1878 reveals, however, a latent anti-employer feeling that could be brought to the surface in times of acute distress. There was considerable violence done to the homes and mills of some of the leading employers in <u>Blackburn</u> and the surrounding area. The majority engaged in the violence, and later arrested, do seem to have come from the ever-present pool of unskilled, low paid and often unorganised labour; the Irish, women and young men figuring prominently. Their conduct indicates an instructive and disarming conjunction of attitudes: on the rampage they shouted 'True Blue' and 'We are Britons and we will burn Blackbun down before we submit'. The union leadership unreservedly condemned what was in fact very unrepresentative behaviour.[74] Blackburn was somewhat more remarkable in combining the most evidently appreciative response to a far-reaching paternalism, with the highest degree of weaving trade unionism in the county. It was also, in the long term, probably the most industrially peaceful of the weaving towns.

The backbone of organisation and prosperity evident in the big spinning strikes made them even more remarkable for their lack of violence and bitterness. The long 1885 Oldham strike, like the great Brooklands Lock-Out of 1892–93,[75] is a case in point. In the absence of picketing and blacklegging, and the inevitable return of the same body of millworkers to the same mill, the ordered, almost ritual quality noted earlier is again apparent.[76] The operatives' journal felt called upon to observe: 'One can't help being struck with the quietude in which this industrial war is being waged, and the historian may learn much from it, and convey to future generations information of a useful kind relating to the peaceful manner in which 25,000 operatives conducted themselves during a trying and difficult period.'[77]

The contrast between Burnley and towns like Bolton and Blackburn is specially instructive. Burnley developed later than the other Lancashire factory towns, and contained a much larger proportion of newly arrived employers, neither confident nor rich enough to afford the paternalism of Blackburn, Preston or Bolton. As was usual in such situations, there was considerable employer opposition to unionism and a primitive system of local labour relations. Burnley was the worst paid of the weaving towns, had the worst working conditions, and the latest established Lists (1867 and 1873), which were constantly evaded by the employers. It was only after 1870 that unionism made headway in the town. Burnley was among the most radical towns in the county.

Comparison between Bolton and Oldham further elicits the importance of the distinction between the private and the public company indicated earlier. Although the long-sustained calm of Bolton was also a product of its relative insensitivity to foreign competition as a fine spinning centre (it did not see the great intensification of work-load Oldham experienced in the 1870s and 80s), the greater understanding and moderation of its private employers was at least as important. The distinction between the types of employer in the two towns was widely recognised among the operatives.[78] Like Blackburn, Bolton witnessed a high degree of union organisation and a powerful employer paternalism.

The Bolton employers seem to have differentiated between themselves and the Oldham employers, both in terms of organisational independence and by working on during a number of disputes.[79] The General Secretary of the Bolton Spinners mourned the gradual passing of the private company in 1900: 'A great change has entered into the method governing the conditions of trade ... the relations of the employer and workman hitherto existing are known no more. The individuality of the two men are gone, and they are now only known as units in a commercial arena.' Five years later he remarked. 'The old system of master and servant, where the private employer knew his individual workman and often treated him generously is rapidly passing away. In its place the limited company, with its shareholders, is largely in evidence ... sentiment has gone out of Business.'[80]

Perhaps the first major area in which employer rigidity was relaxed was that of factory legislation. Although organisations like the National Association of Factory Occupiers (Dickens's 'Association for the Mangling of Operatives') maintained a resistance to further legislative interference until well into the 1870s,[81] the distance between public pronouncement and principle, and private practice and experience, was to be as noticeable in this area of labour relations as in all others.

Factory Inspectors' Reports in the 1850s and 70s testified to a very wide observance of the Acts.[82] In general, master and man were united in praise and observance of the Acts from the early 1850s; the large employers, who could afford the legislation and as magistrates were eager to enforce it against the evasive small employers, leading the movement for acceptance.[83] The Manchester meeting of the General Short-Time Committee in 1859 was representative of operative feeling. Making a presentation to the Countess of Shaftesbury, the Chairman of the Committee declared that few, if any, of the employers would now want ro return to longer hours. There was no hostility between masters and men because their interests were now 'identical'. To loud cheers from the operative audience, his peroration was capped by the lines,

We envy not our masters' wealth,
But gladly we increase their store,
We justly ask, for labour's toil,
Sweet competence, and nothing more.[84]

The differences here between Lancashire and Yorkshire are as
usual illuminating. Evidence before the Royal Commission on
Labour in 1892 given by Bradford and other West Riding
witnesses testified to constant evasion of the Acts, though less
by the big men than by the many small employers in the region.[85]

With the advent of the Lists, there followed a considerable
growth of employers' associations to meet the needs of joint
negotiation. There were certainly considerable local variations
in employer willingness to countenance permanent conciliation
procedures, but of the existence of a growing feeling in favour of
some kind of arbitration machinery there can be no doubt, even
if this represented an interference in the sanctity of the relations
of master and man.[86] Despite opposing stands on many matters,
the Manchester Chamber of Commerce and the Manchester and
Salford Trades Council worked harmoniously over a wide range
of mutual industrial interests in the third quarter of the century.[87]
The general acceptance of the Factory Acts and the welcome
given to organised bargaining and conciliation prepared the way
for the last and most difficult question, that of trade union recognition. This involved the most direct assault on the employers'
notion of themseves as masters in their own houses; a personal
as well as an ideological affront. Because this was so, a determined
resistance to trade union recognition was maintained by many
employers until well into the third quarter of the century.[88]
This took the form of trade associations like the National Association of Factory Occupiers of the textile masters and the Iron
Trades Employers' Association (I.T.E.A.), and confederated
associations like the Manchester Free Labour Society and the
National Federation of Associated Employers of Labour. Though
the Free Labour Society had little impact, the National Federation
was supported by many of the leading employers of Lancashire
and the West Riding and was directly involved as a parliamentary
lobby group in the framing of the Labour Laws of the early
1870s.

Even so, the Federation was the employers' response to the
'newly aggressive' unionism of the late 1860s, rather than the
outright opponent of trade unionism. Much opinion within it
was not opposed in principle to unionism. Its chairman,
R.R. Jackson of Blackburn, testified before the Labour Law

Commissioners in the mid-1870s to the praiseworthy and 'responsible' behaviour of trade unionists in his own area, and to the amicable relations of master and man.[89] There was much of the rearguard action about the protestations of the employers in these years, pressed as they were on the one hand by the 'literary middle class' of revisionist political economists and 'humanitarians', and on the other by the politicians.[90]

By 1881 the journal of the Federation had been turned into an innocuous 'Economic, Financial and Commercial Journal', which considered the Federation to have been 'pretentious and short-lived'. When the few who had joined the Federation in the hope that 'foolish coercion' would be effective were disabused, 'the roll of membership, never numerous, became only nominal, and the funds, never large, dwindled away'.[91] Improperly managed, the Federation was 'now almost forgotten'. The judgement ended on the note: 'The right to combine is now uncontested . . . '

The national acceptance of this right was long preceded at the local level by a practical and *de facto* acknowledgement, at first grudging and then more open-minded, that the unions were essential for the successful running of the industry. This change seems to have taken place mostly in the 1860s, though as early as the 1840s in Bolton the United Cotton Spinners' Association was recognised by a number of employers, and trade relations in the following two decades were excellent. In Ashton *de facto* recognition seems to have been accorded at the end of the 1850s.[92]

The progression from tacit acceptance to full recognition was led by the so called 'New Model' employers.[93] In the localities many more than the well-known names of Salt, Illingworth and Morley qualified for the appellation. Ashton was a case in point, the very largest of the employers, men like Hugh Mason and the Whittaker family of Hurst, concentrating their energies on a welfare capitalism that involved a complete *volte face* in the matter of union recognition. Many more of the big employers, whose established dominance in the industry by mid-century was releasing them from the bondage of competition, were to plough a similar furrow.

Labour relations in iron and engineering were as peaceable as those in textiles throughout most of the period, despite continuing attempts by employers to 'dilute' the status of the skilled man, and despite the rumbling discontent over piecework. The exclusivism of skilled unionism, and its special emphasis on respectability and industry, were directed towards the cultivation of industrial and class harmony.[94] The semi-skilled grades organised themselves from the 1860s, and, like their superiors, seem to have gone out of their way to consolidate industrial peace, an effort given much support by the prosperity of the industry throughout the half-century.

The growth of a wider horizon at the end of the century was the result of the efforts of a younger, often Socialist, leadership, as well as the consequence of the general employer offensive on the status of the skilled worker. Even then, craft unions like the Amalgamated Society of Engineers were reluctant to include the unskilled, the real breakthrough here not coming until the First World War. There does seem to have been a distinction at this time between the more militant and less exclusive new generation and the conservative, old-guard machine-making areas of Lancashire (especially) and the West Riding.[95]

Belief in free labour was specially strong among engineering employers, the I.T.E.A., founded in 1872, numbering among its ranks some of the biggest Lancashire employers, such as the Hargreaves of Bolton and the Lairds of Birkenhead. Like the National Federation this had little success in originating common policies, most of the big firms preferring to go their own way. As in textiles, though somewhat later and less completely, there was a practical, often reluctant, acceptance of the permanent role of unionism in the industry.

The situation in the coal industry differed markedly. In Lancashire the history of industrial relations was one of continual conflict. The opposition of the employers to trade unionism, particularly in Burnley, was equalled by the violence and frequency of industrial disputes.[96] There was a strong rank-and-file militancy, above all in Wigan, which frequently exerted itself against the moderation of the more accommodative union leadership, among whom Nonconformity and teetotalism were especially marked. Union organisation was in most places weak until the 1890s, as is apparent from the slow introduction of the checkweighman system, and the general absence of 'marras' and 'cavilling', the methods of on-the-spot bargaining over wages and the composition of the work team; methods that lessened the force of employer partiality in areas like Northumberland and Durham.

If the failure to establish a stable and mutually satisfactory system of labour relations meant that bitterness was often extreme, this did not mean that it was not often deeply scored by the experience of poverty, defeat and disillusion. The consequence of the continual failures of unionism was perhaps as often apathy, and the acceptance of deprivation and domination, as it was class antagonism and political opposition. The limited opportunities for employer contact and influence in the work situation of the miner, as opposed to textiles, were nevertheless compensated by pressures diluting solidarity: the conflict of the English hewer and the Irish daywageman can be understood in this sense (the Irish were a massive presence in Wigan), as can the organisational weakness that allowed favouritism and economic sanctions to divide and intimidate the workforce. The Lancashire and Cheshire Miners' Permanent Relief Fund seems to have been run by the employers to secure these latter ends.

Two comments by men who knew Wigan and Burnley well are extremely revealing. Burnley, it will be recalled, was the least paternalist and most industrially primitive and troubled of the cotton towns. George Roby, a Wigan working man Liberal leader, glumly characterised working-class reasoning in the town after the 1874 Liberal defeat (the big men of the town were Tory): 'We were enticed by their greatness. We were poor, they were rich; we were workmen, they were masters; we were dependent, they were powerful.'[97]

The S.D.F. leader H.M. Hyndman described the Burnley of the 1890s: 'The same men who had been locked out by coalowners and cotton kings voted steadily for the candidates of their masters (whom they would not trust for five minutes not to cheat them on the weighing bridge or in the sheds), and handed over control of the national interests to the dominant class.'[98]

This was indeed the other face of that radicalism and independence that characterised so much of the weaving north-east and the West Riding. If it was the soil of discontent from which grew an earlier and more widespread commitment to Socialist and Labour politics than was the case elsewhere in the North; with the poorest, the most exploited, and the least organised, an acquiescence and deference born of fear and calculation could also be the consequence of endemic industrial conflict. This kind of ambiguous and volatile social relationship was more characteristic of the West Riding, and it is to this region that attention will now be directed.

In the West Riding a fully developed factory industry came later, and often more suddenly than in Lancashire. Worsted combing in Bradford and carpet weaving in Halifax were mechanised swiftly and completely in the years around 1850. Worsted weaving was mechanised more slowly in the 1830s and 40s, though adult males seem to have come into the industry only in the course of the latter decade.[99] The completion of woollen and shoddy (heavy woollen) mechanisation was not seen until the

1850–70 period, and last of all in some of the country areas. The exception were the male woollen spinners, a part of mechanised factory industry in the first half of the century like the cotton spinners. When it came, this mechanisation was always less sophisticated and capital intensive than in cotton.

The effects of the primitive nature of West Riding textiles were overlaid on those of its historically late technological development. The great variety of specialist processes in woollens and worsted were diversified in terms both of ownership and geographical location. The small firm was more prevalent than in Lancashire, especially in the woollen industry of the Huddersfield area, and in heavy woollen towns such as Batley and Dewsbury. Commission working was common in all trades, especially in Bradford.

There was a much greater number of large and longer-established firms in Lancashire, the continuity of employment offered to the individual operative in Lancashire being of quite basic importance for the easefulness of class relations there. The large firm, the seat of the most effective paternalism, was by no means totally absent in Yorkshire. The old-established worsted manufacturers of Bradford and Keighley, the few very large firms in the heavy woollen district, and the large carpet and worsted firms of Halifax were important instances. Later mechanisation meant later urbanisation, and in all areas the large semi-rural industrial colony continued in seclusion for most of this period, its paternalist sway largely unchallenged.

The predominating character of West Riding industry is nevertheless clear. The structural unemployment endemic in a situation of small, often commission-working firms was intensified by trade fluctuations over and above the market fluctuations experienced in cotton.[100] Season, fashion, foreign tariffs, variations in raw material costs, and a lack of alternative markets, all compounded to depress the condition of the operative and sever the link between master and man which continuous, dependable work created.

Bradford woolmixing and worsted combing are representative of the worst of all combinations of trade pressures upon the operative. A special class of woolbuyers in Bradford attended to the mixing and combing of wool on commission. Both occupations had a seasonal character, unlike the weekly buying in cotton spinning, and were carried on in periods of intensive day and night labour. The comber worked sixty hours a week in 120 degrees of heat for twenty shillings, losing twenty weeks in the year for want of work.[101] Whether large or small (and a few were large), combing firms, as well as the dyeing and finishing trades, combined all the drawbacks of commission-working with the greatest sensitivity to trade fluctuations.

The situation in the waste industries of Bradford and the heavy woollen district was similar. Fred Jowett's experience of partnership in such a firm gave him insight into the parasitic, unregulated, supply and demand system of these trades. He also mounted a wider condemnation of the 'white slavery' of woolcombing, and the irregular work and low pay of even such a skilled and superior occupation as woolsorting.[102] Like Jowett, Walter Bateson was an early trade union leader and Socialist. He saw in his own dyeing trade the same long and irregular hours, the same itinerancy of the underemployed, and the 'driving' or 'whipping up' of those paid on time rates.[103]

The difference in tenor between the evidence of the Lancashire and West Riding witnesses given to the Royal Commission on Labour reveals most directly the regional contrast. Contrary to the satisfaction of Lancashire, representatives of all the Yorkshire textile trades, including the woolsorters, testified to their oppressed condition. Low wages, strong masters and weak unions, bad working conditions, insecure employment, and wholesale evasion of the Factory Acts made up the hard lot of Yorkshire labour, especially the Bradford factory worker.[104]

These differences were not lost on contemporaries. Some, such as Schulze-Gaevernitz, probably over-emphasised the prosperity and peace of Lancashire and the primitiveness of Yorkshire. His desire to trumpet the *Wirtschaftswunder* of Lancashire and its centralised, capital intensive, and technologically developed industry undoubtedly had strong propagandist overtones: Lancashire was to be the harbinger of an even more complete twentieth-century institutionalisation of industrial relations, and the herald of class peace.[105] The German was rightly taken to task by the Bolton Socialist Allen Clarke for gilding the lily.[106] Nevertheless, the comparison drawn was a valid one.

The contrast between the high-wage, high-productivity, and highly unionised French and Lancashire economies, and the West Riding one, was likewise drawn by another contemporary, Arthur Priestman, one of the leading Bradford employers.[107] He pointed to the blind folly of Yorkshire employer opposition to trade unionism, and the better pay, social conditions and housing of the Lancashire operative. Comparisons between standards of living and social amenities were made by others at the time, and always to the detriment of the West Riding.[108]

Thus the history and internal organisation of West Riding textiles meant that only the most primitive system of industrial relations developed. Unlike Lancashire, class tension was unmodified by trade union organisation, and received much more directly political expressions in a continuously lively popular radical tradition and the early receptivity to Labour and Socialist politics. Similarly, because of the nature of industry, the dominant mode of capitalism was much more overtly exploitative than in Lancashire, where the objective conditions for employer paternalism were much more favourable. The conjunction of a 'modern' system of industrial relations and of employer paternalism was to be crucial for the development of Lancashire society. The similarity between the class feeling and political protest of Yorkshire and of parts of Europe with similarly undeveloped industries and labour relations systems struck foreign observers of the 1890s as forcibly as did the difference with 'modern' Lancashire industry.[109]

The nature of West Riding industry was reflected in its trade unionism. Fewer men than in cotton worked in close association with each other, and the great variety of textile trades similarly militated against effective union organisation. The history of unionism between the 1850s and 80s was one of short-term intermittent organisation and great employer opposition. Even skilled trades such as woolspinning, woolsorting and warpdressing were only very sketchily organised.[110] Only with the breakthrough of semi- and unskilled unionism in the 1880s and 90s was there anything more than a thin veneer of sectionalist unionism over the great mass of unorganised male and female labour. This development was led from Huddersfield by young Socialist textile workers like Ben Turner and Allen Gee. First involving the male powerloom woollen weavers in the 1870s and 80s, the organisation expanded into a 'General Union' of textile workers, which included the other grades, and especially women, in the decades that followed.[111] However, even at the onset of the First World War, West Riding textile unionism was far less fully organised than its Lancashire counterpart.[112] This late development was reflected in the late inauguration of Trades Councils in the textile towns, apart from Bradford which was anyway dominated by workers outside textiles.

This movement towards organisation, closely intertwined with the growth of popular support for Socialism, can be related to changes in the conditions of the operatives precipitated by the onset of depression in the 1870s, and its quickening thereafter, especially following the imposition of the Mackinley Tariff in

1891. Wage rates in all woollen and worsted areas, and for almost all trades, rose between 1850 and 1880, then fell fairly considerably and continuously to the turn of the century.[113] At the same time, machine speeds and individual work loads were considerably increased.[114]

There seems to have been a widespread attack on the status as well as the livelihood of many groups of workers in the 1880s and early 1890s. The already depressed machine woolcombers were further threatened by the institution of nightwork in 1891, in some cases a husband and wife alternately working the same machine around the clock. Skilled occupations like sorting were also under intense pressure in these years, employers increasingly using unskilled labour for the job. In the same period there was also an intensified attack on the conditions and status of the dyers.[115]

The loss of whatever hold the employers of the West Riding had over the male workforce was progressively lessened in the 1880s and 90s by the decreasing proportion of adult males in the factories;[116] in the early 90s in Bradford, for example, male workers were being turned out of work by women.[117] While some groups of West Riding textile workers would have shared in those processes making for the retention of formal and debased status distinctions that so characterised the Lancashire experience of social stabilisation, these would have had nothing like as profound an effect in Yorkshire. As indicated previously, indirect wage payment and subcontracting were much less common in Yorkshire than in Lancashire. Piecework was far less common also, as were entry controls, either formal or informal. Thus, although there were still limited possibilities of family employment,[118] the stabilising influence of the family diversified in industry, and more particularly directly linked in the individual factory, was far less effective in the West Riding. Opportunities for the kind of community-maintained employer influence characteristic of Lancashire were far less numerous across the Pennines. The structural elements underlying the integration of the Lancashire operative in the social system of the factory were only partly effective in Yorkshire textiles.

The one conceivable exception to this was the woolspinner. Like the Lancashire spinner, he retained control and primacy in the composition of the workteam manning the mule. However, only outside the Leeds district, chiefly in Huddersfield, were the spinners paid by the piece. Thus only in this limited area of industry does it seem possible that anything approaching to Foster's version of the labour aristocracy would have taken effect. The woolspinner was again unusual in paying his assistants directly.

It is doubtful if a labour aristocracy could have included any larger group of workers. No doubt some sections of the workforce were marked off by superior pay and status, chiefly the warp-dressers, woolspinners, woolsorters, and the well-paid, relatively skilled Huddersfield weavers. Whether they can be considered as an 'aristocracy' is another matter. The depressed and defensive position of the woolsorter has been noted. For most skilled labour, irregular and badly paid work, poor working conditions, partial unionisation, and the lack of any rigorous control over entry to the trade present a totally different picture from that of the Lancashire spinner.[119] Very many of the Yorkshire textile trades were time- and not piece-paid. Sorters, spinners and dyers, though not the more numerous ranks of weavers, were typical of the highly fragmented nature of the trades. In some places they were paid by one method, in others by another. And it seems to have been the piece-paid workers, those qualifying for the title of 'task-master', who were the least inhibited and apathetic, and the most inclined to be trade union members.[120]

On the employers' side opposition to trade unionism continued much more forcefully than in Lancashire. Because of the variegated nature of trade processes and practices, List bargaining, so early established across the Pennines, was a failure in the West Riding. The absence of formalised labour relations was a product of the kind of employer class bred by primitive industrial organisation – a class of small, often commission-working owners, involved in the struggle for existence above which the large employers could stand aloof.

The contrast between the great worsted employers of Bradford and their lesser fellows is especially indicative. Such men as Isaac Holden, the Salts and the Illingworths, complemented by many of the big West Riding employers such as the Halifax Akroyds and Crossleys, were either active supporters of trade unionism or else sympathisers.[121] On the other hand, Arthur Priestman's condemnation of the folly of Yorkshire employers' anti-union sentiment, found little support in his own Bradford Textile Society.[122] Although the 1890s saw a measured acceptance of unionism and organised conciliation – the Bradford Dyers' Amalgamation of 1894 was an important instance[123] – by then the horse had bolted, and labour was ranged in the ranks of political opposition to the employer class. The stronger current of employer feeling was represented by the great opposition all the early union organisers met in the 1880s and 90s.

The nature of much West Riding industry closed the door not only to trade unionism but also to the employer paternalism so characteristic of Lancashire. That there were very considerable exceptions to this will be seen, above all when employers were large, long-established, conciliatory, or isolated in self-sufficient settings. As the examples of Burnley and Wigan make plain, however, the alternatives to endemic industrial conflict and the absence of paternalism were not always class antagonism and independent feeling. Exploitation could act on poverty and defeat to produce acquiescence, and a kind of enforced deference, calculating, grudging, and playing rather more on the surface of behaviour than working at its centre.

The dyers typified many aspects of this. More a sub-culture than merely an occupation, dyeing workers were characterised by extreme poverty and the apathy it produced. Their historian describes them thus: – almost impossible to organise, victimised by their employers, at one moment believing in a minimum of organisation and the impulsive strike, at the next sunk in apathetic ignorance, suspicious of the union and given to support for the notion of free labour.[124] This was especially the case with time-paid workers, characterising combers and sorters as well, without fellow-feeling and alienated from the union by fear and poverty.[125]

These indications of the complex and ambiguous meanings of 'deference', ranging between the affective, the calculative, and the coerced, suggest the need for some definition of terms. It is to a consideration of deference, of the workings of dependence and authority in the factory, and of the meanings of 'community' that attention will now be directed.

Summary
To understand the character of later nineteenth-century factory society it is first necessary to appreciate that it was only in the mid-century decades that a mature industrial proletariat came into being. This re-evaluation of the progress of mechanisation and of the factory system provides the primary means by which the social order of the factory is interpreted in this chapter. In delineating the mentality of this emergent, newly-mature proletariat, and thus in explaining the transformation from social conflict to a striking measure of stability and harmony in the class structure, the notions of a labour aristocracy of the factory and of the functional adaptation of the operative family to the divergence of work and home are examined and found wanting: they mistake the trees for the wood.

Nonetheless, if failing to perceive the human consequences of the consolidation of mechanised factory production at the time, both notions offer useful perspectives. In explaining change the transformation of status within factory industry was of great importance, and as one vehicle of this transformation the division of labour and authority within the family does seem to have been of special effect. Above all, proletarianisation involved the passage of control over the labour process from worker to employer, and the near-extinction of those powerful residues of 'craft' autonomy that are to be seen as marking the factory worker – in so many ways an artisan in the factory – for most of the first half of the century. Thus it is that the power of mechanisation to re-cast the social experience of the worker is given a prominence it does not usually receive: so often this transforming power is innocently seen in terms of the *de novo* creation of a radical, class-conscious proletariat, that the experience of dependence and vulnerability, and the internalisation of authority that sprang from this experience, are completely lost to view (see chapter 3). As the bedrock of deference, dependence worked towards ends very different from those accepted wisdom would have us believe. These consequences of the mid-century consolidation of the factory system affected all workers, those new to industry at the time as well as those living the full experience of the factory system.

Change in these years was wrought upon traditions forged in early industrialism, modifying and amplifying the working-class radical legacy as this change was played out in the second half of the century. Yet, if changes in the mode of production worked upon *something*, and older notions of the factory system inscribing radical class consciousness on the *tabula rasa* of those entering the factory gates are clearly mistaken, then the modulation of tradition could be a source of integration in the social order of the factory as well as of opposition to it. Technological change around mid-century affected the labour of adult males above all, and it is in terms of the partial re-convergence of work and home that one primary source of integration may be found: the patriarchy of earlier forms of production was restored. Whatever the status of this argument, and given the evidence available it is a problematic one to sustain, it is nevertheless clear that it is consonant with the mental framework of the factory worker in the post-1850 years.

The kinds of attitude later described as deferential were informed by the sense of neighbourhood community, and in turn it seems likely that it was the new division of authority within the family that underpinned the cohesion of community feeling, directing it to an acceptance of the routines and authority of work. The problem is clearly one of locating the elusive conjunction between what may be termed 'structural change' and cultural change. Many of the ramifications of this conjunction remain still to be explored, but of its significance there should be no doubt. For what is sought in so much of what follows is the isolation and anatomisation of a kind of mentality hitherto blurred in the historial record; that of the factory proletariat in what may be termed its early maturity, a caste of mind sharing in the outlook of the earlier artisanate and the later fully-mature industrial proletarian, yet distinct from either, a unique epoch in the growth of industrial class consciousness.

The difficulties of marrying structural and cultural change are given due emphasis in this chapter, and many qualifications and reservations are entered: in particular, continuities in the working-class tradition were strongly reflected in the politics of particular towns, and Ashton and Stalybridge are mentioned here to be treated at length later in this work. Many other elements, such as the economic and social improvement of the condition of factory workers at this time are here given their place: clearly, the post-1850 settlement was the product of a plurality of causes. Yet of the fundamental significance of the degree, pace and nature of factory mechanization in shaping the direction of that settlement there is ample indication. The most characteristic expression of the ferment preceding the consolidation of mechanisation was Chartism, for it was Chartism that most clearly mirrored the wider kind of struggle consequent upon the conflict for control over the labour process. A whole way of life was under threat, and this produced an urge for social transformation that fused economic and political forms of protest. However, the source of Chartism's power was also the source of its weakness: essentially an ideology of the artisanate, it spoke directly to the factory worker of the first half of the century, himself so much an artisan in the factory. In the new social order of the factory its purchase on the experience of the proletarian was lost. The ideology and rhetoric of Chartism were unable to comprehend the social relations of the factory, as these were lived after the consolidation of modern industry (see chapter 9 and epilogue). Thus in the second half of the century we witness the loss of control and its re-formation in trade union terms, also the divergence and segregation of economic and political forms of protest and organisation. The passage of control over the labour process away from the worker did not represent a unilateral imposition but was in this respect an active formation, the trade union represent-

ing perhaps the central element in the class consciousness of the
later nineteenth-century factory worker.

But this change did represent a drastic narrowing of aims.
The second half of this chapter seeks to show how the system of
labour relations in Lancashire not only represented a narrowing
of aims to trade union ends but also effectively contained and
moderated class feeling by giving it institutionalised and almost
ritualised expressions. Thus the primary source of class antagonism, the work-place relations of master and man, was in large
measure neutralised and the enormous social force of later
Victorian family, paternalist industry came into the fullest play:
trade unions and deference were not only compatible but in many
respects complemented one another. In this second section the
class harmony produced by perhaps the most 'modern' system of
labour relations then extant is explored.

This exploration involves the tensions and ambiguities in the
post-1850 settlement as well as the growth of moderation, co-
operation, and the assumed identity of interests between employer
and worker. The essential contrast is with the West Riding, and
examination of Yorkshire industry in turn suggests the importance
of the nature of mechanisation. West Riding industry around mid-
century represented an incomplete version of the changes taking
place across the Pennines: upon these differences in the degree
and character of mechanisation turned a more primitive system
of industrial relations. Earlier class feeling – less effectively
transformed in mechanization – was correspondingly less confined
by organised labour relations, and expressed itself in the political
sphere of a popular radicalism that represented such a powerful
continuity with Chartist days. The autonomy of the craft was
more resistant and with it the politics that most represented that
autonomy. Because of the primitive nature of West Riding
industry and industrial relations the objective conditions favour-
ing the emergence of employer paternalism were also far less
present than in Lancashire.

Notes

1. *Cotton Factory Times*, 16 Jan. 1885.
2. J. Foster, *Class Struggle and the Industrial Revolution* (1974), esp.
   ch. 7; N.J. Smelser, *Social Change in the Industrial Revolution* (1959).
3. Foster, *op. cit.* pp. 224–38.
4. For a discussion of the 'cultural' ramifications of Foster's argument
   see below, pp. 288–90.
5. Cf. the evidence in P. Joyce, 'The factory politics of Lancashire in
   the later nineteenth century', *The Historical Journal*, **18**, no. 3,

1975, p. 532, n. 24. See also H. Catling, *The Spinning Mule* (1970), ch. 9, and pp. 165, 178 on the spinner–piecer relationship as something understood and accepted by all concerned: 'There was a tacit assumption that it was a mere oversight that the hierarchy of mule spinning had not been set down in the first book of Moses.'

6. It is assembled in Joyce, *loc. cit.* p. 532, n. 26.

7. See the comment and citations in A.E. Musson, 'Class struggle and the labour aristocracy, 1830–1860', *Social History*, **3**, Oct. 1976, pp. 351–3; A.E. Musson and E. Robinson, *Science and Technology in the Industrial Revolution* (Manchester 1969), chs XII, XV; K. Burgess, *The Origins of British Industrial Relations* (1975), ch. 1; J. Swift of the A.S.E., 'Engineering', in F.W. Galton, ed. *Workers on their Industries* (1893). See also G. Stedman Jones, 'England's first proletariat: "Class struggle and the Industrial Revolution"', *New Left Review*, **90**, Mar.–April, 1975, pp. 63, 64.

8. H.J. Fyrth and H. Collins, *The Foundry Workers* (Manchester 1958), ch. III.

9. K. Tiller, 'Working class attitudes and organisation in three industrial towns, 1850–1875: Wigan, Halifax and Kidderminster' (Univ. of Birmingham Ph.D. 1975), chs I and VI; but see also R. Challinor, *The Lancashire and Cheshire Miners* (Newcastle 1972), pp. 165–6, 168–79, 202–4.

10. Challinor, *op. cit.* ch. 15.

11. Stedman Jones develops these ideas in his very perceptive critique of Foster's work; a critique somewhat vitiated by the combination of sound arguments against the emergence of a labour aristocracy around mid-century with an acceptance of the social and cultural consequences of such an emergence in post-1840s working class life. See Stedman Jones, *loc. cit.*, esp. pp. 61–8.

12. For a useful summary of research see E.H. Pleck, 'Two worlds in one: work and family', *Journal of Social History*, vol. **10**, no. 2, Winter 1976, esp. pp. 183–6.

13. M. Anderson, *Family Structure in 19th Century Lancashire* (Cambridge 1971), ch. 7; W. Neff, *Victorian Working Women* (Cass 1966), ch. 2, esp. p. 27; I. Pinchbeck, *Women Workers and the Industrial Revolution, 1750–1850* (1930), ch. IX.

14. M. Anderson, 'Sociological history and the working class family: Smelser revisited', *Social History*, **3**, Oct. 1976, esp. pp. 326–7.

15. K. Marx, *Capital*, ed., D. Torr (1939), p. 761, quoted in E.P. Thompson, 'The peculiarities of the English', *The Socialist Register*, 1965, n. 52; see also p. 343.

16. Smelser, *op. cit.* ch. IX, esp. pp. 193–205.

17. Anderson, *loc. cit.* pp. 320–2, 323–5; also Anderson, *op. cit.* ch. 9, esp. pp. 114–23. For further discussion of the family in work see below, pp. 111–16.

18. *Ibid.* p. 321.

19. *Ibid.* pp. 322–3.

20. The evidence is inconclusive. See M.M. Edwards and R. Lloyd

Jones, 'N.J. Smelser and the cotton factory family: a reassessment', in N.B. Harte and K.G. Ponting, eds. *Textile History and Economic History* (Manchester 1973). But see also Anderson, *op. cit.* p. 115; though the 1833 figures are for before the widespread adoption of the self-acting machine. Edwards and Jones mistakenly maintain that the change was from the non-parent spinner employer to the master employer.

21.   This is discussed in more detail in K. Burgess, 'The family economy of the Lancashire cotton manufacture, 1700–1945', unpublished discussion paper, Univ. of Glasgow, 1975.

22.   D. Farnie, 'The English cotton industry, 1850–1896' (Univ. of Manchester M.A. 1953), ch. 1; G.H. Wood, *The History of Wages in the Cotton Trade during the Past Hundred Years* (1910), pp. 141–2; N. Smelser, *op. cit.* chs VI and IX.

23.   J. Foster, 'Some comments on "Class struggle and the labour aristocracy, 1830–1860"', *Social History*, **3**, Oct. 1976, p. 366.

24.   See Burgess, *loc. cit.*, and Anderson, *op. cit.* chs 5 and 11 for a discussion of urban household and family structure.

25.   D. Bythell, *The Handloom Weavers* (Cambridge 1969), chs 3, 4, 11. Bythell's own evidence in fact permits a variety of interpretations. See also E.P. Thompson, *The Making of the English Working Class* (Pelican 1968), ch. 9; Wood, *op. cit.* p. 123, Tables 39 and 40; Farnie, *op. cit.* Pt. 1, ch. 3.

26.   Neff, *op. cit.* ch. 2, esp. pp. 26–7, 51; Pinchbeck, *op. cit.* ch. IX; Smelser, *op. cit.* pp. 203–4; S.J. Chapman, *The Lancashire Cotton Industry* (Manchester 1904), p. 112, Table, though this is for cotton factories in the U.K., not weaving in Lancashire.

27.   Neff, *op. cit.* p. 27; Pinchbeck, *op. cit.* pp. 184–5; Bythell, *op. cit.* ch. 11. But see also Anderson, *loc. cit.* p. 236, and Smelser, *op. cit.* p. 209.

28.   Turner, *op. cit.* pp. 199–200.

29.   D.G. Wright, 'Politics and opinion in 19th-century Bradford, 1832–1880' (Univ. Leeds Ph.D. 1966), pp. 30 *et seq.*, p. 62.

30.   Anderson rightly criticises Smelser for underestimating the degree of operative employment of child and youth labour in the 1830s; see Anderson, *op. cit.* p. 115, and Smelser, *op. cit.* pp. 200–1. Anderson's 1833 figures are however for all labour under eighteen years, and for the southern half of Lancashire. The operatives employing these assistants would not usually have been men.

31.   Wood, *op. cit.* pp. 30, 142–3; Turner, *op. cit.* p. 31.

32.   J.H. Clapham, *The Woollen and Worsted Industries* (1907), p. 217.

33.   Anderson, *loc. cit.*, esp. pp. 329–34.

34.   For this and a number of other important factors contributing to the decline of popular radicalism see Foster, *op. cit.* pp. 205–12. See also below, pp. 313–4, 315–7.

35.   On poverty see *ibid.* pp. 91–9, 255–60, and Anderson, *op. cit.* chs 4, 11.

36.   See below, pp. 290–2, and pp. 314–5.

37.   For nineteenth- and twentieth-century combinations of deference

and positive attitudes to trades unionism see R. Moore, *Pitmen, Preachers and Politics* (Cambridge 1974), R. Martin and R.H. Fryer, *Redundancy and Paternalist Capitalism* (1973), and 'The deferential worker: persistence and disintegration in paternalist capitalism', in M. Bulmer, ed., *Working Class Images of Society* (1975).

38. Stedman Jones, *loc. cit.*, esp. pp. 49–52.

39. For the retention of artisan values as the basis of an independent working class, though in the very different industrial and political situation of New England, see A. Dawley, *Class and Community: the Industrial Revolution in Lynn* (1976).

40. Stedman Jones, *loc. cit.* pp. 52–61.

41. G. Stedman Jones, 'The limits of proletarian theory in England before 1850'. Dr Stedman Jones has kindly allowed me to read a pre-publication draft of this paper. The application of its findings that I make to factory workers is not in the original. For a fuller discussion of radical ideology see below, pp. 312–4, 335–6.

42. Stedman Jones, *New Left Review*, **90**, 1975, p. 65.

43. Hobsbawm, *Labouring Men* (1964), pp. 344–71; see also Stedman Jones, *loc. cit.* pp. 64–5.

44. See below, pp. 314–5, 320–2.

45. Bythell, *op. cit.* ch. 9. Again, the evidence Bythell assembles would tend to confirm the link between Chartism and the handworkers, contrary to some of the author's protestations.

46. Thompson, *op. cit.* p. 325.

47. I wish to thank Jim Epstein for his advice on the south-east Lancashire association. It is impossible to detail the bibliography of northern Chartism here, but A.E. Musson, 'Class struggle and the labour aristocracy, 1830–1860', *Social History*, **3**, Oct. 1976 should be seen.

48. J.A. Jowitt, 'Parliamentary politics in Halifax 1832–1847', *Northern History*, (1976); Tiller, *op. cit.* ch. 1.

49. Wright, *op. cit.* chs. 1, 3, 4.

50. W. Cudworth, *Rambles Round Horton* (Bradford 1886), pp. 27–8; Wright, *op. cit.* ch. 5. See below, p. 321.

51. On Oldham see A.E. Musson, *loc. cit.* p. 341; V.A.C. Gatrell, 'The commercial middle class in Manchester, *c.* 1820–1857' (Cambridge Univ. Ph.D. 1972), p. 43.

52. Marriners of Keighley, Brotherton Collection, Univ. of Leeds, VI/Box (47) 97; *Fortunes Made in Business*, Vol. II (1887), p. 23; Wright, *op. cit.* p. 325. On the Fieldens, see also, J. Holden, *A Short History of Todmorden* (Manchester 1912), p. 163.

53. For surveys of labour relations in cotton, all showing the predominance of industrial peace, see Farnie, *op. cit.*; Turner, *op. cit.*; R. Smith, 'A history of the Lancashire cotton industry between the years 1873 and 1896' (Birmingham Univ. Ph.D. 1954); K. Burgess, *The Origins of British Industrial Relations* (1974), ch. IV; P. Clarke, *Lancashire and the New Liberalism* (Cambridge 1971), ch. 4, esp. pp. 81–2.

54. For an invaluable, detailed study of Lancashire labour relations,

outside textiles as well, see N. Kirk, 'Class and fragmentation: some aspects of working-class life in north-east Cheshire and south-east Lancashire, 1850–1870' (Univ. of Pittsburgh Ph.D. 1974), ch. I, 'Masters and Men'.

55. For this in a local situation see *Ashton Standard*, 2 Feb. 1872, *Ashton Reporter*, 18 Jan. 1871; *Ashton Standard*, 12 Mar., 10 Dec. 1870, 13 Jan., 10 Feb., 5 Mar. 1883, and *Oldham Chronicle*, 10 Feb., 14 July 1877; *Ashton Standard*, 2 Jun. 1877, 24 Jan. 1880, 3 Feb. 1883. See also *Cotton Factory Times*, 10 July 1885.

56. Clarke, *op. cit.* p. 83.

57. *Bolton Journal*, 29 Dec. 1894.

58. *P.P.* 1892, XXXIV, Vol. I (6708–111), pp. 216–18, Digest of Evidence.

59. H.A. Turner, *op. cit.* pp. 149, 160–1; E. Thorpe, 'Industrial relations and the social structure: a case study of the Bolton cotton mule spinners, 1884–1910' (Univ. of Salford M.Sc. 1969), ch. 2, sect. II; J.T. Fielding, *Speech on Foreign Competition in the Cotton Trade* (Bolton 1879).

60. R. Smith, *op. cit.* ch. VII, esp. pp. 347, 382; R.V. Clements, 'British trade unions and popular political economy 1850–1875', *Economic History Review*, 14, n. 1, Aug. 1961.

61. *Blackburn Times*, 12 Oct., 23 Nov. 1878; for all cotton and other trade union opposition to political economy in the town see *Blackburn Times*, 2 and 16 Feb. 1861, 8 and 25 Apr. 1865, 16 Jan., 2 Mar. 1867.

62. For much useful information on the weavers' organisation see *A History of the Lancashire Cotton Industry and the Amalgamated Weavers Association* (Amalgamated Weavers' Assn, Manchester, 1969), esp. p. 197.

63. S. Webb and B. Webb, *The History of Trade Unionism* (1950), p. 306.

64. J. Baynes, *Two Lectures on the Cotton Trade* (Blackburn 1857), Lecture II, ch. IX.

65. Information on membership in the third quarter of the century is sparse: see Preston and District Power Loom Weavers', Warpers', and Winders' Association, Correspondence 1860–1868, Lancs. County Record Office, DDX/1089/9/1, for 1864 and 1866 estimates. See also J. Morley, 'Lancashire', *Fortnightly Review*, July 1878, p. 14; *Blackburn Times*, 17 Jan. 1874, 27 Apr., 24 July, 24 Aug., 11 May 1878, *Blackburn Standard*, 20 Apr. 1878.

    For the later period, R. Smith, *op. cit.* ch. VI; S.J. Chapman, *The Lancashire Cotton Industry* (Manchester 1904), ch. X, esp. pp. 232–4; H.A. Clegg, A. Fox and A.F. Thompson, *A History of British Trade Unions Since 1889* (Oxford 1964), pp. 26–31, 97–8, 468. See also *P.P.* 1892, XXXIV (6708–111), pp. 218, Digest of Evidence.

66. Turner, *op. cit.* pp. 122–3. Nominal membership is often a poor guide to trade union strength therefore.

67. Chapman, *op. cit.* chs IX, X; Kirk, *op. cit.* ch. I.

68. Turner, *op. cit.* Pt III, ch 2; K. Burgess, *op. cit.*, ch. IV.

69. Burgess, *loc*.cit., esp. pp. 34–6, and *op. cit.* p. 232.
70. For unskilled trade unionism, and that of the minority skilled grades, see Turner, *op. cit.* Pt III, ch. 2.
71. Burgess, *op. cit.* pp. 266–7.
72. Blackburn and District Weavers', Warpers' and Winders' Association, Minute Books, 1865–1868/9, 1884–1890 (Blackburn Public Library).
73. There are some very interesting ephemera in Manchester Central Library concerning weaving disputes in Manchester, 1853: *Strike Committee Reports*, firms of Penny & Wood, Hadfields of Ardwick, see also *Overlookers' Appeal*, Hadfields.
74. Accounts of the strike in Morley, *loc. cit.*, R. Smith, *op. cit.* ch x. The text account is also based on a reading of the local press, May–July 1878, esp. *Blackburn Times*, 11, 18, 25 May, 1, 15, 22 June, 13 July 1878. The early 1880s was also a disturbed period in Blackburn, police and troops being called out on a number of occasions, see *Blackburn Times*, 29 Mar. 1884, 12 Jan. 1884.
75. R. Smith, *op. cit.* ch. IX.
76. *Cotton Factory Times*, 24 July to 23 Oct. 1885.
77. *Ibid.* 14 Aug. 1885.
78. *Cotton Factory Times*, 7 Aug. 1885 and see Feb. 1893; R. Smith, *op. cit.* pp. 382, 414, 502.
79. Thorpe, *op. cit.* pp. 61, 58–9; R. Smith, p. 475.
80. Quoted in Thorpe, pp. 266, 269.
81. B.L. Hutchins and A. Harrison, *A History of Factory Legislation* (Cass 1966), chs VI, IX: *Capital and Labour*, 4 Mar. 1874, 1 July 1874, 20 Jan. 1875; Kirk, *op. cit.* pp. 50–3.
82. Cf. e.g. Factory Inspectors' Reports, Lancashire and Yorkshire, half-years ending 31 Oct. 1852/*P.P.* 1852–3, XL (1580); 30 Apr. 1853/*P.P.* 1852–3, XL (1642); 31 Oct. 1853/*P.P.* 1854, XIX (1712); 31 Oct. 1875/*P.P.* 1876, XVI (1434); and *P.P.* 1870, XVI (1572).
83. Hutchins and Harrison, *op. cit.* pp. 175–6; Kirk, *op. cit.* pp. 114–16; Baynes, *op. cit.* (1857), p. 67.
84. *Boton Chronicle*, 13 Aug. 1859.
85. *P.P.* 1892, XXXIV (6708–111), pp. 243–8, Digest of Evidence.
86. Rept. S.C. on Masters and Operatives (Equitable Councils of Conciliation), *P.P.* 1856, XIII (343), Lancs. and W. Riding evidence; S. Robinson, *Friendly Letters on the Recent Strikes, from a Manufacturer to his own Workpeople* (1854), Letter VIII: H. Turner, *op. cit.* Appx 1; Burgess, *op. cit.* ch. IV; Kirk, *op. cit.* pp. 119–23.
87. L. Bather, 'A history of the Manchester and Salford Trades Council' (Manchester Univ. Ph.D. 1956).
88. Kirk, *op. cit.* ch. I, sec. A, *passim*, esp. pp. 89–92.
89. Second and Final Report, Labour Law Commissioners on Working of Master and Servant Act, *P.P.* 1875, XXX (1157–1.), pp. 123–4.
90. See the Federation's own journal, *Capital and Labour*, 13 Dec. 1873, also 'A merchant', *Observations on Mr Gladstone's Denuncia-*

tion of certain millowners of Lancashire, etc. (1862).

91.   *Capital and Labour*, 13 July 1881.

92.   For these examples and for the wider change of employer attitude, Kirk, *op. cit.* ch. 1, sec. B, 'Reconciliation'. For a full discussion of the employers, new responsiveness see below, 'The New Paternalism', ch. 4.

93.   R. Harrison, *Before the Socialists* (1965), pp. 33–9.

94.   J.B. Jeffereys, *The Story of the Engineers* (1946), Pt II; H.J. Fyrth and H. Collins, *The Foundry Workers* (Manchester 1959), chs. III, IV; Burgess, *op. cit.* ch. 1.

95.   *Ibid.* pp. 33–4, 52, 55.

96.   R. Challinor, *The Lancashire and Cheshire Miners* (Newcastle 1972); Burgess, *op. cit.* ch. III; Tiller, *op. cit.* chs I and VI; W. Bennett, *The History of Burnley*, Vol. IV (Burnley 1951).

97.   G. Roby, *The Disease of the Liberal Party* (Manchester, n.d. 1874?).

98.   H.M. Hyndman, *Further Reminiscenses* (1912), p. 73.

99.   J. James, *The History of the Worsted Manufacture in England* (1857), see esp. pp. 604–11, 618–21. For the history of mechanisation in West Riding textiles see J. Burnley, *The History of Wool and Wool Combing* (1889); E. Collinson, *The History of the Worsted Trade and Historical Sketch of Bradford* (1854); J.H. Clapham, *The Woollen and Worsted Industries* (1907), esp. ch. 4; S. Jubb, *The History of the Shoddy Trade* (1860); E. Lipson, *The History of the Wool and Worsted Industries* (Cass 1965), esp. p. 176; A.L. Bowley 'Wages in the wool and worsted industries of the West Riding of Yorkshire', *Journal of the Royal Statistical Society*, **65**, 1902.

100.   Clapham, *op. cit.* pp. 180–5.

101.   G. von Schulze-Gaevernitz, *The Cotton Trade in England and on the Continent* (1895), pp. 185–7, 205.

102.   F.W. Jowett, 'Bradford seventy years ago', in F. Brockway, *Socialism Over Sixty Years* (1946), pp. 21, 23–4.

103.   W. Bateson, *The Way We Came* (Bradford 1928), pp. 14–15, 8, 31, 97.

104.   *P.P.* 1892, XXXIV (6708–111), pp. 226–9, 231–5, 237–9, Digest of Evidence.

105.   Schulze-Gaevernitz, *op. cit.* chs III, IV.

106.   A. Clarke, *The Effects of the Factory System* (1899), pp. 134–5, 145.

107.   A. Priestman, 'Our industrial system . . . ', *Journal of the Bradford Textile Society*, I, no. 4, 1895; see also nos 1–3, 1894.

108.   A. Shadwell, *Industrial Efficiency*, 2 vols (1906), Vol. I, p. 113; Schulze-Gaevernitz, *op. cit.* p. 206.

109.   F. Merttens, 'The hours and conditions of labour in the cotton industry at home and abroad', *Transactions of the Manchester Statistical Society*, 1893–94; Schulze-Gaevernitz, *op. cit.* pp. 205–14. See also below, p. 226.

110.   K. Laybourn, 'The attitudes of Yorkshire trade unions to the economic and social problems of the Great Depression, 1873–1896' (Lancaster Univ. Ph.D. 1972), esp. ch. 3.

111. B. Turner, *Short History of the General Union of Textile Workers* (Heckmondwike 1920), *A Short Account of the Rise and Progress of the Heavy Woollen District Branch of the General Union of Textile Workers (Yorkshire Factory Times* 1917), *About Myself, 1863–1930* (1930). See also Bateson, *op. cit.*

112. Turner, *op. cit.* pp. 173–8.

113. Bowley, *loc. cit.*; see also T. Baines, *Yorkshire, Past and Present, including an account of the woollen trade by Edward Baines,* Vols I and II (1871, 1877), pp. 650–5, 669–72, 695–6; 340–3.

114. Laybourn, *op. cit.* chs 1 and 9.

115. Clapham, *op. cit.* p. 220 ; *P.P.* 1892, XXXIV (6708–111), pp. 232–3, 234, Digest of Evidence.

116. Bowley, *loc. cit., passim*; Laybourn, *op. cit.* chp. 3, esp. p. 138; *P.P.* 1892, XXXIV (6708–111), pp. 226–7.

117. *P.P.* 1892, XXXIV ... , p. 229.

118. J. Bornat, 'Home and work: a new context for trade union history', *Oral History,* 5, no. 2, 1977, esp. pp. 111–12.

119. On the flexibility of informal entry controls, cf. Clapham, *op. cit.* pp. 219–20.

120. Bateson, *op. cit.* pp. 8–9, 44; *P.P.* 1892, XXXIV ... , p. 233.

121. For Isaac Holden see E.H. Illingworth, ed., *The Holden-Illingworth Letters* (Bradford 1927), pp. 591–3.

122. 'Trade unions and trade combinations', *Journal of the Bradford Textile Society,* 1, no. 5, Feb. 1895.

123. Bateson, *op. cit.* chs XIII, XIX.

124. *Ibid.* pp. 8, 9; ch. II; 30–2; 42–4; ch. X; 70; ch. XIX, esp. p. 101.

125. *P.P.* 1892, XXXIV (6708–111), pp. 228, 232, 233.

3
DEFERENCE, DEPENDENCE AND COMMUNITY

They have no true idea of life. They believe they are born to work; they do not see that work is but a means to life. ... They think that the masters build factories and workshops not to make a living for themselves by trading but in order to find the people employment. They honestly believe that if there were no mills and workshops the poor people would all perish.

(Allen Clarke, Bolton operative, journalist and socialist, on the operatives of his town in 1899)[1]

... as a rule in the cotton districts where the trade relations between master and man have been ... established on a satisfactory basis, the man, in the truly feudal spirit, takes part with his master, and wears his political colour. This current of things ... 'esprit de corps' interesting the employed in the triumph of this mill over that, is not likely to change immediately nor for a long while to come.

(John Morley, a son of Blackburn, on the Lancashire of the 1860s)[2]

Deference reconsidered

When the factory society of the North in the second half of the nineteenth century is penetrated to any depth it is apparent that the period witnessed a degree of social calm perhaps unique in English industrial society. Rather than the class solidarities and antagonisms so often associated with the development of modern industrial society, the obverse of these feelings constantly suggests itself. More often than not, the tie of employer and worker was one of emotional identification, in which the worker acquiesced in his own subordination. Making sense of these unexpected and contrary feelings presents considerable difficulty.

To characterise them by the term 'deference' is immediately to encounter the chaos of usages that has marked the term's employment. At no time has definition been so elastic as in the 1960s, when sociologists and political scientists turned to the notion in order to explain the considerable electoral success of the Conservatives in the preceding decade. Hindsight has dealt a little harshly with the political scientists,[3] as well as with that sociological neighbour of the deference notion, the idea of the 'embourgeoisement' of sectors of the working class.[4] Yet while labour historians are often still content to trundle forward the labour aristocrat as a kind of prototype of the 'embourgeoisefied' twentieth-century worker, political historians, above all the students of *Hochpolitik*, are no less content with the unexamined premise. The deference of the political historians is a deference without a history and without a society; something God-given in the ether of English political life, there to be nosed, much in the manner of Bagehot, with an exquisite discrimination. Despite the difficulties of definition and multifarious usage, however, the notion of deference can still be a helpful one.

Howard Newby's recent evaluation of the debate is especially useful.[5] In so far as deference has been defined with any rigour, Newby suggestively distinguishes between a concentration upon behaviour and upon attitudes. A concern with the former, whether forelock-tugging or voting Conservative, too often ignores the force of the merely ritual and external, and the presence of purely calculative behaviour. While ritualised behaviour is so often the management of impressions, what has been called 'the necessary pose of the powerless', Tory working-class voting can be even more a matter of calculation.

On the other hand, attitudinal definitions can lead to a concentration upon the attributes of people rather than on the social context. Such approaches tend to oversimplify the coherence of sets of attitudes, often dealing in ahistorical constructs such as a 'deferential personality', which are unable to comprehend the basic and the deviant forms of behaviour within the same explanatory matrix. Such formulations also tend to exaggerate the moral subordination the inferior undergoes. Clearly, those characterised by deferential beliefs are very often steadfast in the defence of their own self-respect. The relationship between superior and inferior is perceived as one of partnership or interdependence, however bogus in reality this may be.[6]

According to Newby, what may be the most valuable way forward is an understanding of deference that encompasses both behaviour and attitudes, and considers deference as a form of social interaction or relationship. This approach nevertheless evades the central problem of evaluating the nature of behaviour and attitudes. The concern in the preceding chapter of this work with the range of responses that may be categorised as 'deferential', varying between the affective and the coerced, illustrates the historian's necessary attempt at elucidating the experience of those held to have shown deference. However theoretically unsatisfactory may be the outcome of the attempt at discrimination, we need to know what deference meant to the object of the 'deferential relationship'.

Newby's resolution of the conceptual difficulties in terms of social interaction or dialectic is nevertheless illuminating. Deference is centrally linked with the legitimation of social hierarchy. More particularly, and in the terms of Weber that do not seem inappropriate to nineteenth-century industrial society, deference is 'the form of social interaction which occurs in situations involving the exercise of traditional authority'.[7] Deference is therefore the social relationship that converts power relations into moral ones, and ensures the stability of hierarchy threatened by the less efficient, potentially unstable, coercive relationship. Deference establishes stabilisation by means of the superordinate's manipulation of the situation; in essence the management of the opposing tensions of differentiation from and identification with the subordinate. These tensions will of course be at their most volatile and disruptive in the market situation of capitalist industrial society.

The various aspects of deference so considered are developed by Newby.[8] What would seem to be the basic element among them is what Newby terms 'ideological hegemony',[9] the means by which legitimacy accrues to the élite, and the 'is' of power relations becomes the 'ought' of moral ones. Construing the terminology of 'hegemony' in a more metaphoric, more concrete, and less formal sense than is usual, I would prefer to describe this inculcation of the élite's definition of the situation as a 'cultural' or 'social' hegemony, rather than an ideological one. This change of vocabulary helps direct attention away from the notion of the ideological 'co-option' of the superior grades of factory labour by the ethic of respectability and 'improvement'; something essentially epiphenomenal in nineteenth-century industrial society. The history of the nineteenth-century English working class has too long been written in terms of the economic and ideological 'capture' of an aristocracy.

On the contrary, the coming of social stability and the acceptance of the power relations of industrial society are to be understood in terms of the family and of neighbourhood community, terms that involved the *whole* of the workforce at the level of quotidian life. While sets of ideas interpreting and reinforcing the power of an élite cannot be separated from the social *milieux* in which they took form, it was in fact the *milieux* that mattered rather more than the ideas. The 'hegemony' the employers enjoyed was only at a second remove an 'ideological' one. The dominance the employers exerted was over the ordinary business of people's lives, inside and outside the factory.

Thus the family in work, and its reflection in the structure of communal status and authority outside work, were instrumental in making the sense of place, of belonging, a source of integration in post-1850 factory society. Acceptance of and accommodation within the new social order of factory industry were enacted in community terms, and the end result was compounded by the employers' permeation of the locale and so of this very sense of place and belonging: deference was so strong because family and community did so much to underpin it. When the term community is used, therefore, it is not only in the limited and Durkheimian sense of society, of the classes, or of master and man that we speak, but also in a much more radical sense of the deep ambiguity of the life that working people made for themselves. The 'communal sociability' that is so often taken as the mark of class selfhood and demarcation was as often the source of subordination and deference. The obverse is of course true: the sense of community that strengthened deference also shot it through with ambiguity, just because it was both self-sustained and deeply marked by the impress of the factory regime.

The sense of mutual constraints, bounds beyond which the superior as well as the inferior could not trespass, is of course integral to any proper understanding of hegemonic social relations. This was particularly marked in *laissez faire* industrial capitalism. Just as Law in the eighteenth century was the prison of the rulers as of the ruled, curbing as it disguised the realities of power,[10] so too in nineteenth-century industrial society the stability of the deferential relationship was at the mercy of the etiquette of mystification. Impermissible behaviour involved the danger of deference being 'seen through'. In this respect paternalism had to deliver the economic goods. In this discussion of the moral significance of paternalism and deference, the economic uses of deference, and the extent to which it depended upon and in turn had to support a certain level of economic wellbeing in order to be effective, should not be lost sight of. R. Moore has shown for the English North-East how the onset of economic depression, and the failure to deliver the economic promise of paternalism, could very quickly result in the disintegration of deference.[11]

Similarly, a paternalist regime that reneged on its implied prohibition of coercion stood in danger of destroying the mechanism which enabled moral relations to root themselves in power ones. The operatives' dislike of the grosser forms of patronage signified another boundary to deference. These prohibitions serve to remind us of other consequences of working-class community being the product of working-class lives. Indeed, throughout this work, the inadequacies of notions of middle-class cultural evangelisation will constantly suggest the powerful resources of independence that remained as a counter to the tide of employer hegemony.

Nonetheless, the northern employer class was skilled in the arts of an élite. Intent on maintaining their own version of the workers' 'independence' intact, yet also sensitive to the sensitivities of the operative, the employers were averse to trespassing on self-respect by ostentatious and demeaning patronage. The extent of the employers' domination of the factory neighbourhood can hardly be exaggerated. The paternalism that gave hegemony form was most effective on a face-to-face basis, and the pre-bureaucratic factory of the North was its most effective vehicle. The inculcation of subordination set the highest premium on the élite's influence over the totality of operative experience. Though never complete, this capacity to delimit the horizons of people's lives meant that the factory worker 'knew his place': the ties of dependency and hierarchy were everywhere apparent, and deference was seen to be the natural exchange for paternalism. Thus the emphasis upon territory and localism was quite central to the success of paternalism. The factory and its neighbourhood reinforced the solidarity and totality of place, and made the identification of master and operative possible.[12]

The foregoing emphasis on the communal basis of deference, and the undoubted significance of the territorial, the local, and the immediate, are congruent with two major developments in later nineteenth-century industrial society that will later be discussed: the ecology of the factory town, and the development, after about 1850, of a far-reaching employer paternalism. These powerfully retarded the growth of impersonality, calculation, and class segregation that are so often and so simplistically supposed to have marked the development of factory life. Later nineteenth-century industrial society developed in such a way as to make localism and territory more rather than less significant, and so to ensure the success of employer hegemony.

It therefore seems apparent that to the extent that hegemony obtained, and the employers' influence delimited and entered into the totality of operative life, and to the degree that ulterior influences were excluded, or else (as in the case of the trade

unions) their effect was qualified and minimised, the more likely
was it that the dominant characteristic of the deferential relationship would be the affective or 'organic' tie. Thus the definition
of deference as a social relationship indicates not only the importance of the élite's attempts to manage the situation, exercise
authority, and thus secure legitimacy and stability, but it also
suggests a means of evaluating the nature of the deferential response. Even so, that response still remains elusive, and deference
so defined is only partly effective in guiding us to a recognition
of what deference was in people's lives and how it can be
identified.

Perhaps there is no answer to these questions. The problem
is ultimately one of evidence, and of the impenetrability of
ordinary lives in the past. Clearly, when it is most effective,
deference involves the subscription to a moral order that validates
the subject's own subordination. Yet, as we have seen, social
situations in which deference worked are invariably full of
tensions and ambiguities. Similarly, the realities of poverty,
dependence and authority are never far from the foreground in
such situations.

This prompts the recognition that the acquiescece born
chiefly of calculation and subjection, typical of parts of Lancashire
but the West Riding in particular, is also deference; a kind of
'subjugatory' deference. Deference is to be construed as a continuum of feeling in which the affective and the coerced are never
strangers, and the inward and outward never distinct. Recognising
which is uppermost throws us back on the evidence and the
concrete historical situation. What the evidence suggests so
strongly, above all for Lancashire but also for parts of the West
Riding, is that deference did have a real inwardness. And this
should be insisted on, in the light of any tendency to envisage
it as a matter of behaviour and manners, and not of attitudes and
morals.

Deference defined as social interaction is the outcome of the
stratification system and not its source. Power relations, in the
present case economic dominance as expressed in the subordinate's experience of authority and economic dependence,
while they do not in themselves elicit the kind of deference that
best ensures stability, are to be understood as the preconditions
of deference. They establish the quality of social relationship and
the habits of mind that enable deference to function. Power
relations are invariably at the back of moral ones. It is with a
recognition of this that authority and dependence in the factory
will now be further considered.

Authority and dependence in the factory

Dependence was the mark of all factory labour. The degree of its effect varied with the extent to which some real measure of craft autonomy was retained after mid-century. The cotton spinner is perhaps the central case in point. Midway between the engineer and the cotton weaver in terms of autonomous work practice and outlook, his subordination to the regime of mechanised factory production indicates the weakness of the skilled man in general, but especially the dependence and vulnerability of the great mass of textile operatives. So much has been made of the spinner's retention of quasi-craft status, reflected in pay differentials, control of the work team, and involvement in production pace, that it is easy to forget how like the rest of the factory workforce he really was. Control over the productive process had passed from man to master, and with that passing the vulnerability that underscored dependence became the common lot of factory labour.

The factory worker was vulnerable in the labour market. Whatever advantage was secured in the more frequent boom years of the third quarter of the century was more than offset by the large reservoirs of trained labour in the factory towns, where cotton was the common experience of men and women from their earliest years.[13] In Lancashire even more than elsewhere, the Irish comprised a pool of often cheaper and unskilled labour. As the 'external enemy' they can also be understood as the 'poor whites' of the North, healing the wounds of dependence felt most sorely by the less skilled. Vulnerability was a consequence of poverty, and poverty a question of proportion. When understood in terms of what had gone before, the increase in prosperity after mid-century was of great effect. Through twentieth-century eyes it is an existence on the margins of degradation that is so often apparent.

The spinner was very far from being his own master. Overlooking in spinning seems to have developed slowly, but by the last quarter of the century it was fairly common. At the apex of one work hierarchy, the spinner was at the base of another in the spinning room.[14] What pressure he exerted on his work team was more than matched by the overlooker's and manager's pressure on him. Complaints that spinners were being driven 'like dumb animals', watched like 'prisoners', and that man was set against man, and mill against mill, were to become commonplace.[15] This was especially so in Oldham, where coarse spinning involved a heavier work load than in fine, and the limiteds practised an impersonal work discipline in keeping with the modernity of their plant. Nonetheless, in fine-spinning Bolton, fines and discharge for minor offences was common, and the tyranny of the spinner-made-overlooker was a staple of contention in the last quarter of the century.[16]

The vulnerability of the spinner's position is underlined by the occasional incursions upon his primacy in the work team that continued to be made throughout the half-century.[17] The spinner was tied to the individual mill for much of his working life by the mill-seniority system of promotion from the trainee, piecer grade. He had to wait, often into his thirties, for circumstances to allow him his 'wheels'. Thereafter, his position was assured only within his native mill.[18] It was this mixture of habituation and dependence, rather than Foster's version of work authority and 'pacemaking', that perhaps best explains the specially pro-employer attitudes of the spinners. It can be remarked in passing, that during the wait for promotion the piecer would often have become habituated to the comparative poverty and the life-style of the less skilled majority of the workforce.[19]

The availability of trained labour always meant that the employers had a considerable latitude in interpreting the mill-seniority system of promotion. That they exerted their authority with success and ease is further testimony to the spinner's vulnerability.[20] There are numerous instances of overlookers and managers exerting their patronage over the dependent piecers.[21] The spinner's work life was a limited one, his manual dexterity representing his value to the employer. On the one hand, the system of promotion encouraged employers to dispense with their older spinners; on the other, dependence in old age could offer opportunities for the exertion of employer patronage and influence. Thus the position of the spinner illuminates the bedrock of dependence. For the rest of the workforce the ties of dependence were stronger still.

The pressures that made for dependence produced a commitment to work which was far more than mere rational calculation. Work got under the skin of everyday life. There is evidence, for weavers and spinners alike, of a willing acceptance, in the cause of work, of both the rigours of authority and of increased workloads.[22] Ill and injured weavers would work flat-out to avoid the stigma of incompetence.[23] These attitudes amounted to something like the tyranny of work over life. In describing a factory population 'conservative', 'slow to change', and unable to understand that trade was the effect of labour and not its cause, the words of Allen Clarke which opened this chapter provide the essential perspective here. The limits of work were the limits of life.

Just as in the factory the worker could only understand his machine, so outside it he had no idea of how the town was governed: 'They have no rational grasp of politics or of political economy.'[24]

The need for security was elevated into the beginning and the end of life. Dependence therefore bred the need for certainty and coherence that the acceptance of caste and hierarchy met. These patterns of dependence, involving fatalistic resignation, suspicion of outsiders, and respect for authority, have been recognised in modern textile communities in both the U.S.A. and England.[25] By providing the foundation that enabled power relations to become moral ones, dependence produced the situation in which deference could begin to work.

Because work was so large a part of life it was perforce a source of pride and meaning. Though not unambiguous in its effect, pride in work further fed the sense of commitment to it. This was not only a matter of the spinner's concern with his machine,[26] but characterised the whole of the workforce, both male and female. Within cotton weaving, status was demarcated by the number and type of looms, the type of cloth woven, and the size and quality of piecework production. Going out to work, and having the 'trade' of weaving to hand, seems to have been a source of pride and respectability to women weavers.[27]

From the Huddersfield woollen districts there is testimony to pride and interest in work and in the individual machine, as well as to the belief that work was the operative's life.[28] In the heavy woollen district, Mark Oldroyd of Dewsbury, owner of the largest woollen cloth concern in the world towards the end of the century, expected and received the highest standards of tidiness and discipline. A Dewsbury woman recalled, and this was the same for all the better class mills, that the workpeople would not allow anyone with dirty clogs into the factory, and that Oldroyd's strictness was answered by a pride in work and the refusal to complain about the long hours of labour.[29] In castigating the 'unworkable theories of Mr Hyndman', the leaders of cotton unionism articulated deep seated feelings in all the textile areas: 'We must not be judged from the standpoint of the scum of some of our large towns, notably of London, who appear ready to jump at any proposals – the wilder the better – which promise the chance of plunder and of living without work.'[30]

The commitment to work was reflected in the popular understanding of the employer as the provider of all. No matter how hard his régime, the employer who provided continuous work and good conditions and materials, and who tempered hardness with fairness, was assured of popularity and a stable workforce.[31] In the oldest firms of all, such as the Low Moor Ironworks in Bradford or the Fison and Forster Greenholme mills, continuous work was answered by loyalty, pride and discipline.[32] These attitudes to work were reinforced by the structure of the cotton market in particular. The failure to provide work was often ascribed by the operatives to the interference of merchants and other speculating middlemen in the proper working of the market.[33] There was much truth in this, but in the attempt to shift the blame for trade difficulties from the employers, and in the frequent joint attempts of masters and men to combat speculation, one working out of the consequences of dependence is clearly apparent.

What seems to have been a near-total absence of upward social mobility within the textile labour force also deepened the psychological consequence of dependence.[34] As the Blackburn journalist W.A. Abram reported in 1868,

Should our typical workman close his career as the manager of a loom-shed, he may set himself down as a favourite of the gods. For one who reaches that elevation fifty superannuated weavers are relegated to the duties of oddmen, messengers, casual labourers, and the like, until death rescues them from the buffetting and contumely of circumstances.[35]

The domination of work over people's lives consequently effected the acceptance of the authority that governed the routines of work. Coercion in the industrial sense was real enough, as the earlier description of West Riding industry indicates. In the small weaving towns of north-east Lancashire, and especially in Burnley, victimisation of union men, the pretensions of petty authority, and continual poaching on the operative's time and wages, were frequent sources of complaint.[36] However, in Lancashire at large, industrial coercion, just as political coercion, was limited in extent.[37] Rather than taking overt, coercive forms, authority in industry worked by being turned inwards under the pressure of dependence. Jeremy Seabrook has found in modern Blackburn the legacy of nineteenth-century industry: authority inculcated in the worklife found both release and reinforcement in the authoritarian personal relations of everyday.[38] The effect of dependence was complemented by the effect of community: figures of authority in the factory were massively present in the landscape of the life beyond work.

The workings of authority in industry involved one of the central problems of paternalism: the delegation of authority

in such a way as to minimise the consequences of the loss of
personal contact. It is in this light that the family economy and
sub-payment in textiles have a special relevance. Such systems of
authority, whether involving the family or not, meant a sharing of
authority with the employer for the skilled and unskilled operative
alike. The force of authority's brunt would thereby have been
deflected. Of supervisory workers proper, more will later be
said about managerial authority.

Probably the most strategic link in the chain of command was
the overlooker. The largest employers were the most concerned
to supervise the hierarchy of authority. W.E. Forster, for instance,
insisted on free access to himself over the overlookers' heads.
In 1856 he stated that 'the good employer got the best overlookers
and was circumspect in seeing they did justice to the operatives'.
The overlookers were at once the 'aristocrats' of the working
class, and very much the employers' men.[39]

When things went well the chain of authority effectively
promulgated the beneficence of the employer's regime. When
they went ill it could often shield the employer from the consequences. No matter how well supervised, the overlooker was
always to some extent considered as 'the boss'.[40] In all industry,
including coal and engineering, authority-holding middlemen
continued to be of importance. While on the one hand a kind of
foreman-based deference could exist, and there are many examples
of overlooker favouritism; on the other, piecework can also be
seen as intensifying the focus of industrial conflict on the foreman,
and thus exculpating the employer who might be seen as the
disinterested arbitrator.[41]

The degree to which the experience of authority comprised
the backbone of the most stable paternal regimes is suggested
by important differences between the role of overlookers in
Lancashire and the West Riding. The West Riding overlooker
was no less the employer's man than the Lancashire one, but
his power was far less extensive. Commission payment to the
cotton weaving overlooker was instituted in 1847, giving him a
direct interest in the production of those in his charge. He also
had a large measure of control over the hiring and dismissal of
workers.[42] The West Riding overlooker seems to have had a much
smaller say in these matters. Though paid on a commission basis
in some areas, and while 'driving' was prevalent in a number of
time-paid trades, the secondary importance of piecework meant
that in the West Riding there was far less scope for the forcing of
production pace than there was in Lancashire.[43]

The coercive nature of the overlooker's authority should not be minimised, though it was in the small weaving establishments of north-east Lancashire that 'driving' was most severe. This was in general directed far more against women than men.[44] The severity of authority was not only confined to the small mill, W.A. Abram characterising the Blackburn overlooker as succeeding by dint of 'a rough force of authority and activity of habit'.[45] One stereotype of the overlooker, reflected in the popular, often dialect 'tacklers tales' of the time, was of the overlooker as lazy and dense, a figure to be ridiculed because he was a figure feared.[4] Nevertheless, the most severe stricture on the overlooker – a 'sod', a 'tin god' – come down to us from the Nelson and Colne area of Lancashire, characterised by small factories, and late industrial development.[47]

The overlooker and the more lowly cut-looker were seen by the employer as his agents. And in the cases of the spinningroom and the cardroom even more than in weaving, this understanding was reciprocated by the overlookers themselves.[48] The 'Rules and Objects' of the Blackburn and Great Harwood Overlookers Association indicate the general attitude to strikes, as strongly held in this case of weaving as in all others. The Association was formed so as to 'render it unnecessary for them to resort to acts which are degrading to themselves, to the association, and an injury to society at large'.[49] An illustration from the political sphere indicates the interaction of force and influence in the operation of authority. If in all mills, Liberal and Tory, the overlookers were a source of considerable influence,[50] there is evidence that in the Tory mills of Blackburn they were often chosen with explicitly political ends in view. Abram wrote of 'the score or so' of managers, overlookers and clerks 'in all large factories':

Each of these is a small centre of authority and combined they form a group whose power is formidable. In the Tory mills political contingencies are seldom lost sight of in the appointment of these persons. Either they are promoted from the ranks as a recompense for their subservience, or they are chosen for their known political basis.[51]

It would, however, be mistaken to consider the relationship of the overlooker and his workers as one based solely, or even mainly, on coercion. The overlooker was a man of parts, doubling as a dentist in some areas,[52] and a man who sat on committees; Co-op, and chapel. Leadership and influence were of the same coin as authority and coercion. The overlooker was popularly regarded as a skilled man, and above all as someone 'respectable'.[53] His position in the factory community as the master's agent and yet part of the workforce gave him a crucial, mediating role in factory life. Although distance had to be maintained in order to preserve discipline and protect the mysteries of his trade from aspiring imitators, the overlooker's family were often cotton workers too. Factory and leisure dress, and perhaps the ownership of a corner-house, signified his apartness. Yet he shared many interests with his male workers, often mixing with them outside work.[54]

The *Cotton Factory Times* did not solely publicise complaints about overlookers. There were many instances of common sentiment – presentations to overlookers on all manner of occasions, cricket matches between overlookers and weavers, a country trip given by an overlooker to his weavers on the occasion of his marriage.[55] The considerable moral influence of overlookers was remarked upon by contemporaries,[56] and was emphasised by leading employer spokesmen such as Samuel Greg. In 1857 he spoke of the overlookers having 'great power placed in their hands, great power for good or for evil. They *must* do much of either one or the other.' Especially in the case of children, right treatment 'may bind them to him by a tie of tenderness that may last through life'.[57]

Changes in the attitudes of overlookers, amounting to what may be termed their proletarianisation, were of considerable significance. A powerful weaving trade unionism always saw it as in its interest to support the organisation of the overlookers, and many overlookers would have had unionised weaving relations. Overlookers often kept on their union cards on promotion to overlooking. The same symbiosis between production and supervisory workers was not seen in the cases of spinning and the cardroom. Where weaving unionism was strong, therefore, there seems to have been a growing awareness on the part of the overlookers of the need to organise. This developed fitfully throughout the half-century, as did the recognition of a community of interest with production workers.[58]

By the 1890s there was still much ground separating the two sides. The kind of organisation the overlookers adopted had only friendly society characteristics for most of this period, reflecting a consciousness of separate identity also seen in their exclusive relief organisations of the Cotton Famine years. Things were much the same in the West Riding, the Bradford Managers' and Overlookers' Society (the overlookers were often organised with the managers) insisting on its friendly society status into the 1880s, and only amalgamating its local organisations in 1896.[59] The change from 'managerial' to 'worker' status was long postponed by the onset of depression in the 1870s and 80s, when the overlookers were re-enlisted in the cause of increased production, and does not seem to have taken a deep hold until the first decade of the new century.

It was then that the overlookers' authority over hiring and firing was being abrogated in Lancashire.[60] The timing of the intensification of overlooker authority, in the late 1840s, and of its diminution, is extremely suggestive. The correspondence with the timing of the decline and rise of independent working-class politics points firmly to the importance of the authority relationship in factory industry. The ways in which this relationship was felt in daily life will now be further considered.

Community and the factory

Population movement beyond mid-century continued to disrupt the stability within which the sense of community could cohere. Continuing migration to the factory towns complemented the consequences of the massive waves of population movement characteristic of industrialisation before 1850. In 1851 70 per cent of the *adult* population of Preston was born outside the town, though somewhat less (50 per cent) in the older factory centres of Bolton, Stockport and Manchester.[61] Despite this flux the second half of the century saw a general slowing of the rate of population increase, as the consequences of mechanisation expressed themselves in a rapidly maturing industrial civilisation (Table 1).

When the two decades after 1841 are compared with the two before a general decrease in the rate of population growth is apparent, the exceptions being the weaving towns of Burnley and Blackburn. After 1861, however, the Lancashire weaving towns shared in the general Lancashire recession in growth. The results of later mechanisation in West Riding textiles are expressed in the 1841–81 population figures.

The table suggests the close connection between the development of population stability and the respective degrees of class harmony in the different towns and cities. Differences existed not only between the Lancashire and West Riding textile towns, but also between the Lancashire and Yorkshire cities. The situation within Lancashire is especially revealing, Burnley once again marking off its special character. Though rates of population growth are only one item on a long agenda, the principal exception to the south Lancashire pattern, Oldham, again suggests the link between population stability and the onset of social calm. The considerable population growth of Oldham after 1850 was a

TABLE I
Rates of population growth in selected
Lancashire and Yorkshire Towns, 1821–1901[1]

	1821–41	1841–61	1861–81	1881–1901
Blackburn	1.605	1.723	1.463	1.226
Bolton	1.582	1.403	1.378	—
Burnley	1.740	1.962	1.709	1.532
Bury	1.909	1.453	1.301	1.061
Liverpool	2.071	1.550	1.245	—
Manchester	1.868	1.438	1.008	1.177
Oldham	1.966	1.698	1.539	1.233
Preston	2.105	1.625	1.151	1.170
Rochdale	1.610	1.568	1.292	—
St Helens	1.914	2.029	1.519	—
Salford	2.084	1.498	1.720	1.254
Stockport	1.601	1.090	1.089	1.324
Huddersfield	1.782	1.358	1.343	1.098
Bradford	2.502	1.590	1.708	—
Halifax	1.664	1.310	1.418	—
Hull	1.512	1.451	1.579	1.452
Leeds	1.815	1.362	1.492	1.388
Sheffield	1.702	1.667	1.536	1.338

[1](a) Each entry represents the ratio of population at the end of the period
to population at the beginning of the period.

  (b) Boundary changes 1881–1901 make continuous comparison 1821–
1901 impossible for towns where no figures given. Earlier boundary
changes allowed for in principal source for table, 1881 Census,
Vol. V, General Report, Table 9. Also 1891, 1901 Census Preliminary
Reports.

consequence of the development of the anonymous limited
companies. These changes were reflected in poor labour relations
and the relative absence of employer paternalism. The endemic
instability of Bradford, by comparison with Lancashire but also
with the other Yorkshire factory towns, is similarly conveyed
in the figures for rate of population growth.

With a few exceptions, the Lancashire Cotton Famine produced
a decrease in growth between 1861 and 1871. Though the slack
in growth was taken up thereafter, it is clear that after 1881
textile and engineering factory Lancashire was becoming a
backwater in the demographic history of the North. The focus
of growth had shifted to west Lancashire, north-east Cheshire,

and the Manchester conurbation, with their new industrial processes (chemicals on Merseyside for example) and their new urban centres.[62] In the last quarter of the century the term 'traditional' begins to be appropriate in describing factory Lancashire.

Even in the mid-century years of considerable population movement the nature of migration to the towns indicates the undue simplicity of imagining a translation from the remote countryside to the unknown, impersonal town. For the rather extreme case of Preston, Anderson shows that of the *total* population in 1851, 48 per cent were born in Preston, and a further 21 per cent within ten miles (the latter comprised 42 per cent of the total immigrant population).[63] Many of the immigrant population would have come from industrial settings, whether in villages or in other towns.[64] Urban, industrial life on the one hand, and Preston life on the other, would not have been unknown to the immigrant, and this knowledge would have worked against those forces threatening the disruption of neighbourhood and community feeling.

Population movement within the town was considerable, but would most often have occurred within the 'charmed circle' of neighbourhood streets. Though only 14 per cent of males ten years and over lived at the same address in Preston between 1851 and 1861 (19 per cent of females), a further 18 per cent were traced within one hundred yards, and 8 per cent within two hundred yards. A further 10 to 20 per cent probably lived within half a mile of the original residence.[65] The present writer's pollbook returns for 1868 (1868 voters traceable at the same address in the 1871 census enumerators' schedules) indicate what may have been a cumulative steadying of this intra-urban movement: between 50 and 60 per cent of *adult males* remained at the same residence over the three-year period, and many more could be traced in the same or neighbouring streets.[66]

Even at mid-century and before, the evidence for a continuity of neighbourhood awareness is striking. Anderson concludes that 'the continual residential mobility of these towns seems to have only rippled the surface of this neighbourhood feeling'.[67] At this time it was kin relationships that supplied the kernel of neighbourhood community identification.[68] John Marshall has described the vigorous social life of distinct communities within the factory towns of mid-century and after,[69] and, for a later period, the Thompson and Vigne oral material on the North is suffused with a sense of the common experience of neighbourhood life. Even in rapidly expanding Bradford, local patriotism was strong, and a man could live his life out at school, home and work within a mile of his birthplace.[70] The second half of the century, then, seems to have seen a lessening of population movement, both into and within the factory town.

As will be seen, the ecological development of the factory town, and the nature of the textile workforce especially, were to be powerful forces emphasising the strength of the neighbourhood community tie. Though the factory was the prime source of local identification, it was not of course the sum total of the occupational life and social character of the town. The occupational spread of adult male employment (Table 2) indicates the diversity of even the most classic factory town.

TABLE 2
Occupational structure of adult male
employment, in selected Lancashire and
Yorkshire towns, 1871

	Blackburn 18194	Bolton 20497	Bradford 37864	Huddersfield 17680
1. Upper/Professional classes[1]	2.07	2.33	2.44	2.95
2. White-collar and official[2]	2.63	2.64	2.96	3.69
3. Retailers and dealers	10.72	10.37	10.00	9.85
4. Small masters/artisanate[3]	8.74	9.51	10.85	11.02
5. Skilled working class[4]	10.01	12.24	18.27	16.01
6. Factory workers				
1. Engineering[5] and iron	6.42	18.24	7.34	4.13
2. Smiths and mechanics	(8.18)	(20.80)	(10.60)	(6.20)
3. Textiles[6]	43.29	27.86[7]	28.43	34.95
7. Labourers[8]	13.53	13.86	15.90	13.69
8. Unclassified[9]	2.59	2.95	3.81	3.71

[1] Factory owners not included.
[2] Includes police, shop assistants.

³ The lack of designation in the Census Abstracts makes it difficult to identify the character of 'makers' and 'dealers'. Dealers who would also be makers have been sorted with identifiable small masters in this category; There would thus be some overlap with the 'retailers and dealers' (group 3), and with the 'skilled working class' (group 5), in the form of such as shoemakers, tailors, tinplate workers and cabinet makers, who have been included in the 'artisanate' category.
⁴ Includes all building workers, smiths, mechanics.
⁵ The bracketed figure includes smiths and mechanics, among whom there would have been some factory workers. These have thus been included twice, amongst category 5, and as bracketed.
⁶ Category includes all factory owners. Only in Bradford and Huddersfield were they anything other than a minute fraction of the total number in textiles. For these two towns their inclusion does not distort the true situation.
⁷ Bolton was somewhat unrepresentative of the factory towns in having a large number of men in engineering and a small number in textiles. In Preston and Oldham textiles accounted for 33.26 per cent and 33.78 per cent respectively, and all iron and engineering (9.54) and (18.90).
⁸ Includes servants, agricultural labourers, and miners (only important in Bradford at 2.60 per cent).
⁹ Includes farmers, military classes, unoccupied.

Source : 1871 Census Abstracts, all males twenty years and upwards.

Textiles provided the largest single source of employment for adult males, and iron, engineering, and textiles between them dominated the occupational structure of manual labour in the towns. However, the prominence of the large bands of small master/artisan and skilled working-calss occupations is particularly striking. Occupationally and socially these middle groups would have merged into each other at many points, and to some degree have extended into the retailer and dealer group as well. These, and the large groups of manual labourers, played a great part in town life, especially in a place like Bradford, where the occupational structure was more akin to that of the city, factory work for men being less significant.

The labourers, most of all the Irish, and elements in the skilled working class – which would have covered a wide range of income and status, especially among building workers – were among the most transient in the town populations. The late mechanisation of Huddersfield industry is reflected in its greater occupational spread and in the large number of adult males in the textile industry. At the other end of the social spectrum, the small number that might have qualified as 'middle-class' is particularly striking.

TABLE 3
Occupational structure, all ages, in selected Lancashire
and Yorkshire towns, 1861

Males

	Blackburn		Preston		Oldham	
	under 20	over 20	under 20	over 20	under 20	over 20
1. Cotton[1]	14434	15706	18365	19703	21167	25052
2. All engineering and iron[2]	26.50	43.42	20.44	32.78	19.89	31.17
3. Mining	1.88	7.69	3.52	9.01	6.99	18.83
	—	—	—	—	2.94	6.31
4. All other under twenty year males employed	7.05	—	9.72	—	6.26	—

Males

	Bolton		Bradford		Halifax		Huddersfield	
	under 20	over 20	under 20	over 20	under 20	over 20	under 20	over 20
1. Cotton/All textiles[3]	16121	17638	22660	26608	7687	9596	7766	8928
2. All engineering and iron	15.71	28.35	14.37	29.43	20.37	29.42	10.07	28.79
3. Mining	8.76	19.26	4.87	11.43	3.04	9.06	1.96	6.38
	—	—	2.17	2.26	—	—	—	—
4. All other under twenty year males employed.	9.73	—	10.49	—	14.84	—	15.98	—

TABLE 3 (*continued*)

	Bolton under 20	Bolton over 20	Blackburn (Females) under 20	Blackburn (Females) over 20	Bradford (Females) under 20	Bradford (Females) over 20	Preston under 20	Preston over 20	Halifax under 20	Halifax over 20	Huddersfield under 20	Huddersfield over 20	Oldham under 20	Oldham over 20
	16330	20306	15352	17634	24233	32717	19594	25323	8202	11529	8022	10161	21391	26734
Cotton	25.12	25.01	30.20	38.48			27.72	35.60					28.31	31.59
Cotton/All textiles					23.33	27.64			27.23	20.20	10.66	9.25		
Domestic service	3.55	7.46	2.87	5.77	4.30	8.45	2.62	6.71	5.30	9.02	7.58	12.33	3.49	5.42

Notes: 1. Cotton alone. There would be small numbers in other textiles industries in these towns. Figures include factory owners.
2. Includes smiths and mechanics.
3. All textile workers in Yorkshire towns.

When the occupational structure of the entire population is considered, however, the importance of factory work, and textiles in particular, is seen to be overwhelming (Table 3).

Textiles can be seen to have shaped the whole personality of town life. The figures for Oldham and Bolton engineering (outside Manchester the great centres of textile machinery manufacture) in fact underemphasise the regional importance of textiles. Coal was of importance in the west and north-east of Lancashire. After 1861 the number of adult females in textiles was to increase, particularly in the West Riding, and above all in the Huddersfield woollen districts. In Lancashire textiles the number of adult males was to remain more or less stable, while the West Riding male operative, though less so in Huddersfield, was slowly forced out of the factory under the pressure of female labour.

The second half of the century seems therefore to have seen the consolidation of a sense of community in the factory towns. At the centre of this sense was the neighbourhood, and very near the heart of neighbourhood feeling the factory. What is so revealing about the nature of class formation at the time is this association of neighbourhood community with the advent of social stability and the harmony of the classes. In particular, the emphasis on territory and the development of a localist or parochial consciousness were to be sources of employer influence and control. To describe the workings of the neighbourhood community of the maturing nineteenth-century industrial town in this way is to encounter important questions concerning the historical nature of community. The association between traditional, or 'classic', urban working-class community and the attenuation of class consciousness demands considerable qualifications to accepted notions of the significance of these community forms. Before addressing the more general question attention will again be directed to forces that may have disrupted community, especially the operation of a labour aristocracy in the factory.

The limitations to Foster's notion of work authority and 'pacemaking' as the mechanisms assuring the accommodation of the worker in capitalist, industrial society have earlier been pointed to. The cultural ramifications of this argument are taken up later in this work,[71] it being doubtful if the kind of cultural polarisation in the working class that would have to exist to support this version of things was in fact at all the case. Any notion hinging on the attractive and repulsive force of variations in skill and status has also to be understood in terms of the bedrock of dependence, vulnerability and authority that underlay the attitudes of all factory labour. As in so many respects, that which factory workers had in common is more important for an understanding of class relations than that which divided them. For all workers, dependence bred the need for security and coherence met by the acceptance of a hierarchic *status quo*.

The factory neighbourhood, in whose workings can be discerned the moral framework reared upon the foundation of power relations, was similarly the common experience of the entire workforce. Dominated by the influence and authority of the employer and his factory regime, the operation of factory neighbourhood feeling would have merged any differences of cultural style and status in a common allegiance to the neighbourhood employer.

It is in this regard that the family may have been of crucial importance, for it was the phenomenon of the family in work that made the connection between the factory and the community such an intimate one. It is in this light that divisions of authority and status within the workforce may most fruitfully be considered, such divisions being primarily reflections of family life and roles. As earlier suggested, the retention of status around mid-century may have been governed by pressures on the family, the resolution of these pressures and the maintenance of the new family equilibrium being of vital importance in inaugurating and perpetuating acceptance of the new industrial system. Because of its family aspect, the new distribution of authority and status in work served to accommodate the whole of the workforce, skilled and unskilled, male and female, in the prevailing order of industrial society. And it did so, as we have seen,[72] by making people's own sense of communal identification a source of the employers' domination over their lives.

Thus the integration of the factory workforce in an industrial system characterised by factory paternalism and deference took place in community terms. Even when the family was not reconstituted in the same factory, its diversification in the whole range of textile occupations would have negated the effect of whatever status oppositions existed. Where direct family, and especially patrimonial, employment was not the case – and it will be remembered that important differences existed between Lancashire and the West Riding in this respect – there were still ample sources of direct family influence and control in the individual factory, in terms of recruitment and training.[73] As reflections of this influence, the destiny of the wage and trade union recruitment were very often family matters, and particularly the concern of the father.[74]

Of the family dimension to textile labour in the second half of the century there can be no doubt. There was an increase in the proportion of married and widowed women (of all women in the cotton industry) from a quarter to a third between 1851 and 1871, the proportion continuing to increase thereafter. Females over thirteen years made up between 50 and 60 per cent of the cotton workforce in these two decades.[75] Fairly accessible figures for West Riding textiles are only available for a later period, but their indication of fewer married women in the industries again points up important differences in the family aspect of labour between the two regions.[76]

It has been estimated that during the second half of the century anywhere between one-half and two-thirds of married female cotton operatives had husbands working in the same industry.[77] The tendency of young people to follow their fathers' occupation was marked in all Lancashire occupations, especially in cotton.[78] There is much evidence that this tendency found expression in the same factory, and very often in terms of either direct patrimonial employment or of supervision. In both Keighley and Bradford, for example, employers expected and received the child labour of their adult workers, employment being secured by the personal application of family members at the mill.[79] Indeed, employers frequently used pressure to enforce family working in their mills. In Blackburn there were instances of employers forcing overlookers to bring their kin to the factory as weavers, and of the dismissal of spinners who declined to bring their wives as weavers.[80] In Lancashire in the 1870s it was commonplace for an employer to tell a man to bring his wife with him if he wanted work.[81]

Patrimonial influence and employment in spinning is clear enough.[82] Although there are considerable difficulties in using census material and factory records to determine the constitution of labour within the individual factory in cotton outside spinning,[83] a range of firm records for Lancashire makes plain the general importance of the family and the particular significance of family and especially paternal influence and employment within the individual factory.[84]

Divisions of authority and status within the cotton workforce may thus be most pertinently understood in terms of family relationships. The most important distinction was between the spinner and the weaver, weaving being highly unusual among all textile crafts in that men and women were paid at the same wage rates,[85] and men worked in the company of women. The principal threat to the weaver was perhaps that to his family authority, in work and at home. It is conceivable that equalities of pay and work experience between men and women in the somewhat exceptional but numerically important case of cotton weaving may have accounted for variations in the degree of attachment to the factory régime. Differences of pay, skill, and work control may therefore have mattered not as reflections of a labour aristocracy, nor of the meaning and worth of work to the male operative, but chiefly as aspects of conjugal dominance and its erosion.

However, when the evidence is considered, what is most apparent is not any source of disequilibrium in the weaving districts, but rather the great extent to which, despite women's work, what may be termed the traditional division of family authority was maintained, and the male weaver's dominance was assured. Although often paid the same basic rates as women, the variations in status within weaving earlier indicated (number and type of looms, and so on) were almost always variations that distinguished male from female labour. By a number of other means as well, such as the allotting and tuning of looms, men almost invariably earned more for work that differed hardly at all from woman's work.[86] By such 'unofficial' means, sanctioned by the employers, the inequality of the sexes was symbolised, and proclaimed to the cotton community.

The stigma of female labour that existed in the spinning areas does not seem to have characterised weaving in Lancashire. Working was a source of pride and respectability to women workers. For so long a part of local life, women's work, and in particular the working mother, was looked on as inevitable and natural.[87] Male and female weavers frequently married, and if the resulting division of labour within the family was somewhat unusual – men helping with domestic work for instance[88] – the traditional pattern was still of the greatest durability. Responsible for both work and home, it is the endless toil of women that is most remarkable. Instead of shame, in situations where spinners and weavers laboured together in any number, it was the pride and respectability of the weaving household that struck contemporaries.[89]

While Anderson has shown the 'instrumentality' of family roles in mid-century Preston, especially the disruptive effect of young women working, his work also points to the primacy of social bonds existing within rather than between the sexes.[90] Margaret Hewitt's work on the following decades indicates the way in which women's employment did not disrupt traditional patterns of influence within the family.[91] In a situation where patrimonial employment was less marked than in Lancashire, and therefore where male dominance was correspondingly less assured,

Joanna Bornat has recently shown for the West Riding textile districts how women's work led not to the disruption of paternal authority but to the economic marginality and dependence of women.[92]

Perhaps the clearest evidence for men assuming and women accepting the traditional division of authority within the family is to be found in trade unionism. Men's involvement and women's lack of interest in trade unionism was a telling reflection in the remainder of the century of the mid-century resolution of disturbance within the family. The significance of these attitudes is the more emphatic when it is considered that from the earliest days men encouraged female trade unionism in cotton powerloom weaving.[93] In terms of trade union activism, membership, and the social life of the union 'clubroom', for most of the half-century women were distinguished for their lack of interest and organisational involvement.[94] In the West Riding also the woman's real domain was still the home, and her daily experience one of housepride and fatigue.[95]

This quiescence was directly expressed in the factory. 'Driving', and other kinds of psychological pressure designed to secure increased production, were most often directed against women. In the Lancashire of 1873 observers noted that women, who were hardly ever in trade unions, were less concerned than men with long-term goals, and far more open to the approbation of the overlooker and the admiration of their companions. Production pressure can be understood in terms of mill rivalry and status as well. A four-loom weaver 'has a certain position and is the object of attention'. Four looms could mean the difference between marriage and waiting: 'Hoo's a four-loomer, hoo's like to be wed.'[96]

The historical development of these attitudes is unclear, given our state of knowledge of women's life in the first half of the century. Whether the profoundly disturbing shock administered to the prevailing distribution of authority within the family, when female and child labour preceded male labour into the mills, was expressed in the social and political activism of women workers remains uncertain. The evidence for the 1830–50 period is conflicting, but when these decades are compared with the ones that followed there is some justification for noting both a higher level of involvement in the earlier period and the possible conjunction of this with the disruption of traditional family roles.[97] Certainly, the new equilibrium between home and work was accompanied by the near-total absence of women from the public and organised life of the working class between the 1840s and the 1890s.

It may in fact be that women were a force of real weight in preserving the *status quo* of the deferential relationship. The family dimension to labour, and a mixture of familiarity and dependence, could have meant that the mill functioned as a kind of second home for many women; a place full of known faces and expectations, often inevitably returned to after marriage and childbearing. As a kind of home outside the home, it supplemented the limited possibilities for a social life represented in the corner shop and the Sunday school. Though the economic motive was undoubtedly primary, there is evidence that the fellowship of the mill also drew women to work.[98]

The mill was an integral part of common life, and of the sympathies and attachments it bred. These sympathies involved the intertwining of the family life of the operative with that of the employer. The central place of the employer–family saga in the social life and ritual of the factory will be considered in due course. There is, perhaps, no more suggestive conjunction than the paternalism of the factory regime and the employer dynasty, and the paternalism of the operative family. The mythology of the family sanctioned the fiction of unity and interdependence that enabled poverty and inequality to be borne.

The awakening of women into the social and political life of the North was a major element in the disintegration of the old, paternalist order. The massive growth of women's trade unionism, in the cotton cardroom, in cotton weaving, and in Yorkshire textiles, was undoubtedly behind this change. Increased work loads, technological unemployment, and the ever-increasing efficiency of male unionism produced the change, especially notable from the early 1890s. The fact that many trades were increasingly becoming the sole preserve of women was important.[99] Women were thrown back on their own devices at last. Nevertheless, the degree of women's trade union membership, more especially of involvement in union affairs, can easily be exaggerated.[100]

The real breakthrough in mentality does not seem to have come until the early years of the new century, with the confluence of the agitation for the vote and the increased unionisation of women.[101] The 70,000 Lancashire women cotton operatives who signed the 1901 parliamentary petition for the vote were an impressive testament to the new direction of change.[102] Even so, the tenacity of the old order was considerable, and one signature did not signify release from political deference and traditional ways. Those who took the greatest strides were a minority, and one always subject to the virulent reaction of their own men.[103] The importance of the Co-op Guild in this was considerable, the organisation providing this minority with a social environment beyond work from which to question the established order of things.[104]

Geographical variations in militancy within the North disclose much about the nature of the society that was fast disappearing. North-east Lancashire, in particular the Nelson and Colne area, fits into the pattern of variation here, as in so many other respects. Women's labour was effectively organised there, and Nelson and Colne seem to have been among the most politically lively of the Lancashire towns.[105] Across the Pennines, in the less patriarchal air of Yorkshire textiles, women responded to the challenge of union organisation very early, taking a leading role in affairs from 1875 in Dewsbury and 1881 in Huddersfield.[106] For decades after the 1870s, however, the old order of affairs was in the ascendant, and it is to its community manifestations that attention will now again be directed.

When the nature of nineteenth-century working-class community is confronted, it is apparent that the idea of the family and the community as themselves in part facilitating the influence and authority of the factory regime, forces a readjustment of traditional notions of the significance of working-class community forms. In suggesting that deference was less a matter of 'ideological hegemony' than of the wholesale penetration of everyday manner and feelings, the necessity of comprehending the complex social effect of the life working-class people made for themselves has been urged: the *milieus* of ordinary life were impregnated with the authority and influence of an élite, so that the habit of neighbourhood community, expressed in the terminology of sociology as 'communal sociability', was the source of subordination as well as of class selfhood. A recognition that this was the case requires a restatement of accepted notions of neighbourhood community feeling as representing 'a life apart' and expressing a simple social image of 'Us' and 'Them'.

Such an understanding would seem to be implicit in Foster's conception of the 'non-aristocratic' working class. It seems to the present writer mistaken to write the history of the working class as if the heart of its experience was inviolate, sealed in some impermeable experience of communal feeling, which when all else failed and the labour aristocracy fled the pale of this culture, subsisted as the seedbed of future change. Change there was, but it was most powerfully shaped by the way in which community was expressed in the much misunderstood years between the end of Chartism and the rise of Labour politics. The history of working-class community needs to be rewritten with the missing years put in.

This is something Meacham's recent work attempts to do.[107] Even so, the years before 1890 are still a dim presence in his work. If we accept Anderson's findings (and his methodology), the dominant orientation to community around mid-century was based on kin, and the characteristic form of kin relationship was calculative rather than functional.[108] With the advent of a measure of prosperity after mid-century, and of population stability and residential continuity, what seems to have happened was that the full extension of community beyond kin, and the growth of functional kin relations, developed very rapidly. In Meacham's terminology, the 'classic' followed the 'heroic' stage of working-class community.

However, not only can it be suggested that this took place rather more quickly than the work of these two writers might suggest, but also that in the coming of 'classic' community the factory had a role the crucial nature of which has not hitherto been appreciated. For it was the factory and its owner that were central elements in the forging of the neighbourhood bond, so that the loyalties and habits of neighbourhood feeling in its most formative years ran across as well as within class lives. Community in a rapidly maturing industrial civilisation was not 'made' by the factory. But, unless the critical role of the factory is understood, we shall rest content with the comforting and sentimental generalisation: the version of 'Us' and 'Them' bequeathed to posterity in the factory North of England was greatly different from that so often supposed.[109]

Discussion of community is set about by difficulties of definition and methodology.[110] The difficulty of demarcating the area and quality of community's effect is perhaps paramount. Until extensive quantitative analysis is undertaken, differentiating between the geographical area of effect (neighbourhood, street or court), between formal and informal patterns of interaction, and between communities of locality and interest, will remain a hazardous business. These difficulties ought not lead us into setting the concept a side.[111] No matter how useful more manageable concepts and methodologies may be, they will almost certainly in the nineteenth century lead us back to the centrality of neighbourhood to community feeling. Despite his misunderstanding of its implications in the factory North, Meacham points firmly to the vitality of local partisanship in the urban 'village'.

The sense of place which was at the time the bedrock of community was moulded by work and its systems of authority and influence as much as by any other force. The character of factory-town growth, and the nature of the factory workforce (above all in textiles), meant that the factory itself was a principal source of stability and local identification in the post-1850 Northern towns.

The factories of the big employers stamped their character on urban life. While the industrial colony continued to be of importance throughout the North, urban agglomeration by no means led to impersonality and mutual ignorance between the classes. The difference between the factory towns and the northern cities was again a crucial one: until late into the century the factory town retained rather more of the village than it acquired of the city. Understood as the 'walking city', the factory town grew by cellular reproduction, the town slowly absorbing factory neighbourhoods in its expansion.[112] An historian of the cotton industry describes the process thus: 'In general the migration of the industry outwards from the towns reveals a tendency, more marked in weaving than in spinning, towards the dispersion of the industry around a group of central urban nuclei, a tendency whose working out turned villages into towns and "country" mills into urban mills.'[113] After the rise of the suburban mills in the Lancashire of the 1820s, the process of absorption was to be characteristic of the region for the next half-century or so, until the town began to grow out of the reach of the employer class.

Around mid-century therefore the pre-established colonial or suburban mill provided one of the few elements of coherence amidst the prevailing rootlessness. As the town grew it retained its territorial identities; the old centres, dominated by the largest and oldest factories, remaining as the real work and social foci of the community. Distinctiveness and reputation remained, just as the old employers remained. Whether in the congeries of settlements that made up Bolton, in Brookhouse, Nova Scotia and Audley in Blackburn, or in the West End and Hurst in Ashton, it was a process that characterised all the factory towns.[114]

Pollbook analysis, explained in a later chapter,[115] indicates the degree to which the great employer's influence was exerted not only over his own workforce, but also over a wide range of occupations in the locale, from labourers to shopkeepers. This influence was to be moderated as much by developments in transport as by anything else. Transport lagged behind the factory system in producing the social system of twentieth-century industry. It was the tram and the bicycle, much more than the railway, that liberated the factory worker from the domination of the territorial.

The link between home and work remained firm until these severed it.[116] In 1905 the Bradford patriarch Alfred Illingworth described the change; knowing well its profound importance:

During the last twenty years a silent change has taken place, and is working a revolution in regard to the housing question in our midst. When first tramways were introduced . . . I foresaw that this change was an important one, and that when the machinery was perfected it would work a revolution. . . . At one time the population was obliged to be concentrated. . . . Nowadays the population can go three or four miles out and for a halfpenny a mile they are taken dryshod to work and not tired . . . by that means a silent movement is going on, and in the city a wider sphere is being opened up.[117]

The effects of ecological development were complemented by those of workforce composition and work practice. Something has already been seen of the loyalty and long-service that answered the large employer's munificence and continuous provision of work.[118] Dependence, and the commitment to work it produced, meant that an operative's connection with a particular firm was often long-term. The mill seniority system in spinning also meant a connection that could be lifelong, and the spinner's working family would consequently have been tied to a particular locale. Using spinners' union records and local directories, Thorpe has shown the longevity of the neighbourhood connection in late nineteenth-century Bolton.[119]

Outside spinning, Anderson's work on weaving Preston shows the increased likelihood, with advancing age, of cotton workers remaining in the industry.[120] This was after the commitment to the industry in youth, and before the vicissitudes of age. Not all cotton trades were as impervious to entry from without as spinning, but for all of them the premium on early factory training and socialisation meant an often long-term attachment to the individual trade and factory. Thus the textile workforce, in particular the adult male in cotton and the smaller groups of skilled and supervisory male workers in woollens and worsted, was a considerable force for continuity and stability in the factory town. It was in many ways both a selected and self-selecting entity, and a chief source of community cohesion.

Employers took a pride in their workforces, weeding out the less efficient and making the utmost efforts to hold on to good workers.[121] In Keighley employer control of housing was used to enforce the return of workers shared out to neighbouring mills during periods of depression.[122] Despite trade difficulties, and stoppages for repairs and fires, the desire to return to the known mill appears very often to have been considerable.[123] Both the unions' journal and the employers were agreed on the need for a constant workforce, the best firms by common consent being those where 'a chap has to wait till somebody dees to get a shop'.[124]

This evidence is supported by factory records. Wage books for a small weaving firm in north-east Lancashire, Grimshaw and Bracewell's, make plain the continuous adhesion of both individuals and family groupings.[125] This was especially the case for adult males, and other Lancashire and West Riding records similarly show the considerable length of stay of skilled and supervisory adult males.[126] Information for Ainsworth's Halliwell bleachworks in Bolton probably exaggerates the persistence of the individual's connection, but is nevertheless reasonably representative of the general state of affairs:[127]

Total Number Employed (1857): 574
Years served in works

over	under	
60	—	7
50	60	11
40	50	12
30	40	40
20	30	44
10	20	22

Workers with over 10 years service   136

These were almost all men, though male youths and young women also tended to stay for the full span of their young working lives, before moving into other trades or leaving for marriage. There would probably have been a larger number of skilled men in such a works than in many cotton factories, but even so the long-stay worker at Halliwell was drawn from all departments in the works. The number of old operatives kept on as a form of dole or pension in labouring and watchmen jobs is also striking. The Respondents' Briefs for the trial of the disputed Blackburn election petition of 1868–69, one of the few early instances of ordinary operatives reporting on their work life, shows the long connection of ordinary male weavers with their place of work.[128]

This degree of labour immobility would not have been duplicated in the case of engineering and iron. The area within which the engineering unions enforced control of entry to the trades was wider than in the highly localised case of spinning.[129] Nevertheless, travelling in these trades was the mark of the young craftsman's career rather than of the mature worker. In old firms of established reputations, such as Dobson and Barlow of Bolton and Platts of Oldham, and where the piecework system worked amicably, the engineering and iron worker would probably have had a long and continuous connection with the individual firm.

Employer ownership of housing was limited in extent in the North, the factory itself rather than direct control of housing acting as the principal focus of workplace influence. Nonetheless, there were considerable variations throughout the North, and employer house-ownership was never unimportant. In the out-districts of towns and in the semi-rural industrial colonies such ownership continued to be of great significance throughout the period. This was especially so in the West Riding, where as late as 1859 in a town as large as Keighley some of the big employers were building or buying large numbers of houses.[130] The early giants of the industrial revolution–the Horrockses of Preston, the Ashtons of Hyde – created the bricks and mortar of community, and often retained control over housing for the remainder of the century.[131] Even so, as early as the 1830s, the employer class as a whole held only a minority of their operatives' housing.[132]

The distinction between Bradford and places like the Fielden's Todmorden or the Foster's Queensbury was important, employer ownership in Bradford in the second half of the century being minimal, with the exception of a few sizeable colonies within the town.[133] The factory town came between those two extremes, though in the northern townships of the city of Manchester in 1870 employers owned as much as between 10 to 12 per cent of all housing.[134] The smaller of these two figures may be considered as the general average for the factory towns. Some perspective on this is gained when the limited number of household heads in textiles is considered. The importance of these holdings was magnified by their frequent concentration in colonies within the town. In Ashton, for instance, the big employers seem to have owned between 100 and 200 houses, the very largest considerably more.[135]

Blackburn and Bury Rate Assessment Books permit a more detailed consideration of housing.[136] In the 1860s and 70s the proportion of town housing owned by employers was around 13 per cent. In the 1850s and 60s the large employers held somewhat smaller blocs than in Ashton, the really big man between

150 and 300. For both towns, as for all northern towns, it was unusual for an employer not to have at least some houses in which key supervisory, and sometimes skilled, workers were housed. The general pattern of house-ownership the books reveal would seem to have obtained for the region as a whole.

The majority of owners held only a few houses, often living in one of a group of houses and renting the others. The majority of houses seem to have been held in large blocs of between ten and fifty. In all this the single owner-occupier is conspicuously absent, and absent in Blackburn for the rest of the century. The speculative builder, the small investor, and the ground landlord, between them had a larger say in determining the physical character of the factory town than the employer and the operative. The piecemeal, opportunistic development of these towns belies their uniformity of appearance. The Co-op and the building society increased their share of the house-market towards the end of the century, though, except in Oldham and Burnley, and especially in some of the West Riding towns,[137] notions of a sturdy, independent, house-owning urban peasantry are without foundation. The exceptions in this regard again point to the geographical distribution of paternalism and deference.

The growth of a greater degree of home-ownership towards the close of the century was, however, a sign of the loosening grip of the employers. In Blackburn, for instance, the largest blocs of employer housing were retained intact into the 1870s. By the 1890s many of these had been broken up and what remained diminished in relative importance as the town grew. This loss of the physical substance of the town was to be one force sounding the death-knell of the old regime. The loss of employer housing similarly heralded the demise of textile paternalism in the mill villages of the U.S.A.[138]

The timing of these changes indicates the force of housing as a social control. Not that a number of employer-owned houses were not always occupied by workers who might have nothing to do with the employer's industry or factory. This was particularly the case in the centre of towns, where a variety of alternative housing usually stood available.[139] Even when houses were built specially for the workforce, as in Halifax and Bradford, their higher rents and better quality often attracted higher social elements.[140] After mid-century, capital investment loomed increasingly large as a motive for employer ownership, displacing the earlier emphasis on managerial necessity.[141] There were, therefore, limitations to both the extent and degree of housing's use as an influence on social behaviour.

But the effect of the employer's holdings should not be mini-mised,[142] whether they were used as punishment or reward: Hugh Mason of Ashton installed bathrooms in his foremen's and overlookers' houses, and in Bolton it was the practice at some mills to grant a piecer his 'wheels' only on condition that he accept one of his master's houses.[143] The moral, reformative use of housing, seen especially in the early industrial revolution, continued to be practised in the remote colonies as well as in the more rigorous of the urban 'villages'. Aside from house provision for key groups of workers, the employer's need of a loyal and stable workforce meant that housing was a bond tying the entire workforce to the neighbourhood.

The employers might forgo rents in bad times, or charge low rents in good. As with the Blackburn Hornbys, the remission of rent could act as a form of dole for the old. There are numer-ous instances of employers enforcing particular work practices through housing, such as the labour of family groups mentioned above.[144] But overt coercion and even moral reform were not the real basis of the significance of employer housing. What really mattered was that the employer so often owned the core of a particular locale, imparting to a neighbourhood its character, shaping its sense of place, and proclaiming this to the town.

The relationship between the operative's vote (from the 1868 pollbooks for Blackburn and Bury), and the ownership of his house, provides a valuable perspective on the relationship between coercion and community.[145] In areas of Blackburn where the operative's house was not owned by his employer he partook of the political allegiance of that employer to an only slightly lesser degree than when the house was employer-owned. In short, community was still effective in shaping men's ideas when control over housing was negligible. In the Liberal area of Park Ward, Walpole Street, Maudsley Street and Audley Range were representative in voting Liberal 52–22 when housing was not employer owned. In three representative Tory streets (Grimshaw Park, Haslingden Road, and Mosley Street) the vote went 144–51 to the Tories. Neighbourhood bloc voting, only slightly affected by employer house-ownership, was borne out by the other Blackburn wards and by the case of Bury as well. This striking validation of the strength of factory-dominated neighbourhood feeling introduces our next concern: the historical genesis of the paternalism that gave this feeling form and direction.

Summary
This chapter seeks to elaborate many of the distinctions made in

the preceding chapter. The first section concerns the usefulness, or otherwise, of the notion of deference. Rather than deference construed as attitudes or behaviour alone there is value in comprehending both by looking at deference as a form of social interaction. This gives us a means not only of examining concrete situations but also of approximating an answer to the question – what are deferential attitudes and behaviour, and to what degree had they an inwardness? Where a totality of influence and direction over people's lives is most clearly achieved, as it was in the factory neighbourhood, the more likely is it that deference bit deeply into social being. Nonetheless, approximation to an answer is all we may hazard, and from the sociological insight we are thrown back to the historical insight. What this suggests most strongly is that deference was pervasive in this way. When we have said this about capitalist, industrial society we have said something argumentative.

The argument is taken up in terms of the vocabulary of cultural, class 'hegemony'. When the familial, communitarian underpinnings of deference are allowed their full import then the inadequacy of notions of hegemony hinging upon the play of ideas between the classes is manifest. The element of challenge in the argument here lies in the claim that the sense of purpose in the occupation and of place in the factory and its neighbourhood were fundamental to the success of Northern employer hegemony. The operatives' acceptance of the social regime of the factory went deeper than the 'negotiated', greatly qualified acceptance of a common stock of ideas and values held to characterise the operation of 'ideological' hegemony. However, no such hegemonic situations can be interpreted in terms of the unilateral imposition of control from above. Such social relations are reciprocal, marked by mutual constraints, bounds beyond which neither party may trespass if the relationship is to remain viable. Many of these barriers and taboos, as well as the tensions obtaining between the deference of the factory and the institutions of working-class self-help, are explored here and in the course of this work (see especially section 3, chapter 8). Nonetheless, if if we are to respond fully to the complexities of class formation in reconstituting the subtleties of contemporary mentality, then the force of deference must be as present to out minds as the qualifications that hedged it about.

Deference is not to be understood without a consideration of the dependence that was its seed-ground, and the experience of dependence is the subject of the second section here. This experience was especially marked at the time. In tracing its consequences the cotton-spinner is given prominence, strategically situated as he was between the bulk of the textile workforce and the craft worker. Rather than the cotton spinner being regarded as an aristocrat of the factory, a consideration of his work situation shows his lack of autonomy, and his dependent status as a proletarian just like his fellow factory workers. The condition of mind to which dependence led is then considered in terms of the commitment to work, and the permeation of daily life by the values and routines of work, a state of things summarised in the term 'the tyranny of work over life' (a tyranny all the more effective when pride in work was behind it). The workings of managerial and supervisory authority are then looked at, the role of the textile overlooker being especially important as a mixture of force and influence.

In the third section considerations broached in the first section are taken up more fully. The fictions of employer paternalist community accorded with the facts of community growth in the factory towns, and indeed took much of their force from those facts. In turn, employer paternalism was buttressed by the paternalism of the operative family, the partial reconstitution of which around mid-century was probably such an important factor in securing the adhesion of the whole textile workforce to the new dispensation. Potential sources of disruption in the workforce – a labour aristocracy and the fact of women's work – are examined in the light of the family in work, as well as the *status quo* of the factory neighbourhood community, itself maintained by, and in turn maintaining, the distribution of authority and influence at work. This potential for disruption was not realised until very late in the century: the eventual emergence of women into the mainstream of life in the factory North is discussed.

The degree and character of population movement is considered, and related to the degree of class harmony in particular towns. What appears to have taken place around mid-century was the consolidation of a sense of community in part dependent on the lessening of population flux. The physical growth of towns around the nuclei of factories meant that this community sense was deeply marked by the impress of the factory and its owner. Workforce composition and work practice also fed this identification of the neighbourhood and the place of work. Housing, as a specially important ingredient of the urban 'village', is given detailed treatment here, preparatory to the more wide-ranging attempt to recreate the culture of the factory made in chapter 5. The impersonality and class segregation of the

126   *Work, Society and Politics*

twentieth-century town is so often read into the history of
nineteenth-century towns that it is forgotten how unlike they
were. It was not until a wide range of social changes began to
converge towards the end of the century that the town, always
unlike the Victorian city, began to take its fully class conscious
modern form. The identification of factory and neighbourhood
was fostered by the powerful re-assertion of employer paternalism
after mid-century. This understanding of the interaction of
change in work and in the town forces a re-appraisal of 'traditional' working-class community as representing a simple
dichotomy between 'Us' and 'Them'. The history of working-
class community needs to be re-written with the missing years
put back in.

Notes

1. A. Clarke, *The Effects of the Factory System* (1889), pp. 145–6.
2. J. Morley, 'The chamber of mediocrity', *The Fortnightly Review*,
    Dec. 1868, p. 690.
3. See the specially useful criticisms and citations in D. Kavanagh,
    'The deferential English: a comparative critique', *Government and
    Opposition*, **6**, no. 7, Summer 1971.
4. J.H. Goldthorpe and D. Lockwood, 'Affluence and the British
    class structure', *Sociological Review*, **11**, no. 2, 1963; J.H. Gold-
    thorpe, D. Lockwood, *et. al.*, *The Affluent Worker in the Class
    Structure* (Cambridge 1969).
5. H. Newby, 'The deferential dialectic', *Comparative Studies in
    Society and History*, **17**, no. 2, Apr. 1975. See also the very interest-
    ing remarks of Edward Thompson, in E.P. Thompson, P. Line-
    baugh, *et al.*, *Albion's Fatal Tree* (1975), ch. 6, pp. 304–8.
6. Newby, *loc. cit.* pp. 141–6.
7. *Ibid.* p. 146.
8. *Ibid.* pp. 146–55, 158–63.
9. *Ibid.* pp. 155–8.
10. E.P. Thompson, *Whigs and Hunters; the origins of the Black Acts*
    (1975), pp. 258–69.
11. R. Moore, *Pitmen, Preachers and Politics* (Cambridge 1974),
    pp. 89–92.
12. See Newby, *loc. cit.* pp. 155–8.
13. K. Burgess, *The Origins of British Industrial Relations* (1975),
    p. 246.
14. H. Catling, *The Spinning Mule* (1970), chs 9, 10.
15. Burgess, *op. cit.* pp. 246, 255, 269; R. Smith, 'A history of the Lanca-
    shire Cotton Industry between the years 1873 and 1896' (Birmin-
    gham Univ. Ph.D. 1954), ch. VII; see also Clarke, *op. cit.* p. 50, and
    Cotton Factory Times, 4 Dec. 1885.
16. See Annual Reports, 1879–96, Amalgamated Association of

operative Cotton Spinners, Bolton (now in Manchester University Library); see also E. Thorpe, 'Industrial relations and the class structure: a case study of Bolton cotton mule spinners, 1884–1910' (Univ. of Salford M.Sc. 1969), ch. 2, sec. III.

17. S.J. Chapman, 'Some policies of the cotton spinners' trade unions', *Economic Journal*, 10, no. 40, Dec. 1900; H.A. Turner, *Trade Union Growth, Structure and Policy* (1962), pp. 135–6; see also *Cotton Factory Times*, 21 Aug. 1885.

18. Turner, *op. cit.* p. 209.

19. Chapman, *loc. cit.*

20. Royal Commission on Labour, *P.P.* 1892, XXV (6708–vi), pp. 746–7; H.A. Turner, *op. cit.* pp. 209–10.

21. Burgess, *op. cit.* pp. 246, 255.

22. *Ibid.* p. 246.

23. W.A. Abram, 'Social conditions and political prospects of the Lancashire workman', *Fortnightly Review*, Oct. 1868, p. 432.

24. Clarke, *op. cit.* p. 146.

25. R. Martin and R.H. Fryer, *Redundancy and Paternalist Capitalism* (1973), chs 2–4; 'The deferential worker: persistence and disintegration in paternalist capitalism', in M. Bulmer, ed, *Working-Class Images of Society* (1975); R. Blauner, *Alienation and Freedom: the Factory Worker and his Industry* (1964), ch. IV.

26. Catling, *op. cit.* chs 9 and 10.

27. J. Liddington, 'Working-class women in the North West II', *Oral History*, 5, no. 2, 1977, pp. 32–4.

28. Oral interview with Joe France, Marsden mill manager. Recorded by Mr Terry Brown, Middleton, Lancs. I acknowledge the assistance of Mr Paul France, Marsden, Huddersfield.

29. Thompson and Vigne (see ch. 1, n. 70) West Riding Interview no. 143 ('Community and Class').

30. *Cotton Factory Times*, 16 Jan. 1885.

31. *Ibid.* 18 Dec. 1885 (John Hawkins of Preston), 17 July 1885 (R. Shaw & Sons, Colne); *Ashton Reporter*, 24, 31 Jan. 1880 (Hugh Mason, Ashton).

32. *Low Moor Ironworks, a poem*, John Nicholson (Bingley 1856), first published 1829; see the biographies of Fison and Forster, also of the Todmorden Fieldens, in *Fortunes Made in Business*, Vol. 1 (1884).

33. Thorpe, *op. cit.* ch. 2, sec. 1; see also *Cotton Factory Times*, 31 Jan. 1890.

34. See above, p. 20, n. 60. These sources refer to upward social mobility into supervision as well as management. Oldham and Burnley in their boom years would have been somewhat exceptional. The Thompson and Vigne Interviews on Lancashire and the West Riding convey a strong sense of the limitations on upward mobility. Of course such mobility could characterise those who left the cotton industry in childhood or youth: see the parliamentary source in n. 20 above.

35. Abram, *loc. cit.* p. 432.
36. For example, *Cotton Factory Times*, 16 Jan. 1885 and succeeding numbers, 'Voices from the spindle and the loom' see also *ibid.* 9 Apr. 1886, editorial and p. 6.
37. On political coercion from *below*, and its spontaneous, community-engendered character, see below, pp. 219–20.
38. J. Seabrook, *City Close-Up* (1971), esp. 'Family relationships', pp. 129–34.
39. *P.P.* 1856, XIII (343), pp. 129, 130, 132, 136.
40. See the Thompson and Vigne Lancs. textile interviews, especially with women.
41. For a discussion of this in a modern setting, J. Cousins and R. Brown, 'Patterns of paradox: shipbuilding workers' images of society', in Bulmer, ed., *op. cit.*
42. *P.P.* 1873, LV (754), p. 806; Turner, *op. cit.* p. 153.
43. *P.P.* 1856, XIII (343), p. 135; G.H. Wood, *The History of Wages in the Cotton Trade during the Past Hundred Years* (1910), pp. 147–8.
44. *P.P.* 1892, XXXV (6708-VI), pp. 752–3, 758; W. Bennett, *The History of Burnley*, vol. 4 (Burnley 1951), p. 106; R. Smith, 'A history of the Lancashire cotton industry . . . ', above, ch. VII; *Cotton Factory Times*, 17, 31 July 1885 (Letters).
45. Abram, *loc. cit.* p. 432.
46. Interviews with Lancashire cotton operatives conducted by Dermot Healey, Manchester Polytechnic: Henry Foulds, weaver, p. 10; Sidney Hookham, p. 4. Copies of these interviews are in this writer's possession. I wish to thank Dermot Healey for his assistance. Source hereafter known as 'Healey Interviews'.
47. *Ibid.*, Henry Foulds, p. 7.
48. Turner, *op. cit.* p. 148.
49. Blackburn and Great Harwood Power Loom Overlookers' Provident Association, Rules and Objects, 1858. Lancs. County Record Office, Preston (hereafter: L.C.R.O.), DDX 1128/1, Minute Books, 1858–78.
50. *Ashton Standard*, 12 Nov. 1870 (leader).
51. Abram, *loc. cit.* p. 432.
52. Healey Interviews, Henry Foulds, p. 10
53. *Ibid.* pp. 11, 17.
54. *Ibid.* p. 17; Sidney Hookham interview, pp. 2, 6; Mr Fairhurst, overlooker, interview, pp. 12–16.
55. *Cotton Factory Times*, July 1885 (cf. Reports, Letters, 'Voices . . . ').
56. P.E. Razzell and R.W. Wainwright, eds, *The Victorian Working Class. Selections from Letters to the 'Morning Chronicle'* (1973), pp. 173–4.
57. S. Greg, *On the Condition of the Working Classes in the Manufacturing Districts* (Macclesfield 1857), p. 9.
58. Turner, *op. cit.* pp. 157–9.
59. *Bradford Managers' and Overlookers' Society Celebrations, 1827–1927* (Bradford 1927).

60. Healey Interviews, Henry Foulds, pp. 7, 9.
61. M. Anderson, *Family Structure in Nineteenth Century Lancashire* (Cambridge 1971), pp. 34, 39–40.
62. R. Lawton, 'Population trends in Lancashire and Cheshire from 1801', *Transactions Lancashire and Cheshire Historical Society*, 114, 1962
63. Anderson, *op. cit.* Table 4, p. 37, and maps pp. 36, 35.
64. *Ibid.* Table 5, and pp. 37–8.
65. *Ibid.* pp. 41–2.
66. See below, pp. 206–11.
67. Anderson, *op. cit.* pp. 101–6.
68. *Ibid.* chs 5, 11.
69. J.D. Marshall, 'Colonisation as a factor in the planting of towns in north-west England', in H.J. Dyos, ed., *The Study of Urban History* (1968).
70. F. Jowett in F. Brockway, *Socialism Over Sixty Years* (1946), p. 25, but see also p. 19.
71. See below, pp. 288–90.
72. See above, pp. 52–8.
73. J. Bornat, 'Home and work: a new context for trade union history', *Oral History*, 5, no. 2, 1977; Anderson, *op. cit.* ch. 9.
74. Bornat, *loc. cit.* pp. 107–10, 112–17.
75. M. Hewitt, *Wives and Mothers in Victorian Industry* (1958), pp. 13–16. See also I. Pinchbeck, *Women Workers and the Industrial Revolution* (1930), pp. 197–201.
76. J.H. Clapham, *The Woollen and Worsted Industries* (1907), pp. 176–7; *P.P.* 1892, XXXIV (6708–iii), p. 236, Digest of Evidence.
77. Hewitt, *op. cit.* pp. 190–3.
78. S.J. Chapman and W. Abbott, 'The tendency of children to enter their fathers' trades', *Journal Royal Statistical Society*, 76 (1912–13). It should be remarked that this study covered the age range of 15–30, with special emphasis on the 17–20 age group. By this age the career pattern would in large measure already have been determined.
79. Thompson and Vigne West Riding Interviews, nos 165, 176, 340 ('Work'); 132 ('Community and Class').
80. *Blackburn Standard*, 9 Feb., 29 Mar. 1884.
81. Hewitt, *op. cit.* p. 13.
82. Burgess, *op. cit.* p. 244; Catling, *op. cit.* ch. 10, esp. p. 165.
83. Census material indicates the family occupational structure one would expect from kin employment, though the material cannot of course tell us about particular factories. Most factory records do not list assistants and their wages separately.
84. It is necessary in most cases to work from name duplications and dates of starting in wage records. The commonness of surnames in the factory districts is one difficulty, though overemphasis on the family dimension to labour as a consequence of this is compensated by kin who would have had a different surname. The following

indicate family labour in the same mill, in cotton and in West Riding textiles: Register of Workers, 1839–1849, Quarry Bank Mill, Styal, Cheshire, in Manchester Central Library, C5/4/3/1, 2; Cloughs of Keighley and Fosters of Queensbury, large range of wages books for 1840s onwards, Brotherton Collection, Univ. of Leeds. The following unequivocally show parental, especially paternal employment; in the former case the record showing a family wage for a family group engaged in the same workgroup: Grimshaw & Bracewell, Barrowford Booth, nr Nelson, Lancs., Mill Wages Book 1846–60 (Warping and Weaving), in Manchester Central Library, L1/16/3/8; Sex and Age Structure of Cobden's Mill, Chorley, calico printing, 1845, in Manchester Central Library, M 87/2/3/16.

The following shows congregations of very distinct names in particular shops within a bleaching firm, *List of Persons Employed by Mr I.H. Ainsworth, Halliwell Bleach Works, July 1857* (Bolton 1857), Bolton Public Library, ZAH/11/4.

For further verification see M. Anderson, 'Sociological history and the working class family: Smelser revisited', *Social History*, **3**, Oct. 1976, pp. 320–2.

85. On wages see R. Smith, *op. cit.*, ch. XII; Wood, *op. cit.*; A.L. Bowley, 'Wages in the woolen and worsted industries of the West Riding of Yorkshire', *Journal Royal Statistical Society*, **65**, 1902; Clapham, *op. cit.* pp. 199–200; *P.P.* 1892, XXXIV (6708–iii.), pp. 216, 219, 226–7, 228–9, 232, 237, Digest of Evidence.

86. Liddington, *loc. cit.* p. 33; Bornat, *loc.* cit. p. 117.

87. Liddington, p. 34.

88. Hewitt, *op. cit.* p. 193. But see also, Beatrice Webb, *My Apprenticeship* (Penguin 1971), pp. 181–2.

89. B.L. Hutchins, *Women in Modern Industry* (1915), pp. 60–1.

90. Anderson, *op. cit.* chs 5, 9, 11.

91. Hewitt, *op. cit.* chs V, XIII. Within the conjugal sphere, the notion of 'traditional' patriarchal authority in the working family of domestic or 'proto'-industry should be handled carefully. See J.W. Scott and L.A. Tilly, 'Women's work and the family in nineteenth-century Europe', *Comparative Studies in Society and History*, **17**, no. 1, Jan. 1975. The co-operative labour of man and wife in domestic industry would certainly have attenuated patriarchy, though it seems apparent that men took primacy in public roles and women in the family sphere, within which their power was 'almost exclusively' limited (*ibid.* p. 48). The complex relationship between the sphere of production and social behaviour in general remains still to be explored. What matters for our argument, however, is not so much that husbands in domestic industry may not have played the dominant role in the family sphere, but that they so often believed that they did play this role (*ibid.* pp. 48–9). And this conception of their work would have reinforced, and been reinforced by, the wider cultural supports for patriarchy. But see

H. Medick, 'The proto-industrial family economy: the structural function of household and family during the transition from peasant society to industrial capitalism', *Social History*, 3, Oct. 1976.
92. Bornat, *loc. cit.*, esp. pp. 101–3, 117–18.
93. Neff, *op. cit.* p. 33; Bornat, *loc. cit.* p. 114; Hutchins, *op. cit.* pp. 104–5.
94. Turner, *op. cit.*, *passim*, see e.g. pp. 293–4; Hutchins, *op. cit.* pp. 92–178; Bornat, *loc. cit.* pp. 112–17.
95. Hutchins, *op. cit.* pp. 105–7.
96. Report to the Local Government Board on Proposed Changes in the Hours and Ages of Employment in Textile Factories, *P.P.* 1873, LV (754), pp. 822–3.
97. Neff, *op. cit.* ch. 2, esp. pp. 30–5, 50–3, 69–70; D. Thompson, *The Early Chartists* (1971), Intro., and pp. 115–30.
98. Hewitt, *op. cit.* pp. 191–3; Liddington, *loc. cit.* pp. 33–4. See also B. Jackson, *Working Class Community* (1968), ch. 5, on community feeling in a modern Huddersfield mill, in a situation of much greater social and ethnic heterogeneity than in the nineteenth century.
99. Hutchins, *op. cit.* pp. 107–8.
100. On woman's unionism, see R. Smith, *op. cit.* ch. VI; Turner, *op. cit.* pp. 139–57, 159–69, 184–5, 293; Hutchins, *op. cit.* pp. 104, 107–8, 115–16.
101. Hutchins, pp. 199–200; Liddington, *loc. cit.*
102. Turner, *op. cit.* p. 185.
103. Liddington, *pp.* 38–9, 41–2.
104. *Ibid.* pp. 39–40.
105. *Ibid.* pp. 37–9.
106. B. Turner, *A Short Account of the Rise and Progress of the Heavy Woollen District Branch of the General Union of Textile Workers* (*YFT*, 1917); *Short History of the General Union of Textile Workers* (Heckmondwike 1920); but see also Bornat, *loc. cit.*, pp. 115–16.
107. S. Meacham, *A Life Apart* (1977), pp. 44–59.
108. Anderson, *op. cit.* ch. 12, 'The wider implications'.
109. For a restatement of the orthodox approach, cf. Meacham, *op. cit.* p. 59, and ch. 7.
110. For discussions of the concept of community useful to historians see A. Macfarlane, 'History, anthropology and the study of communities', *Social History*, 5, May 1977; J. Connell, 'Social networks in urban society', in B.D. Clark and M.B. Cleave, *Social Patterns in Cities*, Inst. of British Geographers Special Publication no. 5, March 1973. For a very useful practical application, R.J. Dennis, 'Community and interaction in a Victorian city: Huddersfield, 1850–1880' (Cambridge Univ. Ph.D. 1975).
111. For a restatement of its importance, D.B. Clark, 'The concept of community: a re-examination', *Sociological Review*, 21, 3 Aug. 1973.
112. For Huddersfield as a late and specially clear example of this,

Dennis, *op. cit.*; see also A.W. Warnes, 'Residential patterns in an emerging industrial town', in Clark and Cleave, *op. cit.*; J.E. Vance, *Economic Geography* (1966), **42**, pp. 294–325; (1967), **43**, pp. 95–127; (1971), **47**, pp. 101–20.

113.   D. Farnie, 'The English cotton industry 1850–1896' (Manchester Univ. M.A. 1953), p. 120.

114.   For a very valuable analysis of urban growth in these terms see Marshall, *loc. cit.*; see also B.T. Robson, *Urban Analysis, A Study of City Structure* (Cambridge 1969), esp. pp. 241–2, and *Urban Growth : an approach* (1973), ch. 3.

115.   See below, pp. 206–11.

116.   For the factory-home link in Blackburn, see *Blackburn Times*, 5 May 1866.

117.   A. Illingworth, *Fifty Years of Politics* (Bradford 1905), p. 45.

118.   See above, pp. 98–9.

119.   Thorpe, *op. cit.* p. 200.

120.   Anderson, *op. cit.* pp. 27–9, esp. Table 2(b).

121.   John Morley, 'Lancashire', *Fortnightly Review*, 1 July, 1878, p. 6.

122.   Thompson and Vigne West Riding Ints, no. 165 ('Work').

123.   *Cotton Factory Times*, 15 Jan., 9 Apr. 1886.

124.   *Ibid.*, 10 July 1885, p. 1.

125.   See n. 84 above.

126.   Horrockses of Preston, Private Wages Book 1900–26, L.C.R.O., DDHs 39; Marriners of Keighley (worsted), Return of Men Employed By Marriners, 18 April 1916, To the Military Representative; Brotherton Collection, VI, Box 97, Univ. of Leeds.

127.   See above, n. 84. The information was publicised in the attempt to combat the extension of the Factory Acts to bleachworks.

128.   Blackburn Election Petition 1868–9, Respondants' Briefs, L.C.R.O., DDX 223 (5).

129.   Turner, *op. cit.* p. 213.

130.   On the Haggases see J. Hodgson, *Textile Manufacture and other industries in Keighley* (Keighley 1879). See also Marshall, *loc. cit.* pp. 225–6.

131.   S. Pollard, *The Genesis of Modern Management* (1965), ch. 5.

132.   *Ibid.* pp. 200–1.

133.   The most valuable source of information on employer housing, and all aspects of operative housing, is S.M. Gaskell, 'Housing and estate development, 1840–1918, with particular reference to the Pennine Towns', 2 vols. (Sheffield Univ. Ph.D. 1974), vol. 1, ch. 2. On the extent of employer housing see also Marshall, *loc. cit.*

134.   Gaskell, *op. cit.* pp. 42–3.

135.   *Ashton Reporter*, 24 Apr. 1869 on Whittakers of Hurst; on the other Ashton employers see *P.P.* 1868–9, VIII (352), Qs 2625–6.

136.   Blackburn Poor Rate Assessment Book 1868 (Blackburn Town Hall); Bury P.R. Assessment Book 1875 (Bury Town Hall). The full run of Blackburn books enabled a comparison of employer ownership for each decade 1840 to 1900.

137. Gaskell, *op. cit.* chs 3 and 5. See also the evidence on operative housing in Royal Commission on Labour, *P.P.* 1892, XXXV (6708–vi), pp. 722, 739, 758, 773–4, 825.
138. H.J. Lahne, *The Cotton Mill Worker* (New York 1944), chs. 3–5; Blauner, *op. cit.* ch. 4. For the same effect in the railway town of Crewe, see W.H. Chaloner, *The Social and Economic Development of Crewe, 1780–1923* (Manchester 1950), pp. 45–51.
139. Gaskell, *op. cit.* ch. 2; Marshall, *loc. cit.* p. 225.
140. On Bradford see Gaskell; on Halifax, K. Tiller, 'Working-class attitudes and organisation in three industrial towns: Halifax, Wigan and Kidderminster' (Univ. of Birmingham Ph.D. 1975), ch. 4.
141. For a full discussion, Pollard, *op. cit.* ch. 5, and Gaskell, *op. cit.* ch. 2.
142. See below, pp. 144–6.
143. Thomson and Vigne, Bolton Spinners' Interviews.
144. See above p. 112, n. 80. See also Thomson and Vigne West Riding Interviews, 176, 206, 341 ('Community and Class'), and *P.P.* 1892, XXXIV (6708–iii), p. 228, Digest of Evidence.
145. Both town's pollbooks were matched with the Rate Assessment Books. For a full discussion of the poll book material see below, pp. 206–11.

4
THE NEW PATERNALISM

The man of looms and spindles, may eventually
come to a position, in which he will have to
arbitrate upon the fate of nations. I do not know
any class of individuals better calculated to
discharge senatorial duties, than those who have
been for years accustomed to the economy of a
cotton factory. Such an establishment is a sort of
imperium in imperio—a model government on a
small scale – a miniature kingdom, in which all
the principles of an enlightened political economy,
receive the authority of a practical development –
the only test by which these principles ought
to be appreciated.

(Jonathan Baynes, employer, Blackburn 1857)[1]

He was not indifferent to the teachings of political
economy, but he should be very sorry if the rigid
and abstract rules of political economy alone
prevailed in his workshops. It would be impossible
for him to buy the labour of his workpeople,
and for the workpeople to sell him that labour the
same as an ordinary commodity over the counter
of a shopkeeper. He felt a deep interest in the
welfare of his workpeople. . . . The bond which
united them was not the cold bond of buyer and
seller.

(Hugh Mason of Ashton, 1868)[2]

The development of industrial paternalism from the 1840s was
of central significance in the evolution of British society, setting
the English experience much more fully in the mainstream of
international change than is commonly allowed. Pre-existing
social structure outside the United Kingdom was nonetheless
considerably more favourable to the transmission of versions of
paternalist social relations from pre-industrial to industrial
situations. In Japan, and to a lesser degree Germany, pre-
existing dynastic élites were more frequently the agents of
industrialisation, and nineteenth-century industrialism failed to
displace traditional hierarchies of authority as effectively as it did
in Britain.[3] Yet, even here, there are significant qualifications,

134

Three generations of spinners at Bank Top Spinning Company, Oldham 1900

A spinning department, Wilton Mill, Blackburn c. 1900

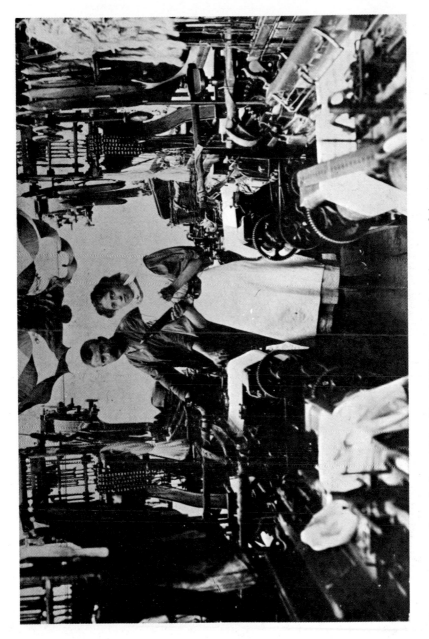

Cotton weaver and overlooker, Albion Towel Mill, Farnworth, at the turn of the century

Decorations at Messrs William Lawrence & Sons, Lyons Lane Mills, Chorley
for Edward Lawrence's coming-of-age, 1899

Townley Street, Chorley, awaits the Lawrence celebrations

as the earlier examination of the landed connections of nineteenth-century industrialists would suggest. The prior cultural climate, like the social structure, was also less favourable to effective paternalism in Britain. Social stability in the industrialising process was most assured in cultures where varieties of the relationship between superior and subordinate were most deeply rooted, as was the case, in differing degrees, in Japan, India, Italy and France.[4]

The character of industrialisation was of profound importance too. The lack of the cultural rootedness of a domestic system in textiles, particularly in the U.S.A.,[5] left the new factory workforces outside Britain especially vulnerable to the operation of authority and dependence, and to the blandishments of paternalism.[6] The long retention of a rural culture in parts of the U.S.A. meant a kind of industrial innocence in the twentieth century not seen in Britain after the early part of the nineteenth. In both Southern and New England textiles, the company town and the mill village continued in seclusion much longer than in England, and offered much greater opportunities for social control. What unity and independence could be asserted was constantly eroded by the divisiveness of ethnicity, whether in the form of successive waves of immigration into New England or the Negro presence in the South.

Perhaps the central difference between Britain and the other nations lay in the fact that Britain was the first to industrialise. For the later industrialisation occurred the more actively did the State participate, whether as the collective *padrone* falling into Marx's category of the Prussian road to capitalism,[7] or in the form of the Japanese transformation from nineteenth-century individual paternalism to twentieth-century corporate paternalism, and most recently, 'welfare corporatism'.[8] Social and cultural case of transition, and the effects of late development, clearly put the British at one end of a spectrum from the Japanese experience.[9]

Nevertheless, nineteenth-century distinctions, especially within Europe, were of degree and not of kind, the spectrum of difference being much narrower than is usually supposed. The international association of paternalism and textiles, the pioneer industry of world industrial development, was especially close and frequent. The special potency of the personal relations of master and man within nineteenth-century paternalism can hardly be exaggerated. Indeed, sociologists inform us that it is on this basis that paternalism may be at its most effective, deference being given not to the abstraction of traditionalism but to the embodiment of that ethic. As Weber describes the situation of the traditional ruler, this involves the legitimation of his power partly in terms of tradition and partly in terms of the free personal decision that the sphere of prerogative leaves open to him. Newby puts the matter thus: 'An individual invested with traditional authority can ... act in untraditional ways by virtue of the legitimacy of his traditional authority.'[10]

It was this personal embodiment, in the family or the family head, that gave paternalism its cutting edge. This edge was at its sharpest in the pre-bureaucratic factory of the industrial North after 1850, and the English experience of industrialism deserves to take its place in the 'golden age' of paternal, dynastic European capitalism between 1850 and 1875.[11] It can indeed be argued that the English family firm of these years confronted the problem of size in a way that was more successful than variants of the military-bureaucratic model of management, whether those elaborated in the twentieth century, or those being evolved in nineteenth-century English and European mining, railways, and steel production. The coming of the public limited company in English cotton around 1900 was of crucial importance in the decline of factory paternalism.

While English industrial paternalism was both pervasive and successful, the predominating employer ideology did set limits to the degree and nature of its operation. Those pre-conditions that favoured the transmission of traditional authority and habits of mind into the era of factory production were less telling: English entrepreneurial ideology attempted to justify the power of a new class, a class ostensibly at odds with the paternalist trappings of the *ancien régime*. In the first half of the century a *laissez faire* ideology was articulated that answered the needs of a fast-developing capitalist industry: the rational organisation of factory production needed the discipline that the social relations of prevailing models of paternalism, no less than of craft production, stood in the way of. In its extreme form, in the hands of certain of its Manchester ideologues in particular, this grim philosophy of rejection continued until very late to spurn the feudal tie and maintain that the relations of employer and worker were to be merely those of the cash nexus. As one Manchester man put it in 1853, 'A mill is not a republic—the hands have no rights.'[13]

From the 1830s and 40s a mellowing of this austere version of things is apparent, a mellowing later reflected in the actual practice of industrial relations that has previously been analysed. This new flexibility was also apparent before mid-century in the social and political attitudes that made up middle-class Liberalism.[14] In this ideological transformation the independent and self-reliant workman was to be helped to help himself. Labour was no longer regarded as a commodity. Aiming at work and hope, the worker was appealed to as a member of the whole community, no longer isolated in the insubordination and poverty that were once taken as the mark of immorality.[15]

This version of 'independence' was to be radically different from the meaning of that term in the vocabulary of radical working-class social and political organisation. In part a response to the assertion of a real working-class independence in the second quarter of the century, with the waning of that independence thereafter, the assumptions of superiority and leadership that always underscored employer talk of independence were to assert themselves with new force. The dependence that mocked independence was to be the experience of the factory workforces after mid-century, and was to be acted upon by the employers with increasing assurance after these years.

The ferment of the 1830s and 40s had nevertheless given birth to a sense of independent identity within working-class life. Versions of 'independence' continued to conflict after mid-century, and this conflict represented one of the boundaries of paternalism's effectiveness. As the preceding discussion of deference has indicated, ostentatious patronage trespassed upon a still lively sense of what paternalism could do to independence.[16] Yet the mutual constraints upon the operation of employer hegemony still left ample room for the successful exercise of paternalism. Indeed, the nature of constraint was paradoxically a source of effective paternalism: conflicting versions of independence nevertheless had sufficient in common, in terms of the fabled, blunt self-reliance of the North, to enable the employers to shape their paternalism to their workers' sensitivities.

That employer paternalism in practice often overstepped the limits of independence is clear. That this was very often done with immunity is testimony to the extent to which the bulwark of independence erected before mid-century was breached in the following decades, as a fully developed factory industry consolidated its social effect. Just as often, employer paternalism overstepped the strict limits of *laissez faire*. Among all these various considerations, to be more fully developed in the rest of this chapter, the constant divergence between the principle of the ideologue and the practice of the employer is perhaps the most striking. There was indeed a certain incompatibility between the stress on modern economic rationality and individualism, and the articulation of notions of social responsibility drawn from feudal, or pseudo-feudal, ideals. Yet, viewed in other terms, employer paternalism was the logical outcome of *laissez faire* ideology and not its logical opposite.

Much of English paternalist practice developed within the matrix of strongly held *laissez faire* notions of what the relations of employer and worker should be. Though such ideas were commonplace among European and American employers of the time as well, these employers were probably more welfare-conscious than their English counterparts, and less amenable to the dictates of the market.[17] The *laissez faire* inflexion in English paternalism may be readily illustrated. Literary representation reflected contemporary practice very closely. Thornton, the employer-hero of Mrs Gaskell's *North and South*, though building the works canteen that represents the growth of a larger sympathy with his workpeople, insists in his dislike of patronising charity that it be supported by the hands.[18] The Halifax Crossleys spent vast sums on the town, yet insisted that the Crossley Institute and works canteen be as far as possible paid for out of the pockets of the operatives. The journal of the employers' federation constantly lauded schemes that stressed self-reliance and promoted the entrepreneurial virtues of thrift and hard work. All forms of education that would reinforce the ethic of improvement were wished well.[19]

The ideological framework of paternalism thus set limits to the imaginativeness with which such schemes were implemented. The mentality of the moral book-keeper is apparent in the case of the Crossleys: their Institute and their Provident Fund were in part paid for out of fines from the workpeople, and this was the common practice in many large firms. Despite a great deal of noise in support of industrial partnership in productive co-operatives, and of profit-sharing, the limitations ideology set on practice are revealed in the actual results of this propaganda. Apart from a real interest in the former by such as W.R. Callendar and Hugh Mason, and some noteworthy profit-sharing schemes like those of the Taylors of Batley, the Priestmans of Bradford, Akroyds and Crossleys of Halifax, as well as several Lancashire schemes, the practical consequences were quite small.[20]

The impress of economic and social individualism is also apparent in the matter of housing. The operatives' education and religion always took priority over their bodily needs. The general failure to provide adequate housing, or to investigate the social conditions of the operative, again indicates the limits to paternalism. Housing such as that of the Akroyds or the Bradford Ripleys was often a mixture of works provision and moral incentive: savings investment in housing was always encouraged, and the good of the buyer's character, whether the employer's workman or not, was at least as important as social provision.[21]

Despite the constrictions of ideology the years around mid-century were to see a dramatic realisation of the need to translate ideals of duty and community into paternalist practice. The so-called New Model employers were then the most publicised (and since the most remembered) examples of what was in fact a profound and widespread change of course. This modification was considerably less onerous for a large body of employers whose individuality is too often lost sight of: the Anglican Tories. For the important minority of Tory Radicals among them, paternalism was indeed a *raison d'être* of their role as employers. Though the majority of employers, Anglican and Nonconformist, were imbued with the social principles of *laissez faire*, there were important differences of degree that will become apparent in due course. For most big employers, and for not a few of the lesser rank, when their numbers are penetrated below the level of an 'historical' Morley or Salt, what becomes clear is a piecemeal, almost instinctive paternalism, unpublicised and unsung in the contemporary annals of the empoyer-hero.

When the grass-roots of paternalism are uncovered, the gulf between theory and the experience of factory town men manifests itself. This division, representing the reality that lay behind public pronouncements decrying paternalism and vaunting the atomised world of liberal individualism, was apparent even in the articulate and public pages of the employers' own journal. On the one hand the interests of capital and labour were regarded as neither antagonistic nor identical: the metaphor of railway lines is used.[22] A most revealing ambiguity is disclosed in the metaphor for industrial organisation: the ancient image of the body is projected, the employer being the head, capital the blood, and the workers the hands and feet. The journal could rage against Harrison's assertion that the 1874 election signalled the consolidation of the new feudalism and serfage, but only because he had made plain the private practice that belied public ideology.[23]

Those of the New Model employers, such as Samuel Morley, who in welcoming trade unionism accorded labour an autonomous identity, could still revert longingly to the practice of paternalism, and regret greatly the degree to which unionism had come between them and the mutuality and personal attention they wished directly to express in their factories.[24] Those less favourable to trade unions, such as Edward Akroyd, could equally

contradict in the factory the public pronouncements of political
economy. Akroyd's neo-feudal ideal of the Guild was as much
the contradiction of individualism as the high-handed interference
of so many employers in the home life of their workers.[25]

Whatever the protestations of employers that they were
employers and their men employees,[26] the terms 'master' and
'man', used by such a cool observer as Frederic Harrison, were
those in common usage, and by employer and operative alike.
Samuel Greg and Mrs Gaskell, while applauding the 'independence' of the workingman, could still employ the images of the
young child and fledgling for the operative, and that of the father
for the employer.[27] This kind of language was the true index of
the feelings of the employers. It symbolised an abiding sense of
superiority which received its logical expression in paternalism.
It is in the inner recesses of employer life that we become aware
that far from being the negation of *laissez faire* capitalist society,
paternalism was its inevitable consequence.

Hobsbawm has discerned the notable contradiction between
the hierarchic and authoritarian bourgeois family, and an economic and political order that emphasised freedom and individualism,[28] and the same distinction just as effectively describes the
family firm in its most paternalist of expressions. Factory paternalism can thus be understood both as an escape from the wilderness
of the industrial town, and as an attempt at the restitution of the
community of the classes. The most compelling nineteenth-
century version of solidarity was perhaps the feudal one of
shared rights and obligations, the employer of course being the
sentient and directing force in whatever metaphor was chosen to
express union.

More than this, however, paternalism has to be taken as the
expression and validation of a sense of superiority, of being
master in one's own factory just as in one's own home. Geoffrey
Best has shown how sensitive mid-Victorian Protestantism
was to threats against fatherhood, and how ready to assert the
claims of paternity against an 'unnatural' Rome.[29] The figure of
the patriarch brooded over the whole of European society.
The superiority that paternalism vindicated was most of all the
expression of the social position of the employers. In the case of the
newly-risen, paternalism shored up the flimsiness of social station;
in those more entrenched it was the living example of their worth,
at once that curious mixture of countering and aping the paternalist style of a landowning class the employers both envied and
despised.

The roots of the new paternalism lay as much in religion as

anything else, not that God and Mammon were ever very far
part in the employer mind. The sense of mission and duty,
complementing the new stress on community around mid-
century, is to be located in the imperatives of a severe northern
religion. It is also to be understood in terms of an almost messianic
faith in the civilising power of industry, itself an aspect of the
nineteenth-century God of Progress. It was during the respite
that the mid-century years afforded the employers that they
began in earnest to consider themselves as Captains of Industry.

The Weberian notion of the 'calling' in Calvinistic theology
would seem to have been quite at home, an idea given the most
robust flesh, in the Nonconformist employers of the North. The
imperative of Duty in the Low Church Evangelical Anglicanism
of the same region, so much emotionally akin to Nonconformity
if so much politically opposed, called with only slightly less
emphasis that personal salvation was to be had in the world of
works. And what better source of Salvation and sphere of Duty
than the works wherein Good Works could be performed?
The employer's works and wealth were held in stewardship for
the Lord. Joseph Wilson, a manager at the Rand Brothers' large
Bradford mills and later a millowner in his own right, put the
feelings of many employers into words.

Such riches as resulted from a successful business career I consider myself
to hold in trust as God's Steward. I never had any love for money: my
wants are few: I live quietly, and seek no wealth. From earliest days the
Sermon on the Mount has been my standard of conduct both in personal
and business relationships, and I have never – so far as memory serves –
consciously departed therefrom. The secret of my highest success has been
simply this – that I have lived for Servce and not for Self.[30]

Although Wilson's style of life was anything but that of many of
the big employers, and while his eye for efficiency was undimmed
('"We could cheat his predecessors but we cannot cheat him."
My eyes were everywhere . . . '), this Primitive Methodist did
put his principles into practice, and as such was representative
of the best of the employers, and the better side of most large
employers, in a very religious age:

I tried to understand the worker's point of view and lean to his side . . . in
times of depression I felt that I must lose rather than the worker, whom I
treated as belonging to me. I loved them individually and so could not
cheat them: I must try to serve them and do what I can for them, so that my
whole business life has been on the lines that have yielded comfort and

peace, and the assurance that my methods would bear investigation on the basis of the highest standard.[31]

As great a family as the Crossleys could in their second genera-tion of eminence still hold to the notion of themselves as of the People that was not merely cant. This notion of kinship with the humble was closely linked to the brotherhood of Congregational-ism, the religion of so many of the employers. John Crossley II, deacon of Square Chapel in Halifax, considered himself to be on a level with the poorest member of the Chapel. His brother Francis, seeing in the American wilderness the command of God to build a park in Halifax, was also complying with the injunction of his mother Martha: 'If the Lord shall aid us in this place the poor shall taste of it.'[32]

The intermarried Holdens and Illingworths of Bradford were others whose lives outside religion, and especially the great factories they ran, were little but evidential extensions of that religion. When translated into a sternly moral care of the work-force, the dissent of Dissent was perhaps at its best. Isaac Holden described his labours thus: 'I have directed labour on a large scale for fifty yeras. [This] has increased my *respect* and *love* for the workers and my appreciation of their good sense and *conscience* and of their energy' [Holden's italics].[33] As a crusading Nonconformst Holden bemoaned the rich ('They should have stayed with the people'), and was always conscious of 'the educa-tional and humanity claims of these crowded populations'. These claims would be met by him and not by collectivism: 'Collectivism would destroy liberty and benevolence with individualism.'[34]

Several of the end-of-century generation of Bradford employers gave voice to a similar concern for their workpeople, none more than Arthur Priestman, a Quaker turned Anglican. We have seen how Priestman rowed against the tide of Bradford opinion in condemning the folly of opposition to trade unionism.[35] He ended his appeal to the employers with some lines of the poet Russell Lowell on the miller not knowing the disruption his wheel caused:

> No more than doth the miller there,
> Shut in our several cells, do we
> Know with what waste of beauty rare
> Moves every every day's machinery.
>
> Surely the wiser time shall come
> When this fine overplus of might,

No longer sullen, slow or dumb,
Shall lead to music and to light.[36]

This awareness of the dehumanising power in the productive process and in naked competition was clearly somewhat rare, and was opposed in the same journal by counter-arguments and counter-lines.[37] Priestman's choice of 'fine overplus of might' was more representative in suggesting the exultant employer belief in the Progress machinery symbolised. Nevertheless, the words of all these paternalists articulated the beliefs of many of the big employers, and especially the Lancashire ones.

The attitude of W.H. Mitchell, the great Bradford merchant, was of a piece with that of the big employers after mid-century, for whom hard work was no longer the end of life, and to whom the knowledge of human nature mattered more.[38] Despite the severity of his strictures, Ruskin's Manchester and Bradford lectures of the late 1850s were not lost on these men, eager to see public recognition of themselves as paternalists, and as the arbiters of the will and work of England.[39] The urge to vindicate economic power and buttress social superiority, the search for community, and the religious notions of duty and accountability, were all interwoven and expressed in the secular motto, *Ich Dien*. Carlyle and Ruskin's elevation of the employer as the Captain of Industry was taken seriously by the big employers, not least in a consolatory sense as the century wore on and showed that entrepreneurial ideology was not to colonise the national culture.

These assumptions were given instinctual expression by Isaac Holden in the 1890s: 'The labour question is not for churches and divines but for working men and their captains.'[40] The official and public justification of Bradford employers in the same decade ran along similar lines: the function of the manufacturer was not to get profit but to provide for his country. Quoting Ruskin's *Unto This Last*, the employers' journal proclaimed that the manufacturer had become 'the master and governor of large masses of men in a more direct, though less confessed way, than the military officer or pastor'.[41] On the merchant and the manufacturer fell the responsibility for the life the masses led. How much more was this grandiose version of industry's mission merited in the mid-century years, when the employers entered upon their inheritance of power and social eminence. Before considering the historical evolution of the new paternalism something of the variety of forms the notions of duty, mission, and community took will be further considered.

The example of Titus Salt is well known and need not detain

us – his move out of Bradford in 1853, and his reconstitution of community in a Saltaire surveyed by his own castellated mansion. The feudal overtones in the cases of the Halifax Crossleys and Akroyds, the Todmorden Fieldens, the Bolton Ainsworths and Ripley's Ripleyville in Bradford are perhaps less known. Employing many thousands in the town, both Halifax ventures, especially the Akroyd's Cropley village and Akroyden (1860), with their use of Gilbert Scott's talent and their deliberate mix of 'squire', 'tenant farmer', and working population, represent the rarer, overtly feudal debt.[42] The deliberate reconstitution of communities outside the squalor of the towns was not unique to Salt and Akroyd, being found also in such as the Mellor family of Bury, and W.H. Houldsworth, who set up his Reddish Philanthrophic Venture in 1860.[43] Motives were of course never unmixed, Houldsworth for instance hoping to draw fine spinners from Bolton to his new colony.

The possibilities for control in those colonies that continued partly rural were to remain enormous, and the same was to be the case for colonies developed with a deliberate sense of community-building within the town, such as Mason's 'Oxford Colony' in Ashton. The arbitrary, near-total domination possible in the former was noted by the young Stanley in 1855, employers refusing to renew dissident workmen's house leases, and one employer imposing the Maine Law on his workpeople.[44] Lord John Manners, about the same time, noted with much approval several examples of the feudal sway of the rural and urban industrial lord in Lancashire.[45] Bolton provided several examples, such as the model, often non-alcoholic, housing estates of H. Shepherd Cross and Peter Ormerod.[46]

Whether built with the feudal parallel in mind or not, and it was much more often a matter of piecemeal development than of wholesale social engineering, such town and country colonies were really far more common than is generally appreciated. The *Morning Chronicle* correspondent described those in south-east Lancashire around 1850: Mason's Ashton community was complemented by the Whittakers' Hurst (the family employed most of the 4,000 population), and by the Buckleys' fiefdom (like Mason's in Ashton's West End) where the family lived among the people and were 'in the habit of familiar intercourse with them'. Bolton was especially rich ground, whether the Arrowsmith and Slater colony in the town, or the Ashworth one outside it, where the family took great pains to oversee the home life of the workpeople. In the Arrowsmith colony the employer again lived among the workpeople (increasingly rare by this time),

and the colony's streets, as in Ashton's West End, were named
after two heroes of Liberalism, Cobden and Bright.[47]

Though employers did not house a majority of their workers in
the North, this had less effect on the exercise of paternalism than
might be imagined. Employer influence was more often expressed
through the factory itself than in the physical reconstitution of
entire communities. John Ryland's great factories in Gorton
and Ancoats were a case in point. Though his Gorton mills were
surrounded by terraces of mean cottages, his works included a
reading room, day and night schools, baths, a library, and an
orphanage.[48]

The paternalism that mattered most widely was in fact a
paternalism largely unknown to the historical record. Below the
level of deliberate community-building and lavish provision in
the factory, what took the greatest effect was a church here, a
school or canteen there, and always the stream of social life that
characterised all factories. That these largely unnoted practices
could add up to such a force for influence, and that the very
numerous examples of a publicised paternalism could be so
effective, was in large measure a consequence of the way in which
the factory regime shaped people's sense of neighbourhood
community as it developed after mid-century. The reasons why
this should be so have been described,[49] in particular the development of the factory town as an amalgam of factory-dominated
neighbourhoods, or 'villages'. What this in effect meant was
that there was little difference in result between clearly demarcated
town colonies, themselves a mixture of deliberate and *ad hoc*
development, and the ordinary, urban factory.

A realisation that this was so forces us to reconsider the continuities in employer paternalism between the two halves of the
century. Foster is clearly right to point to the increasing
irrelevance of eighteenth-century means of work-engendered
social control as urban growth exploded in the nineteenth
century. Though in the many rural and out-township colonies
that continued, and indeed in not a few urban situations, the
eighteenth century model was much livelier than he maintains,
the 'Puritan household' that Foster describes clearly came under
severe strain.[50]

The approximation to a joint life-style, the personal supervision
of the household head, and the fiction of unity manipulated by
the family myth, were indeed transformed under the new conditions of industrialisation, and refracted through the lens of
laissez faire ideology. But the power of continuity in these changes
was great, just as the continuities between domestic and factory

industry were great, both for the employers and operatives. Because the factory town and the sense of community it engendered developed in the way they did they set a premium on this kind of transformation of earlier ways. If in their later manifestations these consequences were vestiges of what had been, there was nevertheless sufficient mutual knowledge, in the form of the neighbourhood's replication of the emotional closeness of the household, to make the modification of traditional forms extremely successful. Some of the elements in this process will be considered in the next chapter. It is in the practical consequences of this modification, rather than in the creation of an aristocracy amenable to the cultural imperialism of the middle class, that what was new and effective about employer modes of social control around mid-century may perhaps be most successfully sought.

Paternalism in English industry was especially marked in the early years of the coming of factory production, when industrial discipline had to be imposed for the first time, and an industrial society created *de novo* in a rural landscape. The studies of early paternalism and of the imposition of industrial discipline that have been made tend to suggest that the paternalist resolution of the problems of production, especially that of factory discipline, was confined to the early years of factory production.[51] The imposition of discipline was not, however, a matter sealed and settled once and for all. The mechanisation of labour, especially of male labour, took place at widely differing rates, and migration into the towns was to continue past mid-century. Paternalism thus continued to suggest itself as an answer to the continuing problems of industrialisation.

The economic uses of paternalism were as important as the social ones, especially in the English situation, where varieties of the carrot, such as piecework and promotion, and of the stick of authority, never went beyond a very primitive level in the nineteenth century.[52] Paternalism was a paying proposition, not least, to one degree or another, because it was paid for out of the low wages and long hours of those who were its beneficiaries. The almost total absence of doctrine and teaching in nineteenth-century labour management[53] – Robert Owen was one of the few who made his knowledge public – should not deter us from understanding the central importance of paternalism in English industrial society. Indeed, this absence was a reflection of the practical and piecemeal effectiveness of that paternalism.

The overweening confidence of the employer class at mid-century is conveyed in the words of the Blackburn employer that opened this chapter. It was then that the employer-dominated

Blackburn Town Council chose the shuttle, the thread, and the olive branch as the town's coat-of-arms. From the Blackburn employers' awareness of the mill as a 'miniature kingdom' sprang the claim to wider recognition. The sub-title of the lecture from which this opening quotation comes speaks loudly for the triumph of optimism: the cotton trade not only had a 'mission', but this mission could be 'politically, socially, morally and religiously considered'. The destiny of cotton was to produce the town, and with it the middle class; then would follow a working class made civil by education, a free press, and religious and political toleration. More than the source of mere money-making, the industry would bring peace and international understanding, bestowing on the world the benefits of British trade, British religion and British civilisation.[54]

At mid-century these claims appeared to be borne out, for it was then that the factory masters of the North stood poised on the brink of the fullest expression of their power. This self-belief has already been considered in terms of relations within the ruling class.[55] By 1850 the employers could afford to be sanguine about their power to move the State. By then the political crisis of the preceding decades had passed, its aftermath sanctifying the role of industrial property in State power. By 1850 or so mechanisation was well on the way to a successful conclusion, and the difficulties of the cotton industry were to be followed by a period of buoyant expansion, seen in engineering and woollens as well. The source of earlier economic difficulties, the imbalance between the industrialised sector and the rest of the economy, was to be rectified above all in terms of railway building.[56] The constraints on investment, growth, and spending of the earlier decades[57] – very few cotton magnates bought into land in the first half of the century for instance – were to be removed around mid-century.

In the following years money was to be minted not only in the employer's own industry, but also in the railways, insurance, stocks and banking through which his capital was increasingly diversified.[58] Diversification within the cotton industry was also accelerated, and there is evidence that capital was increasingly restricted within the charmed circle of the biggest employers.[59] Paternalism was now possible, if for no other reason than the money and time that prosperity brought with it. From the point of view of the patronised, by the 1850s and 60s the large employers were emerging with generations of local attachment built up, unlike the earlier years when reputations were being made, when the firm alone obsessed, and the pretensions of the *parvenu* were unendurable.

This enlargement of the employers' view of their role is charted

most revealingly in the pages of *North and South*. Before his
'conversion', the employer-hero Thornton represents the common
feeling of employers before mid-century: the employer must be
absolute master in his own factory where a wise despotism should
prevail. Thornton penetrates beyond the worklife of the operative,
and this personal knowledge and sympathy convince him that the
interests of master and man are indivisible. If the awakening
is simplistically couched in terms of personal experience and
Christian charity, the work nevertheless reveals the desire of the
employers for a role that was greater than the contractual bond
of employment, and for a say in the life of the worker beyond the
factory.[60] This change was reflected in the wider tide of literary
representation as the 1840s gave way to the 1850s,[61] Dickens's
gloomier picture in *Hard Times* (1854) asserting the older state
of feeling in a period when change was in fact very rapid.

Literature found ample correspondence in fact. Hugh Mason
and the Whittakers in Ashton were representative of a change in
all the factory towns.[62] In the 1840s Mason was the kind of
employer anathema to the Chartists, opposing trade unions
and factory legislation alike. His dramatic change of position is
revealed in the opening quotation. Holding his position to be 'far
more than that of a mere capitalist', he regarded himself as a
'father' but yet one of the 'brothers and sisters' who made up the
mill, marching together for one common end – the mutual
welfare of the workpeople and the employer.[63] The enormous
range of social provision at Mason's mills went far to bearing
out these claims. Ten years earlier John Whittaker was to maintain
that: 'He was of the opinion that those who possessed property . . .
had certain duties to perform towards the great mass of their
fellow creatures; and he had no doubt that what was being done in
recognition of this principle would greatly contrast with what was
done twenty or thirty years age.'[64]

Works dinners and treats, trips to the countryside and the
employer's residence, libraries, reading rooms, canteens, baths,
lectures, gymnasia, burial societies and the like were to become the
rule rather than the exception among the big employers. In 1857
the *Ashton Reporter* felt called upon to remark that it had witnessed
'a great change going on in the right direction, which had the
tendency to bring about that feeling of respect, esteem, and
gratitude between master and operative'.[65] In 1860 'scarcely a
week passes' but some treat was not chronicled in the district,
and such was also the case in Stockport, Stalybridge, and Mossley
(which acquired a special reputation for employer generosity).[66]

These paternalist innovations were not the pure milk of

benevolence. For the many employers still opposed to trade unions in the 1850s these measures were seen as a powerful anti-dote. The magnanimous gesture could be followed by a purge of union activists. As one Stalybridge employer put it in 1857, 'his action would beat all trade unions out of court'.[67] There was a strong element of stage management about the paternalist occasion. When this took too clumsy a form it was invariably seen through by the operatives. At one dinner an Ashton workman was heard to say, 'Our masters think to put us off with a plate of beef and a glass of beer, but he will find himself mistaken. What we want is more wages, and we will have it before we have done.'[68]

Yet the warmth and genuineness of operative responses to paternalist overtures cannot be doubted. This is reflected in the spontaneity of operative testimonials, which were almost as frequent as the benefactions which were their cause. In 1860 John Whittaker's operatives presented him with an inkstand in recognition of 'those acts and principles which have endeared you to every person, from the highest to the humblest'.[69] Such testimonials, expressing 'the warmest feelings of respect and gratitude'; being 'fully impressed with a sense of your kindness towards us' and 'unable to refrain from giving free expression to our esteem for your character as an employer of labour', con-firming 'growing attachment and esteem', and welcoming the 'sudden growth' of 'family spirit', were freely given throughout the Ashton area in the course of the later 1850s and the 1860s.[70]

The change was seen throughout Lancashire, and in many parts of the West Riding. The incidence of treats and trips is one means of measuring this. As early as 1851 the Preston press reported that such events were becoming much more frequent.[71] This was indeed the case. With the coming of the railway the great Preston factory excursions really began to get under way in 1850–51. (These most revealing events will be described later.) The same enormous increase of occasions bringing master and man together can be seen from the early 1850s in Darwen, Chorloy, Blackburn and Burnley as well.[72] At J.G. Potter's second annual dinner at his large Darwen works, one speaker commented, 'This is a new mode of entertaining the working classes. It did not use to be so.'[73] The great railway excursion exodus came later to Blackburn, in 1852–53.[74]

In Blackburn and Preston ten years earlier, such events, and paternalist provision in general, were remarkable only by their absence.[75] At a public dinner given in 1841 by the Hornby operatives in Blackburn as a mark of gratitude for a new gymnasium, it was reported that John Hornby was the first Blackburn master to set such an example.[76] With the passing of the 1847 Ten Hours Act the change was especially apparent: to meet the possibilities of increased leisure several employers organised lectures, and opened reading rooms and literary institutes.[77] By 1853 in Blackburn the operatives of all the great factories of the town were to be on the streets in the political cause of their employers.

By 1855 in Bolton the employers were again being urged to examples of 'liberality' by the press, and the local schools' inspector, in praising the employers' provision of education, was exhorting them to cultivate a personal interest in their workpeople, so as to consolidate the good labour relations their efforts had already brought.[78] By the end of the decade such liberality was much in evidence in the town.[79] Amidst all this Lancashire change the Bradford of the 1850s and 60s stands out for the infrequency of such events. This gap reveals the considerably more muted presence of paternalism across the Pennines, itself a consequence of a very different industrial development. Nevertheless, many of the big employers in the smaller textile centres, and some of the Bradford patriarchs as well, equalled the efforts of their Lancashire counterparts.[80]

The degree to which social stability had been attained by the early 1860s can be gauged by popular reaction to the Cotton Famine. The fact that this profound economic convulsion, in comparison with the social and political consequences of change in the second quarter of the century, produced so little effect is testimony to the effectiveness with which paternalism had done its work. The commonly accepted picture of steadfast endurance in the cause of the North is clearly incorrect. Far from a vindication of middle-class Radical faith in the operative class, a product of the mythology and condescension of latterday Manchester Liberalism echoed in recent accounts of the Famine,[81] it is apparent that the operatives' response was dictated largely by the pattern of economic distress, and that support for the South against the hypocrisy of the North was at least as common as pro-North feeling.[82]

It was not the case that public reaction did not take violent form, indeed popular disturbance was both more widespread and more serious than the latest chronicler of Famine events would lead us to suppose.[83] Rioting was especially severe in the south-east, particularly in Ashton and Stalybridge, but also occurred in Blackburn and Preston on a smaller scale.[84] Despite threats to 'fire the mills' in Stalybridge, there were no attacks

on factories (apart from the one in which the central relief schools
were situated), the greatest opprobium being reserved for the
Guardians. In Lancashire at the time employers were not usually
Guardians, this bastion of petty authority being left to the like of
shopkeepers, who in fact bore the brunt of most of the
disturbances. Indeed, in Ashton and Stalybridge a number of
employers co-operated with the operatives in efforts to relax the
severity of the Poor Law.[85] The Irish had a greatly dispro-
portionate share in the rioting: twenty-eight of the twenty-nine
sent for trial from Stalybridge were Irish.[86] Thus, even in this
most severe case of disturbance, where circumstances were the
most trying, it is the limitations to popular volatility and anti-
employer feeling that are in the end most striking.

Anti-employer feeling was by no means absent. Especially in
Ashton and Stalybridge, Joseph Rayner Stephens and a number
of local Evangelical clergymen led much of the popular discontent
in the Famine years, making it a part of the local political warfare
that will be chronicled in later pages. Though this opposition to
Liberal Nonconformity had much of a 'party' character to it, there
is no doubt that in engaging old political alliances and feelings it
did articulate a measure of operative opposition to the employers,
most of whom were Nonconformist and Liberal. If in the early
stages of the Famine the Lancashire employers responded
sluggishly to the plight of the operatives – as with the middle class
in general, the categories of indiscriminate charity, the 'deserving
poor', and 'pauperisation' still held a great influence over men's
minds – then there is much evidence that employers in their own
works, rather than through the early relief committees, did much
to alleviate the condition of their own workers. As in so many
other respects, it was a matter of personal responsibility finding
expression in the 'miniature kingdom' of the employer's own
works.

The distinction between large and small employers was particularly important. Small-employer Oldham was the seat of much
ill-feeling, whereas the big factories of Mossley made for excellent
employer–operative relations in the Famine.[87] Like many of the
big men of Ashton, the magnates of Blackburn and Darwen took
their responsibilities very seriously.[88] The large employer was of
course better able to modify the effects of economic catastrophe.
The Todmorden Fieldens or the big Wigan employers found an
earlier analogue in the Macclesfield Brocklehursts.[89] After the
imposition of the 1860 silk duties, depression in the industry
was almost as severe as in the Famine. Like the Halifax Crossleys,
the Brocklehursts had pledged to redeem the poor and distressed

of Macclesfield because it was in the town that their money had been made. Like many of the great cotton masters later, the Broklehursts refused to reduce wages at the onset of depression, and were reported to have kept going to the tune of a £70,000 loss.[90]

What long-term effect the Famine may have had will remain unclear until this most significant happening in nineteenth-century English life receives the attention it deserves. It may be found that it did much to take away the independent and resilient heart of Lancashire: 1,700 left Ashton for the U.S.A. in 1862, and Frederic Harrison certainly felt that the Famine had taken the fire out of the operative population. With the increase of employer involvement in the bureaucratic organisation of relief from 1863 onwards, local employers and politicians, echoing the claims of Bright and Codben, were fond of observing that the Famine years had in the end brought the classes closer together.[91] What is more certain, and just as significant, was that the Famine had not driven the classes further apart.

The extent to which a profound measure of stability had been secured is clear from the great acceleration of factory social events and paternalist provision from 1865. This was apparent in the south-east, in Stalybridge for instance the town's employers combining in 1869 to build a public baths for the town.[92] In Bolton and Burnley, with small employers as well as large, these years saw the powerful reassertion of the earlier trend.[93] By 1870 the new paternalism was no longer new, but was the everyday practice of the ordinary employer. It is to the culture in which this paternalism worked that attention will next be directed.

Summary

That industrial paternalism not only existed but thrived in a nation that gave the first and one of the most disruptive examples of factory industry to the world must call in question many of the assumptions by which Victorian society is understood. In a nation where the social structure and the cultural environment were far less favourable to paternalism than elsewhere, the paternalism of the family firm not only co-existed with but in many ways actively complemented *laissez faire* notions of economy and society. Britain was not only part of the 'gloden age' of European dynastic, industrial capitalism, but in many ways its paternalism was a more successful variant of that epoch's representative productive form.*

The account continues with the recognition that *laissez faire* ideology shaped and set limits to industrial paternalism. Nonetheless, a mellowing of the early rigours of *laissez faire* notions is apparent from the 1840s. Aside from this, there were always important differences in the degree of receptivity to such ideas among the employers. The contradictions, indeed the gulf, between the principles of the idealogues and the practice of the employers in the tightly-knit industrial enclave and in the factory town are illuminated: a piecemeal, unsung but pervasive paternalism grew out of the shared sense of community fostered by the industrial and urban conditions of the later nineteenth century. The economic uses of paternalism are seen to be of effect throughout the century, and not merely as a response to the problems posed in the earliest years of factory production. *Laissez faire* ideology was only one shaping influence, and religion, the ideas of duty and progress, but above all the belief in the civilising mission of industry, are all seen to have contributed to the making of paternalism.

Construed as the logical inverse and complement of atomised, liberal individualism industrial paternalism can be seen as the natural consequence of the society represented by that ideology. In fulfilling the need to be master of one's own (hierarchically-ordered) factory, as of one's own hierarchic household, paternalism reflected the need for community, for the restitution of society; needs unacknowledged and negated by the strict logic of individualism. In terms of the class situation of the employers, paternalism shored up an often perilously unsteady social standing, and offered a means of both aping and rivalling landed society. These considerations are traced in terms of the self-conscious implementation of the pseudo-feudal ideal, the less self-conscious workings of industrial colonies outside and within the towns, and the largely instinctual and most widespread form of the ordinary factory town understood as a collectivity of factory neighbourhoods. Discussion of the nature of urban, industrial society in chapter 3 bears directly on this reading of the social effect of the factory, an interpretation which in the next chapter is taken further in terms of the continuities existing between older styles of industrial control and the new meanings they took under the impress of a fully-developed factory system. This chapter closes with the narrative of the new paternalism, locating its genesis in the employers' successful negotiation of the political, economic and technological crises that beset them before 1850. Examination of grass-roots paternalism traces its flowering in the 1850s, its successful response to crisis in the Cotton Famine, and its consolidation as a central feature of industrial society in the 1860s.

*For a valuable re-statement, late to hand, of what may be termed the conventional view of English paternalism, see D. Roberts, *Paternalism in Early Victorian England* (1979). According to this view paternalism did not survive mid-century, in particular the social relations engendered by urbanism and class. Aside from the failure to explore the social relations of classes (the *response* to paternalism), this account does not perceive the degree to which, rather than eroding paternalism, the nature of work and of the town after mid-century actively facilitated paternalism. The same, superficially paradoxical inversion of accepted wisdom may be proffered with only a little less point about the role of *laissez faire* doctrine. Continuing the play of paradox further, industrial rather than rural society may have been the chief seat of paternalism in nineteenth-century England.

Notes

1. J. Baynes, *Two Lectures on the Cotton Trade* (Blackburn 1857), Lecture II, p. 77.
2. *Ashton Reporter*, 18 April, 1868.
3. R. Dore, *British Factory – Japanese Factory. The origins of national diversity* (1973), ch. 14; J.C. Abbeglen, *The Japanese Factory, Aspects of its social organisation* (1958), ch. VIII.
4. C. Kerr, *et al.*, *Industriaslim and Industrial Man* (Pelican 1973), ch. 4.
5. A. Dawley, *Class and Community. The Industrial Revolution in Lynn* (1976), Conclusion, esp. pp. 228–9.
6. On the U.S.A., see M.A. Maclaurin, *Paternalism and Protest. The Southern cotton mill workers and organised protest, 1875–1905* (Westport, Conn., 1971), chs 2, 3; H.J. Lahne, *The Cotton Mill Worker* (New York, 1944); R. Blauner, *Alienation and Freedom. The factory worker and his industry* (1964), ch. 4; L. Pope, *Millhands and Preachers* (New Haven, 1942).
7. E. Genovese, *Roll, Jordan Roll* (1975), Appx, 'The Fate of Paternalism in Modern Bourgeois Society: the Case of Japan'.
8. These distinctions are expertly anatomised by Dore, *op. cit.* ch. 14, also pp. 270–6.
9. *Ibid.* ch. 15.
10. H. Newby, 'The deferential dialectic', *Comparative Studies in Society and History*, **17**, no. 2, Apr. 1975, pp. 155–6.
11. E.J. Hobsbawm, *The Age of Capital* (1975), chs 12 and 13; see also T. Zeldin, *France 1845–1945* (Oxford 1973), Vol. I (1973), pp. 63–8.
12. Manchester Central Library houses a valuable and extensive collection of pamphlets, lectures, etc., explaining the virtues of political economy and the vices of working-class organisation to a benighted operative population. See esp. S. Robinson, *Friendly Letters on The*

Recent Strikes, from a Manufacturer to his own Workpeople (1854);
E. Potter, *A Picture of a Manufacturing District* (1856); see also the
numerous publications of Dr John Watts, Henry Dunckley, and
the Rev. T.G. Lee, all Manchester men.

13. J.A. Nicholls, *The Strike: a letter to the working classes, on their
     present position and movement, by a Lancashire man* (Manchester
     1853), p. 4, (Manchester Central Library). See also his other
     publications.

14. T.R. Tholfsen, *Working Class Radicalism in Mid-Victorian Britain*
     (1976), ch. 3.

15. R. Bendix, *Work and Authority in Industry* (New York, 1963),
     pp. 115–16.

16. See above, p. 94.

17. A. Shadwell, *Industrial Efficiency* (1909), pp. 425–32; Dore, *op. cit.*
     pp. 406, 416–17; see also Zeldin, *op. cit.* pp. 260–4.

18. E. Gaskell, *North and South* (Penguin 1970), p. 446.

19. *Capital and Labour*, 8, 15 Apr., 20 May, 19 Aug., 11 Nov., 1874;
     25 Aug. 1875.

20. D. Farnie, 'The English cotton industry 1850–1896' (Univ. of
     Manchester M.A. 1953), ch. 19, esp. pp. 239–51; S. Pollard and
     R. Turner, 'Profit-sharing and autocracy: the case of J.T. & J. Taylor
     of Batley, Woollen Manufacturers 1892–1966', *Business History* **18**,
     no. 1, Jan. 1976; *Capital and Labour*, 26 Aug. 1874. There is a large
     number of items on industrial partnership, *c.* 1850–70, in the
     Manchester Central Library collection.

21. S.M. Gaskell, 'Housing estate development, 1840–1918, with
     particular reference to the Pennine towns', 2 vols (Sheffield Univ.
     Ph.D. 1974), ch. 2.

22. *Capital and Labour*, 18 Mar. 1874.

23. *Ibid.*, and see above, p. 90.

24. E. Hodder, *The Life of Samuel Morley* (1887), p. 397, from a letter
     of Morley's in 1878.

25. E. Akroyd, *The Present Attitude of the Political Parties* (1874).

26. S. Greg, *On the Condition of the Working Classes in the Manufacturing
     Districts* (Macclesfield 1857), p. 4.

27. *Ibid.* pp. 4, 5; Gaskell, *op. cit.* ch. 15, for the authoress ultimately
     sharing the condescension of the incorrigible Thornton.

28. Hobsbawm, *op. cit.* pp. 237–41, 247–8.

29. G.F.A. Best, 'Popular Protestantism in Victorian Britain', in R. Rob-
     son, ed., *Ideas and Institutions of Victorian Britain* (1967).

30. J. Wilson, *Joseph Wilson, His Life and Work* (n.d.), p. 29.

31. *Ibid.* p. 32.

32. Biography of the Crossleys, in *Fortunes Made in Business*, Vol. 3
     (1887).

33. E.H. Illingworth, ed., *The Holden-Illingworth Letters* (Bradford
     1927), p. 592.

34. *Ibid.* pp. 593, 464–5, 467, 592.

35. See above, pp. 75, 78–9.

36. *Journal of the Bradford Textile Society,* **1**, no. 4, Jan. 1895; see also nos 2 and 3, Nov. and Dec. 1894.
37. *Ibid.* **1**, no. 5, Feb. 1895.
38. *Ibid.* **2**, no. 1, Oct. 1895.
39. *A Joy for Ever,* and *The Two Paths,* in *The Works of John Ruskin,* ed. E.T. Cook and A. Wedderburn (1905), Vol. XVI; *The Crown of Wild Olives,* in Vol. XVIII; see also *Unto This Last.*
40. *Holden-Illingworth Letters,* p. 593.
41. *Journal of the Bradford Textile Society,* **3**, no. 1, Oct. 1896.
42. Gaskell, *op. cit.* ch. 3.
43. *Ibid.* chs 2 and 3. See also *Manchester Guardian,* 26 Apr. 1917.
44. 15th Earl Derby Papers, Stanley notebook, 22 June 1855; Liverpool Record Office, 920 DER 46/1.
45. C. Whibley, *Lord John Manners and his friends* (1925), Vol. 1, p. 100.
46. Bolton Public Library Biographical Files.
47. P.E. Razzell and R.W. Wainwright, ed. *The Victorian Working Class. Selections from letters to the 'Morning Chronicle'* (1973), pp. 183–4, 187–9.
48. Gaskell, *op. cit.* ch. 2.
49. See above, pp. 116–23.
50. J. Foster, *Class Struggle and the Industrial Revolution* (1974), pp. 22–34, 177–86.
51. S. Pollard, *The Genesis of Modern Management* (1965); E.P. Thompson, 'Time, work discipline and industrial capitalism', *Past and Present,* **38**, Dec. 1967.
52. Pollard, *op. cit.* ch. 5; E. Hobsbawm, 'Custom, wages and work-load', in *Labouring Men* (1968).
53. Pollard, *op. cit.* p. 207, and see ch. 4.
54. J. Baynes, *Two Lectures* ... , Lecture II, pp. 56–7.
55. See above, p. 3.
56. J. Saville, 'Class struggle and the Industrial Revolution', *The Socialist Register,* 1974; G. Stedman Jones, *New Left Review,* **90**, Mar.–Apr. 1975, p. 66.
57. V.A.C. Gatrell, 'Labour, power and the size of firms in the Lancashire cotton industry in the second quarter of the 19th century', *Economic History Review,* **30**, no. 1, Feb. 1977.
58. Farnie, *op. cit.* ch. 12.
59. On this latter point I am indebted to A.C. Howe, Oriel College, Oxford, for allowing me to read 'Economic formation and structure', chapter in his Oxford D. Phil. thesis 'The Lancashire Textile Masters, *c.* 1820–1860' (forthcomings at the time of writing).
60. Gaskell, *op. cit.* (first published 1854–55), pp. 166–9, 171, 444–6, 510–13, 524–6.
61. W. Neff, *Victorian Working Women* (1969), pp. 78–85; A. Briggs, *Victorian Cities* (Pelican 1968), pp. 97–105.
62. For further corroboration see N. Kirk, 'Class and fragmentation: Some aspects of working-class life in north-east Cheshire and south-east Lancashire 1850–1870' (Univ. of Pittsburgh Ph.D. 1974), pp. 123–36.

63. *Ashton Reporter*, 18 Apr. 1868.
64. Quoted in Kirk, *op. cit.* p. 130 (*Ashton Reporter*, Mar. 6 1858).
65. *Ashton Reporter*, 22 Aug. 1857.
66. *Ashton Standard*, 14 Apr. 1860; and Kirk, *op. cit.* p. 126.
67. *Ibid.* p. 132.
68. *Ashton Standard*, 23 June 1860.
69. *Ashton Reporter*, 14 Apr. 1860.
70. Kirk, *op. cit.* pp. 134–6.
71. *Preston Chronicle*, 11 Apr. 1851; 12 Jan, 6 Apr. 1850.
72. Preston and Blackburn press, January, Easter, Whit and late summer, 1850–55.
73. *Preston Chronicle*, 11 Apr. 1851.
74. *Ibid.*, 17 July 1852, 13 Aug. 1853.
75. Preston and Blackburn press 1840–43.
76. *Preston Pilot*, 28 Aug. 1841.
77. *Preston Chronicle*, 28 Aug. 1847, 11 Apr. 1851.
78. *Bolton Chronicle*, 13 Jan., 4 Aug. 1855.
79. *Bolton Chronicle*, Jan.–Dec., June–Aug. 1859.
80. *Bradford Observer* and *Bradford Review*, 1852, 1855, 1866.
81. R. Harrison, *Before the Socialists* (1965), ch. 2.
82. M. Ellison, *Support for Secession: Lancashire and the American Civil War* (1972).
83. M.E. Rose, 'Rochdale man and the Stalybridge riot. The relief and control of the unemployed during the Lancashire cotton famine', in A.P. Donajgrodzki, *Social Control in Nineteenth Century Britain* (1977).
84. For a good account of the Famine in a local setting, see Kirk, *op. cit.* pp. 72–85, 127–31; see also W.O. Henderson, *The Lancashire Cotton Famine 1861–1865* (Manchester 1934), pp. 108–13; H.A. Taylor, 'Politics in famine-stricken Preston', *Transactions of Lancashire Historical Society*, **107**, 1955; R.A. Arnold, *The History of the Cotton Famine* (1865) see also *Blackburn Times*, 4, 11 Oct. 1862, *Blackburn Patriot*, 10 Jan. 1863.
85. Kirk, *op. cit.* p. 77.
86. *Ibid.* p. 83. See also 'A Manchester Man' [Rev. R. Lamb], 'Our manufacturing districts under a cloud', *Fraser's Magazine*, Sept. 1863.
87. Kirk, *op. cit.* pp. 76–8.
88. W. Gourlay, *History of the Distress in Blackburn 1861–1865* (Blackburn 1865).
89. On Wigan see K. Tiller, 'Working-class attitudes and organisation in three industrial towns' (Univ. Birmingham Ph.D. 1975), ch. 8.
90. C.S. Davies, *A History of Macclesfield* (Manchester 1961), pp. 136–7.
91. For Cobden see Blackburn Sunday School Union report, *Blackburn Times*, 15 Apr. 1865.
92. Kirk, *op. cit.* pp. 127, 129–30, 131.
93. *Burnley Advertiser* and *Bolton Chronicle*, 6, 13, 20, 27 Jan. 1866.

5
THE CULTURE OF THE FACTORY

> In firms like Alfred Baldwin's, generations of
> workpeople were still familiarly known to genera-
> tions of employers: the nexus was personal, a
> kind of industrial feudalism which had never to
> take much account of banks or trade unions, of
> mechanization or scientific research. In that long
> summer afternoon of aristocracy and industry
> Stanley Baldwin grew up. It was a good world
> for the rich; and no bad world for the labourer in a
> trade where there were no strikes, no unemploy-
> ment, a sound friendly society and a fair-to-
> generous master. ... What [Stanley Baldwin]
> did understand was the relationships in the old
> industry – that curious blend of discipline and
> good nature, fair-mindedness and competition,
> sound workmanship and indifference to science,
> which floats hazily over the great creators of
> Victorian industry.
>
> (G.M. Young on the Baldwins, West Midlands
> industrial magnates)[1]

DESPITE the idyllic overtones, Young's words summon back
the lost world of later Victorian industry. They reveal how
widespread was the pattern of workplace relations seen at its
most completely developed in the factory North, and suggest
the impress of that factory world on the political life of the nation.
In what follows something of the substance of this evocation will
be explored. Any attempt to evaluate the nature of this civilisation
must begin with the basic distinctions that existed between the
régimes of the large and the small factory.

Large factory and small factory
In the second half of the century the economic climate of the
cotton trade was increasingly favourable to the larger firm:
between 1850 and 1890 the size of the average spinning firm
increased from 108 to 165 hands, that of the weaving firm from
100 to 188, and the size of the average combined firm from 310 to
429 workers.[2] These figures for representative firm sizes nevertheless point to the continuing importance of the small employer.

158

In Lancashire cotton in 1877 the average capital of 1,453 firms was £29,927, and that of 880 firms between £2,000 and £20,000.[3] The small firm was important in north-east Lancashire cotton weaving, but especially so in West Riding textiles.

However, when the distribution of a town's workforce by size of firm is considered, the importance of the large and medium-sized firm becomes apparent. Figures for Preston in 1883, where weaving predominated, are particularly useful.[4] A fairly arbitrary definition of 'large', 'medium' and 'small' yields the following information: in Preston large firms of over 700 operatives employed 47 per cent of the total workforce of 36,977 (thirteen firms out of a total of eighty, in twenty-three mills). Firm concentrations of over 1,000 accounted for 38 per cent of the hands (nine firms in sixteen mills). Twenty-seven firms employed 33 per cent of the workforce in 'medium' concentrations between 300 and 700, and forty firms employed 20 per cent in sizes of less than 300.

Concentration of size was a little more advanced in Preston than in the other weaving centres, and a little less advanced than in most spinning towns. Concentration of production in the single establishment was also more marked in the spinning districts. In the spinning district of Ashton in 1882, seven firms in twelve mills (out of a total of forty-one firms) worked 42 per cent and 87 per cent respectively of the total number of spindles and looms, and in Stockport the largest nine firms in seventeen mills (out of fifty-seven firms altogether) accounted for 55 per cent of looms and 61 per cent of spindles.

Gatrell has recently pointed to the persistence of the small and medium firm, as well as the large, in the midst of the very considerable turnover of firms between 1815 and 1841,[6] and it was not only the large firm that persisted in the decades that followed. Yet, after the onset of economic stability around mid-century, the continuity, if not the continual growth, of the large firm was much more assured, the Famine years in particular sending many a small man to the wall. By the 1870s and 80s the continuity of the large capitalist's local attachment was considerable. Of the leading twenty-nine cotton firms in the North in 1877 (in terms of capital accumulation), seventeen were founded before 1840 (and often long before), and three before 1850.[7]

When changes of proprietor occurred, they often masked underlying continuities anyway. In late nineteenth-century Bolton, for instance, the new men who came into the industry were often linked by marriage and previous business interests to the old established family employers.[8] When firms changed hands every effort was made to retain the employees, reputation and goodwill of the original concern. And if the firm could not be passed on to a relative (however far removed) it often went to partners or managers already involved in the firm.[9] The continuous attachment of the workforce was often matched by continuities of employer-outlook.

The prevalence and rootedness of the large company were not seen in most of West Riding textiles. This was especially so in Bradford and in the woollen districts, where industry was intricately subdivided by trade and process. The average woollen firm in 1870 employed only seventy operatives, the average cotton firm 177 workers.[10] In longer-mechanised worsted size concentration could, however, be considerable. Halifax in particular approximated to the Lancashire pattern, especially in view of the massive carpet works of the Crossleys. Information on Halifax firms indicates that a dozen or so of the leading firms may have employed as much as 40 per cent of textile workers in the early 1890s.[11] Concentration was less marked in Keighley, while in the heavy woollens district a situation near to the primitive pattern of Huddersfield woollens existed. Even so, in both woollen areas the large employer was not unknown. Such a one was Mark Oldroyd of Dewsbury, whose firm (out of thirty-eight in the trade) employed about a quarter of those in woollen cloth manufacture.

Later mechanisation, and the greater instability of the Yorkshire textile trades, meant a lesser degree of continuous local connection than was the case in Lancashire. One Bradford historian of the textile trades estimated that of 227 firms at work in the town and its environs in 1841, fifty-six still carried on in 1881, twenty-five had production 'with more or less of means' intact, and 146 had 'failed or in a few cases worn themselves out'.[12] In the smaller textile centres the degree of persistence was greater: histories of forty-one leading firms in the Huddersfield of the 1890s (mostly large ones) indicate that eighteen had started before 1850, and ten after 1870. In Halifax the figures were twenty-one out of fifty-seven, with sixteen starting after 1870.

In engineering, concentration of ownership was even more marked than in cotton in Bolton and Oldham,[13] the chief centres of textile machinery manufacture outside Manchester. Nevertheless, the small firm continued to be important throughout the period in such centres as Bury and Rochadale. The large Lancashire firms were much longer established than the Yorkshire ones, Halifax iron and engineering for instance only coming into prominence in the last quarter of the century.

This discussion of firm sizes provides the basis for a consideration of the social consequences of work in the large and the small factory. One basic distinction that can be drawn is that between what may be termed the 'feudal' and the 'familiar', corresponding to the large and the small factory. The former term conveys the idea of the duties and rights that bound the big employer and his workers, also the notion of the larger master as the 'man of respect' whose worth and dominance were expressed in the locality and in the town. In 1849 the *Morning Chronicle* correspondent noted the distinction between large and small in Oldham. Capitalists providing regular work and well-ordered factories, and who were not operatives within living memory, were far more popular than the small men.[14] In Oldham the shared life-style of small master and man was a source of unpopularity, especially in situations of economic conflict, when the exploitation behind putative camaraderie stood revealed.

It was this finding, rather than conflicting evidence for the popularity of the small masters, that the *Chronicle* correspondent chose to put particular emphasis. In concentrating solely on the conflicting evidence Foster seems to misrepresent the real nature of the size effect.[15] Indeed, his own evidence for the size of cotton firms in 1841[16] presents what appears to be a rather puzzling contradiction to his general position that class consciousness in the town was generated solely in opposition to the hegemony of the big bourgeoisie. The salience of the small firm in the employment structure of 1841 Oldham was probably more emphatic than in most of the other cotton centres. Yet, in the second quarter of the century, Oldham was probably the most radical town in Lancashire.

However the distinction between large and small is to be understood in the early part of the century, the contrast of the 'feudal' and 'familiar' is fairly helpful in describing the situation later on. It should at once be said that there was no absolute demaraction of attributes according to size, the distinction working rather as a continuum of effect. And further, the 'small' firm of the factory North, at below 300 operatives, was in fact really quite large when compared with the size of firms in British industry as a whole.[17] Nonetheless, the smaller the firm the more likely was it that the relationship of master and man would be one of equality. The large master successfully combined the element of identification with the necessary element of differentiation. It was the balance of the two which elicited the deference that ensured the stability of the large, paternalist régime.

In the case of the small man, though paternalism could sometimes be effective, the lack of distance eminence produced meant that deference was not usually the consequence of the small-employer régime. Such employers elicited a wide range of responses, ranging between severe antagonism, and the fellow-feeling of equals, without deference but also without much of a sense of class feeling. Which was to predominate depended on a number of factors: the progress of mechanisation, the fluctuations of a particular trade and its conditions of work, the degree of geographical isolation, the extent of mutual knowledge, and so on. Before taking up this basic distinction in more detail, some comment on the workings of managerial authority in the large pre-bureaucratic factory is called for.

The system of surveillance insisted upon by one generation of the Forsters of Greenholme was maintained in the next. In the early 1890s E.P. Arnold-Forster stated, 'Whatever had been their fortunes in business ... they [had] established such a fixed relationship between themselves and those they employed that it became an absolutely necessary example to those who followed. ... Above all he wished to express his gratitude to the managers and others who had been the connecting link between the firm and the actual workers.'[18] This control over factory authority was the mark of the most successful paternalist regimes. Though not a **northerner**, Samuel Morley was typical of the big employers in using his managers in order to achieve 'the fullest and freest fraternity' with the hands. He combated the effect of size by founding a system of junior partnerships to accrete the firm's experience around his own person.[19] This attention to the chain of command bore fruit in a remarkable lack of conflict in most of the big firms, including those of the West Riding.[20]

Many employers and employers' sons acted as their own managers. When this was not the case, the manager was often seen by the employer as the apostle of his moral purpose and family spirit. Joseph Wilson, the Rands' manager in Bradford, wrote: 'On my appointment to the post of manager in the mill, Mr John Rand said to me, "I would like you to be kind to the workpeople, and do the right thing to them". I replied, "If I could not serve God as truly as their manager as if I were a missionary, I would not accept the appointment". That pleased him.'[21] The Holden family, whether in Bradford or their two French colonies (with their 'English Church', 'English Mechanics' Institute' and 'English School'), similarly saw their managers in a custodial role. Thomas Craig, their old Bradford retainer, lived beside the works and was daily involved in all aspects of their running.[22]

In the northern factory it was not uncommon for the interests of the manager to be made one with the destiny of the firm by the offer of a partnership.[23] Outside iron and coal, 'managerial dynasties' were fairly unusual, though in Bolton cotton custom and inheritance were such that 'managerial family control' characterised the operations of some firms towards the end of the century.[24] In Bradford the Bowling and Low Moor Ironworks were a classic case of managerial clans playing the fullest role in the political, cultural and administrative life of the neighbourhood.[25] The Bradford case reflected the national situation, seen perhaps in its most developed form in the coalfields of South Wales and the North-East, where resident and local-born managers established a kind of paternalism by proxy.[26] In the North, the popularity of managers was reflected in the frequent treats and presentations that marked their work lives, and in the funerals that marked their passing.[27]

Conflicts between the influence of the big man and the small that may have arisen in particular locales were considerably offset by the domination of the large employers over their inferiors. Though taking an overtly political expression in the Oldham and Macclesfied of 1868,[28] the influence of the big man partook equally of the social and the economic. This was seen in terms of the fund of prestige the big man had in town life, but was more directly located in the role the large employer had in the rise of the small man.[29]

Particular employers were special centres of this kind of influence. In the Blackburn of 1853 it was said that many small mills in the town owed their existence to the generosity of the Hornbys.[30] Henry Ashworth of Bolton said of himself: 'He had often heard it said that he had brought up a greater number of factory managers than any concern in the neighbourhood. At the time of the Paris Exhibition, the number was obtained and it astonished a great many that so large a number had become mill managers, active partners, and not a few mill proprietors.'[31] In late-mechanising areas, and where 'room and power' letting from the big men was important, this concentration of capital, technology and experience was especially important.[32]

Oral material on Keighley enables us to understand the differences between the large and small factory more clearly, and to expand on our 'feudal'/'familiar' distinction. Although the material describes the latest and weakest stages of paternalism (most of the respondants were born between 1890 and 1905), there is a clear recognition of the employers as aloof and magisterial, indeed 'gentry' and 'aristocracy'.[33] It was the large employers who most completely crystallised the element of differentiation so necessary to the deferential relationship. As Howard Newby puts it in his analysis of deference as a mode of social interaction, 'one problem with the maintenance of traditional modes of control by means of face-to-face interaction is the risk of carrying the degree of identification too far, so that differentiation, and thence the legitimation of hierarchy, is denied'.[34]

In Keighley there was little danger of familiarity breeding contempt. The big millowners were 'a little better', were 'looked up to', there being 'more of that in those days'. The people were impressed by wealth then, 'not like now', and you were brought up to try and 'live up to' those with money.[35] Nonetheless, conventional notions of deference tend to exaggerate the moral subordination the inferior undergoes. 'Self-respect', being given one's 'due', is quite clearly part of the moral rationale upon which deference subsists. What mattered in Keighley was that one was not taught to bow and scrape.[36] As one respondent put it, in speaking of how he was taught to treat the people who had absolute power over all their lives, 'Cloughs, Haggases – all these people – they were somebody that we were supposed to give a kind of reverence to. But at the same time we wasn't encouraged to do any bowing or scraping. But we was told these people were who they were'.[37]

This conveys most strikingly the delicate balance on which industrial deference in the North rested. What is so interesting, is that this desire for self-respect was reciprocated by the employers, who were intuitively aware of the need to combine the aloof and the familiar. John Clough did not like to be called 'Sir' in the mill, having when young been called by his first name on the shop floor. To his great pleasure, the old hands continued to address him thus when he grew up, the other operatives using the more formal but still familiar 'Mr John', as they did 'Mr Henry' and so on for all the other brothers. The aloof and familiar were combined in his father and mother as well. The father, away from the mill on every committee in Keighley for most of the week, was complemented by the mother, who visited good works on the neighbourhood millhands, and (to her husband's displeasure) spoke broad Yorkshire to those she saw. She knew half the operatives in a very large mill by name.[38]

This source reveals most movingly the liberation of these people from deference; the growth of the knowledge that what obtained then could not obtain now. As one respondent put it when describing the employers' Sunday school treats, 'the rich feeding the poor when you come down to it, these are things you could resent to-day'.[39] It is clear that the generations which preceded that of the respondents was deeply ingrained with respect and obedience. While they did not teach subservience, it was they who actively inculcated the lesson that the employers were the people to whom 'reverence' must be given.[40] Behind the deep conservatism of the older generations was as always the consciousness of the employer as the provider of work. The fear of losing a job or a house, the feeling of total dependence, infects so many of the interviews.[41]

What seems to have been of crucial importance in this liberation from the locale was the injection of an outside influence as the means of distancing and evaluating the experience of deference. It was this that Socialism, and especially the Independent Labour Party, did so much to provide. The transformation was never total, though it was irretrievably hastened by the experience of the First World War. The residue of the past is most revealingly represented in the attitudes of those who had Socialist fathers or who were themselves Socialists in youth,[42] and those who had Conservative or apolitical backgrounds or leanings.[43] The former saw then and continued to see the employers as lacking in feeling and respect; the latter saw them as those who treated them well and for whom they had much respect and affection.

Distinctions between the 'feudal' and 'familiar' firm should not be over-drawn. On the one hand, the stability of the large firm depended very much on the articulation of the myth of the family. As will be seen, the fiction of the family unity was always more effective than the fact of the 'familiar' firm. On the other hand, the small employer with less than 300 hands could effectively combine familiarity and the repute of the paternal provider. Such a man was Joseph Wilson of Bradford, employing 250. He provided an elaborate range of social provision beyond the means and desires of most small owners, and practised a kind of matey version of the paternalist rituals of the big owners. His 'Annual Gathering', 'Yearly Letter', and the tea-evenings at his home, reflected an intimate, personal attention. Each hand was sent his or her own birthday letter. Always using first-name terms, these combined a detailed knowledge of the operatives' personal lives with moral and religious uplift, in particular the injunction to emulate his own and his long-servers' pride in their work.[44]

The small Bradford merchant house could also be the seat of this kind of paternalism, poised as it was on the brink of familiarity's dangers. Sir Gerald Hurst's grandfather taught his illiterate workers and played cricket with them. In his own childhood in the 1880s and 90s the family's household wants were met by relatives of his father's workpeople. As Hurst observed; 'There was thus a sense of personal intimacy and of common interests between master and man. The later growth of amalgamations and large "combines" destroyed this sense. Previously both employers and employed in the West Riding shared most of their unsophisticated tastes.'[45]

Shared tastes and personal knowledge, however, denoted the experience of equality as often as it did of deference. The small mill, in particular the concern that was really more a workshop than a factory, was characteristic of the West Riding in general and the woollen districts in particular. The endemic instability of many West Riding trades, and the situation of the small employer at large, meant that the equality of the small factory more often produced antagonism than the fellow-feeling of equals. Intimate personal relations in work (in sociological terms, 'interactional' as opposed to 'attributional' status) most often led to mutual contempt.[46] The industrial consequences of small-scale production and intermittent employment have already been considered in detail.

Nonetheless, in particular circumstances, the small firm could produce a kind of camaraderie, rather than conflict or deference. In order to plot the real nature of the feelings involved the greatly varied pace of urbanisation and industrialisation must constantly be borne in mind. In the mid-1880s Beatrice Webb recognised the absence of class feeling in small-employer Bacup, by then long mechanised but still geographically and emotionally isolated and inturned; 'class feeling hardly exists because there is no capitalist class; those mills which are not companies being owned by quite small men of working class origins and connected with working people.'[47] The consequences of isolation and mutual knowledge were here complemented by those of cotton weaving employment, when compared with West Riding textiles (and small-scale Oldham industry at mid-century) the source of continuous work and wages. The richest and most revealing combinations of feeling are revealed when workplace relations in the Huddersfield woollen district are considered. There the 'familiar' mill was neither the arena of deference nor the seat of conflict.

In the Pennine valley hinterland of Huddersfield mechanisation was only in process in the third quarter of the century, and many masters were still little but glorified 'putters-out'. It is here that one witnesses a unique prolongation of the craft relationship between master and man. Gradual mechanisation, and the intimate nature of local valley life bred attitudes that reveal much about the whole span of industrial change in the period. Master and man were invariably on first-name terms, the master sharing many of the interests of his workers, such as Co-op membership. In a shared social environment, where craft status and the social relations of craft production were still substantial realities, feelings of class opposition were noticeably absent.[48] The pace of work was leisurely, the relations of master and man being described in the following fashion by a Slaithwaite historian:

... the goodwill and confidence existing at that time between employer and employee stood for something, and was modernly nearest akin to that ... ancient period where Boaz saluted his reapers, saying 'The Lord be with you', and the reapers answered, 'The Lord bless thee' (Ruth 21 : 45). The spirit was all right; of the speed we make no comment.[49]

The religious ingredient was of the utmost significance. Master and man were brought together by a religion in which the democracy of the chapel, and especially the Wesleyan one, was for once more reality than myth: religion too operated in an atmosphere devoid of caste.[50] The individualism of the craft-worker was carried over into political feeling as well. The West Riding Pennine valleys witnessed a perhaps unique blend of excellent labour relations and ultra-radical politics. The Socialism that followed Radical Liberalism as the political creed of the valleys was a close neighbour of the individualistic libertarianism of that Liberalism.

The last quarter of the century was to see the completion of mechanisation and the growth of larger factories. In this change the modern factory inherited many of the characteristics of the social relations of small scale and quasi-craft production. The power of tradition was not only a source of independence. The industry of these Pennine valleys represents perhaps the clearest example of the transformation of older styles of industrial ownership under the impress of fully developed, mechanical factory production. Because of the peculiar local circumstances of continuity and gradualness, those elements comprising what has earlier been called the 'Puritan household' – close, personal supervision, the cultivation of a shared mode of life, and the fiction of a shared purpose imaged in the myth of the father and his 'family' – were transmuted more intact and with less difficulty than was elsewhere the case.[51] As mechanisation developed, and as dependence grew and craft status was finally eroded, a late-evolving but much-qualified deference was created out of the common stock of pre-factory social experience.

With the growth of dependence and size a loyalty to the individual mill and its locality became discernible.[52] Firms like

Cloughs and Robinsons in Marsden were typical of the period of transition, the social relations of master and man being those of putative equals.[53] John Robinson inherited all the benefits of slow transition and long connection, putting them into practice in a notably easeful paternal régime. He is recorded as having chaffed late-comers, urging them to sit down and rest in his office. The discipline of the factory was indeed learned in many different ways in many different places, and at many different times. Robinson was an ordinary member of the Oddfellows for many years. As the firm grew his interests were devoted to Marsden and its welfare. In the classic mill towns the factory had been rooted in the centre of life for decades by this time, and it is to the cultural flower of that root that attention will now be given. The first aspect of this consideration will be the expansion of the employers' interests into the life of the town, in the manner of the Marsden of John Robinson.

The *milieux* of factory life
The large employer's influence was generated in the factory and its locale, and magnified in the arena of the town. Indeed, in many small towns, reputation gained at the level of the town was almost as effective as that at neighbourhood level. One or two great families could establish a long-sustained domination, as was the case in Glossop,[54] and in Hyde, where the Ashtons overawed the town.[55] Similarly, the Pilkingtons of St Helens, the Lairds in Birkenhead, the Northwich Brunners, Brocklehursts of Macclesfield and Garnetts of Clitheroe, were all patriarchs whose fiefs were almost as much the town as the locale.

In all towns, though more especially in the cities, there was a core of endemic poverty, made up chiefly of those who had never known factory work or factory schools. Most employers conceived their economic duty in terms of the provision of employment, a role reflected in the infrequency with which they took up membership of the Boards of Guardinas. Nevertheless, the large employers' view of themselves as the creators and custodians of urban civilisation was sufficiently grandiose to permit a considerable involvement in the control of urban poverty.

The shift of paternalist emphasis from indiscriminate charity and Christian kindness to 'rational' and 'scientific' considerations had been made by mid-century. It was reflected in the foundation of the Manchester Statistical Society (1833), and in the orphanages, almshouses, homes for the aged, and Ragged and Industrial Schools that sprang up in the industrial towns early in this period. Rationality was to be sought in the consequences of the new philanthropy: savings to the taxpayer, an increase in the supply of suitable labour, and the inculcation of a proper respect in the 'deserving poor'.

As well as the response to poverty, employers were fully involved in the provision of urban amenities. The new paternalism was to coincide with the growth of civic Britain. Public libraries and parks, public health, and the building of town halls were all causes to which employers and merchants contributed liberally in terms of land, money and time. Public utilities, such as gas and water supply, were also developed under the aegis of those whose consumer interest was greatest, the employers of labour.

Involvement in the development of civic institutions was reflected in the administrative, judicial and political structures of the town, which were in fact mirror-images of local economic power. In the Blackburn of 1861 twenty-one out of thirty-six town councillors were cotton or iron and engineering employers.[56] In 1899 eight out of fourteen aldermen were substantial cotton employers. In both 1881 and 1891 around 85 per cent of Blackburn borough bench was made up of cotton masters, and other 'gentlemen' mostly from employer families.[57] This degree of involvement was typical of the other towns, and was seen in such as School Boards as well. Influence over town councils was reflected in employer pressure on Corporation officials and workmen during election periods.[58] The influence of John Platt, the great Oldham engineer, moved one Tory observer to note in 1869 that 'hundreds' of Corporation employees were in his power, and that the 'shoddyocracy ... and the shopkeeping classes' were devoted to his interests, no doubt in part because of the hospitality of what were called his 'gilded saloons'.[59]

Interest in the many voluntary organisations of town life was considerable. Employers were avid supporters of the Volunteers, for instance, though corps formed around merchant houses and particular factories were rare after the first flush of interest in 1860. Nevertheless, the Volunteers went far to reproducing the world of the factory on the parade ground.[60] Direct involvement in the organisations of working class self-help was not at all uncommon, and friendly societies, co-ops, temperance societies, and the like will be considered in due course.

Whether in the context of the town or the locale, employer provision can be suggestively interpreted in terms of the gift relationship. In the sense of deference as a mode of social interaction, the gift was one of the most valuable means of managing the tensions of identification and differentiation that characterised deference. The gift celebrated and reaffirmed the bond of master and man. As Marcel Mauss put it, the giver, being possessed by fortune, puts the recipient 'in the shadow of his name'.[61] For the poor, that shadow could be lifted only by hard work and good faith.

Two aspects of the gift relationship as it worked historically in the North are of particular interest. Unlike the situation in London, which G. Stedman Jones has analysed so well, personal paternalism on a local basis in the North long prevented the 'deformation' of the gift, a process set in train in later nineteenth-century London when charity became bureaucratically organised, and thus impersonally dispensed on a less localised and discriminating basis.[62] Secondly, the acceleration of charity in times of social upheaval, when the ordered relations of superior and inferior were threatened, characterised English society at different times throughout the century.[63] The timing of the new paternalism, developing out of the turmoil of the North in the 1830s and 40s, takes on a special significance in this light.

Though the constraints of *laissez-faire* ideology on paternalist practice meant that cultural rather than economic provision always bulked largest, in the case of the big employers economic action was still important. Though proft-sharing and works insurance were uncommon, more primitive sick clubs, savings banks, and provident founds were set up in many large firms. The payment of pensions, relatively common, was a somewhat different matter. Such doles, sometimes given personally, were no doubt used selectively to encourage fidelity (the Potters of Darwen promised the faithful an easy chair, a comfortable cottage, and freedom from care in old age),[64] but there was still much about them suggestive of times more antique than those of economic rationality.

Some of the Keighley employers had a reputation for indiscriminate charity, one of them bankrupting himself by his open-handedness.[65] The difference between Tory and Liberal employers was often marked, especially among those less given to the tenets of economic individualism and more inclined to a Tory-Radical version of social relations. William Wood of Bradford, and the Blackburn Hornbys, were noted for their personal care and open-handedness.[66] Pensions to old hand-workers, and even their continued employment in mechanised days, fitted just as ill with modern, rational times. Yet this was the practice in many of the great West Riding firms, including John Brigg of Keighley, and the Holdens, Akroyds and Fosters.[67]

The provision of facilities for youth and adult education was a principal concern of many large employers. Such bodies as the

Black Dyke Mills Literary and Scientific Institute, and Tootal, Broadhurst and Lee's Sunnyside Institute in Daubhill, Bolton, were to become almost commonplace from the 1850s.[68] So too were factory newsrooms, and even the mill prize-day was not unknown.[69] The Blackburn employers were typical in regarding the aggregation of mills in an area as the inevitable spur to the dissemination of adult education.[70]

Whether the faith of the Blackburn employers in 'improving' education was borne out in practice is another matter. The Sunnyside Institute (at which the Misses Lee played and sang at concert evenings) was typical enough of the limited effect of such institutions. In 1870 complaints were made about the lack of attendance, the number in membership out of the vast throng employed in the mills being only eighty. The recreational rather than the purely educative aspect of such factory provision was probably of the greatest impact, whether in the form of gymnasia, games and smoking rooms, or newsrooms. It is likely that the works brass band drew a more fervent support than the literary institute. The Black Dyke Mills band has certainly weathered the years better than the Fosters' educational efforts. Bands like Hick and Hargreaves' Soho Ironworks Band were to establish themselves in the life and reputation of the North about this time.[71]

The inculcation of thrift, respectability and sobriety, by factory and non-factory institutions of adult education alike, was important enough for the minority whom it touched. But to assume some kind of seminal leadership role for this element is greatly to distort the nature of working class society. When the influence of adult education is considered the great limitations to any notion of the ideological 'infiltration' of working-class life is apparent. Technical education in Lancashire was a notably disorganised failure,[72] nor does the public library movement seem to have extended into popular life with any more success. The same can be said for the Mechanics' Institutes and Church Institutes, into which, with characteristic fervour, the employers poured their time and effort. The education received in these, as in all institutions of adult education, often amounted only to the teaching of basic reading and writing, and was far removed from 'improving' subjects as such.

Estimates of the number and social composition of those touched by the culture of improvement, whether secular or religious, factory or non-factory, suggest how peripheral the impact of this sort of education on operative life actually was. Detailed analysis, which for lack of space cannot be described here,[73] indicates that rather less than 10 per cent of the appropriate age-range (males between fifteen and thirty years) were receiving adult education in most factory towns at any one time in the third quarter of the century. Aside from the considerable difference between enrolment and attendance figures (the estimate is for enrolment), it is clear that very many of these were not of the manual working class at all, and of those who were only a minority were factory workers. On the basis of this information it is difficult to envisage (*pace* John Foster) any great cultural divide at work in the working class.

Of rather more importance, though the fixation of so many historians on the cultural 'co-option' of the 'élite' working class would lead us to ignore it, were the means by which the great majority of the factory workforce was brought within the ambit of employer influence. As with all aspects of factory life, with secular and religious educational provision the integration of the majority occurred because so much of what was an integral part of daily life – a smoke, the reading of a newspaper, playing in a brass band, rather than a lesson in elocution – took place within the territory of the factory. Of course, the social life of the upper Sunday school, the use of a newsroom or lecture hall, and the penny bun and games in the garden of a local benefactor for children, all hammered home the message that thrift and hard work would bring their own reward. Aside from the patently obvious reality that this reward would hardly be in the material world, what mattered rather more for the effect of all this on people was that the reputation of the donor as the big man of the locality was hammered home before all else. The link between the factory régime and the spirit of the neighbourhood was strengthened, the new spirit permeating the recesses of the instincts.

Employer involvement in elementary schooling seems to have counted for more than adult education. What mattered about it was that from his or her earliest days the operative was schooled into the reputation of a paternal élite, and very often into an environment dominated by a particular employer and factory. The employer's interest in education was given particular point by the legal responsibilities for education that the Factory Acts involved him in. Factory schools, entirely paid for by the employer and often run on the premises, were never widespread, but employers continued to finance and manage schools long beyond the 1870 Education Act. This was especially the case in Lancashire, where the School Boards nearly always came a poor second to voluntary provision. The employers often built and managed schools in direct competition with one another. The Hornbys of Blackburn built the Brookhouse schools in 1840 (in 1862 this had a massive 1850 pupils on roll). James Pilkington (a Congregationalist) followed with the Park Road school in 1850, his activity in turn sparking the Anglican Hopwoods into building their school. Prior to this in 1845 the Anglicans had co-ordinated a townwide offensive, setting up an organisation for National and Sunday schools.[74]

In Bolton a similar direct personal interest characterised the efforts of many of the leading employers. The Thomassons spent £30,000 on education in the town, and their generosity was equalled by that of Henry Ashworth.[75] By the 1850s and the 1860s the provisions of the Factory Acts had done much to strengthen the bond between employer and child employee. In both Bolton and Blackburn the awakening of interest was noted in these years.[76] By the later 1860s the Blackburn district schools inspector could maintain that

... throughout a large portion of my district the half-timers Act has brought the employer and employed into a very close relation. In Blackburn especially, but also in a large part of the Rossendale district, the manu-facturers have exhibited the greatest possible interest with schools which the child employed in their factories attend. ... The children have a greater respect for their school, and for school learning; they try to stand well in their classes, and at the inspectors' examinations, which the masters usually attend.[77]

Henry Ashworth for one had a keen eye for the benefits of this close involvement, maintaining that 'If they have been to school they're obedient, they want less licking'.[78]

The competitiveness that characterised educational provision, compounded of status, religious and political rivalries, could sometimes be expressed in direct interference in school life. This was the case in some of the factory schools in the early 1850s.[79] Though sectarian interference in the content of education was rare,[80] the engine of sectarianism in the North being the Sunday rather than the day school,[81] administrative convenience for the employer meant that the majority of young employees usually attended one school, and this school was closely associated with the life of the factory.

Employer pressure to attend a particular school could often be exerted for reasons far removed from the administrative however. As enlightened an employer as Samuel Morley imple-mented an anti-Roman Catholic policy in his firm.[82] In the sectarian battlegrounds of Lancashire things were much worse. In 1870 the Rev. Wescoe of Blackburn complained to the National

Society that his parish was in open warfare, the new British
School built by the manufacturers poaching half-timers from
his school.[83] A number of Tory employers in Blackburn felt
their power so threatened by the 1870 Education Act that they
went against local party policy in their opposition to the new
School Boards.[84] They had little reason to fear. In 1874, Robert
Hopwood Hutchinson, one of the early rebels, was publicly attacked for taking only Anglican half-timers in his mills, a practice
facilitated by his understanding with the local Anglican parson.[85]
In 1880 it was said he would not allow his half-timers to attend
Catholic schools, while in the same year James Briggs, a Non-
conformist Liberal employer, took his children *en bloc* from their
Anglican school to a new one of his own building.[86]

The same kind of pressure was exerted outside Blackburn in
the 1870's. In Bolton it was widespread, and mainly practised by
Anglican employers, though not always for political reasons.[87]
The situation in Ashton and Stalybridge was similar to that in
Blackburn. Coercion of schoolmasters and clergymen was another
variant of the 'screw' in these towns, and children were moved
from school to school at the master's behest.[88] In 1876 the Tory
employers practised anti-Catholic discrimination.[89] The large
Liberal Nonconformist employers did not lag behind. In the
same year an Anglican teacher protested that his pupils were
forced to go to Catholic or British schools, and that the two
millowners on either side of his school had blatantly coerced him.[90]
The presumption of the mighty is apparent in the comment of one
Stalybridge witness in 1876 on the Nonconformist employers and
his own British School: ' . . . a number of gentlemen in the district
entered into a subscription in 1844 to form my school and they
have maintained it ever since, and they look upon my school as
part of their works.'[91] Similarly in Bolton, the proprietary interest
that so many employers assumed in their schools found expression
in Henry Ashworth using his local British schools as meeting
places for his workpeople.[92]

The large employers regarded the building of churches as part
of their duty to the town and its operative population. Their
expenditure in fulfilment of this duty was considerable.[93] It was
stated in 1892 that the majority of Bolton's seventy-seven churches
were built with employer aid,[94] and this was representative
of the factory towns in general. The links between the employers
and organised religion were close. Ties of marriage and blood
were frequent. In the Keighley area the churches and chapels
were popularly understood as the proprietary interest of the
employers, and the parson was seen as part of the social world of

that class, one Shipley Baptist parson even becoming an employer's secretary for a time.[95] An outraged Blackburn working-man Radical expressed the nature of the connection in the following manner (speaking of the Dissenting minister):

... he aims ... to form a large acquaintance with the respectables, employers of labour, as they are the likeliest to raise his salary, fill his pews with managers, overlookers and workpeople; so that he is bound hand and foot to the interests of the wealthy; for on the principle that one good turn deserves another, he must of necessity work into the hands of the wealthy employers who ... mainly build the chapels.[96]

The chapels and schoolrooms that these employers built were as much social and political centres as religious ones. The Park Road Congregational chapel of the Pilkingtons in Blackburn was the unofficial headquarters of Blackburn Liberalism in the third quarter of the century.[97] Meetings of the congregation were often followed by political speechifying, sometimes by the Pilkington brothers, and the Audley Lane Working Men's Reform Club was wont to hold its annual soirée in the schoolroom.[98] The Pilkingtons' Anglican counterparts in Park ward, the Hopwoods and Robert Hopwood Hutchinson, erected and supported the local Christ Church buildings, a duty to the locale which they accepted as their personal concern.[99] All the large employers supported their local town church,[100] splitting their attendance between it and the place of rural residence.

In Ashton and Stalybridge employer interest reached something of a Lancashire peak. The West End employers of Ashton ran large mutual improvement societies and working men's classes in chapels that were little but extensions of their works. The Buckleys were as hand in glove with their 'political parson', the Rev Page Hopps, as Hugh Mason was with J.G. Rogers at Albion chapel. The Gospel of Mason's Oxford Colony was carried to heathen Dukinfield in 1869, a group of Mason's hands helping to set up a workingmen's class in Buckley's chapel.[101]

The assumptions of the powerful were particularly apparent in the case of Jonas Sugden and Brothers of Keighley, who suspended a notice in the works 'wishing' and 'expecting' that all employed in the works should attend worship and school. Jonas Sugden would not employ those who gambled or frequented pubs, and ordered those living in sin either to marry or to leave his service.[102] In Keighley the employers were Sunday school teachers and superintendents, also choir masters (having a voice could be the passport to a job).[103] It was in the chapel that the employer was 'got close to', but yet also in which the physical distance appropriate to station was maintained.[104] In Keighley the employers built and supported the churches and chapels and expected their workpeople to attend them.[105] Judging by the geography of sectarian feeling in Keighley it may appear that many factory workpeople fulfilled these expectations. The Oakworth district of Keighley was dominated by the Haggas and Clough factories, and Oakworth split with geographical precision into church and chapel, Tory and Liberal, Haggas and Clough.[106]

Appearances may, however, be a little deceptive. This kind of local partisanship does not seem to have been a consequence of any deepseated attachment to the institutions and dogma of organised religion. Working-class attitudes to religion, to be considered more completely in a later chapter, were characterised by the indifference of the majority and by a kind of amiable informality in much of the religious feeling that did exist. Yet religion was a staple of political conflict and a badge of political allegiance. This paradoxical situation obtained because religion worked with the grain of experiences located deeper in popular life than formal religious attachments, or even religious feeling itself. Religion was part of a ritualised politics that had little to do with either politics or religion. What it had to do with were the loyalties of work and, to a lesser degree, the loyalties of of race. As a force in the ideological permeation of working-class life by values shaped in the middle class, and especially as a carrier of the ethic of improvement, religion was of limited effect in popular life.

What it may have done rather more successfully than this was to cement the chain of authority in the factory and so bolster the hold of the factory regime on the workpeople. When the links between success at work and religious observance are traced it becomes apparent that rather than expressing a shared ideological perspective between the classes, religion was a measure of the dependence of the operative: the worker attended worship often rather more because of the material consequences of *not* attending than the spiritual ones of attending.

The connections between religious involvement, work advancement and, frequently, political activism, were close. These have been described for Durham mining and in South Wales, and were especially strong in the case of Methodism.[107] In Methodist South Wales chapel attendance often secured a job. The confraternity of Northern Methodism similarly facilitated promotion when a job was secured.[108] In Crewe the unadulterated sycophancy that characterised support for the religious institutions of the local railway company officials was revealed when the Chief Mechanical Engineer's brother changed his patronage from chapel to church. He was followed by the drift of lesser company officials until their influence over the employees in turn brought the former chapel congregation flooding in to fill the Anglican church.[109]

A Lancashire man, looking back on his father's Edwardian times, expressed what must often have been the case (his father was an Anglican-Tory overlooker, the son a devout Anglican):

> ... the main reason people went then was because it was the fashion. I know there was some people came to our church because their employer attended. And they considered it politic to do the same ... whether they thought their job depended on it or not I don't know. ... But I spoke to some of them privately and they'd no time for the Church really. But they considered it was in their interests to come as their boss came.[110]

The links between work advancement and religious and political activism in Blackburn and Ashton have been traced in some detail.[111] Mill salesmen, managers, mill joiners and overlookers all owed as much to diligence in the service of the chapel or church as to diligence in work. One representative case can be mentioned, that of Elijah Holt of Blackburn. Holt started work in the Hornby's Brookhouse Mills at the age of thirteen, and advanced, under the Hornby's auspices, to a managership *via* the overlooking position. A leading political activist in the town, Holt was twelve years in the local St John's Sunday school, from sixteen to twenty years of age a member of its mutual improvement society, and thereafter People's Warden and a lifelong Sunday school teacher at the Hornby church.

It is a truism worth asserting with some force that the religious experience was of complex and elusive social effect. Attempts to explain its consequences in terms of subordination and control by no means exhaust the meaning of this effect. In the Huddersfield area the democracy of the chapel seems to have been a source of independence and egalitarianism in working-class life. This perhaps obtained more often to the east than to the west of the Pennines, though in the small-employer Bacup Beatrice Webb visited in the 1880s this may have been so in Lancashire as well.[112] The religious drive marked the most independent in the working class, the trade union activists,[113] and was a powerful ethical force shaping the Socialism of the West Riding in particular.[114] The language of the Bible, the organisation of the chapel, and the Methodist experience of conversion could teach the dignity, equality and independence of labour as well as the moral community of master and man.[115] Nor was Anglicanism always a source of the *status quo*. In the south-east of Lancashire in particular, popular Anglicanism could articulate a sometimes powerful anti-employer, populist sentiment. When it coalesced with anti-Irish feeling the juggernaut that was born sometimes ran far beyond the bounds of employer control.

Nevertheless, in the historical and cultural context of factory society in the second half of the century, organised religion was in the main a principal support of employer hegemony, the identification of the place of work with the place of worship limiting the horizon of the operative to the local and the known. For the minority of factory workers who were true believers and active churchgoers this effect was no doubt achieved in ideological or theological terms. Particularly in the more Calvinist of the sects, perhaps in sections of Anglicanism too, the 'elective affinity' of economic structure and ideology was apparent: there clearly was some form of consonance between religious and economic individualism.[116] But for the majority religion probably worked most powerfully in a rather different way. As a source of notions of partnership and community, it was one of many elements nurturing the sense of commitment to the employer and his territory. What may have mattered most was the indirect involvement of the nominal Christian, the infrequent attender, indeed the godless many, in the cultural penumbra of church and chapel social life. Religion considered in this wider 'social' sense was probably much more significant than religion considered as the ideological framework of a *Weltanschaung* that legitimated subordination.

The Sunday school illustrates something of this distinction. These schools were rightly called 'the working-class part of religion' in the period. Blackburn in 1875 was reported as having a Sunday school population of 21,000 out of a town population of some 80,000. The Ashton Anglicans claimed in 1869 that nine out of ten of their teachers were operatives, many of them over-lookers.[117] The national Anglican Sunday school magazine in 1863 described the adult bible class and the adolescent upper school as the hallmarks of the factory North of England.[118] It considered this long connection into adult life to be a product of the shared experience of scholar and teacher in the factory and its neighbourhood. The *Morning Chronicle* correspondent at mid-century also considered the factory to be the soil of the Sunday school system.[119] The Blackburn employers viewed the system as 'the grand moving cause of the improved moral and religious condition of the people'; going on, 'And does not the experience of every manufacturer testify to the truth of this eulogy. .... Those workmen and workwomen who are the most sober, steady, respectable and intelligent either have been, or still are, connected with the Sunday schools.'[120]

Whether this employer eulogy was borne out by practical results in quite the way that was imagined seems doubtful. The schools may have produced the 'most sober, steady' and 'respectable', but these were most likely to be the teachers, the mutual improvement society and bible class members, and some of the upper classes. These were at the centre of the schools' ideological purpose, which was anyway more theological than moral, more given to the ingestion of scripture than of respectability. The two sectors overlapped, but were not the same. For the great majority the schools worked in a different fashion.

In our period they became genuinely popular institutions. Social centres much more than devotional ones, attachment to the school (and just as much to 'the old school') would have formed part of the nexus of allegiance defining the feeling of local community. The schools were an aspect of the sense of place which the factory defined. Sunday school marches often went by the houses of the employers and other notables (Hugh Mason often marched with his own Albion Schools). This happened regularly in Bolton and Bury for instance.[121] In Keighley the Clough and Haggas Sunday school marchers were apt to clash in the streets, brass bands and all, with the Radical Free Speech Sunday School.[122] School treats often involved the factories or houses of the employers—'the rich feeding the poor when you come down to it'. The big Blackburn and Bolton employers treated the scholars in their rural retreats.[123] Oldham Whittaker of Hurst sent the whole population of the suburb on a school outing to Anglesey in the 1860s. James Williamson surpassed even Whittaker's munificence in 1887, sending 10,000 of Lancaster's population on a Sunday school excursion to the Manchester Exhibition.[124]

Just as the social effect of religion is commonly misunderstood, so is that of the factory itself. Like the religious institution it functioned as a centre for social life, and was not merely the seat of production, just as the church and chapel were not merely the seat of piety. The factory generated a life of its own.

The most frequent and regular of the constant flow of events in factory life were the dinners, teas and other 'treats' for supervisory and skilled elements in the workforce. Typical of these were the annual dinner for foremen and machine erectors at Asa

Lee's of Oldham, the Preston Birleys' twentieth annual overlookers and mechanics' supper in 1874, and the Stalybridge
treats for carders and spinners.[125] The whole of the workforce
was only slightly less frequently involved. A treat might be given
on a decrease in hours or an upswing in trade,[126] and was almost
mandatory on the departure of any manager or overlooker with
even the smallest claim to popularity. Presentations to old
hands were also frequent, symbolising as they did the spirit
of the factory.[127]

Political factory celebrations will be treated later: in Bolton it
was customary for the hands to be fêted whenever an employer
gained political or administrative office. In small mills and workshops the fare was less inspiring but still forthcoming: a shilling
for the works tea, the donation of a day's wages or a pub. dinner.[128]
Aside from the many testimonials from workers to employers
(considered earlier) workplace activity found form in such as mill
collections for visits to the great Victorian exhibitions, for royal
visits, the Derby memorial fund and Cotton Famine testimonials
and so on.[129]

There was also a considerable degree of sustained activity
throughout the year, seen in bodies like works brass bands and
fire brigades, each with their own dinners and 'do's'.[130] Some
employers, such as Edward Brook of Huddersfield, threw almost
as much energy into their bands as into their businesses.[131]
Mills had their own social committees, organising trips, mill
socials (at which the mill band would play), and sports days. More
informal activities were not unknown, one Marsden employer
turning a blind eye to the pigeon-cote in the loft of his factory.[132]
Factory football and cricket were organised on league bases in
the period.[133]

The ritual quality of so much factory social life is very striking.
It can be understood in terms of the fostering of 'company
cultures'.[134] In a formal and deliberate way this occurred in the
nineteenth century in such firms as Cadburys and Pilkingtons of
St Helens. The general rule was one of less formal cultivation,
which was nevertheless extremely successful. This kind of
socialisation in the company's customs and traditions has taken
the selfconscious form of the modern corporation (IBM for example), and the more successful forms of the Indian and Japanese
factory. The formal integration of Japanese religion and the life
of the factory is apparent in ceremonies like the blessing of the
new year's production.[135] The particularly effective fusion of
cultural *milieu* and factory practice is also witnessed in occasions
like the 'second birth' into the company, and in the keeping

of elaborate firm genealogies and histories. The latter found a more muted precedent in the nineteenth-century English factory, where the culture of the company was to be the culture of the employer family.

The significance of factory ritual can be located somewhat more precisely in the light of the suggestive work of Goffman and Coser.[136] The factory had much in common with the 'greedy' or 'total' institutions which the two sociologists anatomise. Such institutions isolate the individual from competing claims, engrossing as much of his life as possible. The importance of so much of social life of the operative taking place within the orbit of the factory and its neighbourhood will be apparent.

The stream of factory life involved the creation and celebration of symbolic boundaries. Notions of the 'team' and of partnership were central to this. The ritual of the factory extended the symbolic boundary from the factory to the neighbourhood, celebrating the connection of the employer and the community. The basic constituent of this ritual was undoubtedly the mythology of the employer family. The history and destiny of the factory was made one with the saga of family life, so enforcing the fiction of community.

The special significance of status distinctions within labour being considered as distinctions of authority within the family will be recalled. It was these that seem to have been of profound importance in the whole process of social stabilisation around mid-century. The maintenance of paternal authority, and the resulting distribution of authority and status within the textile family, may in large measure have underpinned the accommodation of the later nineteenth-century workforce in the new social order of factory industry. The mutuality of the paternalism and family life of the operative, and the paternalism and family myth of the factory régime, is something that reverberated powerfully below the surface of Northern factory society.[137] As the centrepiece of factory ritual and social life the family found echoes in the fundamental instincts of operative life.

Similarly, the effectiveness with which the family fiction was articulated measure the effectiveness of the employers' retention and modification of earlier means of industrial control. The special circumstances of the Pennine woollen industry, as previously described,[138] seem to have seen a specially clear example of the transformation of the personal style with the coming of a fully developed factory industry. If the transitition was not so gradual or continuous elsewhere, it is still the case that continuities of productive technique, of the living memory of the operatives, and of the ownership of the means of production, were sufficient to guarantee that older forms of influence, associated with the various stages of the mechanisation and concentration of industry that preceded a fully-fledged factory industry, were sufficiently relevant to the needs of the new situation. Remnants of the old system of direct household paternal control they may have been. And no doubt the style of domestic and early factory ownership was transformed under the new conditions of urban industrial life. But, as the foregoing discussion of the new paternalism has indicated,[139] the ecology of the factory town and the developing sense of neighbourhood-orientated community feeling that it in part gave rise to, meant that there was sufficient mutual knowledge and interest in the factory neighbourhood to enable it to act as the surrogate for the direct personal contact and control that characterised earlier styles of management. Similarly, the mythology of the employer family in the ritual of the factory involved a fiction sufficiently plausible to act successfully on earlier ways. It worked in such a way as to make the appearances of a joint life-style and identity, and of direct personal supervision and concern, serve the purposes of their reality.

The Forsters' Greenholme partner, William Fison, was regarded as 'the father of the village', in which 'a kinship seems to extend through the whole community'.[140] Fison did indeed patch up the quarrels of local people. In the giant Low Moor ironworks, despite a plethora of partners and managers, a number of Hardy family members retained a close involvement in the firm, a connection symbolised by the foundation of a memorial 'Harold Club' at the works in 1883.[141] Thus in the enclosed semi-rural colony and the giant, semi-bureaucratic firm the family idea was equally influential.

These efforts found an appropriate response in operative presentations of family portraits to their employers.[142] A typical example of the family saga was that of the Blackburn Hornbys. In the dark days of the early 1840s John Hornby was described as the ideal master before a gathering of his operatives; significantly enough for a Tory-Anglican paternalist, because 'he could never keep his hands out of his pocket when appealed to with a tale of distress'.[143] An interesting sidelight on this occasion was the toast to the 'Six Motive Powers at Brookhouse Mills': on other occasions as well the mill engine was formally celebrated (quite literally christened, with wine) at factory meetings.[144] Just over a decade later William Henry Hornby was lauded as the representative of a continuing family influence that brought work and largesse to the town: 1,900 operatives sat down at the feast table.[145]

Birth, marriage and death comprised the symbolic warp from which the family saga was woven. Typical of occasions celebrating a birth, invariably a male one, were the Sowerby Bridge celebrations of Richard Edleston in 1880, a large dyer and manufacturer.[146] 'Welcome to the Son' was emblazoned above the throng, Master Robert being brought in to general applause and presented to the women present by his nurse. The presiding manager praised the late grandfather, and, appealing to the workpeoples' sense of 'the little one', proclaimed that their master was now even more one of themselves. Eight hundred operatives and their wives sat down to the treat, the trays being presided over by the foremen's wives. The mill fire brigade acted as 'policemen' and general assistants. As was usual at such events the assembly was surrounded by suitable mottos; in this case, 'May Trade ever Prosper' and 'May we never forfeit our master's confidence'. Wives were frequently present on such occasions, whether they worked in the factory or not. If the sexes were sometimes divided at the feast itself,[147] they were united for the dance that invariably followed.[148]

There was no more significant event than a son's coming-of-age, when the rejuvenation of the dynasty and the factory was symbolised and celebrated. Like the other rites of passage, it was male pre-eminence within the traditional structure of family authority and status that was emphasised. In all factory social life there was an element of calculation on the operatives' part: the chance of a free meal or trip was not to be overlooked. There are considerable difficulties of documentation; above all in ascertaining the operatives' definition of these events. Nevertheless, their ritual structure seems plain enough, and, as our previous account of responses to the new paternalism indicates, there is considerable evidence for the spontaneous character of workers' reactions.

This is specially clear in coming-of-age ceremonies. On one such occasion in the Ashton of 1870 the workers were reported as having decorated the mill themselves and contributed towards the cost of the tea.[149] Ten years earlier in the Whittakers' Hurst, banners and ribbons were hung from the area's houses to celebrate John Whittaker's majority: 1,000 workers sat down to dinner.[150]

At the celebration for Hugh Mason's son in 1880 the whole of Ashton's West End was mobilised; the streets and mills were bedecked for the occasion; and the tea was organised by the hands. It was said that the event was mainly the responsibility of the workpeople, working in the mill at night after finishing their daily labour. The meeting, presided over by two spinners and an overlooker, praised the long-servers (most of the hands, but especially the spinners) and Mason as well, as the paragon for all employers. Loyalty, including political loyalty, was pledged to the father and the son. Later on the under-sixteens were given their own 'do', the message being relayed in appropriate terms by the newly initiated son. This included the obligatory injunction to save and prosper.[151]

Workpeople's addresses were invariably fulsome on these occasions,[152] and the whole of a factory workforce might turn out to walk in procession around the mill or through the town.[153] Such activities represented feelings deeply imbedded in the whole of popular society: someone as practised in the arts of an élite as the Earl of Crawford and Balcarves felt moved to comment on the exceptional 'deference' of the 500 members of the Wigan Operative Conservative who had walked five miles to present an address to his son on his coming-of-age.[154]

The life-cycle turned through marriage and was completed at death. On the occasion of the Holden and Illingworth union in Bradford, the hands of each mill left in procession for the railway trip to Morecombe. The employers went on the excursion, addressing the hands from a hotel balcony in the resort.[155] At marriage celebrations a son might be praised for having gone through the factory (as in a Bolton engineering firm),[156] and neighbourhood employers could be drawn into the events. This was the case with the Pilkington-Shaw marriage in Blackburn in 1853, which sent the ripples of the event throughout the whole locale.[157]

There was perhaps no greater an occasion than the employer funeral. One hundred thousand people were said to have lined the streets of Bradford and Saltaire at Titus Salt's passing. Salt died as he lived, the fount of the great factory event. At the inaugural banquet in Saltaire in 1853 2,440 workpeople sat down to feast in his combing shed. The twentieth anniversary of Saltaire in 1873 was signified by the visit of 4000 operatives to his Crow Nest home outside the colony.[158]

Salt's demise was only untypical in the vastness of its scale. The historical record has been almost dumb about the significance of these events. In the history of nineteenth-century popular life, gatherings such as these, as well as the great monarchical congregations of the second half of the century, deserve to take their place beside the massive Chartist and post-Chartist radical throngs. The 60,000 who lined the funeral route of General Scarlett of Burnley in 1871, the 30,000 who saw Alfred Dobson of

Bolton to his grave in 1898, and the 15,000 who saw Robert Shaw to his in tiny Colne, bear an eloquent testimony to the ironies of history.[159]

The smaller funerals were no less revealing, calling forth illuminated addresses of condolence by the hands, which were answered by a day off with wages.[160] The whole of Darwen closed down for James Shorrock's funeral.[161] When two of the Bolton Blairs died in the same year, 1870, the hands attended Sunday service, after which memorial cards were handed out. Three of the longest serving employees led the family in the funeral procession into Bolton, joined by the rest of the hands. Blinds were drawn and streets lined along the way.[162] In 1880 one of the Heskeths of Astley Bridge, Bolton, was borne to his grave by an overlooker, the head mechanic, and an ordinary warper.[163]

The employer's residence played an important part in sustaining the mythology of the family, as of course did the master's lady, invariably the subject of praise.[164] Robert Platt, the Stalybridge cotton master, ran outings to his home in rural Cheshire. In 1858 900 workers marched through the town to the railway station bearing banners which read 'Long Life to our Employers' and 'Britannia Rules the Waves'. They were greeted on arrival by salvoes of artillery fire, and the day was passed in eating, drinking and sporting.[165] Such excursions, especially for young people, were commonplace.[166] Political treats were often held in the houses and parks of the big employer-politicians.

The excursion in fact tells us much about the social effect of factory conviviality. Though in a somewhat attenuated form, there were real elements of 'inversion ritual' at work – in pure form the managing director waiting on his servants and playing the clown, making the high low and the low high for a day, and so reinforcing the acceptance of hierarchy.[167] Employers would frequently go with the hands on an excursion. Although separation was maintained, a judicious measure of mixing was permissible. The employer, and especially his sons, would for instance attend the sports, and occasionally join in the events, as was the case with the Swainsons and Birleys of Preston.[168] The chain of factory authority would have been more directly involved in the topsy-turvy of the day, as indeed in that of all other special days.

The principal forms of popular public ritual and ceremony – the banner, the band, and the procession – began to serve the purposes of integration in the prevailing class system of capitalist society by around mid-century. This occurred in the factory setting as well. It was part of a process, to be described later, whereby the self-

expression inherent in earlier ritual forms of working-class
public behaviour was transformed into expressions of inclusion
in, and acceptance of, the local and national social order.

Something of this can be seen at work in the great Preston
railway excursions that began around 1850. These gargantuan
events, inaugurated by the leading mills, involved the majority
of Preston operatives by the end of the 1850s. The firm of
Horrockses and Miller sent 1,570 workpeople to Blackpool in
1850, Swainson and Birley 1,700 to Liverpool in 1851, and
Horrockses 4,000 to Liverpool in 1860.[169] The form of
these events is particularly interesting. The hands of the great
firms would assemble at the mills in the early morning, and,
accompanied by brass bands and bearing firm banners aloft,
march in procession through the town. They often called at the
residences of the employers, serenading them (at 4.30 a.m.) with
the old favourite, 'A Fine Old English Gentleman'.

In such public processions the solidarity of the mill was reinforced, and pride in identification was affirmed before the town.
Public proclamation did not stop there. At Liverpool for instance,
the train would stop at Edge Hill and the hands march into the
city with bands playing and banners waving.[170] The day itself
was overseen by the overlookers and managers, half 'policemen'
and half servants. It culminated in the assembly of the operatives
in the mill yard to give thanks to the employer. These excursions
got under way during the course of the 1850s, in much the same
form, in other towns, including Blackburn and Bolton.

The tide of social change toward the close of the century was to
work against the magic of such rituals. Those forces ultimately
inimical to nineteenth-century community forms also shattered
the social mould of ritual. The growth of organisation, the
development of transport, and the rise of mass media, produced
the decline of those elements that nourished the ritual forms of
public life: the local view, personal participation, and the premium on the immediate and the concrete.[171] Aspects of this change
were apparent early on. The organisation of leisure began to make
itself felt after the institution of the August Bank Holiday in 1871.
By the 1880s the rise of Blackpool as a commercial leisure centre
was already advanced. In 1885 the Cotton Factory Times noted
that mill excursions were slowly becoming less frequent.[172]
Twenty or thirty years previously the great factory trip had been
saved for and looked forward to with great anticipation. Then,
every one had known each other, keeping together with their
bands and their sports. Now, with the rise of professional enter-
tainment in Blackpool for example, even when people did come

together on trips they were increasingly isolated on arrival.

The importance of conviviality and bonhomie (rather than the moral exhortation of the improving tract) introduces the subject of the range of employer styles, and the great subtlety of their operation. It was certainly not the case that the hard but fair and efficient master was unpopular. The provision of good materials and conditions, and the régime of the disciplined factory in which good work got done, made for mutual respect. Yet what the trade union leader George Howell termed 'geniality and bonhomie', and what J.S. Mill understood as the prerequisites of influence – 'the amiable, the moral, and the sentimental' – were especially important in all the élite's dealings with the working class, whether the factory or non-factory sectors within it. Two fairly consistent styles can be discerned, the Liberal-Nonconformist and the Tory-Anglican.

There was no clearly defined border between the two styles. There were many 'improvement'-conscious Tory employers and 'improving' Tory workingmen, but Toryism in general, rather more than Liberalism, was adaptable, and capable of appealing to all social and cultural levels, the godly and the godless, the 'abstinent' and the indulgent. The Tory voice often spoke of things the chapels knew not, in the accents of indiscipline and unrespectability. It spoke of the poor man's right to his glass of beer and his idle pastime. It spoke to the Blackburn of 1867: ' . . . it is a thoroughgoing Tory community. Strong drink is the secret of its own and Britain's greatness; after that its heart has been given for long years to the Church and cockfighting. Be sober, lead a decent and respectable life and your genuine Black-burner will wax red at the mention of your name, and dismiss you as "a — Dissenter".'[173]

The contrast can best be elicited by a comparison of two rather exaggeratedly different but still representative factory régimes, those of Hugh Mason in Ashton and the Hornbys in Blackburn. Mason's priorities were the same as those of his fellow Liberal employers, the great majority of whom were also Nonconformists, though his ferocity was perhaps unique. The employer-dominated chapel cultures of Stalybridge and Ashton West End were but one front in the fight to impart Improving Taste. The mills and the Mechanics' Institutes were others. The latter were dominated by the Liberal employers in both towns,[174] and their running was closely involved with that of the chapels. By contrast, the Tory-dominated Blackburn Institute withered and died in the course of the 1860s.[175]

Mason's factory and colony were the expression of all he

believed, the opposite of everything against which the universality of his hatred exerted itself (Tories, drinkers, and gamblers were pre-eminent)[176] His streets, among them John Bright and Milner Gibson Terraces, proclaimed the Liberal gospel, his works the moral gospel of respectability. They included, amongst much else, a baths, mothers' classes (Sunday devotional meetings), and a lecture hall (where family members often lectured).

He shared with his fellow employers a notable belief in the saving powers of water, both as a drink and bathed in. His operatives would be 'physically and morally better' for using his baths. The opening ceremony for these was accompanied by panegyrics on Mason's houses and the discipline of his operatives (700 of them marched spick and span through the town).[177] Some years later Liberal employers of Stalybridge donated a town baths, the inauguration of which was similarly stage-managed as an affirmation of their moral purpose.[178] The Anglican Liberal Oldham Whittaker of Hurst was another paragon of hard work (he was at the mill at 5.45 sharp each morning), and shared Mason's keen eye for when the operative family's weekly washing was done (Monday was next to godliness).

The Oxford Colony was moralistic, often authoritarian. It was said that Mason would not employ a man untrue to his wife. The Tory press spoke darkly of the moral supervision exercised in the colony, and the town knew well what an 'Oxford education' meant.[179] Mason's munificence was real enough, but the nature of his giving must often have been trying.[180]

W.A. Abram and William Haslam Mills located enduring differences of style. Abram considered the region as a whole:

Some of our towns which have been reproached with their lapse into Toryism have lapsed simply because the local Liberal leaders have been unworthy of, or unequal to their position, have displayed none of the attributes of boldness, spirit, enthusiasm, pluck and liberality which impress the imagination and inspire the admiration of the multitude.[181]

Looking back on Ashton Mills saw a similar opposition of temper:

The Conservative employers ... had, however, a larger share of original and mundane humanity; they had redeeming vices, and their names slipped easily into the diminutives of Dick, Harry and Tom, Ashton-under-Lyne, for example, being represented for many years by a genial obscurantist whom all the mill and all the town knew gloriously as 'Tommy Mellor'. No one would have ever thought of abbreviating the name – even if any possible abbreviation had suggested itself – of Hugh Mason, and

John Bright remained 'John Bright' to the end, majestic, stark and formidable – somewhat frowning.[182]

It was 'Tommy' Mellor's thought for the Ashton Mechanics' Institute that it made young piecers and grinders get above themselves.[183]

In Blackburn on the Tory side there was nothing quite able to match the Pilkingtons' educational and chapel effort. Their mantle was taken by Eli Heyworth, another Congregationalist. Heyworth opposed his Audley crèche, canteen, and cottages to the people's 'not very ennobling pursuits': 'he believed cockfighting, drinking, and dog racing . . . were uppermost in their minds'.[184]

What there was was Hornbyism, and its fusion of the father and fellow-roysterer. Brookhouse was the centre of things, and Brookhouse took to the streets at the slightest instigation. In 1868 the men, women and children of the neighbourhood attacked the local Liberal club. Brookhouse feeling was described at the time: 'No Liberal to this hour can pass through Brookhouse without having a Tory fist thrust in his face, or being cursed at in a way which even Mr Wescoe might fail to emulate' (Wescoe was a local Evangelical fire-eater).[185] One 'Dicky' Edmundson articulated the faith in 1868 (farmboy to 'gent', he was the kind of 'card' the Liberals were always short on):

I will ask you a question; how does it happen that the least child in the street or lane, if it can prattle cries 'Hornby for ever' . . . [applause, roars of laughter, and cries of 'Good Old Dick'] . . . he is the cock that never stopped crowing. How does it happen that if your make enquiry you find that the hands of Hornby hardly ever make any change. The reason is because they know the worth of their master. I have known the family – not personally, and to have had any conversation with them – all my life, but I have known them as well as my own father and mother.[186]

The gamecock was the century-long symbol of local Toryism; 'Sir Harry' Hornby inheriting his father's title of 'th' owd' Gam' Cock' (the father was a 'cocker' in his youth). The family exercised the virtues of 'spirit' and 'pluck' in sport both ancient and modern, played and patronised. There was a good deal of the squire about William Henry and his son. Abram described the elder: 'Short, thick-set, with very much the similitude of a country squire; . . . a neck like a bullock, and a general expression in which pride is mingled with irascibility, scorn, and dauntless indomitable pluck.'[187]

Abram's words direct us to the relationship between a rural

past and an urban present. The Tory mastery of the common style was in part a consequence of the greater relaxedness, indeed laxity, of Anglicanism when compared with the dissenting sects, and in part an aspect of the Tory-Radical tradition. In a number of cases, however, these were a reflection of the landed origins and connections of Tory employers. As the preceding discussion of élite formation indicates, in a number of Lancashire towns the roots of later nineteenth-century Toryism were to be found in the landed society of the early years of the century.[188] If by the 1860s and 70s landed origins were two or more generations past, some families, such as the Hornby's were still composed of multi-branched lines diversified in both the industrial and landed life of the area. Whether landed in origin or not, most Tory and Anglican employers would have been less opposed to landed styles than their political and religious opponents. Thus, there would still have been an access to the predilections and styles of rural life, and these would have found expression in urban industrial forms of paternal leadership.

The operatives' memory in the third quarter of the century would also have reached back to a rural past. Jeremy Seabrook, for the industrial Midlands at about the same time, has beautifully evoked the power of that which the countryman brought into the town; instincts, desires and memories survived over long decades.[189] It was not merely a matter of memory. As John Marshall has shown,[190] especially in the very numerous suburban mill settlements at mid-century, the rural background and rural ways were still present reality for many workers. Nor had movement into the town after mid-century completely ceased. The small, peasant weaver-farmer of the Pennines is not to be confused with the southern countryman, yet it seems probable that the Tory style was better able to engage past experience than the Liberal. This was partly in terms of the squire-employer, and partly in terms of Toryism's greater openness to the customs of a freer, less organised, and perhaps more violent rural past.

Relaxed and expansive Hornbyism ran counter to the strenuous moralising of a Mason. Hornbyism grew from a capacity to intuit and identify with the constituents of a 'mundane humanity'. The family style was one of personal attention and sympathy—pensioning the old, not collecting the house rents of those in need. An operative remembered 'Sir Harry' thus: 'When he went through the mill yard he would not pass the commonest man in the place without speaking to him.' The 'unstudied directness, almost roughness of his tones' was measured in a dialect that he, unlike the *nouveau riche*, made no effort to conceal.[191]

The family, with considerable justification, considered themselves as having a special place in operative life. Fifteen thousand of the town's population met William Henry at Blackburn station in 1853 to pay homage to Blackburn's benefactor.[192] Hornby maintained that he and his father had a peculiar feeling for the operative class, based on disinterested kindness, and not on the factiousness and insincerity of modern, political days. The true friend of the working class did not bleat about it. This chord in Hornby dynasticism engaged tribal notions of honour and rightness that not only buttressed their success but were an important part of Toryism's wider Lancashire one.

A turn of the century verdict on the family's influence fairly assessed the balance of popular acclaim and answering concern that lay at the heart of a successful paternal régime:

... to be a Hornby in Blackburn is to be a thing apart. There is a suggestion of feudalism and of the constant service of the antique world in the popular devotion to the Hornby crest ... the cult is the product of a very worthy root. It springs from three-quarters of a century of traditions and memories, from men who were strong, honest, clear-headed, clean-living Englishmen, who did solid, unselfish work for their fellows and their town, and whose spirit and deeds have been woven into the 'piece' of Blackburn life.[193]

It is clear that two contrasting cultural styles were developed that drew support from the same social ingredient – the population of the factory *en bloc*. These styles, reflected in so many of the factory regimes of the industrial North, indicate the failure of any schematic attribution of cultural style to social level in the working class to comprehend the real situation. 'Non-abstinent' Hornbyism (in John Foster's terminology) cut a swathe of support through all working-class society. It responded to what drew men together, and not what forced them apart. Having come full circle from the words of G.M. Young that opened this chapter it is now time to consider the political influence of the factory in rather greater detail.

Summary
In the opening section the size variation and turnover of firms is discussed, and the distinction is drawn between the social effect of the large, the medium and the small firm. Contrary to expectation, it is the large, long-established, or 'feudal' firm that was the chief seat of deference. The smaller, 'familiar' factories were the source of feelings ranging between acute class conflict and something like the camaraderie of equals. The Lancashire-

West Riding comparison is used to elicit these distinctions (ones
that were never absolute), and oral material (on Keighley)
further explores some of the subtleties of response to the regime
of the large factory. Large size had its disadvantages, and the
means by which these were overcome are also considered.
Discussion of the Huddersfield woollen districts, the last and
least given to mechanised factory production among the textile
areas, returns us once again to the progress of the factory system
in explaining change. A uniquely late prolongation of the social
relations of quasi-craft production was expressed in the persistence of popular radicalism in the area, though the late consolidation of factory production also represented, in a much attenuated
form, the adaptation of earlier ways to the ends of employer
hegemony.

The major part of the discussion is given over to the means of
employer influence. These are first considered in terms of
employer activity in town life. The Northern manufacturers
dominated the institutional life of their towns, yet all-pervading as
this involvement was it was in their sway over the life of the
factory locale that their hegemony was most deeply rooted. This
neighbourhood influence enables us to contrast the North with
London, where the 'deformation of the gift' by impersonal,
bureaucratic modes of dispensation had long been set in train
mid-way through our period. Local influence is examined first
in terms of economic provision and then in terms of youth and
adult education. The latter broaches the earlier distinction
between 'ideological' and 'social' hegemony, for it was not so
much in terms of ideological 'infiltration' (itself highly ambiguous
in operation), but by pervading quotidian life and permeating
the loyalties of occupation and place that employer influence
worked.

It is at this deeper level that the provision of elementary
education is next considered. These distinctions are also explored
in the light of the 'labour aristocracy' argument, it being doubtful
if anything like the degree of cultural polarisation in the working
class necessary to sustain that argument did in fact obtain (see also
chapter 8, section 3). The place of the employer and the factory
in popular religion is next given extended treatment. Religion
worked less by means of formal doctrinal and congregational
attachments, or as a species of the ideology of 'improvement',
and far more in a looser, social and secular sense, cementing the
hold of factory authority and identifying the workplace and the
locale. The Sunday School in particular is explained in these
senses, as is the factory itself, at the time far more than the seat of
production alone.

The factory was the source of a considerable social life. Particular attention is paid to the ritual form of this life, a form that unified work and community life. The mythology of this ritual, in turn imaging the paternalism of operative family life, turned upon the notion of the team or the family. The saga of employer family life is explored through all the rites of passage occasioning ritual expressions. Something of the same process at work later and less effectively in the woollen districts can be discerned in full operation here: such ritual, working with the grain of a developing community sense, acted upon the rememberances and continuing vestiges of the social relations of industry before mechanisation was consolidated, so perfecting in a surrogate form a continuity that facilitated the success of employer control.

The final section is taken up with a close analysis of styles of employer paternalist regimes. The less definable matters of temperament and spirit are viewed in terms of the contrast between two fairly representative forms, the Liberal-Nonconformist and the Tory-Anglican. In turn, the relaxed expansiveness of the latter and the moralistic restrictiveness of the former are further considered by a description of two very different but not untypical firms, Hornbys in Blackburn and Masons in Ashton. The importance of 'geniality and bonhomie' is looked at in other contexts in chapter 8.

Notes

1. G.M. Young, *Stanley Baldwin* (1952), p. 22.
2. D.A. Farnie, 'The English cotton industry 1850–1896' (University of Manchester M.A. 1953), ch. 16 for a full discussion of firm size. The combined firm decreased considerably in importance in this period. See *ibid.* ch. 11.
3. *Ibid.* ch. 16, citing *Textile Manufacturer*, 15 June 1877.
4. Elsewhere size must be computed from spindle and loom figures. A. Hewitson, *History of Preston* (Preston 1883), pp. 185–6.
5. Computed from *Cotton Spinners' and Manufacturers' Directory and Engineers' and Machine Makers' Advertiser* (J. Worrall, Oldham 1882), published annually thereafter. Limiteds are included in these figures. By this time they had made some inroad in Ashton, less in Stockport, and only in Oldham were they as yet of real significance. For Blackburn size see also P. Whittle, *Blackburn As It Is* (Preston 1852), p. 243.
6. V.A.C. Gatrell, 'Labour, power and the size of firms in Lancashire cotton in the second quarter of the 19th century', *Economic History Review*, **30**, no. 1, Feb. 1977.
7. Computed from information in D.A. Farnie, *op. cit.* ch. 17. No information on three of these twenty-nine.
8. E. Thorpe, 'Industrial relations and the social structure: a case study

of Bolton cotton mule spinners 1884–1910' (University of Salford M.Sc. 1969), chs 5, 7.

9. See the histories of Halifax firms in *Industries of Yorkshire*, 2 vols (1895), and *A Descriptive Account of Halifax and District* (W.T. Pike and Co., Brighton 1895).

10. J.H. Clapham, *The Woollen and Worsted Industries* (1907), ch. 4.

11. *The Yorkshire Textile Directory and Engineers' and Machine Makers' Advertiser*, published annually from 1885 in Oldham. This is the main source on firm sizes, though unlike the Lancashire directories information is incomplete, and there are no town totals of spindles and looms. The longevity of firms, and the distribution of sizes, have to be calculated from a variety of sources. Aside from those already mentioned, the following are especially useful: P. Hudson, *The West Riding Woollen Textile Industry* (Pasold 1975); *The Century's Progress, Yorkshire* (1893); *Yorkshire. Fifty Years of Progress* (Leeds 1887); J. Hodgson, *Textile Manufacture and Other Industries in Keighley* (Keighley 1879); *A Descriptive Account of Bradford and Shipley* (W.T. Pike and Co., Brighton 1895?); *Illustrated Business Guide to Bradford and Keighley* (Manchester 1899); 'Bradford and its manufacturers,' Bradford Public Library photocopy collection of nineteenth-century press articles; *Men of the Period, Yorkshire* (1897). All estimates that follow based on these sources. See also Biographical sources, ch. 1, above, pp. 48–9.

12. J.W. Turner, 'Some old Bradford firms', Ms copy in Bradford Public Library, Case 16/45.

13. On Oldham see J. Foster, *Class Struggle and the Industrial Revolution* (1974), pp. 78, 81–3.

14. P.E. Razzell and R.W. Wainwright, eds, *The Victorian Working Class, Selections from letters to the 'Morning Chronicle'* (1973), pp. 192–3, 183.

15. Foster, *op. cit.* pp. 174–7.

16. *Ibid.* p. 81.

17. R. Samuel, 'The workshop of the world: steam power and hand technology in mid-Victorian Britain', *History Workshop Journal* no. 3, Spring 1977.

18. J. Beckett, *Bradford Portraits* (Bradford 1892), p. 12; see also *P.P.* 1892, XXXIV (6708–111), p. 236, Digest of Evidence.

19. E. Hodder, *The Life of Samuel Morley* (1887), ch. XII, esp. pp. 190–2, 195.

20. *P.P.* 1892, XXXIV (6708–111), pp. 236, 237; *Fortunes Made in Business* (1884), Vol. 1, pp. 455–6. The following useful discussion should also be seen, H. Newby, 'Paternalism and capitalism: a re-examination of the size-effect', in R. Scase, ed., *Cleavage and Constraint: studies in industrial society* (1976).

21. J. Wilson, *Joseph Wilson, My Life and Work* (n.d.), p. 19.

22. See account of Isaac Holden in *Fortunes Made in Business*, Vol. 1 (1884).

23. S. Pollard, *The Genesis of Modern Management* (1965), pp. 150–1.
24. *Ibid.* pp. 154–6; Thorpe, *op. cit.* p. 185.
25. These families and their influence can be traced in W. Cudworth, *History of Bolton and Bowling* (Bradford 1891), *Round About Bradford* (Bradford 1876), and account of Low Moor in *Fortunes Made in* Business, Vol. 1 (1884).
26. Thomas Jones, 'The life of the people', in *Fifty Years: memories and contrasts, 1882–1932* (1932), p. 178 (foreword by G.M. Trevelyan); R. Moore, *Pitmen, Preachers and Politics* (Cambridge 1974), ch. 3.
27. *Cotton Factory Times*, 9 Apr. 1886 (p. 4), 10, 17 July 1885; *Bolton Chronicle* 31 Dec. 1859 (Darwen), 6 Aug. 1859 (Leigh), 6 Jan. 1866 (Bolton).
28. *Oldham Standard*, 28 Nov. 1868 on Platt's influence in Oldham; Reform League Reports, Macclesfield (Bishopsgate Institute, London).
29. For the business, religious, and political links that combined the fortunes of the mighty and the humble see above, pp. 21–2.
30. *Preston Chronicle*, 10 Sept. 1853.
31. Thorpe, *op. cit.*, Biographical Appendix.
32. There are several examples of this in E. Lockwood, *Colne Valley Folks* (1936).
33. See above, pp. 22–3.
34. H. Newby, 'The deferential dialectic', *Comparative Studies in Society and History*, **17**, no. 2, Apr. 1975, p. 158–9.
35. Thompson and Vigne West Riding Interviews, Ints 128, 204, 339 (all 'Community and Class', hereafter C/C).
36. *Ibid.* Ints 165, 146, 172 (C/C).
37. *Ibid.* Ints 181 (C/C).
38. *Ibid.* Int. 282 (C/C and 'Work'); see also Int. 165 (C/C).
39. *Ibid.* Int. 181 (C/C).
40. *Ibid.* Int. 170 (C/C) on respondent's wife's father.
41. *Ibid.* Ints 149, 341 (C/C), 132, 147 ('Work').
42. *Ibid.* Ints 170 (C/C and 'Work'), 181 ('Work'), 147, 206 (C/C).
43. *Ibid.* Ints 340, 162 ('Work'), 165, 270 (C/C).
44. Wilson, *op. cit.* ch. 2.
45. G. Hurst, *Closed Chapters* (Manchester 1942), p. 5.
46. E.A. Nordlinger, *The Working-Class Tories* (1967), ch. 8; M. Stacey, *Tradition and Change: a study of Banbury* (Oxford 1960); see also E. Batstone, 'Deference and the ethos of small-town capitalism' in M. Bulmer, ed, *Working-Class Images of Society* (1975).
47. B. Webb, *My Apprenticeship* (Penguin 1971), p. 180.
48. J. Sykes, *Slawit in the 'Sixties* (Huddersfield n.d. 1926?), chs xv, xvi, xxvii, esp. p. 95; J. Sugden, *Slaithwaite Notes of the Past and Present* (Manchester 1905), chs i, ii, xlv; see also B. Turner, *A Short Account of the Rise and Progress of the Heavy Woollen District Branch of the General Union of Textile Workers (YFT* 1917), pp. 96–7.

49. Sykes, *op. cit.* p. 109.
50. Sugden, *op. cit.* pp. 3–4. For further information on the culture of valley industry see D.F.E. Sykes, *The History of Huddersfield and its Vicinity* (Huddersfield 1897), *The History of the Colne Valley* (Slaithwaite 1906), also the many works of Ammon Wrigley.
51. See above, pp. 145–6.
52. Sykes, *op. cit* pp. 100–1.
53. For these firms see the previously cited works of E. Lockwood and D.F.E. Sykes. See also W.B. Crump and S.G. Ghorbal, *History of the Huddersfield Woollen Industry* (Huddersfield 1935). The process of inheritance and transformation in the passage to factory industry can be traced in full human detail in the Joe France Interview, cited above p. 98, n. 28.
54. Cf. H. Perkin on Glossop in A.H. Birch, *Small Town Politics* (1959), ch. 2.
55. T. Middleton, *History of Hyde* (Hyde 1932), and *Annals of Hyde* (Manchester 1899); cf. also for two other important families, the Hibberts and Darnleys.
56. R. Hopwood Hutchinson, *The Chronicles of Blackburn . . . 1861–2* (Blackburn 1863), pp. 3–4.
57. G.N. Trodd, 'The local élite of Blackburn and the response of the working class to its social control' (Lancaster University M.A. 1974), ch. 3 and Appx 1.
58. S.C. on Parliamentary and Municipal Elections, *P.P.* 1868–9, VIII (352), Qs 2525–32, but see also Qs 3519–21, 3575, 3603–10.
59. *Ashton Standard* and *Ashton Reporter* 2 Jan. 1869.
60. See above, pp. 34–6, also H. Cunningham, *The Volunteer Force 1859–1908* (1975) pp. 20–2, 28–30, 64, 75–8.
61. M. Mauss, *The Gift* (1970), pp. 37–8, 75.
62. G. Stedman Jones, *Outcast London* (Oxford 1971), esp. Pt III.
63. Newby, *loc. cit.* pp. 161–3.
64. *Preston Chronicle*, 11 Jan. 1851.
65. Thompson and Vigne West Riding Interviews, nos 147, 162 (C/C).
66. On Wood see J.T. Ward, 'Two pioneers of industrial reform', *Journal of the Bradford Textile Society*, 1964.
67. For the notable irony of 200 hand woolcombers cheering Sir Isaac Holden to the echo in 1891, see J. Constantine, *Sir Isaac Holden, Bart., and his Theory of a Healthy Long Life* (Manchester 1898), p. 27, also pp. 28–38.
68. *Bradford Review*, 29 May 1858; *Bolton Chronicle*, 5 Feb. 1870; see also *Bradford Advertiser*, 13 Jan. 1866.
69. *Bolton Chronicle*, 3 Jan. 1880.
70. J. Baynes, *Two Lectures on the Cotton Trade* (Blackburn 1857), Lecture 1, pp. 66–8.
71. *Bolton Chronicle*, 8 Jan. 1848.
72. Farnie, *op. cit.* ch. 31.
73. For full information, see P. Joyce, 'Popular Toryism in Lancashire 1860–1890' (Oxford University D. Phil. 1975), pp. 174–7.
74. 'Account of Inauguration, Blackburn United National and Sunday

Schools Association' (1845), Lancs. County Record Office PR 1549/11.

75. For the intimate involvement of the Bolton employers in the whole range of paternalist provision see G. Evans, 'Social leadership and social control, Bolton 1870–1898' (Lancaster Univ. M.A. 1974), chs 2 and 3.

76. *Bolton Chronicle*, 4 Aug. 1855.

77. Factory Inspectors Reports, *P.P.* 1867–8, XVIII (4010), p. 172.

78. *Bolton Chronicle*, 15 Jan. 1880.

79. S.C. on Education in Manchester and Salford, *P.P.* 1852–3, XXIV (571), Qs 235–40, evidence of T. Bazley, the employer.

80. Factory Inspectors Reports, *P.P.* 1852–3, XL (1580), pp. 18–19.

81. Report on the State of Popular Education in England, *P.P.* 1861, XXI, Pt II, (2794–11), pp. 197–9, 234–6.

82. Hodder, *op. cit.* pp. 199–200.

83. Rev. H. Wescoe/National Society, 1 Sept. 1870. National Society Letter Files, National Society, London.

84. *Blackburn Times*, 3 Dec. 1870.

85. *Ibid.* 28 Mar. 1874.

86. *Blackburn Standard*, 27 Mar. 1880.

87. S.C. on Factory and Workshops Act, *P.P.* 1876, XXX (1443–1), Vol. II, Qs 9003–18, pp. 439–40; see also pp. 497–9, 500–1.

88. *P.P.* 1868–9, VIII (352), Q. 2195.

89. *P.P.* 1876, XXX p. 443, Q. 9041.

90. *Ibid.* Qs 9054–6, p. 443.

91. *Ibid.* Q. 9059, p. 444. See also *Ashton Reporter*, 17 Aug. 1883.

92. *Bolton Chronicle*, 25 May 1850.

93. Select Committee House of Lords into the deficiencies of means of spiritual instruction and places of divine worship, *P.P.* 1857–8, IX (387), pp. xiv–xv, 482–3.

94. J.C. Scholes, *History of Bolton* (Bolton 1892), p. 380.

95. Thompson and Vigine Interviews, West Riding, Ints 165, 172, 176 (C/C).

96. *Blackburn Times*, 2 Sept. 1865 (Letters).

97. J.G. Shaw, *Life of William Gregson* (Blackburn 1891), p. 68.

98. E.g. *Blackburn Times*, 4 Dec. 1867.

99. 'Christ Church, Blackburn 1857–1907, a Jubilee Handbook' (Blackburn 1907), p. 6 (Blackburn Public Library).

100. On Eli Heyworth see *Blackburn Times*, 2 July 1892 (p. 5), also 25 June 1892 (p. 6).

101. *Ashton Reporter*, 13 Nov. 1869. For employer chapel involvement in Ashton see J.G. Rogers, *An Autobiography* (1903), pp. 103–19, and for the Albion Working Men's Class, pp. 110–11. For Albion's Young Men's Class turned into a Young Men's Reform Association, see *Ashton Reporter*, 13 Feb. 1869.

102. Hodgson, *op. cit.*, account of Sugdens.

103. Thompson and Vigne Interviews, West Riding, Ints 147 (C/C), 340 ('Work' and C/C).

104. *Ibid.* Ints 143, 165, 172 (C/C).

105.   *Ibid.* Ints 149, 162, 165, 176, 340 (C/C); but see also 341 ('Politics').
106.   *Ibid.* Ints 170, 149 (C/C); see also 128, 270 (C/C).
107.   Moore, *op. cit.*; P. Thompson, *The Edwardians* (1975), pp. 141, 208–9.
108.   C.S. Davies, *North Country Bred* (1963), p. 28; see also J. Seabrook, *City Close-Up* (1971), p. 16, and for many parallels with southern U.S.A. textiles, L. Pope, *Millhands and Preachers* (New Haven 1942).
109.   W.H. Chaloner, *The Social and Economic Development of Crewe, 1780–1923* (Manchester 1950), pp. 153–4.
110.   Thompson and Vigne Lancashire Int, 67, p. 13.
111.   For further information Joyce, *op. cit.* esp. p. 121.
112.   Webb, *op. cit.* pp. 166–85.
113.   B. Turner, *History of the General Union of Textile Workers* (Heckmondwike 1920), chs VI, XVI, and B. Turner, *Short Account of H.W.D. Branch of General Union* ... (1917), pp. 25–6.
114.   E.P. Thompson, 'Homage to Tom Maguire', in A. Briggs and J. Saville, eds, *Essays in Labour History* (1967).
115.   Moore, *op. cit.* chs. 4, 6, 8.
116.   *Ibid.* Intro. and ch. 5.
117.   *Ashton Standard*, 13 Nov. 1869.
118.   *Church of England Sunday School Teachers' Magazine*, Feb. 1863.
119.   Razzell and Wainwright, eds, *op. cit.* p. 176.
120.   J. Baynes, *Two Lectures etc.*, Lecture I, p. 79.
121.   See for example, *Bury Times*, 2 May 1866; *Bolton Chronicle*, 25 May 1850.
122.   Thompson and Vigne West Riding Int, 206 (C/C).
123.   *Bolton Chronicle*, 18, 25 June 1859; *Preston Chronicle*, 14 June 1851; see also *Ashton Reporter*, 6 June 1868 and *Bury Times*, 11 June 1870.
124.   For Williamson see *Northern Advance*, 18 Jan. 1889.
125.   *Ashton Standard*, 5 Jan. 1883; *Preston Herald*, 27 Jan. 1874; *Ashton Reporter*, 22 Apr. 1876.
126.   Cf. Mellor and Heginbotton 'do's' in Ashton, *Ashton Standard*, 28 Feb. 1880; Kelsall and Kemp in Rochdale, *Rochdale Observer*, 16 May 1868.
127.   *Cotton Factory Times, passim.*
128.   E.g. Jan. and 10 Feb. 1866, *Burnley Advertiser; Preston Chronicle*, 5, 12 Jan., 6 Apr. 1850; *Huddersfield Examiner*, 24 Jan. 1 74.
129.   *Bolton Chronicle*, 8, 15 June 1850 (Great Exhibition); *Blackburn Standard*, 25 Aug. 1869, 8, 12 Jan. 1870 (Derby); *Cotton Factory Times*, 3 July 1885 (Preston royal visit).
130.   *Bolton Chronicle*, 5 Jan. 1850; 6 Jan. 1866 (Ormerod and Hardcastle's Annual Fire Brigade Dinner).
131.   Sugden, *op. cit.* ch. 16.
132.   For the pigeon-fancying, and a full account of a mill social committee see the Joe France Interview, cited at n. 53 above.
133.   On Colne football see *Cotton Factory Times*, 7 Aug. 1885.

134. R. Martin and R.H. Fryer, *Redundancy and Paternalist Capitalism* (1973); see discussion and citations in ch. 4, esp. p. 70.

135. J.C. Abbeglen, *The Japanese Factory Aspects of its Social Organization* (1958), pp. 71–2.

136. L. Coser, *Greedy Institutions* (New York 1974); E. Goffman, *Interaction Ritual* (1972), *Asylums* (Penguin 1968). See also the two articles by Newby cited above.

137. See above, pp. 52–8, 111–17.

138. See above, pp. 166–8.

139. See above, pp. 145–6.

140. *Fortunes Made in Business*, Vol. 1 (1884), p. 391.

141. For the Hon. Harold Gathorne-Hardy, son of the first Earl of Cranbrook, who died in 1881. Unlike his father he was an active partner at Low Moor. For this and a full account of the long Hardy connection see *ibid.* on Low Moor Company.

142. E.g. George Harwood of Bolton, Bolton Public Library Press Cuttings, 'Old Lancashire personalities and families' (1932), n.d. for reference.

143. *Preston Pilot*, 28 Aug. 1841.

144. *Cotton Factory Times*, 24 July 1885.

145. *Preston Chronicle*, 10 Sept. 1853.

146. *Halifax Guardian*, 3 Apr. 1880.

147. *Bolton Chronicle*, 13 Jan. 1855 (Thomas Wrigley of Bury).

148. *Preston Chronicle*, 11 Jan. 1851 (Potters of Darwen).

149. *Ashton Standard*, 5 Mar. 1870.

150. *Ashton Reporter*, 14 Apr. 1860.

151. *Ibid.* 24, 31 Jan. 1880.

152. *Bolton Chronicle*, 3 Jan. 1880, as typical example (John Knowles and Son).

153. *Preston Pilot*, 31 July 1841 (Ridgeways of Horwich).

154. *Wigan Examiner*, 12 Apr. 1893.

155. *Bradford Review*, 25 Aug. 1866; see also *Preston Chronicle*, 3 Sept. 1870 (Swainsons).

156. *Bolton Guardian*, 27 Aug. 1870 (John and Edward Woods).

157. *Preston Chronicle*, 28 May 1853.

158. *Fortunes Made in Business*, Vol. 1 (1884).

159. R.P. Cook, 'Political élites and electoral politics in late nineteenth-century Burnley' (Lancaster Univ. M.A. 1974), ch. 3; *Bolton Journal and Guardian*, 4 Mar. 1898; *Cotton Factory Times*, 24 July 1895; on W.W. Cannon's Bolton funeral see *Bolton Jnl and Gdn*, 22 Sept. 1933.

160. *Blackburn Times*, 9 Sept. 1868.

161. *Ibid.*

162. *Bolton Guardian*, 29 Jan., 16 July 1870.

163. *Bolton Chronicle*, 10 Jan. 1880.

164. E.g. *Preston Chronicle*, 10 Jan. 1852 (Accrington).

165. *Ashton Reporter*, 4 Sept. 1858.

166. E.g. *Bradford Review*, 14 Aug. 1858 (Messrs John Rand); *Bury Times*, 28 July 1866.
167. The interpretation of such ritual is of course a problematic matter, see below, pp. 276–7.
168. *Preston Chronicle*, 10 Sept. 1870; see also *ibid.* 23 Aug. 1851 (Swainson and Birley); *Bradford Review*, 25 Aug. 1866.
169. *Preston Chronicle*, 10 Aug. 1850, 23 Aug. 1851, 2 June 1860.
170. *Ibid.*, 13, 20 July 1850; Aug. 1853 and 1860.
171. B. Jackson, *Working Class Community* (1968).
172. *Cotton Factory Times*, 7 Aug. 1885.
173. *Free Lance* (Manchester), 12 Oct. 1867.
174. See Bishop Fraser on the Ashton one, *Ashton Reporter*, 14 Jan. 1871.
175. *Blackburn Times*, 14 Mar. 1868, 18 Jan. 1868 (letters).
176. For accounts of Mason see H.J. Hanham, *Elections and Party Management* (1959), p. 72; W.H. Mills, *Grey Pastures* (1924), pp. 35–9, for a wonderfully evocative description of Mason, 'a capitalist with the accent on the "pit"'.
177. *Ashton Reporter*, 18 May 1867, 18 Apr. 1868.
178. *Ibid.*, 14 Apr. 1870.
179. *Ashton Standard*, 2 July 1870.
180. See descriptions of Mason in *City Jackdaw* (Manchester), Dec. 1875, and *Momus* (Manchester), 11 Apr. 1878.
181. W.A. Abram, 'Social conditions and political prospects of the Lancashire workman', *Fortnightly Review*, Oct. 1868, p. 437.
182. Mills, *Sir Charles Macara* ... (1917), pp. 66–7.
183. *Ashton News*, 28 Jan 1871 (letters).
184. Cf. biography in *Blackburn Times*, 23 Jan. 1904.
185. *Blackburn Times*, 17 Oct. 1868, p. 5.
186. *Blackburn Standard*, 8 July 1868.
187. From *Gossip* (n.d. 1860s) in Blackburn Public Library biographical files. There is a similar, operative's memory of the squire also, in B.P.L. Hornby family file, interview with Mr W. Hulme, 28 Oct. 1929. On 'Sir Harry' see P.F. Clarke, 'British politics and Blackburn politics, 1900–1910', *Historical Journal*, 12, (1969).
188. See above, pp. 1, 5, 9–10, 13, 16.
189. J. Seabrook, *The Unprivileged* (1967), pp. 40–1.
190. J. Marshall, 'Colonisation as a factor in the planting of towns in North-West England', in H.J. Dyos, ed., *The Study of Urban History* (1968), pp. 221–5.
191. *Blackburn Weekly Telegraph*, 18 Nov. 1899. See also B.P.L. Hornby family file, notes of interview with W.S. Livesey, 28 Sept. 1929, and *Lancashire Life*, Apr. 1957.
192. *Preston Chronicle*, 10 Sept. 1853.
193. *Blackburn Weekly Telegraph*, 18 Nov. 1899.

6
THE FACTORY AND POLITICS

> At a contested election in a Lancashire borough,
> one may see the entire body of workers at two
> rival factories pitted against each other, like
> hostile armies, and the deeds of prowess per-
> formed by each are proudly rehearsed by every
> man and boy, by every woman and girl, attached
> to the establishment. Politics resolve themselves
> into partisan warfare, and the real objects of
> political parties are totally forgotten in the zest
> of local clanships.
> (W.A. Abram on popular politics, 1868)[1]

ABRAM'S description goes some of the way to confuting the
prevailing orthodoxies of political history. The discussion of
politics that follows will take us further on the road his words
suggest we must take. There was no inexorable progression to an
individualist democracy in which public opinion, separable
from influence, achieved its free play some time in the third
quarter of the century. The 'national' did not triumph over the
'local'. The deference community did not go to the wall. When
the perimeter of the industrial town is reached, class division
and technological and urban change are invariably held to have
reared their heads; the consequences being unleashed upon the
political system by the Reform Act of 1867 and the Ballot Act
of 1872. Even those, such as D.C. Moore, who have done most to
assail traditional notions, seem content to let the matter rest
there: in the industrial North at least, and for decades after
1867 and 1872, class lines had not become 'too sharp', interest
groups "too jumbled', nor had social and economic categories
'ceased to overlap'.[2] It is only when the explanation begins in the
factory, with a sense for the intimacy of the connections between
the industrial and political systems, that the real nature of political
life will be discerned.

Something of the character of these connections will now be
considered, first in terms of the composition of the electorate,
and then as regards the relationship between industrial structure
and political organisation and ideology. The political nation

after the 1867 Reform Act would have included the most coherent
of the factory blocs, both as a matter of deliberation on the party
managers' part, and because they were amongst the most stable
elements in a fairly mobile electorate. The most stable blocs
would have been most likely to incline to the employer. It is also
the case that the most mobile element in the factory town populations, and therefore the least represented in the electorate, would
have been disproportionately Irish rather than English in
character. The evidence on which these claims are based, the
occupational composition of voters taken from the 1868 pollbooks
for Blackburn and Bury, has been presented in detail elsewhere
by this writer.[3] Owing to residential mobility, about 45 per cent
of the 8,000-strong vote analysed could not be traced by means
of the source of occupation information, the 1871 census enumerators' schedules (movement purely *within* the locality
was however considerable, but could not be established with
absolute certainty from the information given in the pollbooks).

Matching these pollbook census occupational returns with the
occupational structure of the towns as a whole, but also with the
internal grade structure of the textile and engineering factory, it is
apparent that there was a slight (though hardly unexpected)
bias to non-manual elements in the electorate, also a bias in
favour of supervision (especially) and higher status within the
factory workforces. Nevertheless, despite these imbalances, as
the following table makes plain, the electorate corresponded
fairly closely to the occupational structure of the factory towns
(comparison should be made with Table 2, Chapter 3 above).
Park ward in Blackburn was a typical cotton ward.

TABLE 4
Blackburn and Bury 1868 electorates:
occupational returns by general category

	%			%
Bury: Factory Workers	45	Blackburn: (Park)	Cotton Workers	54
Labourers	15		Labourers	13
All craft workers, building tradesmen, small masters	20		Craft and Skilled	10
Retailers and dealers	13		Retailers and Dealers	14
			White collar/respect-ables	1
White-collar/ respectables	6		Iron and Engineering	8

Throughout this period only about 60 per cent of adult males in the factory towns were enfranchised. What is so striking about these occupational returns is that despite the level of enfranchisement, the electorate so closely represented the socio-economic structure of the factory town. The notion, so often mooted,[4] that the post-1867 electorate cannot tell us about the nature of popular political life, must be greatly qualified in the light of these figures. If, at the time, the parties chose the electorate, rather than the electorate choosing the parties, they did so with much confidence that the working-class electorate would serve the ends for which it had been chosen. And, most significantly, it was the factory worker rather than the craft-skilled element among that electorate, who was most heavily relied upon.

Nevertheless, the occupational diversity of the factory town electorate meant that politics itself was diverse and heterogeneous. The party politics of opinion, of the rational and independent individual, had an importance more than proportionate to the considerable size of its non-factory and non-working class electoral constituency because it was from these elements that the most politically active, influential and articulate were drawn. Nor should it be thought that for the factory workforces themselves the politics of conscience or ideology played no independent part in constituting political choice. The three basic motifs in popular politics – ethnic feeling as expressed in popular Protestantism, religion as seen in denominational allegiance, and class as found in the politics of the Chartist inheritence and of trade unionism – each would have exerted political pressures running counter to the identification with the factory regime.

But these constituents of popular politics were most often of the greatest effect among the non-factory electorate, or, among factory workers, were either the direct concern of the few, or, for the many, the form and vocabulary of politics rather than its substance. Ethnic feeling and denominational allegiance (however diffuse the latter was) served the needs of factory influence in the era of the organised mass politics of opinion: they provided the issues around which factory-engendered allegiances could be organised in institutional form, and continuous political activity sustained. The class infusion in politics was important in parts of the West Riding, and for many trade union activists throughout the North. Below this politically articulate level class could also take latent and diffuse forms in the politics of the majority, both within and beyond the factory. In the remainder of this work the complexity of the correspondence between the political and industrial levels will be examined in a number of contexts. There is, however, little doubt that for the majority the most pressing and political of realities was that of work and the life that grew up around it. The factory had a direct, unmediated role in political life. More than this, indeed, urban politics at large was in considerable degree shaped in the matrix of factory life. The immediate task in hand, then, is the reconstitution of the social world of the voters. Only when this is accomplished will the internal structure of politics be apparent, subsisting as it did in concrete form behind the clouds of contemporary political myth and subsequent historiographical credulity.

Those who knew the culture of the factory best knew best the real currency of political life. In the pages of the *Fortnightly Review* between 1868 and 1874 the reactions of John Morley, Frederic Harrison and W.A. Abram chart the gradual realisation of what the new politics meant. W.A. Abram, Blackburn newspaperman and Liberal party manager, was closest to the hard truths. Writing before the 1868 election he explained, 'It is an axiom with election managers in Lancashire boroughs that the politics of a town are determined solely by the relative numbers of spindles and looms driven by Tory and Liberal employers'.[5] He went on to enlarge upon the virtues of the popular master,

It is useless to deny that over their operatives the employers possess a considerable influence ... legitimate influence is the effect produced upon his workpeople by the munificence and kindliness of an employer. Not less is an enterprising character the passport to the respect of the workmen. The influence of an energetic master vibrates to the outermost circle of his dependents. ... The people worship courage and pluck, and will follow the lead of a man who exhibits these qualities without stopping to investigate his opinion. ... It is one of those illogical but natural things which happen everyday, for inferior minds to accept without question the invitation of a man whom they esteem.[6]

At this stage Abram could be sanguine about the prospect of liberated, individual reason afforded by the imminent expression of political reform. The degree to which his confidence was unfounded is apparent in the politics of the street. Table 5 shows how part of one Blackburn ward voted in 1868, all the streets listed being near to large and old-established Liberal and Tory mills:
Abram's fears, and the verdict of Blackburn's own John Morley after the election,[8] were to be echoed by other observers as well: the politics of the factory were there to stay. Engels reported in the aftermath of the 1868 election that in the factory districts,

TABLE 5
Street voting, Park Ward, Blackburn 1868[7]

Liberal factory area			Conservative factory area		
	Lib. vote.	Cons. vote		Lib. vote	Cons. vote
Friday Street	21	3	James Street	17	4
Back Friday Street	13	2	Kemp Street	27	7
Eccles Row	16	3	Peel Street	17	5
Primrose Hill	22	1	Mosley Street	45	16
Russell Street	10	2	Rockcliffe Street	15	2
Fox Street	21	7	Haslingden Road	45	15
Higher Audley Street	48	25	Grimshaw Park	54	20
Audley Range	19	4			

'not a single working-class candidate had a ghost of a chance, but my Lord Thumnoddy or any *parvenu* snob could have the workers' votes with pleasure'.[9] By 1874 Frederic Harrison knew the fruits of Reform in the factory North:[10]

In the cotton and textile trades ... the factory system stimulates a local and domestic partisanship. ... In some of the factory districts they vote by mills and wards in the spirit in which schoolboys play cricket or football by 'houses' or 'forms' ... amongst large masses of workmen, especially millhands, a popular neighbour commands all the influence which the captain of the boats or an athletic tutor has in colleges and schools.

As Abram had seen, the larger mills were the main islands of political influence within the town:

In a large concern of old standing, where, perhaps, 1,000 to 2,000 persons are employed there has grown up with time a strong "esprit de corps" among the hands. Each individual operative comes to identify with the mill at which he works, and if he be not troubled with convictions of his own, readily accepts its political shibbolthes.[11]

Harrison's comment suggests how little difference the Ballot Act of 1872 made to all this. The Blackburn press described the 1873 municipal elections as follows:

Blackburn borough is of course in the thick of it ... everything is seen through blue or green, yellow or red spectacles. Mills and manufactures are for the nonce not places for the manipulation of cotton, but for the manufacture of Tories and Radicals. We hear of 'Tory mills' and 'Liberal mills', or 'Tory shops' and 'Radical shops' ... the borough is divided into 'two bands' between which there are no relations and no contact but that of foe with foe.[12]

Such was to be in the nature of things for the remainder of the century. These descriptions recall Allen Clarke's account of the Bolton operatives in 1899: 'They have no true idea of life. They believe they are bound to work. ... They have no rational grasp of politics, or political economy.'[13] The partisan clan loyalty shown at election times was tellingly evoked by the operatives' own journal, again at the end of the century.[14]

The principal pollbook work undertaken can only be summarised here.[15] It involved charting the relationship between the geographical distribution and occupational composition of the vote, and the ownership, location and political complexion of industry in Blackburn and Bury. Many difficulties attended this work, not least that of the time and labour needed to match the 1868 books with the census enumerators' schedules for 1871. About 8,000 voters were involved. Because of the lack of factory records it cannot be known with absolute certainty whether a particular worker worked in a particular factory. Despite the difficulties, the 1868 pollbooks are the only means we have of penetrating the mass electorate. Pollbooks before 1868 are almost useless for this purpose, and after 1872, of course, they were no longer published.

In Blackburn the street patterns of voting were traced in all six wards and the two townships. These patterns were found to correspond very closely with the siting of Liberal and Tory workplaces. In St Paul's ward, for instance, Liberal power was centred upon the George Street West mills of R.R. Jackson (George Street West voted L.28-C.5). The ward, known as the Liberal 'Rock of Gibralter', was retained by the party most of the remainder of the century. As in all wards, the lesser owners tended to orbit the influence of the large employers. The Tory St John's ward was a citadel of cotton paternalism, and a classic example of the mill-based community (L.536–C.859). The Hornbys reigned in the Brookhouse core of the ward for almost a century after the 1820s. In St Peter's ward the Tory majority was based on the very large Dickinson and Duckworth mills, and located in one half of the ward which voted 2–1 for the Conservatives (Duckworth Street voted C.33–L.12).

Park ward formed the centrepiece of the Blackburn investigation. On analysis it was found to break down into two clearly distinct political areas, represented in the map below. The abruptness of the forntier should be stressed; for example Primrose Hill voting L.22–C.1, and immediately beside it Crosfield Street and Jack Croft C.19–L.4. The owners whose influence is mapped were all front-rank political leaders. They gave their names to streets and pubs within the fiefdoms.

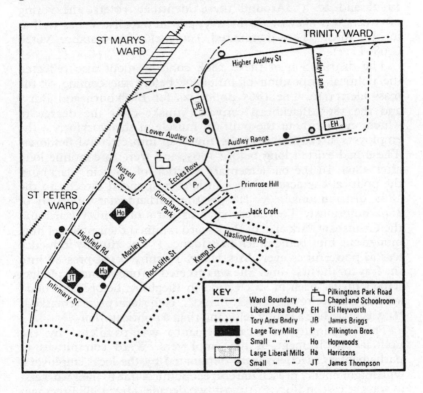

Map 2: Blackburn Park Ward 1868 Election – distribution of cotton industry and the vote

The situation in Bury was much the same. In Liberal Freetown, for instance (a cohesive, old-established colony yet part of the town fabric by 1868), the voting district result was L.289–C.140, the cotton vote being 60–30 in favour of the Liberals. Polling districts 7 and 8 were the centre of Liberal engineering in the town and voted Liberal 552–296, the engineering vote being L.102–

C.41 (the seemingly small size of the engineering vote is a consequence of only 50 to 60 per cent of the electorate being traced
with certainty in the 1871 census). Outside cotton and engineering,
Bury was patterned by minor and quite distinctive areas of influence: in wool, bleaching and dyeing voting concentrations
occurred far from other similar factories, the majorities involved
being quite unambiguous (on the Liberal side for example,
woollen workers supported the local employer to the extent of
17–2, and 22–3). Around these identified voters, the voting
of streets was likewise distinctive, and in out-districts as well as
in the town (Tory-dominated Limefield for instance voted
C.68–L.11).

The distribution of these 1868 concentrations also reflected
the political disposition of influence before the coming of the
mass electorate. The 1865 pollbooks for Blackburn and Bury,
and the 1865 Blackburn canvass,[16] make clear the degree to
which, even without the political muscle of the workforces, the
employers already divided the town up into electoral fiefdoms.
These had existed long before 1865, and were to continue long
after 1868. In the parliamentary election of 1875 in Blackburn
the political character of the wards corresponded directly to the
1868 distributions.[17] As late as the parliamentary election of
1892 notoriously Tory areas such as parts of Trinity ward and
the Grimshaw Park area of Park ward retained their political hue,
orange and blue being much in evidence.[18] The Hornby influence
was as powerful as ever, Mrs Harry Hornby being pressed into
the fray for the first time. She was greeted by one woman's pledge,
'Hoo's nivver been in an election in Blegburn before; but hoo'l
see now that we're real gradely bricks'. As the local press remarked;
'It was more like a family rejoicing than a political affair.'[19]

This continuity of local allegiance was paralleled by the
political involvement of the employers. Ward committees in
parliamentary elections were dominated by the local employers,
who might openly preach the correct political line to their workers,
as was the case in Bury.[20] Almost two decades after 1868 Freetown
and Moorside in Bury (the latter an engineering district) were
still Radical strongholds, and Limefield still enemy territory,
in the proportion of 6–1.[21] The geographical distribution of
employer political power at the time closely resembled the
situation of 1868.

The conclusions that the 1868 Bury and Blackburn books
indicate are strongly supported by the Bradford and Preston
books for the same year. In Bradford the victory of the Liberal-
Conservative Ripley was in large measure owed to his strength

in Bowling ward, where his own dyeworks and the Tory Bowling Ironworks were located.[22] In Bowling 1591 voted for Ripley, 1,055 for Miall and 1,144 for Forster. In Preston, where again the 1868 distribution of the vote reflected that of the restricted electorate before the Second Reform Act,[23] the core of the overall Tory majority lay in Fishwick ward and township. This was the chief seat of the massive Horrockses, as well as the location of a number of other large Tory mills. Edward Hermon, the proprietor of Horrockses, was one of the candidates and was supported in ward and township to the extent of C.974–L.578.[24] Township street majorities were of the following order: Thomas Street C.23–L.2, James Street C.26–L.7, William Henry Street C.9–L.1, and Stourton Street C.15–L.6. In the ward of ninety streets, fifty-nine voted Conservative, eighteen Liberal, and thirteen were tied.

In Oldham borough the spoils were divided between the central Werneth and Westwood wards (centre of the Platt engineering influence), and the cotton and coal Tory out-townships such as Clarksfield and Lees. This division was maintained between 1868 and 1874 regardless of electoral secrecy.[25] There is also some very interesting newspaper evidence that for the three decades that followed 1868 in Burnley the vote continued to be divided by geographical area between Tory miners and Liberal cotton and engineering workers. Ownership of coal was exclusively Tory, cotton and engineering ownership predominantly Liberal.[26]

Particular difficulties attend the use of municipal election results: gross ward results mask the territorial lines of factory blocs, and the lack of ward contests, and lack of political effort (especially when a notable employer was not standing), make interpretation very difficult. Nevertheless, municipal results do show the reality of local allegiance and the continuities of employer influence. Blackburn ward municipal representation in 1879 exactly mirrored 1868 parliamentary distributions: St Paul's had six Liberal councillors, no Tory, St John's six Tories, and Park ward was divided four to two in favour of the Conservatives.[27] Such was the case seven years later as well.[28]

Employers usually stood for municipal election in the ward in which their works were located, and were chairmen and members of ward election committees, just as in parliamentary elections. At election times employers were fond of dwelling on their role as the perfect master, and not above threatening to sell out and go if their operatives did not toe the line.[29] In 1875 the *Blackburn Standard* maintained that in Lancashire, and any adjoining county, the 'average borough' had many wards in which the man of substance who had 'nursed' the ward could return his own nominee without difficulty.[30] In mainly Liberal Ashton, Tory industry was chiefly concentrated in St Michael's ward. In 1869 Tory voters in the ward were taken *en bloc* from the mills to the polls by omnibus.[31] The ward retained its Conservative character in the years to come.[32]

All this evidence strongly suggests that the factory functioned as a political force because it represented a common life. Factory voting expressed the allegiance of the entirety of a workforce and not that of a segment within it. When the occupational composition of the Blackburn and Bury electorates is considered this becomes especially apparent. First the Blackburn breakdown (the Bury figures are given in the appendix):

TABLE 6
Park Ward, Blackburn 1868:
occupational composition of the vote

(A) *Cotton*[1]		*Liberal area*	*Lib. vote*	*Cons. vote*
		overlookers	20	6
		spinners	39	10
		weavers	53	21
		all supervisory	32	13
		all 'skilled'	59	22
		all 'un-skilled'	75	25
		Conservative area	*Cons. vote*	*Lib. vote*[2]
		overlookers	33	5
		spinners	43	13
		weavers	67	32
		all supervisory	42	5
		all 'skilled'	79	22
		all 'un-skilled'	74	34
(B) *Labourers*		*Liberal area*	L42	C27
		Conservative area	C33	L13
(C) *Iron and*				
	engineering	*Liberal area*	L30	C24
		Conservative area	C17	L 4
(D) *Craft and skilled*		*Liberal area*	L32	C28
	(craft shops,	*Conservative area*	C21	L11
	building trades,			
	small masters)			
(E) *Retailers and*				
	Dealers	*Liberal area*	L66	C24
	(inc. beerhouses		7	8
		pubs, inns	16	15)
		Conservative area	C40	L15
	(inc. beerhouses		14	4
		pubs, inns	4	1)

[1] Cotton, supervisory : overlookers, managers, bookkeepers, clerks.
'skilled'　　　　: spinners, carders, warehousemen, clothlookers, sizers, warpers, loomers, tapers; skilled trades in factory – mechanics, joiners, etc.; some trades difficult to classify but pay and some degree of skill place them most appropriately as 'skilled' – twisters, beamers, drawers, twiners (these few in number)
'unskilled'　　　: weavers, card room hands, labourers, stokers, etc.
[2] Only 50% Liberal voters' occupations known for Conservative area, 70% of Tory ones.

Just as the pre-1868 ward distributions of the vote point to a larger employer influence than that measured by the workforce alone, so too do these figures suggest distinct 'village' elements in the make-up of electoral blocs. This tendency was however attenuated by the mainly Tory sympathies of the drink interest (as seen for the town as a whole) and the predominantly Liberal politics of the craft, and retailing and dealing sectors. Nonetheless, especially in the most partisan areas like Tory St John's, the shop and pub could powerfully reinforce the political character of the locale.

Cotton and engineering are, however, the main considerations here. There are signs of a lessening in the degree of local allegiance from supervisors down to the less-attached unskilled. But the differences are hardly great. Contrary to any notion of a political and cultural divide in the working class – a 'labour aristocracy' militating against the expression of unified political feeling – the substantial uniformity of the cotton vote is apparent. The simple voting figures for streets adjacent to the mills also points to this undifferentiated local patriotism. Bury engineering indicates just as forcibly the lack of grade distinctions within the workforce. There was Liberal lead of just under 2–1 in terms of employed adult males. The 500 or so voters traced voted in this 2–1 ratio for the Liberals, overall and in each of the thirteen voting districts. The 200 or so semi- and unskilled workers were in fact even more prone to vote Liberal than their more skilled fellows.[33]

Two last words, the first on labourers. Any idea that popular Toryism was the preserve of a 'lumpenproletariat' receives no support from the Bury figures. Leaving Irish labourers out of the total, and including agricultural ones, Liberal labourers were still in a majority (L.201–C.187). However characteristic of the Tory style a 'pre-industrial' appeal may have been, Tory voting appeared to have no special connection with rural birth. Though such an appeal (described in the previous chapter)[34] undoubtedly had an effect, it served rather to cement allegiances formed at other and deeper levels than to create new ones. And, no doubt, the primary formation was at the level of the workplace. Samples of the vote in Blackburn and Bury were taken, in the form of occupational cross-sections of wards and voting districts, and showed that those born in rural areas were as likely to vote Liberal as Conservative.

The presence of the factory entered into all of political life. Factory workforces had been active decades before this period, in defence of the workplace against Luddite incursions, and in the defences of the 1840s previously noted.[35] In the 1830s Fergus O'Connor could scathingly describe the Operative Conservative Societies as made up of 'the masters and their men – the miller and his dogs'.[36] In the 1840s Rochdale employers, including John Bright, were recruiting and organising their workforces for their own political ends.[37] By 1852 in Blackburn the hands of Feilden and Jackson's mill were parading through the town in support of their politician-employers, and pledging political loyalty to them in the gathering that followed.[38] The Tory riposte in the following year was an even more arresting example of how times had changed. The hands of the Dickinson, Harrison and Hornby factories, together with those of lesser establishments, paraded the streets in orange and blue. Complete with bands, banners and flags they formed part of the 15,000 strong body that met W.H. Hornby at Blackburn railway station for a presentation from the town's operatives.[39]

By 1865 the kind of situation Morley and Harrison were to describe later was already long the nature of town politics. In 1865 the Radical press was thundering against 'the rule of the tall chimneys' and of 'the Lords of Brookhouse and of Grimshaw Park', counselling a Congregationalist minister who dared speak up for liberty: 'Cotton King, cotton rule; liberty afterwards Mr Parkes, that is the way the Blackburn creed runs ... cotton is worshipped in its varied influences to the detriment of free speech and free thought.'[40]

Efforts to mobilise the non-electors in 1865 were furthered by the Liberal millowners closing their mills early.[41] The degree to which the factory had become the known face of politics is apparent from the character of political demonstrations. A vital set-piece in the Blackburn Reform agitation was the large demonstration of December 1866. In this some of the workers marched by trade union and Sunday school order, but the great majority in individual factory phalanxes, led by their managers and overlookers. Roused by the factory brass bands, the operatives of all the leading Liberal mills in Blackburn and Darwen thus openly declared an allegiance to the town that had much more to do with the factory than with Liberalism.[42] The Tory mills refused to allow their workers time off.

The Tory answer to the Reform agitation was of the same character: in 1868 the Hornby hands – men, women and children – were on the streets in the Protestant cause.[43] It was the usual practice for the Hornbys to send a few more operatives off to the polls when things were going amiss.[44] This open use of the workforce was also seen in the town in the 1870s, when in one of the periodic scrambles for the Tory candidacy when a Hornby was not standing, rival employers enlisted their men in the public fight that was to decide the prize.[45] The overt presence of the factory characterised the politics of the North as a whole, down even to Burial Board elections, as much as it did the politics of Blackburn.

In Clitheroe the Tory victory of 1853 was celebrated by the stopping of a large Tory mill, a town procession, and then the march on the victorious candidate's residence. The provision of beer at the latter was followed by violence in the evening, sparked off by a counter-demonstration at the large, Liberal Low Moor works.[46] Even before the advent of the mass electorate, one factory could be crucial to the outcome of an election. In the Clitheroe of 1857, 'there was some talk of an election, but owing to the stoppage of Primrose in 1854 so many Liberal electors had left the town that the prospect of returning a Liberal member seemed so discouraging that no attempt was really made to trot one out'.[47]

The factory premises themselves were often pressed into political service, as when the Marquis of Hartington addressed 3,000 people in a Keighley mill in the 1870s.[48] In the ordinary run of elections this was the case too, as in the Dewsbury election of 1874 and the Halifax one of 1880.[49] In all this activity the ritual character of factory life penetrated political conduct directly. Those elements in the factory social occasion affirming the tie with the factory regime and its locale (described in the preceding chapter) had overtly political uses when the occasion demanded.

The great celebratory and consolatory treats mounted by employer-politicians are especially interesting. In 1869 Angus Holden of Bradford held a large gathering at his mansion as a counter to a similar Tory jamboree in Bradford's Manningham Park.[50] These were fairly regular events in most towns, the candidate's largesse repaying the activism of the minority and the vote of the mass.[51] More than this, however, at such events as the political treats put on by the leading Stalybridge masters at their works in 1869, political strategy and ideology were explained to the workpeople, and the praises of the political chieftains were sung.[52]

At other gatherings in the same year it was estimated that 5,000 attended the Tory occasion, and 4,000 the Liberal one.[53] Large parts of the popular vote saw themselves and were seen as distinct collectivities in town life. These events, marked by eating, drinking and dancing, did not cease after 1872.[54] In 1880, 1,350 employees of the Buckleys and Reyners in Ashton met at the Reyners' mill to celebrate the return of two of the family to the Town Council. A few days earlier 2,000 of another Liberal's hands, J.H. Gartside, met for a similar feast.[55] From the 1880s on the Tory side the Primrose League served to present the employer in a new guise as the political host. Ostensibly non-political events might also have considerable political overtones. The Liberal masters of Darwen were especially inclined to extol the virtues of temperance and liberty during the ordinary course of mill social life.[56]

The political history of a number of firms large and renowned enough to appear above the horizon of the newsworthy can be reconstructed in some detail. A firm like the Wigan Coal and Iron Company had a great and continuous impact on local politics. The coalowners were using the workforce in the municipal elections of the 1850s, when it was already traditional for the firm to parade the colliers at parliamentary elections. Two decades later, in 1874, organised bands of colliers were marching through the town in support of the employers.[57] The local press maintained in 1892 that 'this overgrown and bloated corporation claims for itself the right of returning three Members of Parliament, namely those nominally returned for Wigan, Ince and Westhoughton'.[58]

It was not unusual for Edward Akroyd's hands in Halifax to be sent *en bloc* to the hustings, nor for them to pull their employer's car in triumph after an election.[59] The Crossleys and Akroyds engrossed the political life of the town just as they did the economic. After the 1847 election the Crossley concern took on the hands of Edward Akroyd, dismissed by him as Ernest Jones and Edward Miall supporters.[60]

One of the clearest examples of the influence of the big firm was that of the combined Conservative, sometimes Liberal-Conservative, interest in Bradford, represented by the Ripleys' Bowling dyeworks and the amalgamated Bowling and Low Moor ironworks. In the early 1840s it was the custom then and on every subsequent occasion, when a Low Moor partner had to be proposed on the Bradford hustings, for the foundrymen and colliers of Low Moor to come down in a body to exercise their lungs and hold up their hands in support of their master. This was a matter over which the proprietors had no control; the men had always great admiration for their masters, and were not to be deterred from showing it at such times as these.[61]

In 1867 and 1868 hundreds of workers from Bowling, Low Moor, and the mining districts thronged into Bradford to thwart the Liberals, who termed the entry a 'carnival of ruffianism'.[62] Tory counterclaims that Liberal firms were political 'hothouses' were made with equal emphasis in these same years.[63]

Liberal election cartoons and satires attacked the Bowling 'Warriors' of Ripley in 1867, especially one Strutt, 'the great ornament of Bowling dyeworks'. Thirty-three years with the firm, and a 'gaffer' from 1851, Strutt was one of the Ripleys' chief political lieutenants.[64] The managing partner at the dyeworks, Wilson Sutcliffe (supported by his son), was most important of all in maintaining the Ripley influence. He was typical of the diffusion of factory management and lesser authority in the political and administrative life of a firm's locality, a process described for Bowling and Low Moor in a preceding chapter.[65]

The pervasiveness of the factory connection can be illustrated from the Blackburn example. The most significant figure on the Tory side, Elijah Holt, worked his way up through the Hornbys' Brookhouse mill. When only nineteen years he was described as the 'mad captain' of the Brookhouse band of political workers. Shedding his trade union involvement in later years, he went on to play a central role in the whole Tory effort, linking the Hornby leadership with the popular constituency and co-ordinating with the wire-pulling Thompson family (themselves cotton employers). The Brookhouse link was institutionalised in the party structure in 1880 when Holt was made party agent. Active into the 1890s, it was said of him at the height of his power that 'a breath, breathed in the ear of 'Lijah . . . could put down the mighty from their seats, and exalt the humble'.

The Brookhouse link has been traced in detail, as has the influence of a number of other Tory mills, foundries and workshops in the careers of Blackburn political activists.[66] These men had specially strong links with the political club movement, but also with that central institution in working-class life, the friendly society. The Liberals owed as much to the factory connection. James beads, a small cotton master and the Liberal counter-

216   *Work, Society and Politics*

part of the Thompsons, advanced in life by means of the book-keeping position at the mill of William Eccles.[67] The Congregationalist Eccleses were at one time political leaders in their own right and partners of the most important Liberal employers, the Pilkingtons (the Darwen branch of the Eccles family were to remain front-rank political leaders into the second half of the century). John Norris, who became Liberal agent in 1880, in turn rose *via* Beads' mill, the long, painful way from warehouse boy, cutlooker, bookkeeper, and cashier to manager. Thus, at the level of political organisation nearest to the popular support, the association of the work and political career, and of the factory and organised politics, was of the utmost significance.

When the heights of political organisation are considered the same is seen again to be the case. Power and the real meaning of organisation resided in the understandings that existed between small groups of men, rather than in institutions themselves. These men derived their significance from the economic organisation of town life, their social connections mirroring and perpetuating the prevailing social order. The combination of the Hornbys, the Thompsons, and Holt, was a replica of the industrial society of Blackburn, and of the hierarchy of authority the factory bred. James Thompson, chairman of the Conservative Election Committee between 1865 and 1874, politicised all municipal office in the town. Unworried by scruples and objections, he was the 'complete master' of the Tory forces in the town, the chief of which was 'Hornbyism'. Thompson maintained that the town 'could not contemplate the divorce between Hornbyism and Toryism'.[68] The Liberals felt moved to complain that 'the government of the party is of the truly paternal kind. Each individual Tory has been trained to obey the order of the supreme authority with unreasoning and implicit docility'.[69]

As the unofficial and official agent, and as the chairman of the Central Conservative Club's committee from 1867, Holt worked to mobilise the new popular vote. William Henry Hornby II took the organisational and spiritual mantle of leadership between 1874 and 1886 as party chairman. After a relatively rare interruption the party was by 1893 back in 'the old-fashioned Hornby groove again', William Thompson succeeding his brother James as 'the only dictator Blackburn ever had', until the end of his kingmaking role in 1906.[70]

Liberal complaints about all this typified the sanctimonious self-delusion that was the besetting sin of the party throughout these years. Committee members and officers in the Blackburn Liberal club movement were as much drawn from the ranks of factory authority as were their Tory counterparts. At the October 1868 'indignation meeting' against the Tory 'screw', the Victoria Club was represented by its honorary secretary, the Liberal cotton master Frank Johnston, the Cobden Club by two weaving masters, and the Grimshaw Park Club by the Pilkingtons' book-keeper. The vice-chairman of the Liberal 'Victim Club' was R.R. Jackson's spinning manager.[71] Though the Liberal 'interest' was more diffuse than monolithic Toryism, the factory was still all-important. The function of James Beads differed not at all from that of the Thompsons, the Tory *Blackburn Standard* admitting the indispensibility of Beads to Liberal command of the popular constituency on his death in 1886.[72]

Blackburn was only a somewhat heightened example of what was everywhere else the case. Ashton Liberalism, for instance, was little more than the continuation by other means of the factory and chapel influence of the big employers. And Ashton, as our discussion of the nexus of business, political and religious interests defining groups within the élite has made plain, was no different from the general run of factory towns.[73] In Burnley for example, the links between those who ran the political machines (sometimes, like Blackburn, as families), and the leading coal-owning and cotton employers were especially close.[74] Elijah Holmes and Robert Handsley were leading party workers, and agents and managers at the Tory collieries.

The political club movement did something to take the factory out of direct involvement in party organisation. Nevertheless, the clubs were sited at the centre of the various fiefdoms, and were often patronised by the leading employers of the locale, who also headed the pyramidal ward election organisation.[75] When political organisation is considered in more detail later, the control of the wealthy will be clearly apparent. What lay behind the organisation was oligarchy before 1867 and oligarchy after 1867.[76] The great majority of the working class was excluded from anything but a symbolic role in the exercise of power.

Although the inadequacy of workplace coercion as an explanation of mass political attitudes must be insisted upon, its presence ought not to be underestimated. Behind actual and threatened dismissal lay a range of influences, still potent in the intimate world of the factory long after the institution of electoral secrecy. Appreciation of the extent of intimidation is complicated both by the frequently subjective nature of the experience, and its role in political mythology, especially in south-east Lancashire where it was long used by the Tories.

The following, a Tory dialect attack of 1879 on a new Ashton

Liberal club as the 'Screw Club' composed of overlookers and managers from the Liberal mills, indicates the continuing liveliness of this kind of attack, but also something of the ways in which mill pressure would have worked:

'The book-keepers un th' managers ur th' committee, un then theer's a lot o' sneakin tools ut works ... ' *Jim*: 'Aye, but I'll tell thee abeaut workmen, fust dost see. Thoose chaps hearken owt wot's sed i'th' mill un public heawses un onybody ut happens for't say owt ut they thinkin ul be a tale, they tell th' o'erlooker, un he tells th' manager, un then theer names ur put i' th' black list.'[77]

They could then be 'bagged fro' theer work', a vote on the parish being a vote lost.

However, the investigations of the Hartington Committee and the work of H.J. Hanham both make plain the staggering weight of influence rather than coercion, above all in Lancashire.[78] The Reform League reports on Lancashire constituencies similarly indicate the power of 'legitimate influence'.[79] In Birkenhead for example, the secret ballot came, the shipbuilding Laird family remained, and the town went on its Tory way untroubled. It is most significant that in the Bury of 1868 there were no serious accusations of the 'screw' beyond a few party shouts, the relations of the parties remaining particularly gentlemanly.

But in those constituencies where coercion was uncovered in 1868, chiefly Ashton, Stalybridge and Blackburn, it had fairly systematically obtained in municipal elections for a number of years, and was also exercised by brewers and by the large employers against tradesmen and Corporation officials and workmen.[80] One Stalybridge Tory claimed that coercion had gone on for twenty years in municipal elections, and was 'a general system ... with one portion of the millowners'.[81] In the Blackburn elections of 1868 a few hundred lost their jobs, the municipal election being used as a 'softner' for the parliamentary one. The election of 1869, which followed on the annulled 1868 parliamentary result, was however won with increased majorities by the two sons of the 1868 Tory deposed, a notable victory for the dynastic principle.[82] But for the few who stood out against the masters in 1868 the sacrifice was real enough. The following is a description of what it was like to be in Tory Brookhouse at the time (Margerison was a spinners' union officer and a Liberal clubman):

He [Mr Margerison] replied to the effect that those in Brookhouse dare not give their votes according to their consciences, for if they did they would sacrifice their places. They would not lose their places instantly, the screw coming gradually; they were screwed by one overlooker and then by another, until they were screwed so tight that they could stand it no longer, and were screwed out of the place'.[83]

Forms of pressure were undoubtedly used after 1872. This is how one Bolton spinner described the coming of the Limiteds:

And this was broken down more when ... our new mills was built prior to the first world war when they were limited companies, before that they was all family concerns. They was all family concerns you see and–the workpeople had to be very careful how they voted or how they spoke about politics.[84]

In several other instances too it is clear that influence did not stop short of coercion in the second half of the century.[85] In Blackburn itself employer pressure was noted in the elections of 1885 and 1900.[86] On the latter occasion it was said that the older workers believed that if the result was not the right one the employers would go through the vote again. Workers joining the S.D.F. and I.L.P. suffered the wrath of their employers, who in some cases egged on their operatives into breaking up Socialist meetings.[87] In Keighley, those attending early Labour party meetings in the town sometimes had to do so in disguise, and the police were occasionally used to break up political meetings.[88]

However, it is the limitations to the extent of coercion that are most significant. The Thompson and Vigne West Riding oral interview material, especially on Keighley, corroborates the overwhelming impression left by the Lancashire interviews: of those respondants asked about employer coercion there was only a small minority who detected it in their youth and in the memories of their parents.[89] For most people pro-employer voting was a matter of the understood and expected.[90] Employer influence did not usually extend to coercion, and when it did this was often interpreted as a transgression of the letter of the law rather than its spirit. Nevertheless, political support for the employers was inseparable from the experience of economic dependence and work authority. Political allegiance was based on consent, though a consent that was part of a paternalist exchange to which authority was integral. As our delineation of the connections between deference, dependence and community makes apparent, the means by which authority was politically felt may justly be described as a self-maintained sense of community.

In the limited range of localities where coercion operated to any marked extent it can best be understood in this light. In the

Blackburn of 1868 most of the factory ejections were carried out, and often instigated, by the men themselves. In only two of the thirteen proved cases was the instigation not the men's. The situation in the factories rapidly got out of hand, pressure coming far more from below than from above.[91] Justice Willes testified to the spontaneity of political loyalties in the town:

You did not come to the conclusion did you, that the working men entertained any strong political loyalties themselves – I think they did, I think the Lancashire people as far as I can at all judge have strong political feelings, so much so at Blackburn that the mills adopt colours, blue or yellow, and even a man used to stick up a colour, blue or yellow, upon the machine that he was working at, which seems carrying matters a long way.[92]

The ritual quality of the ejections is of considerable interest. The expulsion and stoning by the body of mill workers was similar to the treatment meted out to others, (such as wife-beaters) breaking community trusts and sanctions.[93] The Respondents' Briefs in the trial of the Blackburn election petition of 1868–69 offer fascinating evidence, in the operatives' own words, for the communitarian spontaneity of political feeling.[94] It was the assembled factory workforces that hooted Radicals out of the works. One employer was met at his works in the morning by forty or fifty of his hands determined not to work with a well-known Radical. Despite the employer reasoning with them, they refused to work unless he was ejected.

This kind of commitment was of long standing. At one of the early Reform meetings in Blackburn Edward Walker, spinner and Liberal, declared that the Ballot was necessary to protect individuals from their fellow-workers – he had several times been punched 'by my own sort', never by a master.[95] In Stalybridge a Liberal activist declared in 1871 that he 'was sorry to see that the working classes ... were the biggest screws out', pressure extending beyond workmen to 'shopkeepers and tradesmen'.[96] Local middle-class public opinion in the late 1860s was in favour of the secret ballot, despite a residue of old-fashioned pride in public accountability.[97] Rather than fearing the consequences, employers of all political hues welcomed the coming of the ballot secure in the knowledge of their own strength, and aware that secrecy would articulate rather than eradicate the legacy of operative support.[98]

This knowledge found expression in the terms in which the employers understood their employees' votes: they were theirs by something like divine right. Robert Stanley, a Stalybridge

Tory activist, was looked upon by the Liberal employers as 'a meddler between employer and workman', and 'a sort of dangerous character'.[99] These assumptions found an approving response in popular attitudes. Frank Johnston, a Liberal mill-owner in Blackburn, declared before the Hartington Committee that the feeling that an employee should vote as his master did was so great that it was followed by all, and was as much the obligation of the Tory-minded in the Liberal mills as the reverse.[100]

A valuable perspective on the whole matter of coercion is provided when it is considered that the Liberals were never accused of coercion in Bury and Blackburn. Yet in both towns, and particularly in the Liberal 'townlet' in Park Ward, Blackburn, Liberal support was as cohesive and forthright as that of the Tories. With this understanding of the nature and mechanics of political loyalties in mind attention will now be directed beyond the factory North to the politics of the nation at large.

Some British comparisons

In placing the politics of the factory North in their national context a crucial question concerning the writing of political history at once presents itself: if such were the politics of the most industrial and urban parts of Britain, whither the orthodoxies of a political history content to assume the urban and the industrial as the hallmarks of a modernity defined as the politics of individual conscience and of ideology? The relationship between an industrial system and a political system is deeply problematic in character, as is that existing between the nature of class-consciousness in a society and the politics of that society. It is to be hoped that a sense of this complexity informs the present work: the realm of the political is governed by its own laws and customs. That this realm is not sovereign is equally apparent. In the industrial North of the later-nineteenth century society defined politics to a degree even more marked than is usual. Only when the non-political life of the voter is reconstructed can this be understood. Only with a sense of society will the true nature of the political system be seen.

A recognition that appearances are not what they seem prompts two questions involving the comparison between Britain and the North. The first is political: what reassessment of British politics does this explication of the factory politics of influence indicate might be made? The second is wider and more difficult: how are we to interpret the links between industry and politics in the factory North, and so the general relationship between urban and labour process and attitudes revealed there, in terms of the life of the nation at large? These two questions will form the matter of the present discussion.

The primary lesson of popular politics in the North is that the politics of influence were really of much wider significance than is usually thought. When the political system is interpreted in terms of how society was rather than how it seemed, many characteristics of the political culture make far more sense than when the ostensibly political is taken for political reality. This is the approach adopted in Chapter 8 below, where the communities of work and religion are allowed to explicate the political culture of the North. It is not unlikely that such an approach might be usefully applied to other parts of Britain. Instead of a rather uneasy periodisation into early, middle and late in the writing of Victorian political history, the northern example suggests that continuity perhaps mattered more. When the increasingly apparent survival of earlier political ways is correctly understood, instead of the notions of modernity and periodisation, an examination of politics in terms of society reveals that the themes of adaptation and renewal are everywhere apparent in the political culture of the time. A good deal of the political history of the later-nineteenth century can be told in terms of the adoption and adaptation of the institutions of the politics of opinion to serve the ends of the politics of influence. Such a reading also indicates that so much in the conduct of politics regarded as peripheral and anachronistic was in fact central, as the politics of influence renewed themselves and prospered.

This sort of interpretation adds its voice to a chorus that is beginning to sound less idiosyncratic and more revealing than is sometimes allowed. As the evidence is assembled, approaches like that of D.C. Moore are seen to involve an originality leading towards the heart of the matter.[101] The value of Moore's work on the county seats lies in his recognition of the disjunction between political myth and social reality, and of the need to consider the social worlds of the voters if this disjunction is to be understood. Whether the work of historical reconstruction has been accomplished by Moore is perhaps doubtful, and a social historian of rural England would no doubt have much to say about his rather uncritical use of the deference notion. While the somewhat patrician reluctance of students of *Hochpolitik* to immerse more than a toe in the troubled waters of social history remains, so too will such difficulties. Despite the gratuitous prudence of closing the curtain on the politics of influence with the advent of urban, industrial England on the political stage, Moore's work does show how much the politics of the North were of a piece with the politics of the nation.

In the industrial areas the recent work of Robert Moore and T.J. Nossiter on North-East England testifies to the great and persistent strength of influence politics.[102] Nossiter's regional study indicates their special force in iron as opposed to coal, though Moore's local study in the region shows how after 1874 the old politics were of predominating weight in the more paternalist of the mining areas. Mossiter's termination at 1874 would seem a little arbitrary, for especially in the many company towns, as well as in county industrial seats, 1874 marked the end of the beginning of the new politics of individualism far more than the end of the old politics of influence. As Nossiter remarks: ' . . . the evidence suggests great responsiveness to the partisanship of the immediate environment, and its magnates. The lower down the nineteenth-century social scale was the voter, the more likely was he to incline – or succumb – to the political complexion of his primary neighbourhood.'[103] These recent forays into the politics of influence serve to accentuate the already considerable evidence that what were earlier thought to have been picturesque survivals were very much at the centre of British political culture.

H.J. Hanham in particular has shown that beyond the cities the politics of influence reached well into the last quarter of the century.[104] This concentration on the towns rather than on the cities is undoubtedly the direction the enquiry should take, though even in the cities the lineaments of influence politics are to be discerned. The work of Paul Thompson, Henry Pelling and Gareth Stedman Jones reveals glimpses, behind the backdrop of class in London politics, of the late continuation and success of both influence politics and employer paternalism and largesse.[105] When this politics is given the attention it deserves it may be that the electoral constituency it described was not a small one. How much that constituency will coincide with popular support for the Conservative party is uncertain: despite the work undertaken on London the nature and extent of this support is unclear, and it may be that in it the politics of influence found its prime object.

However this may be, it seems probable that in the future the politics of the later Victorian town, and especially the industrial town, will be as well described in terms of influence as of class and religion. Clarke's advancement of religion to the forefront of Victorian politics has to be seen in this light.[106] As the next chapter will make plain, far from minimising the importance of religion, its presence in formal politics and in the social constitution of political allegiances is to be emphasised. For many in the electorate religion was probably of first importance in politics, but for the mass electorate work was undoubtedly the primary matrix of political consciousness, however much the communities of work and religion may have overlapped. And, as we have seen, the culture of the factory did much to determine the nature of the general political culture of the factory town.

To describe the political system of the second half of the century in terms of influence is, however, only to begin to ask the interesting questions. Nossiter's description of the politics of influence, of the market and of opinion, not as distinct spheres but as a continuum of effect alerts us to some of the difficulties.[107] Our use of quotation from his work presents others: to what extent was political behaviour in influence politics a product of natural inclination or of coercion? When the terminology of influence is subjected to analysis it is apparent that it covers a multitude of social situations and political responses. The attempt to discriminate between these situations and responses has been a major task of this work. To the continuum described by Nossiter must be added the idea of deference, a term which itself describes a continuum of effect in which the stable and affective mode was never totally divorced from the calculative, coercive and unstable manifestation. Influence politics subsumed both modes, and aspects of influence politics are to be differentiated from the rooted deference that was the predominating element in factory politics. Hanham and Pelling have shown how the economic interests of a trade, an occupational group's rights, and a borough's prestige and economic wellbeing could all comprise influence politics.[108]

When the term 'influence' is employed in this generalised sense it is clear that influence politics does describe a very great deal of the later nineteenth-century British political system. While this is important, because the term fails to engage with the central problem of discriminating the nature of political responses it hides as much of the political process as it reveals. This task can only be begun when the procedure of investigation leads from the social to the political. Because the reverse procedure has characterised so much political history, and because labour history has so seldom met the demands of a rigorous analysis of labour process and popular culture, the evidence necessary to attempt an answer to our second general question remains extremely sparse, so that the answers made here must be correspondingly tentative. Of the priority of that question, of the need to evaluate the relationship between urban and labour process and class formation before analysis of the political culture can begin, there can be no doubt. Thus the question 'What is "influence"?' leads us back to the social context of politics and thence to a range of more general and ultimately more difficult and revealing questions concerning the connections between work, popular culture and class formation. Political analysis depends on the discrimination with which these connections are mapped.

Only the guidelines of a perspective on these underlying questions can be set out here. A comparison between the industrial development of the factory North, especially that of Lancashire, and the industry of Britain as a whole reveals how various was the industrial organisation of the later nineteenth century, and how much Lancashire was to the fore of change. In terms of the application of steam machine power, concentration of ownership, size of unit of production, and sophistication in the division of machine labour Lancashire had a claim to leadership among the factory regions of Britain in the period.[109] A good deal of British industry was either at an earlier stage in the development of a factory system, or else, and just as important, was on a different avenue of industrial development. Modern industry incorporated as well as superseded older systems of production, and the transformation of domestic and workshop manufacture played as large a role as did the development of large, machine-based factory industry: the development of modern industry has been described as 'combined and uneven',[110] and clearly many of the mass-production techniques of the twentieth century were prefigured and explored in the handicraft sector of nineteenth-century industry.

Because of this diversity the social changes and attitudes consequent on the consolidation of modern industry were themselves highly diverse, and the political history of other regions differed greatly from that of the North. The social system that the entrenchment of factory production introduced in the North has been described in detail. Lancashire was far advanced on the road that led to modern factory industry, and it is therefore likely that in other industries less advanced on that road the social consequences of modernity were less marked. Because factory industry was consolidated later and less completely in the West Riding, Yorkshire shared only partly in the social system of Lancashire. Though generalisation is difficult, it can be suggested that in terms of social and political demeanour the West Riding was a kind of halfway house between Lancashire and the nation's plurality of factory and non-factory forms of industrial production. If the kinds of attitude seen in Lancashire were more likely in factory regions that had reached or were reaching Lancashire's level of development, the very different political histories shaped by different occupational cultures must not be lost sight of, and the politics of the craft sector will receive their due attention in our final chapter. Nor should the force of the occupational culture be exclusively emphasised: the greatly changed mental climate and ideological context in which modern, mechanised industry further rooted itself in British economic organisation towards the end of the century will also be considered later.

The situation in Yorkshire textiles can be usefully compared not only with the nation but also with European industry. The relatively primitive organisation of West Riding industry produced social and political attitudes that were not only closer to those of industrially diverse Britain but closer also than those of Lancashire to European textiles. Like the West Riding, mechanisation and concentration were slow to advance in the German and French industries, and trade union organisation and institutionalised labour relations were poorly developed.[111] Paternalism seems to have been furthest advanced where factory industry was most developed and labour relations best organised, as was the case in the French textile industry.[112] As in the West Riding of the 1880s, the advance of what textile unionism there was in the German industry was closely associated with political organisation – in Yorkshire the I.L.P. and in Germany the Social Democratic Party. As we have seen,[113] the similarities of class feeling and political protest marking the textile areas of Yorkshire and Europe struck contemporary observers forcibly towards the end of the century.

Thus in Lancashire the early onset of modern factory production produced those consequences we have described: the loss of control over the labour process experienced by the new factory proletarian, the internalisation of the experience of dependence and authority, the concentration on trade union as opposed to political forms of action, and the interaction of labour and urban process that produced the factory-dominated culture in which industrial deference could thrive. In these changes the special role of the family has been suggested. It seems to have served as the agency of those retained, formal status distinctions accommodating factory labour in the social system of modern industry. Whatever the precise nature of this role, the fact that factory work was family work undoubtedly gave cohesion and amplitude to the types of social attitude that emerged after 1850. No other British factory industry was like textiles in this vital respect. In a similar fashion, Lancashire witnessed the convergence of many other characteristics developed beyond a level reached in most other parts of Britain. The Lancashire situation was a product of a combination of factors never precisely reproduced elsewhere, and thus the type of industrial deference found there was probably unmatched elsewhere. These factors will already be apparent: the size of productive unit, family paternalism and personal management, the nature of the textile workforce and of the textile trades, the geography of the factory town, and the relationships between industrial and urban growth and population movement.

Nevertheless, different combinations of the elements that made Lancashire such a special case could obtain elsewhere, and could lead to attitudes not greatly dissimilar to those found there. In other factory industries, but also in non-factory forms of production, a consideration of the industrial and urban circumstances of Lancashire does illuminate the situation in Britain as a whole. The words of G.M. Young opening our discussion of the culture of the factory indicate that Lancashire was not alone in its industrial and social harmony, nor even in its deference.

The articulation of a useful typology of urban and industrial forms can dwell first on the characteristics of urban growth. We have noted already that it is to the industrial towns rather than to the cities that we must look for the kind of environment in which the politics of influence prospered most. It was in the cities that the processes leading to mutual ignorance between the classes were most advanced, and there that a variety of employment within and beyond the factory was most readily available. Particularly in the case of the great Irish populations of cities like Manchester and Liverpool, population movement into and within the cities involved the kind of communal instability unfavourable to the consolidation of a factory neighbourhood culture. Democracy was to arrive in the towns before the social processes at work in the cities reached them. Thus the climate of the cities was unfavourable to social and political influence, so that cities like Liverpool, Leeds and Manchester receive relatively little attention in this study. The employment structure and demographic patterns of Liverpool, in particular, set it outside the general Lancashire experience. Nonetheless, it was the precise configuration of industry and neighbourhood that mattered, and not urban size alone. The industrial enclave would have existed happily within the city, as in Manchester and Leeds; and across the water from Lancashire, Guinnesses in Dublin and the large Protestant engineering and shipbuilding works of Belfast recommend themselves for consideration.

The type of industry and the social outlook engendered by its work experience can be considered next. Coal is a good example of how complex was the interplay of work, society and politics. Though the work-life of the miner was greatly different to the factory worker, the industry indicates that it was not in factory industry alone that attitudes developed to peak in Lancashire could find many correspondences. The skills and dangers of mining, and the collier's freedom from supervisory authority, bred an independence and solidarity in the industry represented in the work practices and customs of miners throughout the country.[114] But these qualities could be muted as well as accentuated by the life above ground. In isolated mining villages where the owners were neither resident nor concerned, mining produced perhaps the most militant of all nineteenth-century workers. In other such towns and villages where employers or their managers were resident, locally involved and paternalist, the situation could be very different. Work experience, urban ecology, and styles of ownership and management all have to be taken into consideration.

Durham produced both the 'red village' and the dutiful miner,[115] though in suggesting that the latter should have his place in an historical record so far monopolised by his militant counterpart, it is not only R. Moore's work on the paternalist industry of Durham's Deerness valley that comes to mind.[116] Though it is the degree to which the towns were really more like villages than cities that is what matters, and has so often been obscured, the capacity for control and influence in the small industrial towns and villages was greater still. The capacity to define and delimit the social experience of the worker earlier referred to as the employers' social hegemony could be almost as marked in coal as in textiles, especially in situations of geographical isolation. Tom Jones's description of his boyhood and youth in South Wales is particularly revealing.[117] The local coal and iron firm in Rhymney employed 90 per cent of the town's workers, translating this potential for influence into domination over the town: the shop, the brewery, the pub, the doctor and the vicar were all under the control of a resident managerial class itself fully involved in the life of the town. The town was compressed into a long narrow valley, its geography contributing to the possibility of domination. Though the family ownership and control of the North was not present, the proxy paternalism of local managers was an effective substitute.

Jones described a society without what he called an 'economic sense' and 'class consciousness':

Standing over against the miner's miner's home life in the old days were

two authorities – the minister of religion and the employer of labour, and
for both there was usually a real respect. The miner was contented because
his responsibilities were limited and clearly defined. What was asked of
him he did.[118]

When religion and work overlapped, religion could be of great
importance in cementing the authority system of the old industrial
order. Moore's work on Durham points to this, and Jones was
quick to see one fundamental difference between the nineteenth
century and the twentieth: 'The difference between this generation of working-men and the men who were in their maturity
at the turn of the century lies just here: in the difference between
a primarily political and a primarily religious consciousness.'[119]
Religion was often an aspect of the inturned, almost hermetic,
community culture upon which the employers' economic power
capitalised and elaborated. The degree to which so much of
later nineteenth-century industrial society was like this, and the
degree to which employers translated this potential into industrial
deference has not hitherto been properly appreciated. Jones's
own words got to the nub of the matter – when men knew where
they stood they did what they were asked.

The waning of religion and the almost simultaneous rise of
socialism contributed much to the distintegration of the old
order: at the end of this work it will be seen how both were part
of a larger process of social change opening society out and thus
destroying the monopoly on people's outlook that the closed
culture of the factory had enjoyed.[120] It can be suggested that it
was less as a received ideology and more as an abrasive, disruptive
outside influence that socialism took its greatest popular effect.
This capacity to brush the scales from men's eyes gave it that
messianic missionary quality so often noted. As Jones described
South Wales: 'During this crusading period Socialism swept
through the valleys like a new religion, and young men asked one
another, Are you a Socialist? in the same tone as a Salvationist
asks, Are you saved? In one generation the outlook of the miners
was transformed.[121] Writing in 1932 Jones described the larger
change: 'The servility and civility of the eighties gradually
gave way to the arrogance of twenty years ago ... '[122]

In this transformation the resurgence of trade unionism from
the 1880s played a major role. The comparison with West Riding
industry again strongly suggests itself: in industries where trade
unionism was not strongly rooted, the confluence of socialism
and trade unionism towards the end of the century resulted in
a quicker and more complete breakthrough to class politics than

in Lancashire, where the union was the uniquely representative working-class institution, and its centrality in popular culture deeply affected the history of labour relations and thus the nature of the class consciousness which sprang from the work situation. Such comparisons must however be made in the light of the diversity that obtained not only between the British regions but within them as well. A central element in this diversity was the tradition of working-class ideology and organisation, and any typology of industrial and urban forms must include this element. The experience of particular industrial *milieux* was refracted through the tradition of working class political, trade union and self-help organisation. Thus the trade union in one industry or trade could exert a profoundly different effect from that in others, and this difference was a consequence not only of the shaping power of particular industrial environments but of living traditions as well.

Nowhere were traditions of political and industrial organisation more potent than in South Wales, and it is with a recognition that this was so that attention is again directed to the region. For, if the effectiveness of paternalist influence can be discerned in this most inhospitable climate, then it seems likely that in the nation at large it was not without effect too. Though mining was not outside the sphere of industrial feudalism, its chief effect was always to be found in the large factory. This could be the case in iron and engineering, though the breakdown of craft autonomy and control had not reached the level found in textiles at mid-century. Iron and engineering factories have figured in our description of Northern factory culture and factory politics, especially where they were large, long-established, and under paternalist, family control. Nossiter has shown the influence possible in the iron industry of the North-East, especially in a company town like Darlington.[123] The large, paternalist iron firm played a major role in the economic development of South Wales, where in towns like Merthyr Tydfil and Aberdare industry permeated the life of the communities that had grown up around it. Tom Jones drew a distinction between industrial relations in coal, differing markedly between pit and pit, and the 'unruffled peace of the tinplate and metallurgical industries'.[124] It was to the old, paternalist firms that much of this peace could be ascribed, and it was on this peace that industrial feudalism thrived.

The advent of the mass electorate in the 1860s saw the confluence of a powerful working-class radicalism and middle-class Liberalism in the common assault on the privilege of an English Establishment.[125] Though class feeling was powerful, a common

Welshness and Nonconformity united the classes, and this unity involved many of the industrialists. This sort of bond, especially when it was subject to the qualifications of a political alliance in which the class constituent was important, is not to be confused with the deep-seated, communal influence exerted in the factory North. Neverthless, it could work with the grain of the structural elements underlying this kind of influence.

Whatever the situation on the Welsh side of the fence, behind the eruption of class feeling in 1868 the lineaments of industrial feudalism are nonetheless discernible in the politics of South Wales iron.[126] Industrial paternalism was strong after 1868 and it is unlikely that the response to it was solely a matter of coercion. The politics of religion and of class should not be allowed altogether to obscure a persistent and powerful theme in the history of the valleys. The evidence of the *Morning Chronicle* correspondant in the area is not to be ignored.[127] At mid-century the popularity of the founding fathers of South Wales iron – the Guests, the Crawshays and the Forthergills – was considerable enough to cancel much of the effect of their non-local origins and religion. By 1850 their paternalism was sufficiently ramified in the communal hinterland of industry to make their influence a dangerous adversary to the radicalism of the region in the fight for the allegiance of their workpeople. As in Lancashire, this kind of identification with, and permeation of, the locale could not have amounted only to a matter of coercion and dependence.

The association of industry in a town with one or a few large firms was fairly common in the second half of the century. As in South Wales, where industry was created *de novo*, the employers were almost as fully involved in the growth of the town as in the industry which gave birth to the town. Examples that come to mind are Jarrow, Hartlepools, Birkenhead and Barrow, and smaller centres like Seaham and Goole. Towns like St Helens and Middlesborough were the result of economic growth later in the century. The possibilities for employer influence in boom towns like St Helens were always immense, in this case the Pilkington family establishing a benevolent despotism that has reached into the present day.[128] The railway towns were another species of the company town. Above all in Crewe, where industry was *in situ* and the company responsible for the childhood and adolescence of the town, the social influence of the limited company could be immense.[129] Elsewhere, the military-bureaucratic model of paternalism imposed by the nature of the industry, and seen across the Channel in the iron industries of Europe, was never as successful as the personal, family paternalism that characterised so much British industry. The fundamental distinction between private and limited company ownership is again suggested. What mattered about nineteenth-century industry, however, was not so much the company town but the capacity of the ordinary family firm to reproduce the social effect of the company town within the environs of the large town. Other towns that come to mind in this respect are Norwich, Stirling, Lincoln and Macclesfield.[130]

Thus the myriad of 'company towns' within the large towns, or in another sense the congeries of 'urban villages', represented a distinct and long-lasting stage in nineteenth-century urban and industrial growth. Because the widespread representativeness and fundamental importance of this development have not been recognised, the dimensions of employer power and influence in the later-nineteenth century have not been understood. Extrapolation from the characteristics of the Lancashire situation suggests that elements developed to an extreme there were nevertheless to be found at different levels and in different combinations elsewhere. The Northern example indicates a necessary respect for the concrete particular and for the diversity of towns and regions. Nevertheless, this brief and selective survey of the nation begins to show that the similarities of culture and attitude in industrial Britain were as important as the differences. Only when these similarities are further explored will the new social history of politics be possible.

Summary

The political system that was built upon the culture of the factory is considered here. A recognition that the factory was at the centre of political life suggests a major revision of the notion that the third quarter of the century saw the inevitable triumph of the politics of individualist, democratic opinion. The centrality of the factory voting bloc is established by the use of pollbooks, and the composition of the electorate is examined by the same means. Though the autonomous play of political motive among factory workers is recognised at the limited level at which it operated, and the very important occupational and political diversity of the factory towns is given its place, the factory is nonetheless seen to have dominated urban political life in a direct and unmediated manner.

This refutation of Whiggery demands the detailed reconstitution of the social words of the voters and non-voters: the long history of the factory in politics is narrated (one stretching long before and long after the Second Reform Act and the institution of electoral secrecy in 1872); and the pervasiveness of the political workplace is itemised by means of a detailed account of Blackburn politics, and of the political history of particular factories in a variety of towns. Municipal and parliamentary results, but especially parliamentary pollbooks are used: they indicate the influence of factories over the entire occupational structure of locales, point to the limited importance of coercion, and help indicate the limited operation of a 'labour aristocracy' in popular politics.

The second section considers the re-assessment of British politics in the period that this explication of the factory politics of the North gives rise to. Given that influence politics characterised the most urban and industrial part of England, and that industry and the town are invariably construed as the hallmarks of a modernity defined as the individualist politics of opinion, the necessity of a re-assessment will be apparent. It is clear that the breadth, depth and longevity of influence politics were far greater than is commonly realised, especially when our categorisation rests content with the term 'influence', as opposed to the more positive, inward and elusive attitudes we have analysed in the factory North under the name of deference. The necessity of understanding society and politics as they were rather than as the hindsight of posterity would have us believe they were in fact leads to a more responsive and comprehensive account of the contemporary political culture, and in chapter 8 the business of re-assessment begun here is taken further in terms of the North.

The second and major concern is to establish the relevance to the nation at large of the link between labour and urban process, and political culture, established for the factory North. Discriminating the nature of the political response, and thus penetrating the smoke-screen that surrounds the term 'influence', requires the interpretation of politics in the light of industrial structure and culture. The work that would enable national comparisons to be drawn is not always to hand, though certain broad correspondences can be suggested. Lancashire was in the van of industrial change and the kind of society and politics produced by its highly developed factory system were not seen in other less developed areas. Nonetheless, and the West Riding and European textile industries provide a useful comparison, in areas approaching the Lancashire mode of production approximations to the Lancashire instance would have obtained in this period. However, the argument from the Lancashire example is one not solely dependent on the proletarianisation attendant upon advances in mechanisation and the division of labour:

Lancashire was an example of the convergence of a great range of factors, the presence and particular combinations of which were not precisely duplicated elsewhere. But a number of these industrial and social characteristics were present elsewhere, and were often combined in such a way as to make the Lancashire example of prime importance for an understanding of later Victorian society and politics. In particular, the special configuration of industry and the town seen in Lancashire is urged as of widespread significance: the value of interpreting the industrial town as a congeries of urban villages, of company towns within the town as it were, is especially clear. The wide variety of elements making up any typology of industrial and urban forms is recognised, and starting from the premise of Lancashire's difference the conclusion that Lancashire was structurally related to British society and politics is drawn.

Notes

1. W.A. Abram, 'Social conditions and political prospects of the Lancashire workman', *Fortnightly Review*, Oct. 1868, p. 439.
2. D.C. Moore, 'Social structure, political structure and public opinion in mid-Victorian England', in R. Robson, ed, *Ideas and Institutions of Victorian England* (1967), esp. pp. 45–6, 56–7; and *The Politics of Deference* (Hassocks and New York 1976), ch. 10.
3. P. Joyce, 'The factory politics of Lancashire in the later nineteenth century', *Historical Journal*, **18**, no. 3 (1975), pp. 534–5.
4. E.g. P.F. Clarke, 'Electoral sociology of modern Britain', *History*, **52**, no. 189, Feb. 1972, p. 33; and *Lancashire and the New Liberalism* (Cambridge 1971), ch. 5.
5. Abram, *loc. cit.* p. 437.
6. *Ibid.* p. 437.
7. Computed from Blackburn Register of Electors 1868–69, marked with the vote and canvass for the whole constituency. Two matching copies, 324.8024 used. Blackburn Public Library.
8. See above, p. 90.
9. F. Engels to K. Marx, Nov. 18 1868, *K. Marx and F. Engels on Britain* (Moscow 1953, London 1954), pp. 499–500.
10. F. Harrison, 'The Conservative reaction', *Fortnightly Review*, March 1874, pp. 303–4.
11. Abram, *loc. cit.* p. 437.
12. *Blackburn Times*, 1 Nov. 1873 (leader).
13. Cited above, p. 90.
14. *Cotton Factory Times*, 5, 12, 19 Oct. 1900; see also *ibid.*, 28 Sept. 1900.
15. For full details see Joyce, *loc. cit.* pp. 533–41. For the occupational composition of the 1868 Bury electorate see Appendix below.
16. Bury 1865, 1868 and Blackburn 1865 pollbooks in respective

public libraries. Blackburn 1865 canvass in Lancashire County Record Office (L.C.R.O.), Preston, DDX 223, Box 5, 'Analysis of the Register for the year 1864–5'.

17. *Blackburn Standard*, 2 Oct. 1875.
18. *Blackburn Times*, 9 Aug. 1892.
19. *Blackburn Standard*, 9 July 1892.
20. *Bury Guardian*, 31 Jan. 1874.
21. *Ibid.* 31 Oct. 21, 28 Nov. 1885.
22. For ward vote see W.W. Bean, *The Parliamentary Representation of the Six Northern Counties* (Hull 1890), p. 794. The Bradford 1868 pollbook is in the Institute of Historical Research, Univ. of London.
23. See distribution of Preston pre-Reform vote in L.C.R.O., DD Pr/131/31 and 39.
24. 1868 pollbook in Preston Public Library.
25. *Oldham Standard*, 21 Nov. 1868, 7 Feb. 1874. The Oldham 1868 pollbook is in the I.H.R., Univ. of London. It contains no addresses for the voters.
26. R.P. Cook, 'Political élites and electoral politics in late nineteenth-Century Burnley' (Lancaster Univ. M.A. 1974), ch. 5.
27. *Blackburn Standard*, 25 Oct. 1879.
28. *Blackburn Times*, 16, 30 Oct. 1886.
29. *Preston Chronicle*, 3 Nov. 1860; *Blackburn Times*, 1 Nov. 1879.
30. *BS*, 30 Oct. 1875.
31. *Ashton Reporter*, 6 Nov. 1869.
32. *Ibid.*, Nov. 1879, 1880.
33. See Appendix.
34. Above, pp. 189–90.
35. See above, pp. 63–4.
36. *Northern Star*, 10 Nov. 1838 (at Preston).
37. G.L. Molesworth, *Life of John Edward Nassau Molesworth* (1915), pp. 58–61.
38. *Blackburn Standard*, 22 Sept. 1852.
39. *Preston Chronicle*, 10 Sept. 1853.
40. *Blackburn Times*, 7 Jan. 1865 (leader).
41. *Ibid.*, 8 July 1865.
42. *Ibid.*, 2 Jan. 1867.
43. *Blackburn Standard*, 18 July, 28 Oct. 1868.
44. J.G. Shaw, *Life of William Gregson* (Blackburn 1891), p. 257.
45. *Blackburn Times*, 11, 18 Sept. 1875.
46. *Preston Chronicle*, 4 June 1853.
47. S. Clarke, *Clitheroe in its Railway Days* (Clitheroe 1900), p. 68, and p. 67.
48. See account of J. and J. Craven in *Industries of Yorkshire*, Pt I (1890).
49. *Huddersfield Daily Examiner*, 29 Jan. 1874; *Halifax Courier*, 27 Mar. 1880.
50. D.G. Wright, 'Politics and opinion in nineteenth-century Bradford,

236   *Work, Society and Politics*

1832–1880' (Leeds Univ. Ph.D. 1966), p. 828.
51. See e.g. *Bolton Chronicle*, 27 Aug. 1859.
52. *Ashton Reporter*, 6, 20 Mar. 1869.
53. *Ibid.*, 3 Apr., 8 May 1869.
54. For other examples see *Ashton Standard*, 2 July 1870, 12 July 1884; *Ashton News*, 15 Apr. 1871; *Ashton Reporter*, 31 Oct. 1868; *Blackburn Standard*, 28 Feb. 1880.
55. *Ashton Reporter*, 1, 8 May 1880.
56. *Preston Chronicle*, 4, 11 Jan. 1851; *Bolton Chronicle*, 13 Dec. 1859.
57. K. Tiller, 'Working-class attitudes and organisation in three industrial towns' (Birmingham Univ. Ph.D. 1975), ch. 8.
58. *Wigan Comet*, 23 July 1892.
59. B. Wilson, *The Struggles of an Old Chartist* (Halifax 1887), p. 31.
60. Tiller, *op. cit.* pp. 411–12.
61. *Fortunes Made in Business*, Vol. 1 (1884), pp. 117–18.
62. Wright, *op. cit.* pp. 740–1.
63. *Ibid.* pp. 771–2.
64. 'A lay of the Bradford election of October 1867', Bradford Public Library Election Ephemera Collection; *Bradford Review*, 24 Oct., and 5 to 11 Nov. 1868.
65. See above, p. 163.
66. For further information see P. Joyce, 'Popular Toryism in Lancashire, 1860–1890' (Oxford D.Phil. 1975), pp. 106–8.
67. *Blackburn Standard*, 1 May 1886.
68. Joyce, 'Popular Toryism . . . ' pp. 250–1 (information on 'Hornbyism' and the Thompsons in *Blackburn Times*, 28 Nov. 1874, 13 Mar. 1875, 26 Jan. 1889, 26 July 1902, 27 June 1908; *Blackburn Weekly Telegraph*, 7 Oct. 1899).
69. *Blackburn Times*, 14 Feb. 1878 (leader).
70. *Ibid.*, 17 Dec. 1927.
71. *Ibid.*, 31 Oct. 1868.
72. 1 May 1886.
73. See above, pp. 16–22, 33–5.
74. Cook, *op. cit.* ch. 2.
75. For employer involvement in a political club (Trinity Conservative), see *Blackburn Standard*, 29 Apr. 1868; for Liberal employers as ward chairmen, *Ashton Reporter*, 1 Aug. 1868, *Ashton Standard*, 12 Nov. 1870.
76. J. Vincent, *The Formation of the Liberal Party 1857–1868* (1966), p. 94, also pp. 82–96.
77. *Ashton Standard*, 8 Nov. 1879. See also the Ashton Public Library broadside and cartoon collection for reiteration of the 'screw' charge in elections after 1868. For the belief in intimidation where none was intended, election reports, *Oldham Chronicle*, 21 Nov. 1868, and H.J. Hanham, *Elections and Party Management* (1959), p. 84.
78. *Ibid.* pp. 77–9, 81–2; Select Committee on Parliamentary and Municipal Elections, *P.P.* 1868–9, VIII (352), e.g. evidence on

Bolton and Warrington, pp. 69–82, 570–9.
79. Reform League Reports, Bishopsgate Institute, London.
80. *Blackburn Times*, 14 May 1859; *Blackburn Standard*, 31 Aug. 1864, for the shopocracy under the thumb of 'Mr This and Mr That'; *P.P.* 1868–9, VIII (352), Qs. 2761–83 (Ashton tradesmen); Qs. 2525–32, *Ashton Reporter*, 2 Jan. 1869 (both on the Corporation; but see also Stalybridge Liberal rebuttal, Qs. 3519–21, 3575, 3603–10); for employer-workman coercion see esp. Qs. 2536, 2692–7, 2564–79 (on Ashton Liberal masters).
81. *P.P.* 1868–9, VIII (352), Qs. 2276–8; see also Q. 2321, 2441–2500; for further information on duration of coercion see also, *Ashton Standard*, 14 Apr. 1866, *Blackburn Times*, 1 May 1869 (letter columns).
82. On 1868 in Blackburn see H.J. Hanham, *op. cit.* p. 83; *P.P.* 1868–9, (352), pp. 586–7; J.C. Lowe, 'The Tory triumph of 1868 in Blackburn and in Lancashire', *Historical Journal*, 12 (1969); and for a Tory version of events see Blackburn correspondent's reports in *Manchester Courier*, 6, 10 Nov. 1868.
83. *Blackburn Times*, 31 Oct. 1868.
84. Thompson and Vigne Lancashire Int, 122 ('Politics').
85. Clarke, *op. cit.* p. 139; Wigan broadside collection no. 33, March 1880 (Wigan Public Library); Wigan Election Petition Evidence, *P.P.* LXXIV (207), 299.
86. *Blackburn Times*, 24 Oct. 1885; *Blackburn Weekly Telegraph*, 6 Oct. 1900.
87. *Blackburn Times*, 15 Oct. 1898.
88. Thompson and Vigne West Riding Int. 181 ('Work'), 339 ('Politics').
89. For the Keighley minority see Ints 176, 180, 181, 206 ('Politics'), but see also Int. 282 ('Work' and 'Community and Class'); for the Lancs. minority see esp. Ints 32, 47, 86, 87, 131, 135 ('Politics').
90. *Ibid.*, West Riding, no. 176 ('Politics').
91. *P.P.* 1868–9, VIII (352), Qs. 10730, 10718, 10724, and pp. 586–7.
92. *Ibid.* Q. 10720.
93. *Manchester Daily Examiner and Times*, 24 Nov. 1868 (Blackburn report).
94. L.C.R.O., Preston, DDX 223 (Box 5).
95. *Blackburn Times*, 20 July 1864.
96. *Ashton News*, 25 Mar. 1871.
97. *P.P.* 1868–9, VIII (352) pp. 87, 94, 99, 140 (but see also pp. 157–8); pp. 77, 112–13, 121–2, 577–8.
98. *Ibid.* pp. 128, 136, 151–2, 183.
99. *Ibid.* Q. 2306.
100. *Ibid.* Qs 3096–8.

SOME BRITISH COMPARISONS
101. D.C. Moore, *The Politics of Deference: a study of the mid-nineteenth-century English political system* (Hassocks 1976).
102. R. Moore, *Pitmen, Preachers and Politics* (Cambridge 1974).

T.J. Nossiter, *Influence, Opinion and Political Idioms in Reformed England: case studies from the North-east 1832–1874* (Hassocks 1975).

103. *Ibid.* p. 94, see also pp. 95, 202–3. For the orthodox view restated see D. Fraser, *Urban Politics in Victorian England* (Leicester 1976). Unfortunately, Fraser ignores the society of the voters, and underestimates the importance of the non-voters before 1867 and the mass electorate after. To dismiss the working class as without class consciousness is as egregious an error as to magnify that consciousness into the central element in politics.

104. H.J. Hanham, *Elections and Party Management. Politics in the time of Disraeli and Gladstone* (1959), Pt 1, esp. chs 1–4.

105. P. Thompson, *Socialists, Liberals and Labour* (1967), pp. 73–4, 85–9; H. Pelling, *Social Geography of British Elections, 1885–1910* (1967), pp. 39, 45, 46, 48, 50–1, 53; G. Stedman Jones, *Outcast London* (1971), p. 269, and 'Working-class culture and working-class politics in London, 1870–1900', *Journal of Social History*, 7, no. 4, Summer 1974. pp. 482–3.

106. P.F. Clarke, *Lancashire and the New Liberalism* (Cambridge 1971); also 'Electoral sociology of modern Britain;, *History*, 57, no. 189, Feb. 1972.

107. Nossiter, *op. cit.* ch. 12.

108. Pelling, *op. cit.* pp. 40, 44–5, 49, 50, 51, 52; Hanham, *op. cit.* pp. 59–62, 63, 70.

109. R. Samuel, 'The workshop of the world: steam power and hand technology in mid-Victorian Britain', *History Workshop*, no. 3, Spring 1977.

110. *Ibid.* pp. 57–60.

111. W.O. Henderson, 'The labour force in the textile industries', *Archiv für Sozialgeschichte*, 16, 1976.

112. T. Zeldin, *France 1848–1945* (Oxford 1973), Vol. 1, pp. 63–8, 260–4.

113. See above, p. 76.

114. K. Burgess, *The Origins of British Industrial Relations* (1975), ch. III.

115. On the militancy of the Durham miners, Nossiter, *op. cit.* chs 5, 6.

116. Moore, *op. cit.*

117. T. Jones, 'The life of the people', in *Fifty Years: memories and contrasts 1882–1932* (1932), foreword by G.M. Trevelyan.

118. *Ibid.* pp. 186, 180.

119. *Ibid.* p. 186.

120. See below, pp. 335–40.

121. T. Jones, *loc. cit.* p. 182.

122. *Ibid.* p. 185.

123. Nossiter, *op. cit.* ch. 8.

124. T. Jones, *loc. cit.* p. 184.

125. K. O. Morgan, *Wales in British Politics 1868–1922* (Cardiff 1963), chs 1, 2; I.G. Jones, 'The election of 1868 in Merthyr Tydfil: a

study of the politics of an industrial borough in the mid-nineteenth century', *Journal of Modern History*, **33**, no. 3, Sept. 1961, and 'The Merthyr of Henry Richard' in G. Williams, ed., *Merthyr Politics: the making of a working-class tradition* (Cardiff 1966).

126. Morgan, *op. cit.* p. 39 (In 1874 'Political nonconformity and industrial paternalism were still the most important factors in the political structure of the valleys ... '); I.G. Jones, 'The election of 1868 ... ' pp. 274, 283–5, and 'The Merthyr of Henry Richerd', pp. 55–6.

127. P.E. Razzell and R.W. Wainwright, eds, *The Victorian Working Class. Selections from letters to the 'Morning Chronicle'* (1973), pp. 256, 258–64.

128. T.C. Barker and J.R. Harris, *A Merseyside Town in the Industrial Revolution: St Helens 1750–1900* (Liverpool 1954).

129. W.H. Chaloner, *The Social and Economic Development of Crewe 1780–1923* (Manchester 1950); see also Hanham, *op. cit.* pp. 85–90.

130. *Ibid.* pp. 71, 74–8.

7
RELIGION AND POLITICS

Popular politics in the second half of the nineteenth century present at first sight a striking paradox: for the great majority of the working class attachment to the institutions and dogmas of organised religion was informal, often vestigial, yet the conflict of religious denominations was as near the centre of political life as any other matter. In explaining the compatibility of religious apathy and political sectarianism the role of religion in articulating the loyalties of the factory has already been put forward.[1] This seeming incongruity applied to the political culture and the electorate of the North as a whole. The present discussion will explore some of the diverse influences which combined to make the equation of religion and politics perhaps the most revealing in the politics of the godly and of the 'indifferent' alike.

Contemporary observers, new to Lancashire but aware of its nationwide reputation for sectarian bitterness, noted with some surprise this combination of political strife, religious indifference in the many, and a certain tolerance and flexibility in the everyday affairs of the different denominations and sects.[2] This degree of amiability characterised the religion of those outside the working class as well, though the higher up the social scale opinion was sought by the parliamentary enquirers of the 1860s the more keenly was denominational rivalry felt, especially among those middle-class Dissenters who established their own kingdom of pedagogic righteousness.[3] Nevertheless, if the denominational links of the majority of people were informal, and their loyalties often tenuous and diffuse, both were of sufficient strength to be of great importance in politics. At election times these persistent subterranean allegiances were magnified and excited into often unreasoning and violent sectarian feeling.[4] However nominal it was, a man's religion was the surest guide to his politics.

The work of Peter Clarke indicates that it was 'religion in a social sense' which underpinned the 'cultural' politics of Lancashire.[5] With this notion of religion spilling over beyond the congregation into the lives of those only informally connected with organised religion there is no essential disagreement here, aside from the considerable proviso that for the factory populations

240

the conflict of church and chapel was itself an expression of allegiances formed at the level of the factory and its environment. In the first section of this chapter the impact of organised religion will be traced outwards from the immediate circle of the congregation in order to explore the extent to which religion invested the social worlds that defined politics. It was not that the congregation itself, as the directing force in political argument and organisation, did not have a profound impact on politics ; when the 1851 religious census is examined for those who did attend, rather than for those who did not (the usual direction of historal enquiry), the influence of organised religion is seen to have been considerably more significant than is often supposed, and of an altogether different character from the nominal Christianity of the twentieth century.

What lent special urgency to the residual denominational allegiance of the indifferent mass of the population was the presence of a large Irish Catholic minority, above all in Lancashire. The popular Protestantism of Lancashire forms the second main object of enquiry in what follows. Though ethnic tension seems to have been the primary constituent in this Protestantism, the phenomenon displayed several different aspects. These were often combined with anti-Irish feeling, but were not always reducible to it. Protestantism articulated a widespread popular dislike for the narrowness and restrictiveness of Nonconformity. It also took the form of a Tory populism that sometimes capitalised on this opposition of temper, combining it with elements of class feeling that were of special effect in certain localities and at certain times. Such a time of acute social stress was the cotton famine,[6] and such a locality the south-east of the county.

The circumstances that made Ashton and Stalybridge in particular such special cases were noted earlier,[7] the presence of a poorly paid and badly unionised weaving sector and the influence of exceptional local leaders being of special local significance. Men like Joseph Reyner Stephens, aided by local Evangelical clergymen, gave a Tory bent to a legacy of independent political feeling that was perhaps stronger in these two former strongholds of Chartism and popular protest than was elsewhere the case in Lancashire. Despite its diversion away from old-fashioned *laissez faire*, the continuing dominance of the Liberal-Nonconformist millowning interest into the third quarter of the century also did something to keep antagonisms alive that were fading fast elsewhere in Lancashire, though not of course in much of the West Riding. Exceptional though the two towns were, an examination of political life in them helps locate an underlying class identification, and the remnants of an independent tradition in politics, that were nowhere ever completely transformed into industrial deference and pro-employer politics. Yet, as the account will show, Protestantism seems to have called most directly to the most insulted and injured, and these were far more often the labouring poor outside rather than inside the factory. What makes the phenomenon so interesting however, is that it spoke with only a little less urgency to the prejudices of all of society, both high and low. Both the ethnic and populist elements in Protestantism united society in the same moment as they divided it. The richness of social detail revealed by popular Protestantism make it perhaps the most illuminating of all the expressions of religion in politics.

The institutions and ideas of religion supplied most of the form and vocabulary of popular politics in the period. The degree to which religion dictated party preference is apparent from W.A. Abram's description of what he called the 'politico-religious alignments' of the average factory town:

On the side of Toryism:
1. Churchmen by conviction, sentiment and tradition
2. Minority of methodists, and small minority of other Nonconformists
3. So many of the Indifferents as may be moved thitherward by secular convictions or interests

On the side of Liberalism:
1. A small party of Liberal Churchmen
2. Dissenters of all sects with few exceptions
3. Vast majority of all Methodists
4. Roman Catholics, almost without exception
5. Free-Thinkers
6. Indifferents, not otherwise influenced ...

... the issue of this appeal will hinge mainly upon the action of the class of Indifferents, who compose ... a moiety of the operative population.[8]

The issues and the electioneering that gave these alignments form were religious in character. Church and chapel clerics, school-rooms, bands, choirs and Sunday school teachers and scholars, were an integral part of most election campaigns. The pressure groups that mattered were denominational ones. Even ostensibly political organisation might sometimes grow out of denominational institutions, as was the case in the transformation of church mutual improvement societies and Protestant halls into Tory clubs, and chapel societies into Liberal ones.[9] The clergy and the congregation shaped the whole character of politics,

providing much of the larger language of political exhortation
and identity.

Religion left a deep impression on the 'working-class poli-
ticans' themselves. The following is a Wigan radical's description
of the Tory activists, though the same association of religion and
politics could be found for just as many Liberal party workers:
'The Tories have many excellent and able men among the
working-class politicians ... they have entered the political
temple through the ecclesiastical gate. They are Tories because
they are Churchmen and anti-Papists. Their best men belong
to the Orange Societies or some of the Church Associations.'[10]
The writer felt that Tory success owed much to the party's
connection with 'the church, the school, the workshop, the
various (religious) societies and associations', 'an agency in
capable communication with the meanest electors'. In such
ways did religion in politics become the stuff of political partisanship. The degree to which sectarianism entered into the political
emotions of the people at large is reflected in the following, an
attack by 'Dickie' Edmundson on the Radicals, delivered to the
men of Blackburn's Bank Top Conservative Club in 1868.
'If they had been heathens they could not have conducted
themselves worse, they forgot to sing the National Anthem,
and they did not open the meeting with a prayer. ... Let not
the cry be "What are your politics" – but, "What do you intend
to do with regard to the Church". (Applause) Let us hear nothing
else but that.'[11]
The Bank Top Club oath began, 'I, being sensible of the blessings
this country has enjoyed under a Protestant government ... '.
It is to the social force of religion-pervasive, informal, and often
entirely unconnected with religion as a system of beliefs and
practices – that we shall first turn in the attempt to explain the
peculiar strength of religion in politics.

The impact of organised religion

1 CHURCH AND SCHOOL

The most accessible indication of popular response to organised
religion is the attendance at public worship measured by the 1851
Religious Census.[12] Nonconformity increased in strength west-
ward from Liverpool to Leeds, and Catholicism decreased in
strength. This disposition of denominational strengths corresponded closely with the disposition of party strengths. The
calculation of individual attenders, still more of 'the worshipping
community' at large, remains a matter of guesswork. Perhaps the

most reasonable method would be to take the figure of two-thirds of all attenders as a guide to individual attendance.[13] Some account should however be taken of the proportion of the population unable to attend at any time on a Sunday, and in Table 7 half of Horace Mann's figure of 30 per cent has been taken, so that two-thirds of the total attendance figure is expressed as a percentage of 85 per cent of the total population.[14] Any generosity of estimate is counteracted by the fact that a number of places of worship, especially Anglican ones, returned no attendance figure at all.

TABLE 7
Religious attendance, Lancashire
and Yorkshire boroughs, 1851

	%		%
Ashton	36	Salford	30
Blackburn	30	Stockport	34
Bolton	29	Warrington	46
Bury	35	Wigan	40
Liverpool	35		
Manchester	28	Bradford	34
Oldham	26	Halifax	36
Preston	20	Huddersfield	46
Rochdale	40	Leeds	37

Attendances in some of the industrialised urban registration districts were higher than in some of the smaller towns. If in both settings attendance was swollen by the large number of afternoon Sunday school scholars, the relationship between increased town size and decreased religious attendance is clear enough. The big factory towns of Blackburn, Oldham, Preston and Bolton were only a little less centres of indifference than the cities, the Manchester and Liverpool attendance figures being inflated by the large Roman Catholic element. Attendance in the strongly Nonconformist West Riding was more significant than in Lancashire.

It seems likely that the great majority of attenders were from the upper levels of society. Taking the non-manual sector of the population as 20 per cent, and assuming that *all* in this sector attended, then the range of manual worker attendance would have varied between less than 10 per cent in Oldham, 10–15 per cent in Blackburn and Bolton, around 20 per cent in Ashton and 25 per cent in Rochdale and Huddersfield. Though by twentieth-century standards these figures are striking, particularly in the smaller towns, the general conclusion is undoubted: the great majority of the working class went nowhere, and were not directly influenced by church or chapel. Information on the situation after 1851 is scanty, figures for 1882 suggesting that attendance levels may only just have been maintained.[15] In 1880 the Blackburn clergy were preaching on the theme of why the masses did not go to church, eighty out of every hundred then being non-attenders.[16]

Attendance is however only the beginning of an understanding of the churches' influence. The indifference or latitudinarianism that characterised popular attitudes was subject to the constant proselytisation of the day schools, both Anglican and Non-conformist. The religion the schools brought into people's lives was often bitter and aggressive. Robert Robert's assessment of the education the Anglican schools offered is borne out by the words of Joseph Howes, a Liberal political lecturer: 'The only education I ever received was in a Church of England day school where I was taught to stamp my feet, clap my hands, sing God Save the Queen, repeat the catechism, and I was sent out into the world unable to write my name.'[17]

The voluntary school system mattered in Lancashire as nowhere else in England. Education was a staple of political conflict at all levels, the School Board elections themselves being fought out on unashamedly party lines. The sectarian rivalry that permeated the building and management of schools, seen in the account of employer involvement in education, marked the entire provision of schooling. Clarke has shown for the late nineteenth century the close connection between Anglican day school predominance and Tory voting.[18] Something of the substance of this is conveyed by the experience of a Keighley couple: the husband went to a church school and was a Tory; the wife to a Board school, retaining her Liberal sympaties until marriage when she quietly adopted her husband's colours.[19]

Within the community the parson often held an authoritative position, not only as another version of the 'gentleman',[20] but also as one focus of community identification within the town. Even when the denominational attachment was nominal only, the church and the schoolroom imparted their character to the growing suburbs; the effects of a 'laborious clergy', supported often by small groups of working men, doing much to give religion a good name.[21] As centres of social activity as well as of worship, the influence of the church and chapel would have been felt far beyond the circle of the congregation alone. Bishop Knox remarked on this kind of loyalty in describing a church worthy who never entered the church but was indignant at the charge that she was not a churchwoman after twenty years of washing up after the Sunday school teas.[22] Occasions like 'Sermon Sunday', as well as the round of teas, bazaars and outings, would have included many outside the active faithful.[23] Women may have been the most closely involved. One irate Ashton Liberal certainly thought so, in attacking the political consequences of an atavistic allegiance:

Their great idea was to go to church with Uncle John leading them in gold buttons. . . . Certainly a majority of women is Tory. The reason is that they were born churchmen, the father was a churchman, they were christened at church, they were wed at church, and the poor simple things said they'd like to be buried in consecrated ground, as otherwise they would not go to heaven.[24]

The main effect of church social provision and leisure activity was nevertheless felt among the congregation itself, which was in many ways a self-sufficient entity. St Matthew's in Blackburn represents the range of activities common in the whole of the North: burial society, temperance society, book club, savings and holiday club, cricket and football teams, cookery and dressmaking classes, scripture union, and men's institute and club.[25] The very autonomy of the inturned community of the faithful itself contributed much to the partisanship of political feeling. Where religion really began to operate widely in a 'social sense', however, was in the Sunday school rather than in church or chapel life itself. The Sunday school was the one great institution that reached into the lives of the mass, transmitting the partisanship of denominational loyalties into political attitudes.

2 SUNDAY SCHOOL

In 1851 the Lancashire Sunday school population, including teachers, represented 17 per cent of the county's population, the West Riding schools 20 per cent. In some of the boroughs the proportion was greater still, the relationship between town size and attendance at worship being repeated in terms of school enrollment. Attendance ranged between 60 and 80 per cent, and the number of teachers was vast, in the ratio of one to nine scholars.[26] The usual situation as regards the proportions of the sexes is reflected in the example of Rochdale: in 1861 there were 9,293 male scholars and 10,997 female ones.[27] This enormous presence was not to diminish. There was a quickening of energies on all sides from the 1850s, the Anglicans making up much of the leeway that existed in 1851, when their day school predominance was matched by the Nonconformist Sunday school lead. Increased provision, and the improved local and national organisation, were directly linked to the new militance of Nonconformity in the 1850s and 60s, and the equally forthright Anglican resistance. The men who ran the Nonconformist Sunday School Unions and the Anglican organisation were the same individuals who conducted the daily business of Liberal and Tory politics.

The profound influence of the schools is best appreciated by an understanding of the age-range of the scholars. The schools were the preserve of adults and adolescents as well as of children, a state of affairs owing much to deliberate policy realised with particular effect in this period. Local sources indicate that between a third and a quarter of scholars stayed on beyond fifteen years, though very many would have left soon after. Nonetheless, sizeable groupings were congregated in particular schools, which were among the chief islands of political activism in the towns (grandfathers and grandsons might be registered at the same school). Though it was to the older scholars and teachers that the schools meant most, and these would often have been members of the congregation, the influence of the schools on children and adolescents spread far beyond that measured by church attendance alone. The teachers came from all social levels, the lower middle-class and higher working-class occupational levels figuring most prominently.[28]

After mid-century the schools relinquished their role in the teaching of reading and writing and became much more directly the agency of religious proselytisation.[29] Parallel with these changes, what seems to have an earlier emphasis on regimented discipline and unadorned social control gave way to a more relaxed and conciliatory approach on the part of the authorities. The schools became genuinely popular institutions, in large measure developing under the influence of the school populations' wishes, and with the frequent misgivings of the school authorities. If the schools were to involve the older scholars then the price had to be paid.[30] In 1868 the Blackburn S.S.U. bemoaned the way in which the schools were becoming social centres, young girls dressing in their Sunday finery for reasons far removed from the devotional.[31] Charles Rowley's youth at the Manchester Bennett Street school was spent more often in discovering the countryside, dancing, playing cricket and going to the theatre than in reading improving tracts.[32] As the century wore on the contrast between the secular present and the theological and political earnestness of earlier days was increasingly made.[33] The unbending of the schools to working-class manners meant that the enjoyments of a social life were at least as important to the older scholars as the improvement of their taste and intellect.

This is not to say that a fairly determined assault was not made on the morals of the scholars by the school authorities. Temperance took on the proportions of a crusade, especially in the Nonconformist schools, and there was an unflagging effort to inculcate the other virtues that made up the Victorian middle-class gospel of self-help, an effort reflected in a Sunday school literature of 'improvement' which proclaimed the advantages of getting on and narrated the success stories of those who had.[34] And no doubt this all had some effect, especially on the upper school. However, judging by the manner in which the schools developed after mid-century, the degree of this success could not have been more than minimal.[35]

Thus far one can agree with Thomas Laqueur's version of the nineteenth-century Sunday school:[36] the schools do seem to have been much more genuinely popular working-class institutions and much less part of the cultural apparatus of the middle class than is often supposed, though this would seem to have been a development of the later rather than the early part of the century. However, to suppose that because of this the schools were the source of an independent working-class culture is surely to overstate the case. This notion of the schools' function ignores the way in which in the North after mid-century the schools were an integral part of the culture of the factory.[37] Not only this, the schools were also the agency of a party politics organised and directed by the middle-class party hierarchies and the political clergy. The scholar was institutionalised in a political culture that was far removed from independent working-class politics.

Laqueur is surely also incorrect in envisaging school funds, organisation and teaching as being primarily in working-class hands.[38] The direct involvement and the donations of employers and other middle-class patrons always characterised school organisation and funding. National, regional and local organisation was directed by those outside the working class: the local Sunday School Unions for instance were the preserve of the Nonconformist *menu peuple*. However it was received, centrally produced school literature and propaganda certainly shaped the individual teaching effort. Although the older scholars and teachers had a say in the daily running of the schools, ultimate authority was always in the hands of the usually superior lay superintendents on the Nonconformist side and the local parish priest on the Anglican side.

The upper school was trained for public life by its involvement in school committees and clubs, and above all in the mutual improvement societies. A union of Nonconformist societies was set up in Ashton in 1867 to prepare for the coming struggle.[39] At the centre of the organisation was the Albion school, where addresses were frequently given on 'the art of reasoning and public speaking'. The school claimed that it had 'no small part in the creation of the intelligent interest in social and political questions that has always been shown by the people of this neighbourhood'.[40] Sunday school records show that party political debate was a staple of society activity, especially in the course of the 1860s as the era of mass politics came nearer.[41]

The teachers in particular formed something like political 'flying columns' on both sides, actively packing and disrupting meetings. Their reputation went before them: at a ward meeting in the Huddersfield campaign of 1874 it was reported that 'the room was quite full, and at the outset it was evident there were bible teachers present from the great noise and uproar they occasioned when the proceedings began'.[42] In 1880 Sunday school teachers and pigeon-fanciers (an instructive Tory conjunction) packed the invariably political and invariably riotous meetings of the Blackburn Philanthropic Burial Society.[43] Hugh Mason complained bitterly about the Orange ribbon in the Sunday school,[44] and Alderman Knott of Oldham felt called upon to remark in 1869 that: 'The Church Institutes and Conservative Clubs endeavoured to make a political association of the teachers in their Sunday Schools. Every agency was at work that was possible, and the Liberals would have to form counter-agencies.'[45] And counter-agencies they indeed formed: in 1881 Nonconformist day and Sunday schools in Ashton were making open financial contributions to local Reform Associations.[46]

The political influence of the schools on the mass of scholars was less direct but often just as intense. The highly political teachers had a considerable influence, on the Anglican side for instance passing on the 'no-surrender' Christianity of the Evangelical clergy to the school at large. The great event in school life was the annual Whitsun march. Invariably organised as a show of sectarian strength, the event concentrated denominational, ethnic and school loyalties on the great day. William Haslam Mills evoked Whit most tellingly:

In Ashton-on-the-Hill we 'walked' on Whit Friday and had done so immemorially . . . two by two, between lines of spectators, behind banners and bands of music, in a state of intense consciousness both of self and schism. I have said 'schism' because the proceedings were indeed frankly

and unblushingly sectarian. We who were Dissenters 'walked' in the
morning . . . the Church had seized the afternoon.[47]

The Anglicans of Ashton, with their poor scholars' banners
('Fear God and Honour the Queen', 'Sunday Schools are
England's Glory'), were every bit a match for the Dissenters.
Bishop Fraser's wish that the local murches celebrating the
schools' centenary in 1880 should not be one more occasion for
the display of denominational pomp and rivalry went unheeded.[48]
In Ashton crowns, bibles and blue ribbons decorated the Anglican
march as usual, and outside Ashton as well, most marches went
their seperate ways as they had done for decades past.[49] Political
occasions often brought the scholars on to the streets. Large
numbers of the ordinary school populations marched in the
massive Reform demonstration of 1866 in Blackburn, and the
Irish Church controversy brought rival scholars into confrontation in the town in 1869.[50] Scholars were often present at Orange
Order meetings.[51] In the Crescent district of Salford the ultra-
Protestant cleric Hugh Stowell had established by his death in
1865 a Sunday school system sufficiently strong to make Crescent
a Tory stronghold for years to come.[52] The kinds of tension in
society that made the schools such a forceful presence in popular
politics will now be further considered.

Popular protestantism
Protestantism was never solely a synonym for anti-Catholic or
anti-Irish feeling. The complexity of the nexus of emotions and
traditions it represented must constantly be borne in mind. It
was dedicated to the confusion of the designs of Dissent as well
as of Rome. From the late 1850s in particular the conflict of church
and chapel was to be at the heart of politics, as Nonconformity
asserted its strength within Liberalism and Anglican Toryism
responded. The opposition of Nonconformity and Evangelical
Anglicanism reached a peak of ferocity in Lancashire perhaps
unparalleled in any other part of England. Just as these two
elements were not simply expressions one of the other, so too was
anti-Catholicism never simply anti-Irish feeling in other terms.

Geoffery Best has illuminated the interplay of theological,
moral, political and even sexual attitudes that defined popular
Protestantism.[53] Opposition to what was taken to be papist
tyranny and backwardness was as prevalent in middle-class
Nonconformist circles as among the Anglican respectables. The
notion of the 'free-born Englishman', and the defence of English
rights, liberty and truth were concerns as dear to the heart of

many a Liberal workingman as they were to his Tory counterpart. In the end, however, there is no doubt that it was the clash of two very different cultures which gave these traditions social force and political direction. And it was this conflict that articulated the often passive but nonetheless considerable denominational allegiances previously examined. Toryism stood to be the beneficiary of ethnic loyalty because it was the chief spokesman of Englishness. But the tradition and bigotry that compounded Englishness were not the monopoly of any one part of the electorate, and Liberal workingmen are not to be regarded as a bastion of tolerance and far-sightedness. If a distrust of Rome that might not be a contempt for the Irish was widely dispersed in society, so too could a contempt for Rome masquerade for anti-Irish feeling among large parts of the electorate. For Liberal workingmen it was often merely that the loyalties of chapel and of work, and the exigencies of the alliance between English Liberalism and Irish Nationalism, overrode the political expression of deep-seated ethnic loyalties.

1 THE IMPACT OF THE CATHOLIC IRISH

The growth of ethnic feeling in the 1850s and 60s was primarily a consequence of the massive immigration following the Irish Famine. However, the Irish had long been a part of northern life, especially in Lancashire, and disturbance and riot were by no means unknown before the late 1840s.[54] In the chief centres of immigration, such as the ports of Liverpool and Preston Protestant traditions stretched back many decades, strengthened as they were by the arrival of Protestant Ulstermen as well as Catholic Irishmen. In Wigan, already an old Irish centre by 1850, Church and King Jacobite traditions coalesced with Orangeism to make Tory Protestantism rather than Chartism the popular cause in the 1830s and 40s.[55] West Lancashire, and above all Liverpool, was to be the stronghold of Protestantism until well into the twentieth century.

The increase in sectarian violence followed the pattern of the arrival and dispersal of the Irish poor. The early consequences of this population movement were intensified by the Hierarchy Controversy of 1850–51. The Operative Protestant Associations and other bodies formed as a reaction to the creation of an English Catholic hierarchy were the first great increment in Protestant organisational growth. The Irish-born population increased from 6 to 10 per cent of the total Lancashire population between 1841 and 1851. The absolute number of Irish-born rose slightly to 1861, but their proportion in the population decreased with every decade after 1851, amounting to 6 per cent in 1881. This great influx made first for the big urban centres of Liverpool, Manchester and Salford, dispersing itself in the 1850s and 60s in the north-west as a whole, even though in 1861 two-thirds of the county total of Irish lived in the three cities, and 40 per cent in Liverpool alone. The pattern of communal disturbance in the west of the county in the 1850s was a reaction to the first geographical location of the 1841–51 influx, and the disturbances of the 1860s similarly seem to have been a consequence of the later movement into east and south-east Lancashire. The public tumult which culminated in the Murphy riots and the general hysteria of 1867–69 was especially marked in towns like Ashton, Stalybridge, Rochdale, Oldham and Bacup, but was also seen in the West Riding where the Irish were increasingly prominent.[56]

The exceptional bitterness of the late 1860s was the product of exceptional circumstances, and was the last great paroxysm resulting from the post-Famine influx. 1868 witnessed the combined effect of the first election under the new franchise, the economic depression of 1867–68, and the Fenian scare. After the long-drawn-out consequences of the great Irish immigration had worked themselves out community relations were to be more placid. Ethnic violence lessened considerably in the 1870s and 80s: the twelfth of July was examined in a number of northern towns throughout these decades and the level of disturbance, even in election years, was negligible.[57] Similarly, the ethnic aspects of anti-Catholic propaganda were greatly moderated after the orgy of the late 1860s. The decline in extremism was in so small part due to declining central Conservative party interest in Protestantism after 1868.

Even if the overtly ethnic aspect was muted, Protestantism remained probably the central element in Tory electioneering after 1870. The Irish did not easily become English, and the determined and volatile identity they maintained continued to buttress the other loyalties which fed English Protestant feeling. The social life of the Irish (outside the public house) was generated at every level by the Catholic Church. Despite the 'seepage' of attenders once the shores of heathen England had been reached, and despite the tensions with Irish nationalism, the identification of Irishness and Catholicism was wellnigh absolute. Differences of religion were reinforced by differences of occupational status. The Irish invariably had the most menial and lowest paid jobs, more often in outdoor labouring than within the factory. The existence of 'Little Irelands' in most northern towns presented further visible proof to the English of Irish inferiority.

A Lancashire correspondent of the London *Times* described, in 1868, a state of affairs that could not have applied only to that year: the Irish were the 'mean whites' of Lancashire, earning 'the class animosity and contempt, the white man in America and Jamaica reserves for his blacks'. Working for lower wages, eating cheaper foods, the Irish were 'a sort of "knobsticks" in a great national trade union'.[58] Decades later, in Robert Roberts's Salford, English disrespect for the Irish was a commonplace of slum life.[59] In much the same years oral material makes plain the continuance of job discrimination against the Irish, and the ever-present charge of priestly control.[60]

2 'THE CHURCH OF THE PEOPLE'

The notion that the Church of England was the National Church, 'the church of the people', differentiated from the congregational ethos of Nonconformity by its parish system and the pastoral care of all, was an idea that received considerable support in the Lancashire of the time. Such a vision of the Church had been integral to the religion of many of the Evangelical forerunners, especially the Lancashire favourite Lord Shaftesbury. It received expression in organisations like the aggressively Evangelical Church Pastoral Aid Society, as well as in the Free Pew Movement, which had one of its two headquarters in Manchester.[61]

The identification of Anglicanism as the peoples' church was strengthened by the actions of several clerics as industrial conciliators, among them Bishop Fraser and the Rev. Verity of Clitheroe, a leading supporter of the operatives in the long weaving strike of 1859 in the north-east, and a Burnley Tory committee chairman in the election of 1868.[62] In Blackburn the clergy played a major role in the Cotton Famine relief organisation, one operative spokesman of the Church Operative Schools praising their work in 1863, and defending them against the detraction of 'Mr Miall and his like' as the true representatives of 'the Church of the People'.[63]

The foremost centres of Anglican attention to the popular cause was in the towns of Ashton and Stalybridge. In areas where Tory employers and politics dominated, the Anglican clergy was far less ready to disturb the local *status quo* of which they were a part. Even in the south-east there was a good deal of opportunism about the involvement of the Evangelical clergy. Their chief champion, Joseph Rayner Stephens, recognised that only a minority of the Anglican clergy were worthy of respect: the majority, like Prince Lee, the Bishop of Manchester before Fraser, he condemned for neglecting their duties to the poor.

The kind of Tory populism seen in the two towns at its most extreme capitalised on a widespread temperamental disaffinity between Nonconformity and popular manners. Nonconformity's obsession with temperance lay at the root of this opposition of feeling, giving it a special value for the Tory party. In Ashton and Stalybridge Stephens preached what almost amounted to a gospel of beer, going so far as to declare that he would welcome the 'infidel' before the narrow and bigoted Nonconformist 'type'.[64] Though in most localities this temperamental opposition contained only vestiges of class resentment, in the two towns the action of Stepehns and the Evangelicals magnified these vestiges into an often considerable political force. The political symbolism of clogs and unrolled sleeves could often be potent. In 1869 the Rev. Heffill of Audenshaw defended the 'ignorant' workingmen Tories as wearers of clogs, declaring himself to be a clog-wearer in defiance of the 'Radical hat and silk umbrella' of local, establishment Liberalism.[65] At the end of a Tory meeting in the previous year one Mossley clergyman rolled up his sleeves, hitched up his robes, and, to the delight of his audience, sprang forward in clogs.[66]

These associations were a product of the long local involvement of Stephens and the Evangelicals. The combination of strident Evangelicalism with the attack on the mainly Nonconformist opponents of factory legislation and exponents of political economy was specially characteristic of the local Tory appeal in the first half of this period, and was seen in the case of the Rev. Hugh Stowell of Salford as well.[67] Though the employers' change of outlook was far advanced by the 1860s, Stephens's reputation, gained in days when the issues were more clearcut, was sufficient to keep old antagonisms alive in the two towns. Stephens's schismatic Methodism and romantic Toryism led him to espouse the National Church as the church of all degress and kinds, and most of all of the helpless and excluded poor. The clergy that he championed – most notably Williams in Ashton, Eagar in Stalybridge and Audenshaw's Heffill – he regarded as the true parish priests of the people, in battle with the presumption of local, propertied Dissent.[68] However, Stephens's support for this clergy contained no measure of the anti-Catholicism that was so much a part of their religion.[69]

Of considerable use to Toryism, though never fully or happily integrated in it, Stephensite populism touched a nerve of class feeling more exposed in these towns than in most others. In times of exceptional social difficulty like the Cotton Famine years, Stephens came into his own, though events in Ashton and

Stalybridge at the time represented an extreme and most unusual deviation from the norm of social calm. At meetings
hours-long and tumultuous Stephens defended the Englishman's
right to beef, bread and good beer.[70] For the support they gave
the operatives the Evangelical clergy were condemned by the
mighty of Stalybridge as *agents provocateurs*, and 'only fit for
the hulks'.[71]

The same disposition of political slogans and individuals
characterised party politics when they came. In particular, a
small group of workingmen who had surrounded Stephens from
the 1840s into the 1870s played an important part in Tory
organisation, though their political loyalties were often a maverick
strain within Tory politics.[72] The Rev. Williams was active
in the Ashton Tory club network, and Heffill and Eagar led the
party in Audenshaw and Dukinfield. In Dukinfield Eagar was
in open conflict with the Nonconformist coalowning and cotton
Buckley family, as well as the Buckleys' Congregational minister
Page Hopps. At the miners' galas of the 1870s in Ashton Heffill and
Eagar sometimes took the chair, and both were popularly regarded
as the miners' champions.[73] At a Tory meeting in Dukinfield in
1869, when Irish and English colliers were in direct industrial
conflict, Sidebottom the Tory candidate was greeted by the cry
that he was 'no Ranter' and Heffill was praised to the skies by the
assembled audience.[74]

It is to the dominant element in this populism, the ethnic
loyalty which in the hands of the widely influential Evangelical
clergy often moved far away from the more civilised concerns
of Stephens, that attention will next be directed. In the special
appeal of populism to the colliery workforce we recognise already
the most characteristic source of support for anti-Irish demagogy,
the poorest and least assimilated in society.

3 GRASS-ROOTS PROTESTANTISM

Even before the arrival of Prince Lee as Bishop of Manchester
in 1848 the Evangelical clergy had made inroads in a number of
Lancashire towns. The Church Pastoral Aid Society, founded in
1836, accelerated a process which Lee completed. In Blackburn
for instance, by 1862 Evangelicals were to be found in most of
the town's parishes.[75] On his arrival in 1870 Bishop Fraser was
faced with a *fait accompli*.[76] The new self-confidence of politicised
Dissent in the 1850s and 60s drew forth Church Institutes and
Church Defence Associations that were of vital importance in
co-ordinating the party effort of Toryism in all northern towns
in the 1860s and 70s.[77] The anti-Ritualism of the clergy and of the

typical Lancashire congregation provided another focus for the confluence of anti-Catholic and anti-Irish feeling, and for the co-operation of clergy and laity in political activity. Anti-Ritualism also acted as a link between the concerns of the party leadership and the proclivities of the mass electorate: in times of strain such as the late 1860s anti-Ritualism could spread over into public disturbances.[78]

Below the social level of many in the Anglican congregations, and often with only the slightest links to the religious life of the Church, Orangeism presents the first of the truly proletarian faces of Protestantism. At once the diversity of Protestant feeling is apparent, its capacity for engaging the support of all levels in society. The more extreme forms of sectarian feeling were not at all the sole preserve of those in the most direct contact with the Irish, namely the unskilled English. The Liverpool Tory leader A.B. Forwood stated that the Liverpool Orangemen were the most sober, respectable and intelligent of the working classes, and the evidence of the Reform League in 1868 bears out his description of their skilled character if not his encomium on their virtue.[79] In Ashton, Stalybridge and Blackburn, where their ranks were less swollen by Ulster craftsmen than in Liverpool, the most active Orangemen came from the social level defined by the following occupations: tinplateworker, overlooker, self-acting minder, earthenware dealer, watchmaker, mason and bootmaker.[80] The Orangeism of the coal areas, long the godchild of the oldfashioned, landed Tory coalowners, was something of an exception to this.[81]

The Order was established in Lancashire around the turn of the century, and was always strongest in Manchester, Salford, and the west of the region. Between 1850 and 1870 it grew considerably throughout the North of England.[82] An understanding of the Order's size must depend upon somewhat unreliable press reports. The figures of 700 members in Wigan, 300 in Rochdale (both for 1869), and 1,400 in Blackburn (1880) are probably reliable, though a combined total of 5,000 in Manchester and Salford in 1880 may be somewhat exaggerated.[83] Many of these would not have been benefit-receiving members: in 1874 there were only 341 such members in Preston, the remaining 1,000 having joined only for political purposes.[84] Nonetheless, these figures argue a considerable presence for the Order in town life.

The leading Manchester Orangeman was William Touchstone. A warehouseman and clerk, he later became a full-time Tory lecturer and a leading figure in the Manchester organisation, alongside the working printer S.C. Nicholson and the employer

W.R. Callendar. All three gave voice to the characteristic combination of support for Protestantism and opposition to Manchester
laissez faire. The 'holy alliance' of the Manchester School and
Fenian Catholicism defined the politics of the skilled trade
unionists who gave Protestantism their support in great number,
'respectable' men who campaigned for the same changes in labour
legislation as did all other skilled trade unionists.[85]

Touchstone, a Sunday school teacher and temperance advocate,
represents this very considerable respectable side to the Order.[86]
This was also apparent in the Order's involvement in the life
of the Church, though this was usually far more social and institutional in character than religious: lodge members were often
castigated for not attending church, but the Order took its part in
church rituals (such as foundation stone-laying ceremonies),
sometimes met in Church schoolrooms, and generally received
the backing of the clergy.[87] In 1875 the Blackburn Orangemen
were opening newsrooms and recreation rooms, and in 1889 a
large new Orange Hall was inaugurated. Juvenile lodges, for the
sons of Orangemen, were also formed about this time.[88] One of the
few personal accounts of Orangeism, that of a Burnley weaver,
suggests the strong hereditary element as well as the respectability
of the Order: the writer and his father were both fervent Orangemen and Sunday school teachers.[89] There were a number of
female Orange lodges in most towns, and wive and 'sweethearts'
were often guests at lodge anniversaries.[90]

The lodges should not be equated with Methodit tea-meetings.
A number of lodges continued to meet in pubs in the 1880s.
The violence of Orange language was often equalled by that of
Orange behaviour. In 1868 Orangemen led violent incursions
into Irish Blackburn.[91] Relations between the Order and the
disreputable Protestant lecturer William Murphy were often
close – significantly enough, particularly so in Ashton and Stalybridge – and Orangemen everywhere exulted in Murphy's attacks
on the Irish in their 'bug-ridden Popish cabins'.[92] The more
violent and sinister side to Orangeism also gave pause to the Tory
leaders from time to time. The Manchester leaders condemned its
violence, and in Ashton the wildness of the Orange leader Booth
Mason's fantasies of conspiracy and dissolution often alienated
Tory opinion in the town.[93] If Orangeism and Murphyism were
sometimes indistinguishable they were not the same thing: the
Order could be controlled, Murphyism was wellnigh uncontroll-
able. The Order was integrated in and subservient to Tory party
organisation. This received the highest recognition in 1872, when
on the occasion of his much-heralded visit to Manchester,

Disraeli accepted the honorary membership offered by the Salford lodges. He rose to the august moment, observing that it was 'one of the greatest distinctions I ever received, and I hope I shall be a loyal brother'.[94]

The fantastic Protestantism of William Murphy presents a rather different picture. The Protestant Electoral Union was founded in 1865 to expose the enormities of the Catholic confessional. For the next five years, and again Ashton and Stalybridge were exceptional in being centres of the Union's efforts, Murphy and his fellow lecturers were to reap a rich harvest in a period of plenty.[95] The fundamentalist Protestantism of these 'Ultras', mostly Ulster Protestants or renegade Catholics, was by no means unique. The 'Baron de Camin' was a source of disturbances throughout the North in the 1850s and 60s, and the Salford-based 'Protestant missionary' Henry Mead also enjoyed a considerable notoriety.[96] Mead preached against the 'Unholy League' of 'Infidels, Independents, Reformers and Fenians', united in the cause of priestly despotism. Most typical of these lurid wanderers were the self-described ex-priests and 'escaped nuns'. Part of a travelling Protestant roadshow that also featured a 'Protestant Red Indian Chief', one 'Brother. Stanislaus' was especially popular: when in Stalybridge he walked through the town in monk's robes to the appointed hall where he officiated at a mock-altar.[97] After 1870 this kind of popular theatre was to decline, Lancashire being part of the national pattern in which the nunnery craze of the 1830s to the 1860s gave way to the anti-confessional frenzy of the later 1860s.[98] Despite the occasional sideshow in later years,[99] no one was to match the success of Murphy.

Among the many chords Murphy struck with his audience the sexual one was not the least important. The prurience of his manipulation of the nunnery and confessional motifs can be understood in the sense Best suggests: it involved the exposure of the dominant Protestant father, in the respectable classes as well as among the poor, to the threat against his idealised womanhood posed by the priest as the rival, corrupting moral father.[100] Women were as appreciative of the lewdness Murphy dealt in as men. In Stalybridge he drew large crowds of women to specially arranged meetings, which his wife also attended.[101] He pledged himself to change the law and forbid women working. Murphy seems to have been repaid for his pains: in Bacup 1,000 women, armed with staves were reported to have marched in his defence.

Murphy's success was in large measure a matter of brilliantly achieved popular theatre. He assaulted his audience with sensations, often waving a revolver as he entered his meetings flanked by his stormtroopers (the latter were often formed from his specially faithful Stalybridge 'lads'). The entry set in train a carnival that often culminated in a singing, shouting excursion into the local 'Little Ireland'.[102] The constant arrests and triumphant returns of Murphy and his assistants, together with Murphy's advanced persecution mania, all fed the mounting fever.[103] At one Manchester meeting in 1868 his supporters massed for a violent rescue and revenge, chanting 'Shall Murphy die? Shall Murphy die? Then forty-thousand Lancashire clogs shall know the reason why'.[104]

What is perhaps surprising about Murphyism is that it received a willing ear, and not seldom a willing hand, in respectable society, and not only working-class society. One description of the impact of the phenomenon on Ashton suggests that the pillars of the congregation, and those with a skill to hand, were closely involved: 'It gave an impetus to Protestantism, and no doubt Christ Church was built much earlier than it otherwise would have been. Not only was monetary assistance given, but a number of working men, many of them Murphyites ... gave their services free every evening.'[105] The Irish counter-attacks of May 1868 were said to have forced the 'respectable' working class into opposition; and not only the working class, for 'very respectably dressed people with their silk umbrellas' were reported as having broken up stones for ammunition in the Ashton fight. In Bacup and elsewhere tradespeople and artisans were involved in the disturbances. The *Ashton Reporter* remarked that Murphyism had split the whole life of the town, even breaking up the unity of the family.[106]

The darkest and most sinister side of Protestantism was not solely the expression of the humblest in society. All the other manifestations of Protestant feeling as well, including the populist dimension, served to unite the interests not only of the working class but of all the classes in society: Tory employers, for instance, were perhaps the chief beneficiaries of Protestantism in all its different aspects. But the line between unification and potential social disruption was indefinite, and the lower in society the Protestant reflex was sought the more was that line crossed. Murphy's principal appeal was to the poor and excluded in society, and it was they who most completely translated his message into violence against the Irish. In releasing that violence Murphy also spoke to the condition of the very poor. The forces so unleashed by the unashamed use of the Irish scapegoat in the late 1860s went beyond the bounds of control, threatening the peace and prosperity of the propertied classes and the political parties that chiefly represented their interests.

Murphy and his like seem to have found a special source of support among colliers and quarrymen, and these were particularly prominent in the disturbances.[107] The Liberal press usually characterised the rioters as the young, the rough, and sometimes the non-voters.[108] Illiteracy is some guide to social level: only a few of those arrested in the Ashton riots were able to sign the riot depositions with anything but a cross.[109] The Protestant Halls of Rochdale in 1869 made a special appeal to the very poor.[110] The fury of the rioting in 1868 is striking: Catholic churches and houses were torn to pieces rather than merely ransacked. Murphy represented a threat to order and property, a threat that lay in what Murphy said as well as in the actions of the rioters.

For, when the Murphy phenomenon is penetrated to the lowest levels of its social support, it reveals further uncharted deeps. Contained within the sectarian fanaticism was another message, an attack on authority and its pretensions which answered to the needs of those who were most shut out from that authority, the poorest of the poor. Murphy's continual conflict with the magistrates of the towns in which he lectured presented the oppositions openly: Murphy and his workers were against the 'tyranny' and 'respectability' of the upper classes, especially as these were represented in the magistracy and the police.[111]

Most significantly, the attack was couched in religious terms as well. Murphy confronted a real spiritual destitution among the poor, a need that organised religion had failed to meet. His meetings were not only circuses. The intensity of feeling they showed was similar to that of the revivalist congregation, particularly the early Methodist camp meetings. The Protestant Tent set up in Rochdale was in fact called the Protestant Camp.[112] 'The Lion of Judah' was a Murphy anthem as well as 'Rule Britttania'. In Ashton on three Sunday's in January 1868 Murphy was reported to have preached to between 6,000 and 8,000 people, many of whom had not attended a sermon in years.[113] Murphy presented himself as a Messiah to Rochdale in a similar fashion. In these sermons he preached against the hypocrisy of the respectable, 'There is hope for ruined sinners, but none whatever for religious ones', and in favour of the poor and ignorant against a rich and uncaring clergy: ' . . . the grace of God was better than Grammar . . . the Brass-Knocker and the Mansion receive too much attention, and the wooden knocker too little'.

From this the mighty drew back. The most extreme Evangelicals, however, again displayed how deeply they were enmeshed in the toils of grass-roots Protestantism. In Ashton, characteristically, a number gave their support to Murphy, including the Rev. Heffill. Elsewhere the excesses of Murphy earned the condemnation of the Tory press, Tory employers, and many of the Anglican clergy.[114] But it was the violence of rhetoric and action in Murphyism that was condemned and not the message of ethnic solidarity. The events of the 1860s had shown the political uses as well as the dangers of ethnic feeling. In the future the lessons were to be learned, and the Protestant reflex controlled in the interests of the party. The Tory party and its leadership were not again to lose the initiative in the period.

Summary
The political culture of the North as a whole, of those outside as well as within the factories, is now considered systematically. This treatment of religion in politics takes its bearings from the initial observation that the North combined apathy in the formal religious affiliations of the majority with an often unreasoning sectarianism in popular politics. Explaining this equation is the principal aim of the chapter, though the hold of formal religion, especially over the politically active, should not be minimised. The way in which religion could articulate loyalties formed at the deeper level of work has been considered: here the growth of near-secular cultures around the institutions of formal, organised religion forms the first principal means to be considered by which religion entered politics. These diffuse yet often strong loyalties were one of the raw materials of politics, but probably more important was the matter of the Catholic Irish-Protestant English opposition. Religion and ethnicity could combine with undercurrents of class antagonism to compound a kind of Tory populism, especially in south-east Lancashire towns like Ashton and Stalybridge where the nerve of class was unusually exposed. Because it reveals such an extremely rich mixture of attitudes, popular Protestantism, the banner of the outcast and the bond of classes, receives especially close attention in this chapter.

The way in which the form and vocabulary of politics was shaped by religious categories is considered, and the peculiar ferocity of the Nonconformist-Anglican opposition in the North is suggested. The social aspect of religion is explored first in terms of church, chapel and school, and then by means of a consideration of the Sunday schools. Between them, these institutions engrossed much of the social life of the working class, a life that was institutionalised in an often blatantly political culture. The dimensions of popular Protestantism are then drawn, and something of the culture of the Catholic Irish is considered. Protestantism is related to the nature of this culture and the timing of the Irish influx. Under the heading of the 'Church of the People' the populist aspects of Anglicanism are looked at in relation to class feeling. The probably more important ethnic ingredient in populism is first examined on its 'respectable' side, that of the congregation and of Evangelical influence. The less respectable side, represented by Orangeism is next considered, though any simple correspondence between Protestantism and the 'undermass' is clearly mistaken. Indeed, Protestantism united all levels in society, and was often 'respectable' in the extreme. Nonetheless, in its most sinister guises it called most loudly to the most insulted and injured. A consideration of the fantasy and inchoate social rebellion of Ultra-Protestantism completes the treatment of religion in politics.

Notes

1. See above, pp. 174–9.
2. *P.P.* 1861, XXI (2794–11), Pt II, J.S. Winder's report on education in Rochdale and Bradford, esp. pp. 197–9 (S.C. on Popular Education); Schools Inquiry Commission, *P.P.* 1867–8, XXVII (3966–viii), Pt VIII, Vol. IX, pp. 509–12, 517–18, 758; see also H. Pelling, 'Popular attitudes to religion', in *Popular Politics and Society in Late Victorian Britain* (1968).
3. See above, pp. 30–2.
4. Thompson and Vigne West Riding Ints, 28 ('Politics'), also Ints 170, 181 ('Politics'); and Lancs. Ints, 122 (p. 18), 136 (C/C).
5. P.F. Clarke, *Lancashire and the New Liberalism* (Cambridge 1971), esp. pp. 14–19, 53–76, 252–67; see also A.D. Gilbert, *Religion and Society in Industrial England, 1740–1914* (1976), Pt III, on the combination of popular 'secularism' and sectarian politics.
6. See above, pp. 150–2.
7. See above, p. 60.
8. W.A. Abram, 'Social conditions and political prospects of the Lancashire workman', *Fortnightly Review*, Oct. 1868, pp. 435–6.
9. For further elaboration of the points raised here see P. Joyce, 'Popular Toryism in Lancashire 1860–1890' (Oxford Univ. D. Phil. 1975), pp. 142–9.
10. G. Roby, *The Disease of the Liberal Party* (Manchester n.d. ? 1874).
11. *Blackburn Standard*, 8 July 1868.
12. *P.P.* 1852–3, LXXXIX (1690), Report and Tables.
13. The method followed by H. Perkin, *The Origins of Modern English Society* (1969), p. 201.
14. *P.P.* 1852–3, LXXXIX (1690), Rept pp. CXIX–CXXI (esp.), clii-

cliii; also H. Mann in *Journal of the Statistical Society of London*, 18, June 1855, esp. pp. 152–3.

15. A. Mearns, *Statistics of Attendance at Public Worship in England and Wales, February 1882* (1882).

16. *Blackburn Standard*, 6 Dec. 1880 (Rev. Hignett).

17. J. Howes, *Tory Trickery: Joseph Howes versus the Duke of Buccleuch* (n.d. ?1888), Manchester Central Library; R. Roberts, *The Classic Slum* (Manchester 1971), ch. 7, and *A Ragged Schooling* (Manchester 1976).

18. Clarke, *op. cit.* pp. 67–9, also pp. 64–6.

19. Thompson and Vigne W. Riding Int. 180 ('Politics').

20. J. Seabrook, *City Close-Up* (1971), p. 23.

21. On the association of church and neighbourhood see *Christ Church Blackburn 1857–1907. A Jubilee Handbook*, and *St Thomas's Church, Blackburn Centenary 1865–1965*, Appendices A and E (both in Blackburn Public Library); also *Blackburn Patriot*, 3 Oct. 1863.

22. E.A. Knox, *Reminiscences of an Octogenarian* (1935), pp. 239–40, and ch. XII.

23. *Ibid.* p. 230; W.H. Mills, *Grey Pastures* (1924), chs 1 and 2; J. Seabrook, *op. cit.* p. 16.

24. H. Heginbottom, *Thomas Heginbottom His Life and Times* (1913), p. 62. A comment made during the 1874 municipal elections.

25. *St Mathew's Church, Silver Souvenir ... 1906* (Bb. P.L.).

26. *P.P.* 1852–3, XC (1692), Tables R and S, and pp. 36–9. Catholic schools were of little account.

27. *P.P.* 1861, XXI (2794–ii), Pt II, report on SS in Rochdale, esp. p. 192.

28. For further information on this and the preceding paragraph see Joyce, *op. cit.* pp. 162–8.

29. See remarks of speakers at regional SSU conference, *Blackburn Times*, 27 Mar. 1875, also leader. See also J. Foster, *Class Struggle and the Industrial Revolution* (1974), pp. 215–16.

30. W.A. Watson, *The First Fifty Years of the Sunday Schools* (1873), ch. xvii, esp. p. 151; *C. of E. Sunday School Teachers' Magazine*, July 1863; *Ashton Standard*, 6 Dec. 1879.

31. *Blackburn Times*, 2 May 1868.

32. C. Rowley, *Fifty Years of Ancoats, Loss and Gain* (?1899), p. 7; see also E.A. Knox, *op. cit.*, ch. XIII, and pp. 230, 239; and Thompson and Vigne W. Riding Int. 134 (C/C).

33. W. Bennett, *The History of Burnley*, Pt IV (Burnley 1951), p. 153; see also R.W. Wainwright and P.E. Razzell, eds, *The Victorian Working Class. Selections from letters to the 'Morning Chronicle'* (1973), p. 175.

34. See e.g. G. Milner, ed., *Bennett St Memorials* (1880); also *C. of E. SS. Teachers' Magazine*, Mar. and June 1863; *Oldham Chronicle*, 15 Aug. 1877; *Ashton Reporter*, 11 Sept. 1880.

35. See above, p. 179.

36. T.W. Laqueur, *Religion and Respectability, Sunday schools and working-class culture 1780–1850* (1976).
37. See above, pp. 178–9.
38. Laqueur, *op. cit.* chs 3 and 5.
39. *Ashton Reporter*, 11 Dec. 1867.
40. *Souvenir of Albion Schools 1862–1912* (Ashton Public Library). The Albion MIS was founded in 1840. For its influence see also J.G. Rogers, *An Autobiography* (1903), pp. 109–11; see also *Ashton Reporter*, 13 Feb. 1869.
41. Culceth Street (Methodist), German Street and Bennett Street (Anglican) MIS minutes in Manchester Central Library, Archives Dept.
42. *Huddersfield Daily Examiner*, 4 Feb. 1874.
43. *Blackburn Times*, 6 Nov. 1880 (letters); see also *Ashton Reporter*, 7 Mar. 1868 (on SS in Volunteer agitation).
44. *Ibid.*, 24 Nov. 1868 (Milner Gibson meeting).
45. *Ibid.*, 17 Apr. 1869; also 5 June 1869.
46. Audenshaw Reform Association Contributions Book, Ashton Public Library.
47. W. Mills, *op. cit.* pp. 27, 29.
48. *Bolton Chronicle*, 19 June 1880.
49. *Ashton Reporter*, 3, 10 July 1880.
50. *Blackburn Times*, 7, 14 Aug. 1868.
51. *Blackburn Standard*, 3 Oct. 1868.
52. R.L. Greenall, 'Popular Conservatism in Salford 1868–1886', *Northern History*, 9, 1974, pp. 125, 132–4.
53. G.F.A. Best, 'Popular Protestantism in Victorian Britain', in R. Robson, ed., *Ideas and Institutions of Victorian Britain* (1967).
54. The best narrative account of Irish–English relations in the period is N. Kirk, 'Class and fragmentation: some aspects of working-class life in north-east Cheshire and south-east Lancashire 1850–1870' (Univ. of Pittsburgh Ph.D. 1974), ch. 4. The author's emphasis on early political and social amity, and class union, is not altogether borne out by the considerable counter-evidence he presents for the first half of the century. On the early years see also A. Redford, *Labour Migration in England 1800–1850* (Manchester 1964), ch. ix, esp. pp. 164–5; J. Jackson, *The Irish in Britain* (1963), chs 3, 6; E.P. Thompson, *The Making of the English Working Class* (1968), ch. 12, sect. III. See also Foster, *op. cit.* pp. 243–6.
55. K. Tiller, 'Working-class attitudes and organisation in three industrial towns' (Birmingham Univ. Ph.D. 1975), chs 2, 8.
56. On sectarian public disturbances see Kirk, *op. cit.* ; *Bolton Chronicle*, June, July 1850; *Preston Chronicle*, July 1852; *Bradford Review*, July 1858, Sept., Oct. 1862.
57. Cf. July in *Blackburn Times*, 1879, 1886, 1892; *Burnley Advertiser* 1879; *Bury Guardian* 1874, 1880, 1885; *St Helens Newspaper and Advertiser* 1885, etc.
58. Reprinted in *Manchester Daily Examiner and Times*, 25 Nov. 1868 (a 'knobstick' was a blackleg).

59. R. Roberts, *The Classic Slum* (Manchester 1971), pp. 7, 9.
60. Thompson and Vigne Lancs. Ints. 122, 136, 139 (C/C); Int. 131 (pp. 13, 16).
61. Cf. *The Church of the People and Free Church Penny Magazine*, 1867–1875; see also E.R. Wickham on Sheffield Anglicanism, *Church and People in an Industrial City* (1957), pp. 140–7.
62. *Blackburn Weekly Telegraph*, 28 May, 18 June, 9 July 1859.
63. *Blackburn Patriot*, 23 May 1868.
64. *Ashton Reporter*, 13 Apr. 1867 (Sunday-closing meeting); see also *ibid.*, 30 Mar. 1867.
65. *Ibid.*, 6 Feb. 1869.
66. *Ashton Standard*, 19 Sept. 1868.
67. Stowell's Operative Protestant Association, founded in 1839, was still going strong in the 1860s. For Stowell's popularity and Ashton as an early centre of Evangelical organisation see *The Protestant Witness*, 1849–1851 (Manchester Central Library), esp. 2 June 1849; see also H. Stowell, *A Plea for Working Men. Do not lower his wages* (1848), and J.B. Marsden, *Memories of the Life and Labours of Hugh Stowell* (1868).
68. See Stephens's own publication, *The Champion of All that is Right, and True, and Just*, published in Stalybridge 1849–50, esp. Vol. 2, nos. 12, 13, 24; *The Protestant Operative*, printed in Stalybridge, was circulating in the early 1850s; see esp. poem 'The Parson and the People' in 15 Feb. 1851 number.
69. *Ashton Reporter*, 17 Oct. 1868, 21 Nov. 1869.
70. *Ibid.*, Feb. 1863, and *Ashton Standard*, 31 Jan. 1863.
71. *Ibid.*, 11 Apr. 1863 (letters), and *Ashton Reporter*, 28 Mar. 1863; see also Home Office Papers, H.O./45. O.S. 7523A, A. Aspland to Secretary of State Gathorne-Hardy, report of Williams telling Dukinfield operatives to duck offending town councillors in a pond (22 Mar. 1863).
72. See below, p. 325.
73. *Ashton Reporter*, 9 Nov. 1872, 15 July 1876.
74. *Ibid.*, and *Ashton Standard*, 24 Oct. 1868; see also *Reporter*, 25 Jan, 8 Feb. 1868.
75. *Blackburn Standard*, 15 Feb. 1862.
76. For Fraser and the party spirit in Anglicanism see *ibid.*, 15 Mar. 1871, *Ashton Reporter*, 14 Jan. 1871, and P. Clarke, *op. cit.* pp. 58–61.
77. Rev. Canon Molesworth, *The Necessity and Design of Church Defence Associations*, delivered Manchester 1860 (in Manchester Central Library); see also the organ of these bodies, *The National Church*, and on the role of militant Dissent in Liberalism, J. Vincent, *The Formation of the Liberal Party 1857–1868* (1966), pp. 65–76.
78. E.g. *Manchester Courier*, 6 Sept. 1869, *Rochdale Pilot*, 18 Dec. 1869; see also H. Nicholson, *Autobiography* (Rochdale 1892).
79. Information on Forwood from Philip Waller's MSS, forthcoming book on Liverpool politics; Reform League Reports, Liverpool and Birkenhead, Bishopsgate Institute, London.

80. Census and directory identifications based on press accounts of lodge meetings.
81. On Oldham collier Orangeism, *Oldham Chronicle*, 15 July 1854 and 7 Apr. 1855. This indication of a long-established collier Orangeism must serve to qualify the chronology of political transition Foster posits for the Oldham miners, see Foster, *op. cit.* pp. 234–7, esp. p. 235.
82. For the early history of Orangeism see E. Taylor, *An Account of Orangeism* (Manchester 1868), and H. Senior, *Orangeism in Ireland and Britain 1795–1836* (1966); on its growth, Kirk, *op. cit*; Foster, *op. cit.* pp. 219–20.
83. *Manchester Courier*, 19 June 1869; *Bury Guardian*, 17 July 1880.
84. *P.P.* 1874, XXIII (996), Pt II, p. 305.
85. *Manchester Courier*, 14 Nov. 1868.
86. *Manchester Evening Times*, 17 Dec. 1912 (obit.); also *City Jackdaw*, 10 Dec. 1875, 28 Jan. 1876.
87. *Blackburn Standard*, 18 July 1868, 9 Sept. 1870, 20 Sept. 1871, 28 Sept. 1872, 9 Sept. 1876; *Blackburn Times*, 23 Sept. 1865; *Preston Guardian*, 9 Nov. 1870.
88. *Blackburn Standard*, 13 Oct. 1875, 6 July 1889; *Blackburn Weekly Express*, 6 July 1889; biography of S. Holden Hanna in Bb. P.L. biographical files.
89. W.L. Rawstron (b 1874), *Reminiscences*, a paper read to the Burnley Historial Society, 10 Nov. 1954 (Burnley P.L.).
90. E.g. *Bradford Review*, 17 July 1858.
91. *Manchester Daily Examiner and Times*, 19 Nov. 1868.
92. *Ashton Reporter*, 17 Oct. 1868, 21 Nov. 1869; *Blackburn Standard*, 13 Nov. 1867.
93. *Ashton Standard*, 22 Nov. 1873. Booth Mason was Hugh Mason's brother, surely the most bizarre coupling in the whole political history of the period.
94. *Manchester Courier*, 3 Apr. 1872.
95. *The Monthly Record of the Protestant Evangelical Mission and Electoral Union*, 1871–73.
96. For Camin in Bradford, *Bradford Review*, Sept. 1862; for Mead, Greenall, *loc. cit.* p. 132.
97. *Ashton Standard*, 27 June 1868; *Rochdale Observer*, 30 May 1868.
98. Best, *loc. cit.* pp. 128, 133, 138–42.
99. *Oldham Chronicle*, 4 Aug. 1877; *Ashton Standard*, 9 Feb. 1884.
100. Best, *loc.cit.* pp. 134–7.
101. Ashton press, Jan. 1868.
102. *Ashton Reporter*, 18, 25 Jan. 1868; *Blackburn Times*, 22 Jan. 1868.
103. *Ashton Reporter*, 21 Nov. 1868; for a paranoic outburst in Blackburn, *Blackburn Standard*, 28 Nov. 1868.
104. *Manchester Courier*, 12 Sept. 1868.
105. W. Chadwick, *Reminiscences of a Chief Constable* (Manchester 1900), pp. 94–5.
106. *Ashton Reporter*, 25 Jan, 16 May 1868; Home Office Papers,

H.O./45 O.S. 7991/170, Chief Constable of Manchester's Report to Dublin Castle, 2 June 1868; see also Kirk, *op. cit.* ch. 4.

107.   *Ashton Reporter*, 25 Jan., 8 Feb., 25 Apr. 1868.
108.   *Ibid.*, 25 Jan, 30 May 1868; see also evidence of James Kirk, Mayor of Stalybridge, *P.P.* 1868–9, VIII (352), esp. Q. 3849.
109.   Riot Depositions, Ashton 1868, Lancs. County Record Office, Preston. Details for only a few of those arrested however: in one set of ten only three were able to sign their names.
110.   *Rochdale Pilot*, 12 June 1869.
111.   *Blackburn Standard*, 22 Jan., 23 Oct. 1868; *Ashton Reporter*, 25 Apr. 1868.
112.   *Rochdale Pilot*, 15 Aug. 1868. For the atmosphere of a Murphy meeting well described, *Ashton Reporter*, 25 Jan. 1868.
113.   *Ibid.*, 8 Feb. 1868.
114.   *Blackburn Standard*, 16 Oct. 1867 (on Protestant violence in Belfast), 23 Oct. 1868 (letters); *Ashton Reporter*, 8 Feb. 1868, for Darwen Anglican clergy urging their people not to attend Murphy's meetings; *P.P.* 1868–9, VIII (352), Q 2732.

8
POLITICS AND SOCIETY

Political organisation

In the factory towns the significance of political organisation
inhered chiefly in its institutional representation of economic
power and the social leadership based on it.[1] When the full range
of the organisation is considered in relation to society as a whole
the same oligrachic rule is apparent. Excluded from political power,
the working class was nevertheless included in the political
process by means of the manipulation of the fiction of consultative
democracy. As John Vincent describes the new political machinery
of the 1860s and 70s: 'What was conceded was not democracy
within the party, either really or in form, but a broadening of
participation by the many, in decisions necessarily taken as
before, by the few.'[2] That the symbolic role of the working
class in the exercise of power sufficed was of course a consequence
of very few working people asking for more, and never too many
asking for even this much.

Those who manned the party apparatus in the northern
industrial boroughs – spanning the distance between the notables
in their Councils and Associations and the working men in their
clubs – were most often the small men of local society. In both
political parties it was the shoemakers and tailors, the retailers and
dealers, the small manufacturers and other minor respectables
who did most to fight elections and keep the machinery running
between them.[3] A great deal of the story of activist recruitment
has to be told in terms of individual churches and chapels and the
social, religious and business links of their congregations.[4] Some
of these connections have been traced for the Blackburn chapels,[5]
the activists forming a vital leaven between the leadership and the
working class, not only in the political sphere but also through
their involvement in such causes as Temperance and the Sunday
schools, and even more importantly, in the co-ops and friendly
societies. The *menu peuple* were the indispensible drones of
popular politics. As Ostrogorski saw, the caucus and the rest of
the organisation functioned principally as a 'safety valve', and a
means of getting the donkey-work done.[6]

The direction of the organisation was centralised in the hands of
the urban social and economic leadership and its servants, and

served to perpetuate the ascendancy of that leadership. As the work of Vincent and Hanham[8] makes clear, this was as much the case for Liberalism as for Toryism. The records of local party associations make plain the access to strategic positions that money brought. In the last quarter of the century Liberal Caucus and Tory Council served merely to perpetuate the dominance of wealth and streamline the machinery of a make-believe democracy.[9] The composition of the Blackburn Liberal Council in 1884 indicates the dominance in the organisation of industry and wealth: of the twenty-nine on the Council, sixteen were substantial employers (twelve of them cotton masters), four were well-established corn-millers, and seven were of lesser but very respectable standing.[10]

In considering the regional co-ordination of political organisation the 'unofficial' links of marriage, trade and social life among the élite families must constantly be borne in mind. Although the official regional framework cannot be considered here,[11] some remarks can be made: within the context of the developing professionalisation of politics (seen in such as the Agents' Associations), a strong sense of regional and local autonomy was maintained until at least 1900. This autonomy reflected the ideological concerns of the local notables and activists who controlled the regional bodies. The hierarchical structure of the local organisation and the different rates at which it was developed have been treated by other scholars and need not concern us here. At the bottom of the pyramid were the workingmen's political clubs.

On the Conservative side the Operative Conservative Societies of the 1830s and 40s established something of a tradition in the organisation of Tory workingmen. They appear to have been patronised by the local notables in a particularly unblushing fasion, one reason perhaps for the animosity with which they were greeted by Whigs and Radicals.[12] There were continuities of individual patronage and organisation from the early years into the 1860s and 70s in Wigan, Oldham and Bolton, as well as in the case of Conservative Sick and Burial Societies in a few other localities. For both sides, however, the real spurt forward came from the later 1860s. Of the great hold of the clubs there can be no doubt. The Club and Institute Union hardly got a foothold in the nineteenth-century North, least of all in Lancashire. In 1871 there were twenty-two party clubs in Bolton, in 1889 forty-three in Oldham, and in Rochdale seventeen out of twenty-nine clubs in the town in 1885 were political. In 1867 the first flush of renewed activity produced membership figures for the Conservative clubs as follows: 500 in Ashton, 700 in Stalybridge, 1,000 in Rochdale and a reputed 5,000 in Manchester. After the second wave of club development in the late 1870s and 80s there were nearly 3,200 members in thirty-one Bolton Conservative clubs.[13] Of these no less than thirteen bore the names of big Tory employers. Liberal club membership would have been as considerable. Not all members were voters: perhaps two-thirds were,[14] and levels of membership also varied with degrees of economic prosperity.[15] Estimation of the proportion of the electorate in the clubs and total membership relative to the electorate is therefore hazardous, but in the period of maximum activity in the 1880s figures of 10–15 per cent and 15–20 per cent respectively may not be too far off the mark.

Given these kinds of figures it is unlikely that the clubs were not mainly made up of working-class people. Hanham's contention that the clubs were chiefly centres for the insecure of status (clerks, artisans, shopkeepers), caught between the working-class pub and the middle-class hotel, would seem incorrect.[16] This may be so for the club committeemen, but hardly for the rank-and-file. Moreover, what is specially striking about the clubs in their early years is the enthusiastic political feeling that working men brought into their organisation. Rather than the clubs being formed by activists and notables to create political interest, they seem to have been more often freely generated by workingmen themselves, as social and political outlets for the expression of allegiances already established. In 1867 and 1868 Tory organisers in Salford and Rochdale pointed to the ubiquity of organisation and partisanship in Lancashire.[17] Edward Hardcastle in Salford rightly pointed to his thousand unpaid canvassers as evidence for this enthusiasm. The Oldham Tory clubs were usually set up by workingmen, sometimes in private houses. It was constantly maintained, for the Oldham Liberal clubs as well, that members were from 'the labouring classes' or 'workingmen', and that it was the membership that projected and did most to run the clubs.[19] Information on the club rank-and-file after the expansion of the 1880s similarly suggests the presence of the entire range of labouring occupations.[20]

As striking as this spontaneity of interest was its location against the background of popular acceptance of élite leadership, and of a secondary and symbolic political role. Hardcastle of Salford thought in 1868 that all that was wanting was the leadership of 'gentlemen of influence and social position', and there is every sign that the club membership agreed with him. The links between the clubs and the employers have already been seen.

The Oldham clubs ultimately looked to the patronage of 'gentle-men', and particularly on the Tory side there is every evidence that this was forthcoming.[21] In 1868 the Hornbyite Elijah Holt moved into the affairs of the Blackburn Central Working Men's Club to urge the replacement on the committee of the 'demo-cratic' by the 'aristocratic' element, and the same transformation was successfully accomplished in Rochdale a year later.[22] The reactions of a member of the Cockbrook Conservative Club (Ashton) were widely representative: 'Working men, however, liked to be surrounded by a higher station in life, and liked to work in harmony with them'. The leadership, gentlemen in good position, had to lead and to say 'come on' to the led.[23]

The conventions of consultation had to be looked to, however. This was especially so on the Liberal side, where the diversity of opinion within the party often made management difficult, and the qualified commitment of elements in organised labour frequently involved a real independence of mind. Open revolt against the 'dictation' of wealth was highly unusual, though there is evidence for this kind of eruption of feeling during the difficult years of the Reform agitation in the later 1860s.[24] On the Tory side, the failure of the leadership to soothe the sensitivities of the club movement resulted in an open row in Preston between 1881 and 1883.[25] This, however, involved the clubs' defence of their own moneyed candidate (himself supported by many among the respectable leadership), and amounted to an assertion of the local and the paternal against presumptuous outsiders and local cliques, rather than any real attempt at gaining a say in policy or control.

The rules of the game were nearly always followed, and the necessary minium of consultation accorded. This was especially the case with the procedures governing the selection of parlia-mentary candidates, both before and after the institution of the Caucus. The necessary illusion of the process lay in the faith-fulness with which 'electors' and 'representatives' were consulted once the real choice had emerged from the deliberations of the local 'magic circles'. The acclamatory meeting characterised all the constituencies, and found a parallel in the annual meeting of the MP with his constituents, invariably propagandist exercises in which the member 'accounted' for his year at Westminster.[26]

For decades on end the clubs slumbered peacefully in the party breast. Most in the Liberal clubs were not a whit less respectful than their Tory counterparts. The ends for which consultative democracy were required in Stalybridge were expressed by one Liberal clubman in 1868: the new system would result in workingmen mixing with their betters, and thereby fostering the spirit of class harmony.[27] The subserviency of the Tory club movement is apparent from the Blackburn conflict of the 1870s, when one section of the leadership fought another for the parliamentary candidacy, using the club movement as its political hammer.[28]

The conduct of political life

The institutional arrangement of the organisation represented what was new in mass politics, and were a response to the problems posed by the coming of the mass electorate; an electorate numerous, voting in secret, and decreasingly amenable to the old and often corrupt methods of electoral management. But the institutional arrangements were only one means of meeting the challenge of 1867 and 1872. What was of at least equal importance was the physical character of politics, what is called here the conduct of political life. The texture of political action has gone largely unvalued by political historians in the past, and this is a further reason for considering it in detail here.

The character of the campaign and the election had its own effect, and one in which the conduct of politics was at least as important as the content. Electioneering was about the 'manufacture of sentiment' and the creation of enthusiasm. The emotion and imagery of the racecourse and fair day were brought into politics, sharpening pre-ordained antagonisms and creating new ones among the less attached and partisan. The 'irrationality' Ostrogorski considered such a distinguishing mark of English mass democracy in this period had perhaps its fullest play in the Victorian North, and most of all in Lancashire. But there the message was not at all the medium alone, for it was first voiced loud and long in the factories and the denominational and sectarian institutions of the localities. Thus the forms of political conduct had a kinship with the nature of clan and sect loyalties.

Developments in political conduct involved the creation of new political forms to manage the new electorate, though forms that owed much to the old ways of going about things. The themes of continuity and adaptation will be prominent in what follows, and both themes in their concrete expressions were to owe much to the characteristics of community life and loyalties. The success with which the politics of influence adapted to the politics of opinion was remarkable. In the 1860s and 70s developments in the conduct of politics complemented the new institutional arrangements in perfecting the political effectiveness of those included in the collectivities of work and religion, attempting to involve those outside them, and ensuring the continued dominance of the established social and political leadership.

The election campaign built up through tumultuous weeks of meetings. Election day itself remained a great day in town life long beyond the Secret Ballot and the general slackening of the ancient reliance on drink and corruption.[29] In 1873 political excitement in pre-election Blackburn was described as obliterating all other considerations, and causing men to leave their work and businesses.[30] Election day itself was both a celebration of allegiance and a popular sport of the greatest participatory intensity. It was preceded by a welter of broadsheets, songs, placards and 'squibs', the motifs of which were often sporting – the parties as opposed football teams for instance, or the much used billiards and horserace handicap fictions.[31] Pigeons and dogs, especially bulldogs – all alike fancied in the industrial North – were often tied with political colours. Nor was the human specimen reticent: one Oldham man, dyed and dressed in blue, paraded the town in the Tory cause in 1874.[32]

Though in a form heightened by an unusual dedication to the use of drink and violence, Clitheroe elections in the days of the hustings represent much that was typical about the old electoral regime, and much that was to continue in more subdued forms after 1872. The keenness of the contests characterised the whole of this period, elections being 'little else than Civil War', as did the tribalism of loyalties: 'My feyther wer ollus a liberal (or tory) and soa am I', or, 'a notoriously ignorant landlord'; 'I'se for th' Church and Staate'. Elections bred their own heroes: in the Clitheroe of 1868, 'Dick Unlicked' (over thirteen rounds with a radical stonemason), 'Smut Varley', 'Jolly Tar' and 'Young Twid'.[33]

In 1852 Marx was somewhat precipitate in noting the decline of the politics of mayhem. More than other contemporaries, however, he saw the significance in electoral events, the social ends that drink and violence served. The celebratory aspect is apparent in his understanding of the people as a Greek chorus massed behind their official heroes, 'rioting in bacchanalian carouse, at the creation of parliamentary divinities, like the Cretan Centaurs at the birth of Jupiter, and taking pay and treat for participation in their glory'.[34] Marx similarly perceived the function of the saturnalian election; 'the master then turned servant, the servant turned master. If the servant be master for one day, on that day brutality will reign supreme.'[35]

Much in the conduct of politics as it developed in the 1860s and 70s was to meet the needs of participation and celebration by other means, as national and local efforts to curb 'corruption' took effect. But the 'reign of brutality', if decreasingly severe, was to persist long, and carnival was to be a defining mark of elections into the twentieth century. Liberal electioneering was only a little less given to bacchanalian excess than the Tory version, and in the factory towns, more intimate and less under the eye of the world than the cities, the institution of electoral secrecy moderated rather than eradicated the general mayhem.[36]

Popular acceptance, indeed popular demand, for this kind of politics was reflected in the lack of public feeling against treating, and in the widespread dislike of election petitioners: in 1881 the Liberal petitioners' effigies were carried on gallows through Wigan.[37] Popular attitudes were bound up with the conception of the politician, and especially the employer-politician, as the town patron. Treating was but one face the candidate presented as the fount of largesse, and the representative of all the varied interests of the locality.[38] Continuities of conduct and expectation in politics were rooted in a *milieu* in which the personal, the local, and the concrete mattered most of all.

The odium attaching to the non-local candidate was universal and automatic: even the Darwen manufacturer J.G. Potter was execrated as a foreigner when he stood in neighbouring Blackburn. Analysis of the social composition of parliamentary candidates in the North-West Region between 1860 and 1886 indicates the overwhelming weight of landed, commercial and industrial wealth, and the primacy of the local candidate:

TABLE 8

Social composition of parliamentary candidates,
North-West Region, 1860–1886[39]

	Total candidates (not including Lancashire county seats)		Total candidates (including Lancashire county seats)	
	Liberal	Conservative	Liberal	Conservative
Industrial	45	41	48	42
Commercial	34	11	40	12
Professional	33	32	36	32
Landed	11	20	17	30
Working-class	3	0	3	0
Local	68	67	86	79
Non-local	48	37	48	37

The situation in the West Riding was very similar, and, as other work on Liberal candidates in the North-West between 1886 and 1900 makes plain, these characteristics were as prominent after 1886 as before.

The kind of propaganda mounted on behalf of the great Wigan Tory coalowners Lord Lindsay and Thomas Knowles was used whenever possible: in 1880 it was claimed that between the two £634,000 in wages and £12,000 in rates had been paid to the

town. Their Liberal opponents had contributed nothing.[41]
John Lancaster, a Liberal candidate of former years who had
severed his once considerable coal connection, was ridiculed in
Tory propaganda as having 'toddled off to Rugby' and the
effete South.[42] The papers of M.P.s in the period illuminate
the workings of political largesse. At the turn of the century, in
the Westhoughton Division and in Bolton, Lord Stanley had
to meet the needs of chapels and churches, friendly societies and
workingmen's clubs, football and cricket teams, and cottage
hospitals and orphan funds.[43] As the election drew near such
claims became overwhelming.[44] Elections might indeed revolve
around the competition of patronage claims, as in Warrington
where the Tory brewer Gilbert Greenall was examined in the
Liberal placards of 1868 and found wanting.[45] Below the level
of principle and intelligence shown in the best urban politicians,
such as the Radical-Nonconformist worsted manufacturers
and merchants of Bradford, the run-of-the mill local candidate
was in politics to buttress his own social standing and represent
the interests of his trade.[46] His mediocrity and narrowness of
vision itself strengthened the hold of patronage politics and
maintained the parochialism of politics intact.

The patronage turney drew its force from the still considerable
isolation and local patriotism of towns, and often involved the
exploitation of an elephantine popular memory. Hugh Mason
of Ashton was being pilloried in the 1880s for his transgressions
of the 1860s.[47] The degrees of the notables' generosity in the
Cotton Famine were similarly remembered long after the event.
The usual medium of charge, insult and their invariably immediate rejoinders, was the wall placard, though the itinerant balladeer
still plied his trade in the Wigan election of 1874. Such efforts,
often highly skilled, depended for their effect on the immediate
recognitions possible in the intimate life of the factory town.[48]
The following is fairly typical in style, an attack upon one
Napoleon Clare, a lieutenant of Warrington's Gilbert Greenall
in 1868:

> Swagbelly grunts like a Chinese pig,
> When Gilbert he adores;
> Clare drunk you'll in the Griffin find,
> The sty for Greenall's boars ...
>
> Ye shallow pated Orangemen,
> Of number one take care,
> And work to be made jerrylords,
> Like old Swagbelly Clare.[49]

This type of local satire, often in dialect form, continued power-fully into the twentieth century, and in municipal elections as well.[50]

Political largesse was a continuation of the politics of the market by other means, but for large parts of the electorate the politics of the market were nothing other than an adjuct of the politics of influence. Beer, money and largesse, as elements in the gift relationship, cemented the social ascendancy of wealth and assured the adhesion of the electorate to the parties. As previously indicated,[51] it is in these senses, and not as some quaint industrial remnant of 'Eatanswill', that the political culture is most fruitfully approached. Similarly, this emphasis on the personal, the local and the concrete as the defining and delimiting marks of the political culture suggests the persistence of traditional authority and of communal loyalties. Only when the force of this persistence is understood do these cultural characteristics assume their central place as the logical political expression of the wider culture, and not as residues peripheral to the onward march of the politics of individual opinion.

The Conservatives seem in general to have been better able to respond to politics as participatory, local and convivial, and to maintain these elements in political conduct as a means of managing the mass electorate. Many Liberals failed to appreciate, as a grass-roots Liberal like W.A. Abram in Blackburn did, the need for 'visible symbols' and 'curt formulae'. The greater responsiveness of Toryism can also be seen in the party's more calculated adoption of the public ritual forms of working-class life for political purposes.

Any historical discussion of ritual enters difficult terrain. The detailed evidence needed to produce close analysis of a ritual and so evaluate its full social meaning is not usually available.[52] More particularly, this means that we are unable to evaluate the variety of contexts within which any given ritual had social meaning. Nor can we very often know the subjective meaning of events for the participant. It is too easy to rest content with the sacramental Durkheimian understanding of public ritual as society's worship of itself. Aside from an inherent historical credulity, the functionalism usually implicit in such approaches fails to recognise, as Leach says,[53] that rituals 'do things' as well as 'say things', and can have a conscious effect for the participants.[54] What perhaps requires saying with some emphasis is that the same ritual can have a variety of social contexts and meanings, even pulling in opposite and contradictory directions.

Discussion of the place of ritual in class relationships bears directly on this point. A friendly or trade society procession in the context of a civic or national ritual can both augment and attenuate the element of class identification among the participants. Both Edward Thompson and more recently Robert Gray have persuasively shown the articulation of class mutuality and independence in such rituals.[55] And, undoubtedly, in the factory North there existed powerful continuities of class assertion between the early part of the century, when these feelings were strongest, and the years that followed.

Reservoirs of solidarity were tapped with special effect by the endemic forms of public display and ceremony in working-class institutional life, above all in the friendly societies and trade unions. Not only did these societies have their own ritual, they also had ritual occasions in galas, outings and 'anniversaries'.[56] In the great range of non-factory trades especially, though also as a residue of earlier ways within factory production itself, an intense trade consciousness and pride marked the time, being reflected in such events as the Preston Guilds celebrations.[57] Yet, if large parts of working-class public life were a world unto themselves, in the second half of the century this only begins to describe the nature of that public life. For it was then that public ritual began most fully to display a diversity of context and meaning, becoming more an aspect of inclusion in the social and political nation, and less an assertion of a unique identity than was earlier the case.

The chief constituents of this public language were the procession, with its banners and bands, and the meeting. Bishop Knox of Manchester described the peculiar Lancashire addition to processions, and their peculiar style – the banners, the bands, the attendant swarms of women and children, the robed Corporation figures, and the mounted leader.[58] The great Lancashire Anglican Workingmen's White March on London in 1906 was one culmination of the adaptation of the ritual forms of public life for the purposes of party politics.[59]

In the early part of the century such ritual involved the creation of a sense of identity and worth among those shut out from involvement in the corporate life of the nation. The second half of the century was to see the development of at least the fiction of involvement. The excluded were increasingly to be the included, one great symbol of the changed condition of things being the extension of the franchise. This process of integration was accompanied by the closer interaction of working-class ritual with that of the nation and of the town.

The creation of the incorporated boroughs in the mid-century years, and the new civic life this brought about, involved a new range of rituals in which working-class ceremonial could be exercised in new settings. Not that the pre-established administrative structure was unable to offer its own grandeur too, such as the ceremonial departure of a High Sheriff to office. In 1850 Clement Royd's leave-taking in Rochdale involved the friendly societies in the procession and the whole town in the subsequent carnival.[60] Such occasions, marked by the consumption of a whole roast ox and a superfluity of beer and plum-pudding, offered an élite the opportunity to practise the arts of an élite. Civic developments certainly windened the span of possibility, the various Corporation processions like that on Mayor's Sunday reconstituting the reputation of the élites in the new setting of a shared political and administrative identity.[61]

The special significance of civic ritual seems to have lain in this notion of a corporate town identity. The fostering of the idea of identified interests was apparent in the ceremonial openings of the great northern town halls, such as the Rochdale opening in 1867 and the no less splendid Manchester occasion in 1877. At the latter the procession comprised sixty-four groups of trade and friendly socieites, marching with fifty-one bands, making up a total of 44,000 people.[62] The correspondence accompanying the organisation of the event indicates the great eagerness of the societies to be part of the town hall 'movement' and of the great day itself. Although a Trades Commitee had a hand in the organisation the event was orchestrated by the Manchester Corporation.[63] Municipal activity could vary between the distinctly parochial, such as 'Hospital Sunday' – involving the whole range of town institutions and sometimes an organised procession – and civic representations of the national event.

Royal events came increasingly to occasion the mixing of working-class ritual in the civic celebration. This role of the town as the catalyst of the larger event has been illuminated by the Mass-Observation study of the 1937 Coronation.[64] This indicates the centrality of the local dimension, the emphasis on town patriotism and social cohesion to the exclusion of obtruding sectional interests. The deflection of ritual to the purposes of town unity was considerably furthered by the growing cult of monarchy in the 1870s. The local event involved the whole range of minor town bodies, as well as the ranks of the Sunday school, and the trade and friendly societies. On the death of Prince Albert in 1861 the Volunteers, the Cadet Corps, the town clergy and the Corporation workmen of Blackburn all walked in mourning, attired in the costume of their status and calling.[65] In the 1893 Clitheroe celebrations for the Duke of York's marriage, temperance organisations, bicycle clubs, 'the mounted knights of the cleaver' and the ubiquitous brass bands all formed 'a grand torchlight procession'.[66]

Jubilees, coronations, marriages and funerals all offered the chance for display, though the royal visits themselves were the most momentous. The 1873 visit of Prince Arthur to Lancashire combined the royal with the civic event, Bolton Town Hall and a new infirmary in Wigan being officially opened.[67] In Wigan the Crawfords were a considerable supporting attraction. They did most to manage the visit, assembling and treating their tenants as part of the show. The large processions in both towns included friendly society members dressed in trade costume, bearing all the insignia of trade and lodge aloft. In Bolton the trades carried the town coat-of-arms, and the other banners bore the devices 'May Bolton maintain its province in the cotton trade', 'A thing of beauty is a joy for ever', but also, 'Justice' and 'Labour is the source of all wealth'. And, indeed, what the participants had in such events was a kind of justice, one more symbolic than real. In the day itself recognition and status were accorded and the sectionalism of labour was subsumed in the wider social order.

The appropriation of so much working-class public ritual for the purposes of party politics was primarily a natural consequence of the political implications this ritual had to begin with. Politics was based on the communities of the sect and the factory and inevitably adopted the characteristics of communal life, among which was the recourse to the habit of ritual and ceremony. The ritualised public observances of the congregation, the Sunday school, the Orange Order and the factory were implicit political occurrences. As religion and the workplace came to the centre of politics in the 1850s and 60s, they carried with them the loyalties of the clan and the sect, and the means by which these loyalties were maintained in being, the social language of ritual.

This process of political appropriation involved, as well, an active understanding on the part of the political parties. In the matter of 'curt formulae' and 'visible symbols' the Tories had something of an advantage. The Liberals, deficient in the visible symbol, could not hope to match the mute but evocative Tory emblem, whether the mace, the open bible, the likeness of a Derby or the monarch, the allegorical representation of 'Altar, Throne and Cottage', or the ossified history of the Orange banner. Ritual and symbolism was the mother-tongue of the party of unspoken tradition. And, in the active shaping of public ritual, the Tory party does seem to have had the greater intuition and imagination.

Contemporary observers, both English and American, noted the outrageously partisan character of English political meetings, and above all the 'curious volatility' of the Lancashire audience.[68] The orchestration of the campaign, and the integration of the procession and meeting, represented the chief elements in the political manipulation of the ritualising habit. They provided the semblance of power in the feeling of numbers, necessary, as Ostrogorski saw, to shape emotions for the ends of party politics.[69] This engineering of political excitement served many of the same ends as had the now waning politics of the market. The politics of undisciplined mayhem gave way to the politics of disciplined mayhem. Acting on the 'favourably disposed will' most often, and not on the mind, the torrent of words that made up 'the golden age of the platform' is best understood in the context in which the words were experienced. Elections were 'speaking matches' in which the game was at least as important as the words.

The election campaign usually built up to the climactic mass meeting. Nine thousand Tory working men gathered in the Preston Corn Exchange in 1868,[70] and this was after unremitting weeks of meetings at club and ward levels.[71] The periods between parliamentary elections were also exposed to the torrents of rhetoric: at club functions, during the visits of national politicians, in the gatherings of denominational and pressure groups, and in the municipal and School Board elections, the parties saturated the remainder of the political year. The organisation of political emotion was characterised from the 1850s and 60s by the movement indoors – itself an aspect of the increased level of organisation in town life – and the use of Manchester as the chief centre of political pilgrimage, though the ritual of the town meeting remained very strong, especially as part of the Liberal ideology of incorporation.

The great Manchester congregations best reveal the ways in which the political event was arranged to tap the vein of working-class ritual. Both parties organised such meetings, but the Tories were always more adept, almost commandeering the vast Pomona Gardens for their special blend of the indoor and outdoor in the mass rally. The Liberals were usually content with the Free Trade Hall.

The great demonstration in support of the Irish Church in 1869 was typical. Estimates of the number present varied between 100,000 and 500,000. Political clubs, Orange lodges and Sunday schools formed a 30,000-strong procession through Manchester, fighting with the Irish along the way. The Lancashire Tory mighty held forth from eight platforms, amid continual singing, band-playing, banner-waving, and the organised tumult of the passing of motions.[72] The impression these meetings made is best conveyed by eye-witnesses. The following, describing the 1878 Pomona demonstration on the Eastern Question, suggests much but leaves unmentioned much of importance – the dramatic entrance, usually from the rear of the hall, and the use of effigies. Gladstone, representing the 'Woodman' cutting down Burke's Tree of State, was burned in effigy at the Pomona meeting. A newspaper reporter described the scene:

The chairman then rose for the purpose of putting the resolution to the meeting. Then followed a scene of the wildest enthusiasm. The vast assembly cheered vociferously and it was in vain that the chairman endeavoured by voice and gesture again and again to obtain a hearing in order that he might read out the resolution. ... Suddenly a large canvass scroll stretching from one side of the platform to the other and bearing the words 'Both hands up for the resolution' was elevated and instantly every hand shot up, both on the platform and on the floor. Hats were waved in the air ... on walking sticks ... and on umbrellas. The scroll was lowered and another raised bearing the words 'Hands up against the resolution'. The cheering now gave place to groaning and hissing mingled with shouts of 'He's gone out'. ... Directly the scroll was removed 'Rule Britannia' was heartily sung. A gentleman at the rear of the hall then held up a portrait of the Queen. This was the signal for another outburst of cheering and 'God Save the Queen' was sung with thrilling effect, all the heads being uncovered and those on the platform rising from their seats. The sight from the platform at this moment was something to be remembered. Veteran politicians remarked as they looked down upon that sea of up-turned faces, that they had not witnessed anything like it for many a day.[73]

These occasions were solemn enough: in 1876 30,000 people paid for the privilege of participation at Pomona.[74] The organisers, men like S.C. Nicholson and William Touchstone in Manchester, and Elijah Holt and the Thompsons in Blackburn, had the closest possible links with all the institutions of working-class life. Nicholson's greatest triumph was the demonstration for Disraeli in 1872.[75] Twenty-thousand marched through Manchester in the rain, accompanied by the inevitable banners and bands, women and children. The Orangemen marched with oranges stuck through their umbrellas. At the great congregation afterwards Disraeli confessed himself not unmoved, remarking that the demonstration was 'one of the most remarkable incidents, perhaps I may say an unparalleled one, in the life of any public man'. It was not, however, the gospel of Sanitation nor even of Tory Democracy which marked the real significance of the day. That lay in the event as one symbolic culmination of the appropriation of the characteristics of popular public life for the purposes of party politics.

The grand participatory theatre of the Pomona meetings reflected that of the more sinister Murphy ones, where revivalism and music hall were mixed in the anticonfessional dumbshow.[76] The jingo demonstrations throughout the region in 1877 and 1878 took on the same character too, with their marches and countermarches, torchlight extravaganzas, and their systematic use of effigies and banners. The Liberal demonstrations of the 1870s were less grandly orchestrated, but popular passions were still very effectively excited and dragooned. In tracing the continuities between the old politics and the new, and in revaluing the newness of the new, the association of politics and ritual will have a central place. This discussion merely commences the agenda of analysis, the political day, and especially 'Voting Day', offering itself strongly as the next item for consideration: between Marx's description of the meaning of political conduct in 1852 and the 'fustian-clad' cab-riders of Huddersfield in 1874, kings for a day at the expense of the parties,[78] there was no essential difference despite the passage of almost a quarter of a century. These further possibilities can only be suggested here, but of the instructive power of the association between politics and community public life there seems little doubt.

Political cultures and class cultures

Popular politics was rooted in the communities of work and religion, and bore the marks of entrenched, partisan conflict. In explaining the failure of the radical-tinctured Blackburn labour candidate in 1885, the *Blackburn Times* remarked:

It was because the operatives and artisans in Blackburn, like the middle class people, the millowners and the tradesmen, are very strong political partisans. They take sides and stick to their sides tenaciously. The Tory working men would not support Mr. Boothman because he had been as a Radical. ... The Irish vote is the only sectional vote that can be turned around in the mass.[79]

The community base to politics meant that politics permeated the the daily and ostensibly non-political business of men's lives. For some working men it so forcibly entered life as to make of politics a kingdom of its own, and a direct expression of social life in such as political co-ops, friendly societies and clubs.

If for most workingmen this expansion of the political culture was not so complete, in Lancashire perhaps more than anywhere else in England politics crossed the threshold of ordinary affairs.

Conservative, Radical and Protestant Sick and Burial Societies enjoyed a continuous existence in some localities from the 1840s into the last quarter of the century. The politicisation of social life was given a strong impetus by the Second Reform Act, finding expression in the formation of political co-ops, especially in the strongly Liberal West Riding and east Lancashire, where the original movement was endemic and not a little tinged with Liberal sympathies. Strong Conservative co-ops were formed in Rochdale and Darwen for instance,[80] as a consequence of the same kind of political volatility seen in the Colne Valley in 1880, when the Liberals' use of the co-op horse in a political demonstration forced the Tories into forming their own society. 'Yellow' and 'Blue' building societies as well as co-ops were also formed.

In the political coloration of leisure which the workingmen's Liberal and Conservative clubs represented there was a much wider effect. For those most intimately involved in club life, especially the somewhat higher social elements which made up the committees, the clubs could cocoon the member in a self-sufficient environment, much as with the social life of the religious congregation. For the clubs looked after their own: in the Oldham cotton strike of 1885 for example, the Tory clubs provided strike relief.[82] The seriousness of purpose workingmen brought to the first great wave of club development in the 1860s has already been noted. The early clubs were often spartan, little more than newsrooms, and the rigour of the surroundings was reflected in the attitudes of many of the members. For some of the ordinary members as well as the committee men the clubs represented an escape from and not an excuse for drink: the desire for 'permanent instruction and amusement' and the hope of 'social elevation and temperate regulation' found expression in the written histories of the early clubs.[83]

But very quickly the accent on 'amusement' rather than instruction became the dominant one, and party political work took on the subsidiary role it was thereafter to retain. The clubs developed under the pressure of what the members wanted rather than what their betters thought they should have. Instead of lectures and reading rooms, what mattered was the round of comedy evenings, bazaars, tea parties and outings.[84] Billiards, bowls, and above all the bar, rapidly dominated club life, especially in the elaborate clubs of the 1870s and 80s, the solid, square presence of which is still a considerable feature of northern recreational life.

This expansion was paid for out of the proceeds of drink, suplemented by members' subscriptions, club share sales, and the usually liberal donations of the local political élites. The attempt at remaining 'dry' was doomed to failure: by the 1880s complaints about gambling, and the primacy of 'bacca, billiards and beer', were legion in respectable circles. In the 1880s and 90s the clubs became big business, taking on something like their modern form. As usual, the Tories were more alive to developments, their Association of Conservative Clubs (founded in the early 1890s) co-ordinating the national and local organisational effort in the clear recognition that politics would be secondary to the social side, but also that the social side would do no harm to the political effort.[85]

For, however well developed the social aspect, the political name was nowhere ever solely a cover for social pursuits. The clubs all made some attempt at party propaganda, and they were the centrepiece of an election organisation which employed a much greater manpower than in modern elections. On the Tory side, the interest of the brewers in the affairs of the clubs, and the conviviality of the Orange Order, comprised two direct connections between politics and leisure. It is, however, the indirect links which are perhaps even more revealing than any formal involvement in party organisation. The fact that a good part of working-class social life in the North, and especially in Lancashire, developed within the framework of politics suggests how fully the popular electorate was institutionalised in a political culture. Though the club movement developed under the influence of its members' wishes, this was always in the context of a popular acceptance of middle-class patronage and political direction. Elsewhere in England the political club movement was not as deeply rooted, and the non-party Club and Institute Union dominated. The C.I.U. developed in a similar manner to the political clubs but the assertion of working-class tastes in the C.I.U. led not to social and political quiescence but to the rejection of middle-class patronage and condescension, and the articulation of an independent political position.[86]

The development of club life is of a general significance as well in suggesting a certain continuity of cultural style in working-class life. Of the existence of the extremes of the temperance, mechanics' institute man and the demoralised slum-dweller, and of the presence of a certain degree of mutual repulsion between them, there is no doubt. Yet to put the opposition of cultural styles in the working class at the centre of our understanding of contemporary society is to distort our understanding. The centrality of these kinds of opposition represents the import of John Foster's work.[87] In a rather less rigorous way it also represents a good deal of the logical implication in other versions of the 'labour aristocracy' notion.

Despite Foster's disclaimers that the opposition of 'abstinent' and 'non-abstinent' cultural styles represents 'poles' or tendencies in social behaviour, the logic of his argument would seem to require that the two 'sub-cultures' be mutually exclusive, internally coherent, and operate widely in working-class life: if they were not this then it is difficult to envisage how they could have acted as a real principle of social differentiation between the two labour 'sub-groups' whose identity they are supposed to have represented. If the sub-groups of the 'skilled' and 'unskilled' are to remain identifiable and intact then their cultural expressions must be sufficiently distinctive to provide the necessary level of mutual repulsion. In fact, cultural style and social level in the working class did not correspond in any simple sense, least of all in the sense of some primal cleavage: once this is acknowledged status disintegrates into a myriad of gradations and contexts. Before moving to a closer discussion of this, something more concerning the relationship between working-class culture and party politics remains to be considered.

Contrary to the supposed centrality of opposed differences, what one would like to suggest here is the continuity of a broad and dominant popular culture; humane, 'free and easy', and broadminded in its respectability. Arnold Bennett was perhaps as near to the heart of the matter as anyone: his picture of the 'Bursley Mutual Burial Club' in the 1870s, with its evenings of drink, songs, recitations and clog-dancing-inseperable from the joys of dog-breeding and coursing-conveys the essential picture of a stoic common endeavour and the fellowship of pleasure.[88] It was to this culture that the Tory style, more relaxed and responsive than the Liberal, made the most successful of the party appeals. At the social extremes, among the very poor least rooted in community life, this culture veered into demoralisation and self-defeat, and the Tory party was undoubtedly not averse to fishing in the waters of Bright's 'residuum'. But to equate the Tory style with the politics of the slum is to misjudge it. Similarly, to underprize the reserves of self-sufficiency and independence in working-class life is equally to misjudge a culture, which, though especially unresistant in these years to the social and political appeals of the upper classes, nevertheless kept much of its own counsel in co-op, friendly society and trade union. Something of this apartness will be considered at the close of this section.

   The continuity of cultural priorities represented in the development of the club movement was one reflection of the more general failure of the 'improving' middle class, intent on creating a respectable and temperate working class in its own image. The music hall, the sports stadium and the popular press triumphed over the mechanics' institute and the temperance society. In the transition to a more stable and organised urban life the legacy of older and more violent and spontaneous ways was a powerful one. The 1850s and 60s was still a time of hard drinking, hard sports and hard gambling.[89] As late as 1877 the *Oldham Chronicle* noted that 'cock-fighting and prize-fighting are no doubt practised to an alarming extent at the present day, but it is done under cover'.[90] What followed in the train of the older and still lively pastimes was directly related to them: the 'purring' (clog-fighting), 'ratting' and wrestling still particularly prevalent in the mining districts were but the coursing, pigeon-fancying and horserace mania of the majority writ large.[91] Especially in the early years of this period, the debt to rural life was still a considerable one.

   Thus the pint and the bet remained as much distinguishing marks of popular leisure as they had always been. The extent to which the Tories' greater command of 'geniality and bonhomie' struck a dominant chord in working-class life has already been considered in a number of contexts, particularly in terms of employer paternalist styles.[92] Posterity has too long credited contemporary Liberal propaganda with the substance of fact. The Liberal stereotype of the Tories, and of themselves, took widely representative form in Manchester political cartoons of the 1870s[93]: the Tory workingman, drunken and vicious, grovels at the feet of a bejewelled Disraeli; the noble features of the decent artisan Liberal are framed by a savings bank. It is clear that 1868 came as a profound shock to many Liberals. Not only was Toryism not vanquished, but it went on in Lancashire to consolidate a massive success. This success owed as much as did Liberal support to the adhesion of the 'respectable workingman' Liberalism had so long flattered and blithely appropriated to its cause. The Liberal stereotypes of themselves as the party of Progress and their opponents as 'the stupid party' were long retained as a comfort against the coldness of this fact.

   To so much in Liberalism that was strenuous and restrictive Toryism opposed the figure of John Bull, tolerant, frank and hearty. In the terms of one example of the frequent Tory use of the horserace handicap fiction, John Bull was a mixture of 'John Jolley', 'Old Honesty' and 'Live and Let Live'. To the laughter and applause of a large gathering of Preston Tory workingmen in 1868 one speaker proposed the virtues of 'good, plain, homely Constitutional food such as we ourselves can live and get fat upon – myself for a specimen'.[94] In 1885 a recitation was delivered to 5,000 Tory workingmen in Blackburn praising the virtues of John Bull, for whom the glass and the heart were to brim: 'Honest John Bull' was industrious, good humoured and brave, also 'Not afraid of his betters when mellow/Since betters he knows he must have'.[95] John Bull was the opposite of everything the Nonconformist and Temperance wings of Liberalism stood for.

The figure took a variety of incarnations in Tory politicians. Lt Col. Feilden, a relative of the Blackburn Feildens, was usually assured of the Chorley seat, and played up the plain, honest military man who was no politician or speaker. Courteous and condescending to his Liberal opponent in 1885, he described himself as speaking 'in a sort of colloquial style', a manner that drew the shout from the floor – 'That's John Bull for you'.[96] The 'gallant general' found a counterpart in Burnley's General Scarlett, the hero of Balaklava. Squire John Bull was the foremost advocate of England's beer and its glories. John Morgan Cobbett of Oldham, a parody of his famous father, was very much the embodiment of Oldham Toryism in the third quarter of the century. His hobby-horse was the repeal of the malt-tax, the Tory *Oldham Standard* in 1861 joining him in affirming the efficacy of home-brewed beer in improving the health and morals of the people.[97] What Cobbett represented in his person, J.R. Stephens embodied in his principles, defending beer and good living as part of Old England and its rights and liberties.[98]

The Tory access to good feeling was reflected in the invariable Toryism of the butcher fraternity, who had their own special rural connections. The butchers were active in Tory electioneering,[99] and at play were the Tory type *par excellence*, dog-fanciers and horse-trotters to a man.[100] The occupational cultures the Liberals could call upon, such as the tribes of often Nonconformist travelling drapers, were hardly a match: the Tory trinity of the publican, bookie and butcher presented a more raffish and successful political image than the Liberal recourse to the shoemaker and draper. In castigating the 'mean pride' of Wigan Liberalism, the workingman George Roby noted the paucity of Liberal talent in this area.[101] The Tories had all the 'cards'.[102] Like Arnold Bennett's own 'good old Denry' Machin they had 'good old Dickie' Edmundson and 'Lijah Holt in Blackburn. Further up the social scale they had 'John William' Maclure ('Mr Fix-It' and 'the apostle of Conservatism to the masses') in Manchester, and in Salford, William Charley, in Liberal eyes 'the darling of the unwashed of Salford'.[103]

Sport was particularly important in mediating this aspect of the party appeals. There were of course a number of Liberal, though mainly Anglican, exceptions to the Tory rule: A.B. Rowley of Ashton, Oldham Whittaker's son-in-law, owed his considerable popularity to his reputation as a strike arbitrator and a 'genial sportsman'. The coursing craze in Blackburn affected the masters as much as the men. The Quaker James Briggs owned a winner of the Waterloo Cup, 'Bed of Stone'. His sporting interests were shared by his brother William, an Anglican and the town's M.P. As the Liberal party manager saw, these interests were of great political value.[104] Known as 'Willie' Briggs or 'Eawr Billy', he was in appearance the jolly Englishman, with a perfect command of dialect. A contemporary magazine described him as having 'much of the appearance of a Wapping butcher out for a holiday'.[105] The Tory association was always closest however, and nowhere more so than in the world of the turf. The intermarried brewing families of Blackburn were devotees, William Ward, 'the sporting brewer', having some success in both the Derby and the Waterloo Cup. His uncle, 'Dan' Thwaites, was an avid follower of the hunt. Col. Sir John Rutherford, for long Darwen's M.P., was a leading racehorse owner of his time and a footballer for Blackburn Rovers.[106]

These indications of common cultural preoccupations in popular life return us once more to the notion of status fragmentation and opposition in working-class culture. The idea has been examined in a number of contexts and found wanting:[107] not only are the mechanics of its operation at the level of work suspect, so too are the cultural dynamics held to have given these differences social definition; and this applies alike to textile workers and other factory workers, and those outside as well as inside factories. Without the correspondence of work and life, without the *necessary* level of cultural coherence, exclusiveness and breadth of operation, differences between craftsman and labourer remain mere sectionalism, as old as time and very likely as long-lasting.

There is of course ample evidence from the time for the recognition of superiority and inferiority among craftsmen and labourers, and these trade-derived differences did find expression in social life.[108] Craftsman and labourer would for instance drink in different bars of the same pub (though the relevant point here would be that they all shared in the culture of the pub). The exclusiveness of the skilled man – fearful of the dilution of his skill and of the abyss of poverty below – also hardly stands in need of further documentation. But this is worlds away from some kind of internecine cultural strife between the 'aristocrat' in his temperance society, mechanics' institute and Sunday school, and the 'undermass' in their pubs and friendly societies, alienated from the 'respectability' of the 'pro-employer' aristocrat.

When leisure life outside work is considered what becomes apparent is not only that work-derived status differences operated within a broad, shared culture, but also that these differences were very often muted, often completely unrecognised, in the hours outside work: 'a lot of people was on the same level and treated on the same level.'[109] The distinction that really mattered was the one between clean and dirty hands, shoes and clogs, non-manual and manual work.[110] What struck John Morley about his own Blackburn was the broad majority of the self-respecting, 'respectable' despite liberal admixtures of what Morley called 'poor religion' and 'aims too personal', as well the habit of drinking.[111] A consideration of working-class institutions makes plain the common purpose of all occupational levels in social and economic activities that had little to do with 'abstinent' self-improvement.

It is unlikely that the co-op worked to disseminate somehow non-proletarian values among the working class. If respectability was the mark of membership, then this seems to have characterised the majority of working people, especially in the cotton towns.[112] And this majority was composed of all occupations and statuses.[113] After the decline of the idealism of early days the 'respectability' of the membership meant little more than keeping on the financial straight and narrow path. In their provision of benefit and fellowship the friendly societies were perhaps the central institution in working-class life. Far from insulating one part of a class from another, the societies' vast membership involved the entirety of working-class society in the common pursuit of 'mirth' and conviviality. The pub long continued to be a vital part of society life, and society rules enjoined a respectability that had nothing to do with the aping of middle-class values.[114]

When the societies were threatened, as in the years of the Sunday Closing and Licensing Act agitations, they responded forcefully and with unanimity.[115] The political capital to be made in these circumstances went mostly to the Tories, particularly in Ashton.[116] Though there were all manner of exceptions, a Liberal interest in the mechanics' institute and a Tory one in the friendly society does sum up the trend of patronage interests and sympathies among the respectable classes. The Tory party itself was indeed more alive to the needs of the societies and sensitive to the style of their social life. If the societies were not the institutional cocoon of the 'undermass', nor were they insulated from society at large. Like the co-ops, not only were they patronised by the wealthy – an interest represented in the case of the societies by the honorary office-holding of Tory employers and local politicians in particular – but their organisation involved those outside the working class as well.

The gap between the 'far superior directing agents' (in the regional administration of the societies) and the local lodges, was filled at town level by many of the same individuals who formed the cadres of the party political organisations.[117] These often self-made men (small manufacturers and dealers mostly) were specially prominent on the Tory side, and had close links with the co-ops and political clubs as well as with the societies. Thus, at the levels of both élite involvement and party organisation, the foremost institution of working-class self-help was never severed from society at large.

Nonetheless, just as trade union and friendly society ritual continued to assert attenuated but still considerable traditions of solidarity and independence throughout the period, so too did the economic and social life of the co-op, the friendly society and the burial society constitute a social world potentially counter to the communities of the factory and of the religious denomination in its widest sense. The individual worker was often a member of all three social worlds, which may be conceived as spheres of social effect, each partly superimposed on the others. Because the degree of superimposition in the period was so considerable, and because the communities of work and religion were of such immense influence, the possibility of translating the world of self-help into a powerful class identification and thence into independent political action was severely limited at the time. Yet the institutions of working-class self-help were born and reared in the working class and no other. The attempt at self-sufficiency was a remarkable one: economic benefit, the disciplines of organisation, leisure, and a measure of education as well, were areas of activity in which an impressive assertion of a seperate identity was made.

The trade union completed this institutional constellation, and it did so not only as the source of organised industrial bargaining, but also of sickness, death and unemployment benefit, and of outings, 'anniversaries' and a club life of its own. The unions, operating at the foremost point of antagonism, the workplace, were the one institution capable of transforming the residual element of class identification latent in the other institutions of self-help into independent politics. This was to occur with only a minority of trade unionists, and even then these were to come mainly from outside the factory. This was so not only because in textiles especially labour relations reached a new level of institutionalised calm in the period, but also because the effect of the factory was felt in the entire community life of the worker. Work tended to fill up the space the institutions of self-help would otherwise have entered. For non-factory workers, and especially craft ones, work did not engross society in this way, just as for them labour relations never evolved to the point of bureaucratised stability reached in many of the factory trades.

The perception of a separate identity and purpose, however qualified in the period, was accentuated when union membership was most fully attended by a distinct cultural environment: it was then that the limited sense of class involved in the economic operations of union life – a sense most developed in those with the practices and traditions of a sought-for craft to hand – was strengthened by a truly social dimension, and the union most effectively offered itself as a counterweight to the other, obtruding, social worlds upon which politics was based. Because of the strength of the contrary, communal currents in politics, and because of the influence of ideologies of class co-operation in the period, such a recourse to the social life of union membership seems to have been necessary if independent labour politics were to develop.

The insulation of trade unionists in an autonomous social life was felt most completely by the activists, and it is the politics of this minority which will form the chief focus of the last chapter of this work. Their experience combined the fullest contact with the daily business of labour relations and the most complete exposure to the social life of union pub, clubroom and institute. In the next section the links between the Blackburn weavers' leadership and the public house will be noted, connections that distanced these men's radicalism from Liberalism and their daily life from contact with the other classes. For these activists negotiation and relaxation were one. For the ordinary trade union membership this was not so. With many textile unionists the social life the union offered was vestigial.

This owed something to the vast size of individual town unions and something to the centralisation of union affairs in the hands of a small bureaucracy. The Preston Weavers' Union is a case in point. Although it founded a burial society in 1861 and a weavers' institute in the early 1870s, this seems to have been the limit to which an organised social life developed: the burial society had no associative life and the small institute building catered for the town's 15,000 unionised weavers.[118] Occasions like the Preston Weavers' Field Day in 1870, attended by only 1,500 operative, were few and far between in Preston, and in Lancashire weaving in general.[119] The quasi-craft organisation of the spinners, their more lavish provision of benefit and more highly developed social life, made them a rather different case.[120] For all textile trade unionists, as union organisation gradually became firmly implanted, the cultural surround to union membership was fortified in the 1870s and 80s: it was in the early 1870s that spinners' institutes were formed in Oldham, Preston and Blackburn,[121] and in the 1880s that weavers' mutual improvement societies, newsrooms and libraries began to multiply.[122] This development may have contributed to the weakened hold of the traditional communities, though it would still have been only a small minority which would have had access to what was often only the most primitive kind of organisation. And for all textile workers, the culture of the union was always in competition with the powerful culture of the factory.

The line between the trade union and the friendly society was a thin one in many of the craft trades, and the social was inseparable from the economic side of union life. In 1896 twenty-six out of thirty-eight trade societies in Blackburn continued to meet in pubs, where business and pleasure were mixed.[123] For many of the minor trades the possibility of a whole town's membership knowing and regularly meeting each other was considerable. Though within the pale of factory influence, the engineering and ironworkers' combination of economic and cultural organisation offered considerable resources with which to offset that influence. When the politics of the labour interest are considered it is apparent that it was from the craft trades in particular, where a social world was most fully developed and where cultural worlds overlapped least, that the primary impulse towards independence came.

The politics of beer and Britannia
The Conservative party's electoral success owed much to its involvement with the drink trade. In 1862 there were 462 drink outlets in Blackburn borough, reputedly one for every twenty-three houses, and seventeen for every one clergyman, place of worship, or public school.[124] The pub and the beerhouse were

not merely drink shops, they were also the primary focus of a great deal of working-class institutional life.[125] As the fount of all knowledge, the drinkseller had his own local fame and standing, and is in many respects best understood as a leader of street and neighbourhood opinion. The Mass-Observation study of Bolton pubs in the 1930s suggests this understanding, and Roberts similarly points to the pub as providing a niche in neighbourhood society, perpetuating in its own character the *status quo* of the surrounding streets.[126] It was as much more than a source of electoral organisation and largesse that the pub and beerhouse made themselves felt in popular politics.

The drink interest was socially and politically complex. Though it was predominantly Tory, especially from the 1850s under the impact of the mounting political influence of Temperance, local pollbooks reveal the greater likelihood of Liberal voting among the beerhouse keepers, smaller fry than the publicans and less a part of the trade ethos of the publican-dominated Licensed Victualler Associations. The connections between Blackburn radicalism, the beerhouse and the trade unions explain much of the recalcitrance of this minority of beerhouse keepers. James Craven (licensee of 'The Standard of Unity') and William Crossley, both weavers' leaders, had close drink connections. Detailed reconstruction of local political groupings indicates the tension between these union radicals and a workingmen Temperance group with strong links to the club movement, organised Nonconformity and the Liberal mills.[127] The beerhouse and the temperance question in Blackburn served to articulate the radical unionists' sceptical and much-qualified acceptance of Liberalism.[128]

For the majority of drinksellers, however, the interests of the trade were uppermost, and where there was any doubt the powerful influence of the brewers made itself felt. An unusual document, the canvass of publicans and beersellers for the 1865 Blackburn election,[129] enables us to evaluate this influence (Table 9).

Considerable as brewer influence was at this stage, the 1865 vote shows how much the screw must have been turned between the canvass and the vote (though the free-house figures in Table 9 do indicate the Tory sympathies of the interest in general)—

	Conservative	Liberal	Split-vote
Pubs	80	15	24
Beerhouses	76	28	35
	156	43	59

TABLE 9
Publicans and beersellers in the Blackburn election, 1865

	'Would work for two Conservatives'	'Would work for one Conservative and one Radical'	'Would work for the Radicals'	Total
Thwaites	44	20	18	82
Dutton	40	4	16	60
Cunningham (Tory brewers)	14	7	7	28
Shaw (Liberal brewer)	16	7	32	55
'Free from any brewery'	36	8	21	65
	150	46	94	290

In some towns the power of the brewers was almost irresistible. It operated through an interest in sports and by means of the dispensation of charity, as with Gilbert Greenall of Warrington. In 1869 the Liberal press remarked that Greenall, who owned two-thirds of the town's pubs, 'had a pub in every street in Warrington except one and in that one he had helped to build a church' (his election expenses were twice those of his rival).[130] Although brewing workforces were small, influence seems to have been widely exerted over them.[131]

In the 1870s and for long afterwards Daniel Thwaites of Blackburn was the largest owner of property in the borough, most of it situated on street corners. A local man looked back on the years before the First War; 'Them days the brewers always played a big part in the town. They used to give out licences for public houses as if they were tickets to go on a bus. ... That was the only amusement the workers had.'[132] Thwaites's connections with the political clubs, as well as his own tied houses, helped further his considerable political ambitions, and the other brewing clans of Blackburn were an enormous force in local politics in the last quarter of the century. Like 'Dan' Thwaites, the others were adept at speaking in what a contemporary called 'a language suited to their hearers'.

The association of Temperance and Liberalism was close, but by no means complete. The important Conservative-Anglican involvement cannot be considered here.[133] Many Liberals, especially those who were not Nonconformists, were hostile to the fanaticism of sectarian temperance. And, as has been seen, when it came to the electoral crunch Liberals were often no less forward than the Tories in drowning events in a flood of beer. The differences between strident Temperance and moderate Liberalism manifested themselves in most localities,[134] and Liberal politicians continued to pay court to the Licenced Victualler Associations.[135] The LVAs sometimes endorsed Liberal candidates, persisting in considering themselves an interest group anxious not to enter 'the vortex of politics'. Local Associations reiterated the theme frequently, and as late as 1880 'the dinner table first', 'no politics' and 'look after your own bread and cheese' were typical sentiments.[136]

By this time, however, the pugnacity of Temperance had taught the interest on which side its bread was buttered. Though the identification with the Tory party was never complete the agitations surrounding Sunday closing and the 1872 Licensing Act had considerably hastened the marriage. In Blackburn, where the two sides were always well matched, the drinksellers gave up running independent candidates after 1869 (complete with their fighting fund of beer, blankets and coal) and worked directly through the party thereafter.[137] Stephens's intervention in Ashton gave the issue the populist edge characteristic of the town's politics. The embodiment of Temperance in the person of Hugh Mason only served to heighten the effect of Sunday closing and licensing regulation in bringing the poor to the side of Toryism: there were minor disturbances in the town between 1867 and 1872, when 'John Barleycorn' was an anthem of local Tory electioneering.

The continued political efficacy of representations of the established order such as the John Bull figure suggests that the idea of Queen and country, even the notional union of monarch, lord and multitude, may have found a response among the electorate. The symbolism of this mythic communion was certainly take up by Tory workingmen. In the 'Jingo' demonstrations of 1877–78 representations of the Queen, the Mace, the Bible and Lord Derby were carried in the processions.[139] In Blackburn allegorical representations of the 'Altar, the Throne and the Cottage' were held aloft.[140] In municipal elections in the 1870s Tory cabs bore pictures of the open Bible inscribed 'Teach thy Sons and Thy Sons' Sons', and somewhat earlier Disraeli was greeted in Manchester by banners bearing the likeness of Victoria on one side, and the bible on the other, inscribed 'The Secret of England's Greatness', also by the likeness of Lord Derby, 'A Heart Noble, A Mind Dedicated'.[141]

Much of the reference made to the established order, like the *ad nauseam* use of the Union Jack, was no doubt little more than the stuff of which party shouts were made. In the era of Disraelian, business Conservatism notions of 'organic' class union held only limited sway. Neofeudal chains of dependence and obligation aside, however, it seems clear that the constituents of this union, the monarch and the aristocracy, individually had much popularity and were used to considerable political effect. There were quite concrete reasons why this should have been so, and why even Tory ideas of class union were not altogether picturesque anachronisms. The presence of the Irish magnified the value and majesty of all things English. The Lancashire aristocracy and gentry were not divorced from industry, nor from the social and political life of the towns. Above all, factory paternalism bolstered the currency of older and more distant versions of class union: Tory politicians were adept at smuggling the Tory employer into the trinity of monarch, lord and commoner. In the region at large, and especially in south-east Lancashire, the aristocracy existed not only in the mind of the young Disraeli but also as an aspect of the popular identification of the Tory party as the anti-*laissez faire* party of the Factory Acts.

It was in the south-east town of Stalybridge that was formulated the most consistent, unrelenting and bizarre version of 'organic' class union, that of Joseph Rayner Stephens. His texts were 'The Altar, The Throne and The Cottage' and 'The Aristocracy and The People'. Their meaning was perhaps closest to the religious Tory radicalism of Oastler, but also shared something in common with Ashley's social vision and the romantic Toryism of Disraeli and Young England. Much of Stephens's message developed consistently out of his early experience of the Factory Acts and Chartist agitations: politics was no more than the means to larger ends and was always to be distrusted. In the third quarter of the century he still taught the rejection of industrial society in favour of a mythical pre-industrial social bond: 'From the monarch to the peasant . . . gradations are measured, are relative, are reciprocal.'[143] Against the mechanisation of society he set a Tory individualism and a recognition of the mutuality of rich and poor that were both anchored in an historical conception of the rights and liberties of an old and lost England. Like Oastler, he can in many ways be understood as a last flower of eighteenth-century Tory populism.

His greatest influence was felt in the 1830s and 40s, in the years when the outcome of factory mechanisation was still a matter of conjecture. Despite his romantic overtones, memories in the third quarter of the century were often near enough to those days to give his words a meaning. But in the years after mid-century his accommodation with party politics and his glorification of the aristocracy were to represent an improverishment of his large, early spirit. Not that the accommodation was not always uneasy: he rejected the anti-Irish feeling of Tory and Evangelical politicking, and in one of his periodic political returns in Stalybridge, under the title of 'What is it you want?', he castigated the people for putting politics first.[144] Yet he often campaigned actively for the Tories: all denominations were to shelter under the protection of the Conservative Associations as well as the Church and Crown. The people were to be saved from the treachery of the Whigs by the 'devoted loyalty' and 'chivalrous spirit' of a Derby. Between the aristocracy and the people existed the bond of innate nobility: the workingman and the aristocrat were equals in goodness and manliness.[145]

Elsewhere in Lancashire similar notions were voiced, but without the force of Stephens's peculiar vision and local popularity, and much more as a matter of electoral strategy. W.R. Callendar, the Manchester cotton manufacturer and M.P., frequently praised the Ashley tradition and its supposed custodians the Lancashire aristocracy, above all the Derbys.[146] Lord John Manners survived as the living embodiment of this tradition of aristocratic support for the Factory Acts.[147] Aristocratic families like the Lindsays and Egertons had extensive industrial interests in the region. In 1867 the Rev. E.G. Hornby of Bury praised Alfred Egerton as a great employer, the superintendent and protector of his men, and a prime example of how all the interests of the region were intertwined.[148] Through men such as Egerton employer Toryism introduced itself into the union of lord and commoner. The Wigan example shows this well. In 1874 the Tory candidate Thomas Knowles, a large local coalowner, presented the unity of interests thus: the Earl of Crawford was the captain, Knowles the mate, and the working-class Tories the crew.[149] Callendar's address to 7,000 Manchester workingmen in 1867, entitled 'Historic Conservatism', indicates the usual Tory capacity for having the best of all worlds. Extolling the union of monarch and multitude, castigating the Whigs and the middle classes as the betrayers of the people, he yet extricated the Conservative middle class (via Peel and the Peelites) as the custodians of national unity and of the Bolingbroke–Burke tradition.[150] The involvement of Tory employers, and especially their wives, in the pseudo-feudal flummery of the Primrose League also reflects this desire to be at one with the communion of aristocrat and plebeian. The Liberal equivalent, the Red Rose League, was no match and quickly passed into oblivion.

In the West Riding more gradual urbanisation and the potency of the working-class radical tradition meant that antagonisms between landed wealth and urban interests were maintained longer and more passionately than in Lancashire. In the 1840s and 50s the Earl of Dartmouth relegated mills and Dissenting chapels to the confines of his Colne Valley estates. The arrogance of the lord of the manor and his Slaithwaite parson fuelled radical passions for years to come.[151] Similarly in Huddersfield and Halifax the Whig Ramsden and Wood families earned the wrath of radicals of all hues. Indeed, Oastler was the arch-enemy of both families, and working men Tories long carried forward the attack on them. Joshua Hobson of Huddersfield, Chartist, Oastlerite, and later a leading Tory activist, was a moving force in the Tenant Right agitation of the 1850s, joining forces with orthodox radicals against the Ramsdens who owned most of Huddersfield borough.[152] Time was to do much to moderate feelings. The Dartmouths' local standing was strikingly reflected in later and less acrimonious decades, when the Slaithwaite populace was wont to pull the lord and lady's carriage into the town in triumph on the yearly 'Rent Day', when the family, amidst great celebration, collected its dues in rent and homage.[153]

If the alacrity with which the Tories displayed their aristocratic ornaments is anything to go by, the lord found a much readier response in the Lancashire commoner. At a 'monster' Manchester demonstration for Lord Salisbury and the regional aristocracy in 1879 the following song circulated among the throng,[154]

> But we have got Lord Salisbury, a clever man you'll say
> With Sandon and Stanley to help him upon this glorious day
> And then the noble ladies, daughters of Dukes and Earls,
> Show they're not afraid to meet factory chaps and girls.

Political literature in Wigan echoed the same themes:

> 'Lord Lindsay is our friend boys
> As his past deeds do show
> So pay the House of Haigh boys,
> A tribute that you owe.[155]

This literature found a parallel in the statements of working men. One Rochdale man in 1867 regarded the 'Conservative

Aristocracy' as the founders of commerce and industry, and the root of all labour legislation.[156] A Manchester sweep in the same year, defiant in defence of his worth and status, could nevertheless ask to be raised to the level of the aristocracy and not they lowered to his.[157] Liberal workingmen as well, such as one in Blackburn in 1866,[158] could round on the Nonconformist clergy for daring to attack the aristocracy. W.H. Mills described the Stalybridge of the 1880s as follows:[159] 'It is one of those towns that exhibits – perhaps it exhibits better than any other – the combination of a slight industrial turbulence with an almost servile respect for the House of Lords, the Bench of Bishops, the Union Jack, the bull-dog, and every institution disliked a distrusted by the soul of John Bright.'

Dwarfing all other reputations was that of the Derby family. Their large Lancashire estates were to sustain an influence that reached well into the twentieth century.[160] The family's popularity owed much to its close attention to these local interests, as the papers of the 15th Earl make plain.[161] Bury's sewers received the ducal scrutiny, and then its parks, for which £10,000 was forth-coming in 1884. The borough influence was a jealously guarded one: Derby would not surrender his Bury church patronage to the Bishop of Manchester. A considerable devotee of technical education, the 15th Earl moved with the Disraelian tide. Nor was he laggard in political affairs, appropriating the Secret Ballot to the Tory cause as early as 1857. He was no mean judge of the new democracy, maintaining that the Ballot would release the store of respect, affection and deference the mechanic and the tenant felt for their employers and landlords. Until its coming these virtues would be unexpressed, the working man disliking dictation as much as he was freely deferential.[162]

The popularity of the family owed most to the 14th Earl, and his Factory Acts and Cotton Famine activity. In 1867 one Black-burn man compared Derby with John Bright in these terms, Bright being away salmon fishing in Scotland during the hour of greatest need.[163] The death of the Earl called forth a very considerable popular response in Lancashire, 'The Lancashire Penny Testimonial to Lord Derby' reportedly receiving 85,000 donations in 1869 alone.[164] In Blackburn collections were taken up in the Tory mills. The unveiling of the consequent Preston memorial in 1873 was yet another occasion for the public celebra-tion of the dynasty.[165]

The revival of the fortunes of the monarchy was to be hastened by Disraeli's championing of Empire and Empress. Even before this renaissance, and before the nadir of Albert's death too,

Lancashire seems to have been no enemy to the Crown. The two visits of Victoria to Manchester in the 1850s were occasions not only for the flunkeyism of the new rich but also for the loyalty of a population 'painfully unhealthy' but the best ordered of any British city visited.[166] In the decoration of the streets and factories (off the main route as well as on it), and in the massing of bands and choirs, there were signs of a real popular enthusiasm. In 1857 it was estimated that one million people came into the city from south Lancashire.[167]

The revival of the monarchy's fortunes was in part fostered by the Paris Commune and the spread of Republicanism in England. The Prince of Wales's illness and recovery in 1871 was followed by an unsuccessful attempt on the Queen's life.[168] The promulgation of the decree of papal infallibility in 1870 could not have hindered matters either. Events, and Disraeli's interference in them, conspired to set the Crown on a road to popular approval that has had few turnings in the past hundred years.

The visits of royal family members to Lancashire in 1873 set the seal on popular acceptance. The *Wigan Observer* felt called upon to ask, 'Mr Bradlaugh . . . where do you keep your eyes'.[169] The London press described the visits as the biggest show of popular enthusiasm in years. In the years that followed the Lancashire day schools inculcated the cult of monarchy with a particular energy.[170] By the early twentieth century in Liverpool vast armies of children were being deployed on a scale of public theatre more reminiscent of twentieth-century China than typical of England.[171]

Republicanism got short shrift in Lancashire, spurring a particularly vicious kind of Tory backlash.[172] At the inauguration of the Bolton Republican Club in 1871 an organised Tory mob disrupted the meeting, killing one man.[173] Whenever possible the Tories attempted to commandeer the Crown for political purposes. On the occasion of royal visits and jubilees local parties were able to represent Nonconformist reticence about licensing extensions, and any hint of municipal parsimony, as a kind of spiritless disloyalty. A number of Conservative clubs put on their own, alcoholic, celebrations for the 1887 Jubille,[174] as they had fifteen years earlier for the Prince of Wales's Thanksgiving Day.[175]

Popular support for the cause of Empire seems on the other hand to have been somewhat muted. The most notable effusion of sentiment in this period was the 'jingo' demonstrations of 1877–78.[176] In Manchester and Salford the Tories certainly recruited the service of the 'lambs' and the 'pothouse warriors', but chauvinist violence seems to have been limited to these elements and the lower middle-class mob. These findings reflect recent descriptions of the limited popular appeal of imperialism in the years of the Boer War.[177] Not that the demonstrations of 1877–78 were not massive and highly ritualised. But the allegiances these expressed were either the creation of the event itself and not of its pretext, or else, more often, were buried far more deeply in the local culture than imperialist sentiment ever penetrated. For a working population whose attention was so firmly fixed on the immediate and the concrete the appeal of the far-flung and exotic fell on deaf ears. The electorate did not take the road that led from patriotism to imperialism.

Summary

The work of re-evaluating the political culture of the North in the light of industry and religion is entered upon here. When society is allowed to explicate politics, the uneasy periodisation and unhappy use of the concept of modernity that characterise teleological readings of political development give way to the recognition that the political culture was above all marked by the characteristics of continuity and adaptation. Survivals in their various transformations were not anachronistic and peripheral but central: they reflected society as it was. Thus the political culture engaged areas of feeling far removed from the politics of individual opinion. When viewed in social terms politics makes more sense than when it is seen through the prism of the Whig interpretation.

Political organisation is first considered, and found to be chiefly the institutional representation of economic power and social leadership in the localities. Reflecting oligarchy at one end, organisation projected the purely symbolic nature of participation at the other end of the social spectrum. The adaptation of the institutional components of politics to the ends of influence politics was only one means of organising political sentiment and action, and it is to the conduct of political life, the texture of political action, that attention is next directed. The conduct of politics was invested with the marks of the communitarian allegiances of work and denomination, and in turn gave these loyalties party content and political direction. Political conduct also created and consolidated allegiances among those outside the communities. In showing how clan and sectarian loyalties were brought into politics; the campaign, the election day, and the true significance of both 'corruption' and political rhetoric are all examined. The hallmarks of this culture of celebration and participatory excitement were the personal, the local and the concrete.

Ritual is considered as politics, in the looser sense of that term, as bearing upon the relations of classes. In the second half of the century working-class ritual converged with and was partly subsumed in the rituals of the nation, the Empire, the monarchy, but above all the town. The natural language by which the loyalties of the clan and sect were maintained, the social language of ritual, fed directly into politics, but in considering politics as ritutal a more deliberate adaptation is apparent too. The ritual means by which emotion was politically exploited and organised are analysed, and the greater Tory sensitivity in this region is noted.

The third section delves further into the social foundations of politics, showing how the strength of the loyalties that informed politics in turn gave politics a society and culture of its own. For the activists this is seen in the political community of party co-ops, friendly societies and clubs; for the rank-and-file the less complete but still significant permeation of life by politics is located by means of a discussion of the working men's political club movement. Because politics was informed by society the parties engaged a positive response when pitching their appeals to popular culture at large. The ways in which politics engaged diverse aspects of popular manners is examined *via* political stereotypes, party leaders, the reputations of parties, and sport. The question of style takes up aspects of the club movement, as well as the discussion of employer styles in chapter 5. Attention is directed to the way in which in popular culture new pursuits were generically related to old. It is to the continuity of a broad (and broad-minded), dominant popular culture that the Tory party appealed with the most success. Interwoven in this discussion is a critique of the cultural ramifications of the labour aristocracy argument. Though it is the lack of resistance of popular culture to outside influence at the time which is most striking, the elements of independence and resistance in working-class life must not be under-valued, and it is these that concern us under the heading of 'class cultures'. Here something of the conflict rather than the congruence of the worlds of self-help, religion and work is evaluated, particularly so in terms of the trade union, and those workers most effectively sealed from the kind of politics described in this chapter, the non-factory skilled and craft workers (see chapter 9 also).

The final section is a case study of working-class Conservatism, though it also forms a continuity with the preceding section in that tensions within social politics are again considered. These were felt within beerhouse radicalism and temperance, but also within popular Toryism itself, especially in its south-east Lancashire populist aspects. The politics of the pub and the drink interest is the next topic, followed by an account of popular partiotism, and of attitudes to the monarchy and the aristocracy. Ambiguities within popular Toryism are discovered in these areas also, though it is also the case that many of the feelings described, not least a positive support for Queen and Country, cut across party lines.

Notes

1. See above, pp. 216–7.
2. J. Vincent, *The Formation of the Liberal Party 1857–1868* (1966), p. 94.
3. For the sociology of these activists see P. Joyce, 'Popular Toryism in Lancashire, 1860–1890' (Oxford Univ. D. Phil. 1975), pp. 233–9.
4. See above, pp. 16–18, 21–2, 175–7.
5. Joyce, *op. cit.* pp. 236–7, also p. 351.
6. M. Ostrogorski, *Democracy and the Organisation of Political Parties* (1902), Vol. I, pp. 346–7, also 329–70.
7. Vincent, *op. cit.* p. 82 and H.J. Hanham, *Elections and Party Management* (1959), chs 6, 7, esp. pp. 114–17. For the local notables' manipulation of the party apparatus see also J.D. Baxendale, 'The development of the Liberal Party in England with special reference to the North West, 1886–1900' (Oxford Univ. D. Phil. 1971), ch. 2.
8. N.E. Lances. Cons. Registration Assn., Subscriptions Book, 1874–1880, and Minute Books 1876–86; PLC 2/1/1, Lancs. County Record Office (L.C.R.O.), Preston.
9. Ashton-under-Lyne Cons. Assn., Minute Books 1885–1901; occupations from 1888 town directory; in Ashton Conservative Party Offices. Knutsford Division Cons. Reg. Assn., Minutes of Central Committee and Executive Council, 1885–1927; see esp. Executive Committee meeting and report, 1 Aug. 1885; in Knutsford Cons. Assn. Offices.
10. Two unknown; *Blackburn Times*, 26 Jan. 1884, and 1884 directory.
11. Cf. Joyce, *op. cit.* pp. 262–7.
12. On the O.C.S., see W. Paul, *History of the Origin and Progress of Operative Conservative Societies* (Leeds 1839); R.L. Hill, *Toryism and the People* (1929), ch. 2, esp. pp. 47–57.
13. *Bolton Chronicle*, 30 Apr. 1887.
14. *Ashton Standard*, 13 Aug. 1881.
15. For account of a club's vicissitudes (Grimshaw Park C.C.), *Blackburn Standard*, 28 Feb., 13 Mar. 1880.
16. H.J. Hanham, 'Liberal organisations for working men 1860–1914',

304   Work, Society and Politics

Bulletin Society for the Study of Labour History, 7, 1973.

17. Manchester Courier, 16 Nov. 1868; Rochdale Pilot, 9 Nov. 1867.

18. 'Oldham Toryism', bound volume of press cuttings on Conservative Clubs in Oldham (Oldham Public Library).

19. E.g. Oldham Chronicle, 24 Mar. 1877; see also Ashton Standard, 1 June 1867, 13 Aug., 29 Oct. 1881; Blackburn Standard, 9 Oct. 1880; Blackburn Times, 24 Apr. 1880.

20. Ashton West End Conservative Club Nominations Book 1893, in club premises, Ashton/1888 town directory.

21. 'Oldham Toryism'.

22. Blackburn Times, 22 Jan. 1868; Rochdale Pilot, 16 Jan. 1869, opening of Bluepits Club.

23. Ashton Standard, 14 Mar. 1883.

24. Ashton Reporter, 17, 21 July, 20 Mar., 25 Sept. 1869; Blackburn Times, 25 Feb. 1865 (letters).

25. For an account, Joyce, op. cit. pp. 276–8.

26. For further information, see Ashton Reporter, 31 Jan. 1874, 3 Jan., 21 Feb. 1880; Ashton Standard, 1 Aug. 1868, 22 Oct. 1881, 9 May 1885; Blackburn Times, 6 June 1868; Blackburn Standard, 21, 28 Nov. 1866 (leaders), 6 Mar. 1867.

27. Ashton Reporter, 28 Nov. 1868.

28. Joyce, op. cit. p. 359.

29. For the diminution of earlier practices, Hanham, op. cit. ch. 13; C. O'Leary, The Elimination of Corrupt Practices in British Elections 1868–1911 (Oxford 1962).

30. For the rhythm of the political day, Blackburn Times, 1 Nov. 1875 (leader).

31. For the 'squib' and its authors see S. Clarke, Clitheroe in its Railway Days (Clitheroe 1900), pp. 63–4; for use of the sporting metaphor, Oldham Public Library, election ephemera collection.

32. Oldham Chronicle, 7 Feb. 1874.

33. Clarke, op. cit. pp. 61–2, 62–74; and on Oldham elections see B. Grime, Memory Sketches (Oldham 1889).

34. K. Marx 'Corruption at Elections' (London, Aug. 20 1852), in K. Marx and F. Engels on Britain (Moscow 1953, London 1954), p. 361.

35. Ibid. p. 359.

36. Joyce, op. cit. pp. 293–6, for the persistence of these aspects.

37. Wigan Election Petition, P.P. 1881, LXXIV (207).

38. P. F. Clarke, op. cit. ch. 7, esp. pp. 220–1, 224, 241–2.

39. These figures include all Lancashire constituencies, except Liverpool, and the Cheshire spinning ones of Stockport, Stalybridge, Hyde, also Northwich and Barrow. Liberal Unionists in 1886 are counted as Conservatives. For further information see Joyce, op. cit. pp. 7–9, 60–1.

40. Baxendale, op. cit. Appendices 2 and 3.

41. Wigan Public Library, Case 3:1, Broadsides, 1. Parliamentary Elections, no. 41.

Politics and Society 305

42. *Ibid.* no. 48, 'John Lancaster, My Jo', and no. 33 (by 'Jack Plane').
43. 'Westhoughton parliamentary division. Lord Stanley's subscriptions'; bound volume in Bolton Conservative Club.
44. Crawshaw MSS, L.C.R.O., Preston, DDX/821/2/9 (12), Marquis of Hartington to Sir Thomas Brooks, 26, Sept. 1891 (on Rossendale).
45. Warrington Public Library Broadsides W329, 'John Bradshaw's Odes to the Tories' (1868).
46. T.J. Nossiter, *Influence, Opinion and Political Idioms in Reformed England* (Hassocks 1975), p. 83.
47. For the full litany of Mason's failings, 'Twenty facts for the consideration of the working men of Ashton', Ashton Public Library Broadsides Collection; see also Wigan broadsides for 1868, 1874, 1880.
48. See e.g. Warrington Broadsides for 1868, esp. 'The Last Great Battle . . . ' for the array of local figures in the contending political armies.
49. *Ibid.*, 'Ode to Swagbelly Clare'.
50. *Ibid.*, esp. 'Styx' and 'Pluto' in the 1880s and 90s. There are good collections of political ephemera in the public libraries of Rochdale, Preston and Blackburn as well as the other collections cited in this chapter.
51. See above, p. 222.
52. R.K. Merton, *Social Theory and Social Structure* (New York 1963), ch. 1, esp. pp. 50–60.
53. E.R. Leach, 'Ritual', *International Encyclopedia of the Social Sciences*, Vol. 13 (1968).
54. For a specially valuable historical analysis of ritual see N. Zemon Davis, *Society and Culture in Early Modern France* (1975), ch. 4, esp. pp. 101–3.
55. E.P. Thompson, *The Making of the English Working Class* (1968), ch. 12, II; R.Q. Gray, *The Labour Aristocracy in Victorian Edinburgh* (Oxford 1976).
56. *Bolton Chronicle*, 14 July 1866 (Ironfounders' Gala and Anniversary); *Bury Times*, 28 July 1866 (Oddfellows' Manchester Gala); see also T. Shimmin, *Town Life* (1858), ch. XVI.
57. W.A. Abram, *Memorials of the Preston Guilds* (Preston 1882).
58. E.A. Knox, *Reminiscences of an Octogenarian* (1935), p. 243.
59. S. Clarke, *op. cit.* pp. 73–4.
60. *Illustrated London News*, 30 Mar. 1850.
61. *Blackburn Standard*, 19 Nov. 1873 (leader).
62. R.D. Mattley, *Annals of Rochdale* (Rochdale 1899), p. 55; Manchester Central Library Broadsides, 1877/1/B.
63. Miscellaneous papers re Trade Procession, Manchester Town Hall Opening 1877, Manchester Central Library Archives Dept., M68/1/1
64. Mass-Observation, *May the Twelfth* (1937), Mass-Observation day surveys, ed. C.H. Madge and H. Jennings; see also Mass-Observation, *First Year's Work 1937–38* (1938), pp. 111–15.
65. R.H. Hutchinson, *Chronicles of Blackburn 1861–1862* (Blackburn 1863), p. 12.

66. Clarke, *op. cit.* p. 154.
67. *Wigan Observer*, 6, 7 June 1873; *Bolton Evening News*, 6 June 1873; *Blackburn Times*, 7 June 1873.
68. The American Lowell, and Sir Alfred Pease in P. F. Clarke, *op. cit.* p. 139, and Hanham, *op. cit.* p. 303.
69. Ostrogorski, *op. cit.* pp. 390–9, 403–4, 465.
70. *Preston Herald*, 7 Oct. 1868; and for other such meetings, *ibid.*, 31 Mar. 1880; *Manchester Guardian*, 31 Jan. 1874; *Manchester Courier*, 14 Nov. 1868.
71. For the deluge of meetings, Clarke, *op. cit.* pp. 134–5.
72. Manchester press, 19 June 1869.
73. *Manchester Courier*, 9 Feb. 1878.
74. *Blackburn Standard*, 4 Nov. 1876.
75. *Manchester Guardian*, 3 Apr. 1872, also 30 Mar.
76. See above, pp. 258–9.
77. *Blackburn Times*, 18 Feb. 1878.
78. *Huddersfield Daily Examiner*, 5 Feb. 1874.
79. *Blackburn Times*, 12 Dec. 1885. For an identical comment on Rochdale, H. Brierley, *Reminiscences of Rochdale* (Rochdale 1923), p. 112.
80. *Rochdale Pilot*, 19 Dec. 1868; J.G. Shaw, *History and Traditions of Darwen and its People* (Blackburn 1897), pp. 192–3.
81. D.F.E. Sykes, *The History of the Colne Valley* (Slaithwaite 1906), p. 461.
82. *Ashton Standard*, 27 Sept. 1885.
83. 'Born in a cellar', from *The Hollins Grove Conservative Club Diamond Jubille Handbook 1877–1937*; *Darwen Central Conservative Club Diamond Jubilee Handbook 1868–1935* (both Darwen Public Library).
84. *Ashton Standard*, 23 Oct., 27 Nov. 1869, 29 Jan., 5 Mar. 1870, 5 Mar. 1870, 19 Oct. 1872; *Blackburn Standard*, 16 Feb. 1870.
85. *The Monthly Circular of the Association of Conservative Clubs*, is a useful guide to club life.
86. R.N. Price, 'The working men's club movement and Victorian social reform ideology', *Victorian Studies*, no. 2, Dec. 1971; T. Taylor, *From Self-Help to Glamour, the Working Man's Club 1860–1972*, History Workshop 1972; K.T.S. Dockray, *The Manchester and District Branch of the Working Men's Club and Institute Union Ltd. A survey* (Manchester 1927).
87. J. Foster, *Class Struggle and the Industrial Revolution* (1974), pp. 212–38, esp. pp. 237–8.
88. A. Bennett, *Clayhanger* (Penguin edition 1970), ch. 10, 'Free and Easy'.
89. For the contrast between these decades and the later part of the century, C. Rowley, *Fifty Years of Ancoats Loss and Gain* (Manchester 1899); also C. Aspin, *Lancashire : the first industrial society* (Helmshore Local History Society 1969), pp. 102–4, 177–8.
90. 28 July 1877; see also *Ashton Standard*, 30 Apr. 1859, Jan. 1876.

91. On the coursing craze in Blackburn, *Free Lance*, 12 Oct. 1867; on the betting mania in Manchester, *ibid.*, 25 May 1867, and 'A Manchester man', 'A Whit Week in Manchester', *Fraser's Magazine*, June 1856, p. 644.
92. See above, pp. 187–191.
93. Manchester Central Library Cartoon Collection, Manchester Elections, 1874–1900.
94. *Preston Herald*, 7 Oct. 1868.
95. *Blackburn Standard*, 24 Oct. 1885.
96. *Blackburn Times*, 7 Nov. 1885.
97. 26 Jan. 1861.
98. *Ibid.*, for a meeting of Stephens, Cobbett and Joshua Fielden, the 'squire' of Todmorden.
99. J. Clegg, *Annals of Bolton* (Bolton 1888), Sect. II, p. 135; J. Vincent, *Pollbooks, How Victorians Voted* (Cambridge 1967).
100. C.S. Davies, *North Country Bred* (1963), p. 129. For a Tory butcher, 'Tom' Mullineaux, see W.A. Abram, *Blackburn Characters of a Past Generation* (Blackburn 1894).
101. G. Roby, *The Disease of the Liberal Party* (Manchester n.d., ?1874).
102. On the rise of the card, and the role of philanthropy, audacity and football in making a local name, A. Bennett, *The Card*.
103. *Comus*, 14 Feb. 1878, *City Jackdaw*, 19 Oct. 1877; *ibid.*, 24 Dec. 1875, *Comus*, 20 Nov. 1877.
104. *Blackburn Times*, 5 Dec. 1885 (letters).
105. *Whitehall Review*, 14 July 1877; *Bb. Times*, 7 Nov. 1903 (obit).
106. For Rutherford, Clarke, *op. cit.* pp. 149, 225.
107. See above, pp. 50–2, 110–11, 171–2, 191, 211.
108. E.g. Thompson and Vigne Lancashire Ints 122 (pp. 24–5), 134, 140, 151, 106, 36, 46, 54 ('Work').
109. *Ibid.* nos. 134 (C/C), 131 (p. 9); and on miners, 90 and 139 ('Work').
110. A. Clarke, *The Effects of the Factory System* (1899), pp. 46–7, 32–3.
111. J. Morley, 'Lancashire', *Fortnightly Review*, July 1878, pp. 5–7, and see table showing two-thirds of town's operatives with money deposited as savings.
112. G.D.H. Cole, *A Century of Co-operation* (1947), pp. 183, 188; see also *Bb. Times*, 14 May 1873; 20 Mar. 1875.
113. Information on Co-op leadership in Blackburn, *ibid.*, 10 Feb. 1872.
114. Some societies were of a higher social level than others, though all shared the same kind of associational life. The basic source of information is R.C. on Friendly and Benefit Building Societies, *P.P.* 1874, XXIII, Pt I (961), Pt II (996); esp. 34 (Table) (961); 280–1, 283–5, 288, 295 and 290–303 (on Oldham), 304–7 (on Preston), (996).
See also *P.P.* 1867–8, XIV (402), evid of Lancs. witnesses, pp. 362–7, 410–20; P.H.J.H. Gosden, *The Friendly Societies in England 1815–1875* (1961), Foster, *op. cit.* pp. 216–18.
115. *Manchester Guardian*, 1 July 1872.
116. *Ashton Reporter*, 13 Nov. 1869, 6 Jan. 1872; P. Smith, *Disraelian*

Conservatism and Social Reform (1967), pp. 227–30, 264, *City Jackdaw*, 26 Nov. 1875 (on W.R. Callendar of Manchester).

117. See above, p. 268, and Joyce, *op. cit.* p. 351, also Gosden, *op. cit.* pp. 88–93.

118. Preston and District Power-Loom Weavers, Winders and Warpers' Association, Minutes 1864–83, and Operative Burial Society Minutes 1861–68: DDX 1089/1/1–3 and 1089/2/1, L.C.R.O. Preston.

119. *Preston Chronicle*, 9 July 1870.

120. *Bolton Guardian*, 30 July, 13 Aug. 1870 (spinners' excursion); *Cotton Factory Times*, 23 Jan. 1885 (spinners' dinners).

121. *Oldham Chronicle*, 10 Feb., 14 July 1877; *Blackburn Standard*, 24 May 1871.

122. *Cotton Factory Times*, 23, 30 Jan. 1885.

123. Blackburn and District Trades and Labour Council Annual Reports.

124. *Blackburn Standard*, 27 Aug. 1862; see also W. Edward Moss, *Life of Mrs Lewis, The Drunkard's Friend* (1927), on Blackburn.

125. B. Harrison, *Drink and the Victorians* (1971), chs 14, 15.

126. Mass-Observation, *The Pub and the People* (1943), esp. pp. 52–6, 65; R. Roberts, *The Classic Slum* (1971), pp. 6, 15.

127. For further details, Joyce, *op. cit.* pp. 361–3.

128. See below, p. 319.

129. 'Analysis of the Register for the year 1864–5', DDX 223, Box 5 (Robinson and Sons, Solicitors), L.C.R.O., Preston; 1865 pollbook in Blackburn Public Library.

130. *Manchester Daily Examiner and Times*, 6 Feb. 1869; see also Reform League report on Warrington, 1868.

131. Thompson and Vigne Lancs. Int. 47 ('Politics'), on Salford brewer.

132. J. Seabrook, *City Close-Up* (1971), p. 15.

133. Joyce, *op. cit.* pp. 368–71.

134. *Ashton Reporter*, 28 Feb., 6 Mar. 1880; *P.P.* 1867–8, XIV (402), pp. 362–7, 371; *Manchester Daily Examiner and Times*, 25 Nov. 1868 (on Bolton).

135. *Blackburn Standard*, 9 Nov. 1864, 7, 21 Oct. 1868; *Bb. Times*, 17 Apr. 1869 (Leader).

136. *Ashton Reporter* 28 Feb. 1880; for the Lancs. LVA spokesman William Candalet, *ibid.*, 22 Mar. 1884.

137. *Blackburn Times*, 30 Oct., 6 Nov. 1869.

138. *Ashton Reporter*, 9, 30 Mar., 13 Apr. 1867, 25 Sept. 1869, 28 Feb. 1880.
Ashton Standard, 26 Oct., 9, 16 Nov. 1872.
Ashton News, 25 Mar., 29 Apr. 1871.

139. *Manchester Courier*, 8 Sept. 1877.

140. *Blackburn Times*, 16 Feb. 1878; *Blackburn Standard*, 11 Apr. 1885 (Leader).

141. *Ibid.*, 19 Feb. 1876; *Manchester Courier*, 3 July 1872.

142. Both printed and in Manchester Central Library. For the latter

delivered in Manchester, *Ashton Standard*, 22 Feb. 1868. For the early Stephens see J.T. Ward, 'Revolutionary Tory: the life of Joseph Rayner Stephens (1805–1879)', *Trans. Lancs. and Chesh. Antiquarian Society*, **68** (1958) and T.M. Kemnitz-Fleurange Jaques, 'Joseph Rayner Stephens and the Chartist Movement', *International Review of Social History*, **19**, 1974, Pt II. See also Stephens obit., *Ashton Reporter*, 22 Feb. 1879.

143. *The Altar, The Throne and The Cottage*, p. 11.

144. *Ashton Standard*, 2 Apr. 1870.

145. *Ashton Reporter*, 13 Apr. 1867.

146. *Manchester Courier*, 4 Apr. 1872.

147. *Manchester Guardian*, 31 Jan. 1874; *Manchester Courier*, 2 Apr. 1872 (factory workers' delegation to Disraeli, also quote from London *Standard* on the 'Coningsby' tradition), also 4, 5 Apr. 1872.

148. *Ibid.*, 27 June 1867.

149. *Wigan Examiner*, 31 Jan. 1874.

150. *Manch. Courier*, 27 June 1867.

151. D.F.E. Sykes, *The History of the Colne Valley* (Slaithwaite 1906); J. Sugden, *Slaithwaite Notes of the Past and Present* (Manchester 1905), p. 80.

152. J.T. Ward, 'Some industrial reformers, *Bradford Textile Society Journal 1962–3*; 'Idem', *The Tenant Right Question* (Huddersfield 1860).

153. J. Sykes, *Slawit in the Sixties* (Huddersfield, n.d., 1926), ch. XXIII.

154. Manchester Central Library Broadsides, 1879/4/B.

155. Sung to the tune of 'God Bless the Prince of Wales', Wigan Broadsides no. 48.

156. *Rochdale Pilot*, 4 May 1867.

157. *Manchester Courier*, 27 Feb. 1867.

158. *Blackburn Standard*, 28 Nov. 1866.

159. W.H. Mills, *Sir Charles Macara, Bt. A study of modern Lancashire* (Manchester 1917), pp. 65–6.

160. Randolph Churchill, *Lord Derby 'King of Lancashire'* (1959), chs 7, 17, 26 and p. 97 for map of estates; see also Hanham, *op. cit.* pp. 287–8, 79–80.

161. Fifteenth Earl Derby Papers, Liverpool Record Office, 920 DER/41 and 42, Private correspondence.

162. *Ibid.*, 920 DER/47/2, Essays: 'Secret voting: a Conservative measure'.

163. *Blackburn Standard*, 1 Apr. 1867.

164. *Ibid.*, 25 Aug. 1869, 8, 12 Jan., 9 Feb. 1870; *Bb. Times*, 8 Jan. 1870, 26 July 1871.

165. *Ibid.*, 7 June 1873.

166. Vincent, *op. cit.* p. 149; *The Victoria History of the County of Lancashire*, Vol. 4 (1911), p. 184.

167. *Manchester Courier*, 20 June; *Manchester* Guardian, 27 June, 4 July; *Ashton Reporter*, 4 July 1857.

168. B. Kingsley Martin, *The Magic of Monarchy* (1937), ch. II.
169. *Wigan Observer*, 6, 7 June 1873.
170. Roberts, pp. 110–12; also *A Ragged Schooling* (Manchester, 1976).
171. Cf. Ephemera, re opening of Liverpool Cathedral, Liverpool Public Library.
172. *Manchester Guardian*, 3 May 1872.
173. *Blackburn Standard*, 29 Nov., 6 Dec.; *Manchester Guardian*, 1, 2, 4 May, 6 June 1872.
174. *Ibid.* 4 July; *Manchester Courier*, 20 June 1857; *Blackburn Standard* and *Oldham Standard*, June 1887.
175. *Manchester Courier*, 27, 28 Feb. 1872.
176. Joyce, *op. cit.* pp. 384–91.
177. H. Pelling, 'British Labour and British Imperialism', in *Popular Politics and Society in the Late Victorian Britain* (1968); R. Price, *An Imperial War and the British Working Class: working-class attitudes and reactions to the Boer War, 1899–1902* (1972)

9
THE PARTIES, THE LABOUR
INTEREST AND RADICALISM

Organised labour in the period offered little by way of an alternative to the collectivities of work and religion upon which
politics was based. Between 1885 and the beginning of the new
century the journal of the cotton workers gave ample evidence
of a real attachment to party and of the widespread absence of
class animosity. In the 1890s it remarked, 'It is evident . . . that
the millworkers in Lancashire are still strong adherents to party,
and that the time is far distant when the bulk of the operatives will
give up their political principles.' Even more revealing was the
remark: 'If a workman votes for a man with a carriage and pair it
is because he believes that his views will be more adequately
and effectively represented by him than by his opponent, who may
have to do his business on foot.'[1] Attitudes so marked in the late
nineteenth century were more deeply embedded still in the
decades before 1885.

This adherence to party, and refusal to countenance the
involvement of trade unions in party politics, characterised the
entire union movement outside cotton as well, and marked
many in the union leadership as well as in the rank-and-file. The
history of the Blackburn Trades Council was typical enough of
the factory towns. Although uneasily enlisted on the Liberal
side in 1868, 'politics and prejudice', as one Council member put
it, meant that the Council quickly disintegrated thereafter, and
was inactive until 1884, when it sprang briefly into life to foster
the parliamentary labour candidacy of 1885. There was no
permanent organisation until 1889.[2] This division represented on
a broader scale the political dissension and suspicion that
characterised the largest union in the town, that of the weavers.
The radical inclinations of the original weavers' leadership
spurred on the creation of a powerful and Tory-inclined rival
organisation in 1885.[3]

Although Trade Councils were more active in other towns they
were no less politically divided than in Blackburn. The Stalybridge Council was typical: in 1877 it declared itself to be made
up of all political opinions and of none, meeting always without
discussing politics.[4] Individuals unions almost always declared

311

that they were above politics, and in 1868 the Reform League reports on the North-West testified to the reality of political division among the leadership as among the mass of unionists.[5] Thus the political wishes of the great majority of the organised working-class electorate were accommodated within the prevailing party system.

This accommodation, however, was at the price of economic and political reform. Whatever the degree of failure, and it was large, the agitations of the 1830s and 40s later bore fruit in trade union recognition, factory reform and the granting of the vote. And these advances represented gains in labour's awareness of its own power and status. Some of the reasons why these gains were not translated into independent working-class politics were examined in the previous chapter.[6] Pre-eminent among those forces blocking the emergence of a class-based labour politics was the community pressure of work and religion. Those who most successfully eluded the sway of these pressures were those most directly involved in the economic and social life of the trade union, namely the union activists. This distinction applied within the factory, but most fully outside it, where the highly evolved social life of the craft unions set their social and political life apart from the upper classes, and where the traditions and practices of a still powerful craft autonomy established a potential for independent action impossible for the great majority of factory workers.

Our central distinction between retained and relinquished control over the labour process will be recalled:[7] unlike the factory worker, the craft worker had not been subjected to the profound social effect of the consolidation of modern, factory industry. Thus he was most free of the cultural spheres of community politics. Whether the craft worker, and the factory union activists, were similarly free of the compromises of alliance with the established parties is another matter. To appreciate the degree to which the potential for independent action was translated into practice we must briefly return once more to the problematic of the 'labour aristocracy'. Once the tautological reductionism of the notion is put to one side, and we revert to the idea of class formation as the product of concrete historical process, the craft sector can be seen as the vanguard of working-class politics. This is something the recent work of Gray and Tholfsen in fact shows, despite their concern with hegemony, compromise and mediation.[8]

Compromise and mediation there certainly was, but it can be suggested that the most appropriate context in which this can be understood is the social aftermath of the consolidation of modern industry. It was seen earlier that the possibility of the union of political and industrial action was at its greatest when the struggle for control over the labour process was at its height, and when the whole social and economic order of the worker was under threat.[9] This was the case with textile workers before 1850. With the craft workers, on the other hand, the threat to control over the labour process was much longer drawn-out and discontinuous. Thus the craft worker responded with less urgency than the early factory worker to the threat modern industry posed, and the fusion of political and industrial action was itself discontinuous. It is in this general sociological sense that the compromises and ambiguities of alliances with the political parties can be interpreted. But to evaluate these alliances correctly we must understand the social situation of the craft worker in terms of the available tradition of radical theory and rhetoric.

In this task the recent work of Gareth Stedman Jones is most illuminating.[10] Stedman Jones locates the early 1830s advance over the old constitutionalist rhetoric in terms of the articulation of a class-based theory of exploitation. Chiefly under the influence of Owen's perfectibilism and Hodgskin's labour theory of value, the radical critique moved away from the state and corruption and towards an understanding of the capitalist, and the role of property and power. To the rights of man were added the rights of labour. Yet it is the limitations of the 'new' critique that are to be stressed: the hold of natural right theory was sufficiently strong to make property a natural right. The goal of a non-capitalist economy of free producers did not encompass the changed social relations modern industry was ushering in. The employer's rights of direction in industry were not attacked, merely his role as middleman. Industrial capitalism was equated with a politically based system of unequal exchange. Thus for both 'old' and 'new' critiques the political was in the end sovereign: the causes of poverty were political and not economic. The failure to evolve an economic rhetoric and theory was grounded in the ineradicable individualist assumptions of the language of natural rights. The relationship between radical theory and the work situation and social assumptions of the craft sector will be apparent: to the craft worker the employer was a nebulous figure, for it was only in his role as capitalist and not employer that he could compose a class.

We have previously remarked upon the link between the artisan core of Chartist theory and the factory workers.[11] For the factory worker of the 1830–50 period – in so many respects an artisan in the factory, responding to the destruction of his craft status – Chartism spoke with force and direction. But with the completion of mechanisation the factory worker was increasingly bereft of a radical critique capable of comprehending the changed class relations of his position as a factory proletarian. For the craft worker the situation was rather different.

With the failure of Chartism, and especially of the prophecy of a commonwealth of free producers, the radical, transforming power in Chartism was greatly diminished. The consolidation of factory industry in one sector affected all of labour: the 'immovable horizon' of capitalist industry enforced compromise and alliance with the two established praties. It is in the correspondences and continuities between Chartism and Liberalism that we may trace much of the political history of labour in the years to come. For, the limitations of Chartism considered *par excellence* as a political theory of the artisanate – the validity of property, the individualist assumption, the sovereignty of the political – led to an affinity with much in radical Liberalism, itself an ideology which stressed the classless union of individuals in the struggle not against industrial capital but against Privilege. In such areas as land reform, anti-aristocratic feeling, franchise reform, or popular self-education, the compromises were to be emphatic; in other areas, republicanism, secularism, internationalism, much less so.

Yet the radicalism that was bequeathed to the second half of the century was not the same as Liberalism, and the lived experience of the conditions of modern industry in the later period constantly recalled the independence of the past to present days. The autonomy of work practice and tradition the craft worker possessed similarly meant that his accommodation with the political system was the most qualified and distanced. The craft workers especially, together with those factory trade union activities free of community politics, represented an attitude in politics that was to lead directly to the fully-fledged independence of the Labour party in years to come. The compromises of the party alliance, but much more the real core of independence that was maintained, will form the subject of the remainder of this chapter.

In all this the factory rank-and-file must not be lost to view. Where domestic and craft traditions were the last to fall among factory workers, and where factory industry consolidated late and least completely, there the association of Chartism and the craft-cum-factory worker was especially close. This was the situation in the relatively primitive textile industries of the West

Riding, where Chartism was a living presence in the decades after 1850. In Lancashire the structures of work and denomination did not give a full account of the politics of the factory majority. Something of the recalcitrant populism of Ashton and Stalybridge has been indicated, though this was probably the preserve of those outside rather than inside the factory. In Lancashire at large the muted class identification large-scale unionisation nevertheless made possible could receive occasional expression. Just as the factory trade union activist could be fully enmeshed in cultural politics, so too could something of the reverse of this obtain: the cultural politics of the mass could at times be transformed into the politics of the labour interest.

One expression of this was the Preston parliamentary election of 1874. While the outcome confirms the primacy of cultural over class politics it also indicates the tensions within the political socialisation of the Northern factory worker. In 1874 the great majority of the town's working class voted for the two Tory candidates. The single opponent, James Mottershead of the Labour Representation Council, received the support of the Liberal working class and of the union leadership. Twelve hundred of Mottershead's vote of 3,756 split with Edward Hermon, the greatest employer in the town and the embodiment of Lancashire textile paternalism. Hermon received a massive 6,512 votes.[12]

Though the number of labour activists owing their allegiance to the Conservative party was probably greater in Lancashire than anywhere else in the kingdom, the predominant Liberal inclination of the labour interest in the North testifies to its liberation from cultural politics. In Blackburn, for instance, these unionists steadfastly allied with the Liberals in the face of what was usually a majority of Tory employers in the town. Some indication of the size and composition of this independent constituency is provided by the attendances at a series of meetings organised in the town in 1868, when the co-operation of the Reform League and the Liberals represented a high point in the political activism of the labour interest. The weavers' meeting drew only 300 of the thousands of unionised male weavers in the town, while the iron and building trades between them were able to assemble 450. An aggregate meeting of unionists, when the craft sector was well represented, later drew an attendance of about 2,000.[13] The politics of the labour interest was always the politics of a minority.

In our second sense of independence – resistance to assimilation in the ideology and organisation of the political parties – the history of the politics of labour was one of ambiguity and uneasy compromise. The varying degrees of class awareness and political independence seen in the politics of the 1830s and 40s were deeply qualified in the following decade as the old leadership divided along the lines of support for Reform and Disestablishment on the Liberal side, and the Factory Acts and anti-Poor Law causes on the Tory side.[14] Most were to take the Liberal road, the priorities of the Liberal alliance yoking together the radical *menu peuple*, the employer leadership and the labour activists in the once-unlikely marriage of the politics of anti-Privilege. That times had changed greatly was evident from the speed with which the Liberal alliance displaced Chartism in the course of the 1850s.

By 1852 in Blackburn the Chartist rump was backing the Liberals in the cause of political reform, and even marching in support of Liberalism and Free Trade (at a march organised by one of the Pilkington brothers' spinners).[15] Only five years previously Bright and Free Trade had been the objects of Chartist scorn in the town.[16] At the end of the decade organised Chartism had disintegrated, and former Chartists like William Crossley, the weavers' leader, were backing Bright and Reform. Despite the transformation of the 1850s, however, tensions within the Liberal alliance very quickly asserted themselves. The pressure of the labour interest for political reform was exerted not only against the obstruction of the Tory party and press in Blackburn but also against the suspicion and laggardness of many among the Liberal leadership. The situation in Blackburn reveals how important the attitude of the local party establishments was: in towns where the Liberal leadership was more amenable than in Blackburn (and there were probably as many of these as there were parallels to Blackburn) the impetus towards scepticism and independence was less marked.

In Blackburn Reform was fought for most of the way. In 1859 the first engagement in the campaign against the Tory-Liberal electoral 'compact' opened in this two-member constituency, with the *menu peuple*, the labour interest and the Secularists working in close alliance.[17] Failure to dislodge the alliance of moderate Liberalism and Toryism resulted in the full-scale conflict of 1865, when Ernest King, the ultra-radical editor of the *Blackburn Times*, thundered against 'slavery' and 'What Capital is doing to Labour'.[18] The amenability forced on the leadership resulted in a period of edgy peace after 1865, symbolised by the Reform League–Liberal co-operation of 1868. In the course of the 1860s the same understanding between popular radicalism and the moderation of propertied Liberalism was reached in most towns, including Oldham, Preston and Macclesfield.[19]

As was apparent from our discussion of political organisation, and particularly of the club movement, very many workingmen Liberals were satisfied with this accommodation.[20] The place in the Liberal sun that was all many radicals desired was provided by involvement in the organisation, an involvement which concerned the fiction and not the reality of democracy. However, of the shock troops that made up the most recalcitrant element in radicalism, it would seem probable that it was the *menu peuple* and not the labour activists who were most content with the life of the political drone.

Both Vincent and Nossiter have interpreted the *menu peuple* to be the soul of radical Liberalism in the 1850s and 60s.[21] However this may be, what robustness that soul may have had in the days of agitation seems to have been rapidly restrained when Reform was achieved and the organisation took the erstwhile *enragé* to its bosom. In 1874 a keen observer of this class remarked that the 'once sturdy wart' of radical Dissent 'had become a slim shopkeeper; its eyes are dim with Gaslight; with reading invoices and Bills of Lading its attention is distracted'. The ethos of this timeserving Liberalism was the chapel tea-meeting; and its philosophy, 'God bless the lucky ... and the kindred creed of poor is damnable'.[22]

Secularism was one important influence steering the labour interest away from complacency, and transmitting to the present something of the independence of earlier days. In the 1850s and 60s the small group of Blackburn secularists was aggressive and well organised. The principal leaders were William Billington, Shelleyan pantheist, tapesizer and poet; Henry Baker, Owenite tailor and newsman, and the mechanic Thomas Stephenson.[23] The editor of *The Times* Ernest King, had close links; he and Baker leading what was called the 'extreme faction' in the 1860s. Though King and Stephenson emigrated in that decade, and Baker died in 1866, this autodidact, artisan tradition left its mark. Secularism's most important capture was William Crossley, Blackburn's foremost labour leader. Starting as a factory labourer, his career progressed by way of beerhouse keeping, co-op mill management, and small manufacturing. He was secretary of the weavers' union from 1859 until his death in 1875, and active on the Town Council, the School Board, and many other town bodies. In his youth a Wesleyan lay preacher, he shed religion on acquaintance with the works of J.S. Mill and Comte, with which his mind was 'saturated'.[24] The compliance and

recalcitrance existing between Crossley and Liberalism symbolised the feelings of many of the active element within organised
labour.

The succession of W.A. Abram (a passionate Gladstonian),[25]
to the editorial chair of the *Blackburn Times*[26] as well as the greater
flexibility of the employer leadership after 1868, meant that
relations within the Liberal alliance improved considerably in
the 1870s. Nonetheless, labour's alliance with Liberalism was as
much the product of Tory opposition as of any ideological
commitment to the Liberals. If the Tory leadership and press
were receptive to trade union recognition, they long held out
against the Reform process, and against transforming union
recognition into a say for labour in the life of the town.[27] The
activists were able to look for light to the national centres of
politics, but it was still in the arena of local, town life that the
heat of independence was generated.

The one issue that did most to fuel anti-Tory passions was the
question of the appointment of a stipendiary magistrate. The
union leaders, directly concerned with the influence over the work
situation that control of justice could bring, were obdurately
opposed by the Tories for over two decades after the issue was
first aired in 1861. This question was only one of a number in
which labour's desire for a say in the life of the town was supported
by the Liberals: in the 1860s Liberals supported demands for a
relaxation of the property qualification for Town Council
candidatures (*The Blackburn Times* letter column in these years
was headed 'Open Council'), and Tory plans for the reform of the
police were opposed by the Liberal–labour alliance, this time
backed by Ernest Jones.[28]

There was no essential difference between the demand for a
say in things in Blackburn and the demand for a say at Westminster. The first realistic attempt at a labour candidacy in
Blackburn, that of J.N. Boothman in 1885, was thus a continuation of a long-established attempt at self-determination by
labour. The failure in 1885, like the failure to elect a single
independent to the Town Council on the stipendiary magistrate
ticket in the 1870s, serves to put the politics of the labour
interest in perspective. As in 1880, when cotton masters
were returned with massive votes after the tumult of the great
weaving strike of 1878, in 1885 it was clear that the stranglehold
of cultural politics had barely been relieved. The 1885 result was
as follows:

Coddington and Peel (Cons.)	8,239
Briggs (Lib.) and Boothman (Ind.)	4,738

Briggs	1,382
Boothman	182
Coddington and Briggs	550
Coddington and Boothman	342
Peel and Briggs	70
Peel and Boothman	79

Not only did the mass of electors spurn this attempt at a labour candidate (Boothman had a Radical pedigree), but the union leadership was itself split. As the *Cotton Factory Times* testified, Boothman was a genuine independent, but he had to be put forward privately by a small group of the less partisan labour activists, and individual unions washed their hands of the whole affair.[29] Nonetheless, the degree of unity then reached by former Tory and Liberal unionists was the most considerable yet, and from the failure of 1885 the long-established tradition of independence was to receive the momentum that led to full political autonomy. In the same year the Northern Counties' Weaving Amalgamation voted for the discussion of political matters at the Trades Union Congress.[30]

The tensions existing between Liberalism and the labour group found expression in many spheres. The preceding discussion of the radicalism of the Blackburn beerhouse indicated the cleavage that existed between the union radicals and other politically active workingmen with strong links to the party organisation, the Liberal mills and the chapels.[31] And, while the labour group attended political and pressure group meetings, its absence from the Liberal party apparatus is particularly striking. Nor were the quintessential causes of Liberalism much patronised – the Peace Society, but above all Temperance.

The daily life of the union radical cut him off from much that was socially as well as ideologically a part of Liberalism. The association of drink and Secularism, for instance, was very close: Baker was a notorious boozer, and Billington kept a pub in his later years. Cultural differences threw the common assault on Privilege into perspective. Though part of a politics that concerned the class interdependence of those without Privilege uniting against those with Privilege, it was clear enough from the experience of town life that those with Privilege were rather the employers of Blackburn than the aristocracy of England. Despite his Liberal sympathies, William Crossley could declaim against all the employers of Blackburn as the real enemies of the working class.[32] As our discussion of labour relations makes plain,[33] whatever the degree of co-operation and moderation marking labour relations, organised labour rejected the tenets of political economy. Employers were employers more than they were politicians, and this realisation was present to the radical unionists and the employers alike. In 1874 the election of the Liberal cotton master William Briggs was greeted with delight in the best Blackburn circles.[34] King Cotton had again triumphed. Despite the limitation to a purely political analysis that the radical critique imposed, the economic reality of daily life constantly confounded the logic of that critique. In the end, class was at the bottom of the politics of the labour interest.

It was, however, most qualified in expression in towns, unlike Blackburn, where labour worked with a more amenable Liberal leadership and did not confront a monolithic and unreceptive Toryism. Such seems to have been the case in Bolton, where J.T. Fielding, the fine spinners' leader and Trade Council secretary from 1874 to 1894, was a member of the Liberal Executive and more receptive than most union leaders to the tenets of political economy.[35] Fielding's political stance was probably representative of the feelings of Bolton activists, just as the person of Crossley summed up much in the Blackburn situation. Burnley represented almost the complete opposite to the Bolton example.

There the Liberal employer leadership was comprised of *parvenu* late-comers, in cut-throat competition with each other. Burnley's labour relations were among the worst in the county, and its paternalism very limited. Its pattern of industrial urban development was similar to that of the West Riding: later mechanisation and urbanisation preserved intact more of the Chartist tradition in politics than was elsewhere the case in Lancashire.[36] This radicalism was fed by the influx of victimised trade unionists into the town's galaxy of small, anonymous·mills, and by the migration of Yorkshire labour, carrying its own political traditions westwards.[37] The particular impact of socialism on a north-east sharing a number of Burnley's characteristics is especially revealing. The influence of Hyndman and the Social Democratic Federation was strongest of all in Burnley, where in 1893 1,000 of the north-east's 2,000 membership was to be found.[38]

In Yorkshire the links between the Chartism of the late 1840s and the protest of the textile handworkers was very close. The onset of the mechanisation of male labour, later in Yorkshire than in Lancashire, was latest of all in the woollen districts. Thus Chartism lived on as a powerful force in the popular radicalism of the region.[39] Indeed, the Chartist tradition and the experience of the handworker were to coalesce in later socialism: Allen Gee and Allen Stringer for instance, were socialist leaders of the textile unionism of the 1880s who began their work life in the domestic industry of the woollen districts in the 1850s and 60s, and Ben Turner himself was born into this hand-working culture in 1865.[40]

The politics of the Chartist inheritance were especially strong where handworking traditions were the most tenacious. In Bradford the Chartist journal, *The Voice of the People*, was published in the old hand woolcombing district of the town, a bastion still in the 1850s and 60s of O'Connorite Chartism. In Horton and Great Horton, a Democratic Institute and a Political Union continued to exert a strong Chartist influence on the politics of Bradford from the early 1840s to the late 60s.[41] Feargus O'Connor, the Chartist leader who spoke most directly to the handworkers, was as alive in the political mythology of these old handworking centres in the late 1860s as were the present tribunes of Cobden, Bright and Gladstone.[42] In the late 1880s the old Chartist Ben Wilson stated that the majority of old radicals still living had taken their political opinions from 'The Lion of Freedom'.[43]

Because of its greatly different industrial history and structure, popular culture was more resistant to outside influence than was the case in Lancashire. It was upon these reserves of in-dependence, upon a tradition of self-help rooted in a sense of class identity much less penetrated by the factory than in Lanca-shire, that West Riding socialism drew much of its strength in the 1880s.[44] Work on Halifax in the second half of the century testifies to the vitality of a self-help culture anchored in the co-op, the friendly society and building society, and in popular education.[45]

This cultural autonomy received a political and not an industrial expression: unlike Lancashire, in Halifax as in much of the West Riding, textile unionism was weak and class identity in the majority was not contained by union organisation. In Halifax especially, Chartism was only one expression of a tradition of radical politics which stretched back into the eighteenth century and forward to the foundation of the political labour movement.[46] Among the factors contributing to this tradition of political independence Positivism was not the least important, particularly in Halifax and Bradford.[47] Acting on the Secularist tradition, Positivism further diverted labour away from any easy accord with Liberalism. In Lancashire Positivism had nothing like the influence it enjoyed in the West Riding.

Comparison between the great Reform demonstrations of the 1860s in Lancashire and the West Riding indicates the depth of the popular radical tradition in the east, as well as the degree to which the Yorkshire factory workforces were more resistant to the pull of the politics of the factory. It was variously estimated that between 80,000 and 300,000 people thronged towards Leeds for each of the two Woodhouse Moor demonstrations in 1866 and 1867. Many had to walk as the railway companies declined to put on excursion trains. Friendly societies, co-ops and trade unions all marched in the cause of political reform. Bearing in mind the poorly organised condition of Yorkshire textile unionism the textile presence in the trade union contingents was considerable. Across the Pennines the Manchester demonstration of 1866 was not only considerably smaller (around a third of the Leeds size), but the absence of the textile unions in a region of high textile unionism was especially notable. In the Blackburn Reform demonstration of 1866 it will be remembered that the marchers were organised by the mills and marched in mill order.[49]

Yet, neither the political nor the structural and industrial differences between the two regions should be overstated. If factory industry in its fully developed state came later in the east, many of the social consequences of modern industry eventually made themselves felt in the West Riding. Especially in early-mechanised worsted, and in the large and long-established factories outside the competitive and subdivided industries of Bradford and the heavy woollen district, the effect of factory paternalism was powerfully felt: Keighley, for instance, has figured prominently in our description of the factory culture which maintained industrial deference in being. As in Lancashire, political independence was most fully the preserve of a minority of labour activists, and of those outside rather than within the factory. As in Lancashire, too, the politics of the labour interest were marked by compromise and conciliation.

Whatever, his debt to O'Connor, Ben Wilson ended his days as an 'advanced' Liberal and a religious radical. In radical Halifax itself, the groundswell of popular feeling in support of the radical candidatures of Ernest Jones and E.O. Greening in 1868 was in turn met by considerable popular support for establishment Liberalism, a support which included the voice of the Trades Council. It was the official Liberals who won the electoral day in the end.[50] Like the other West Riding Trade Councils, the Halifax one usually did its best to remain officially non-political. Just as in Lancashire, independence was most muted when Liberalism was most receptive to the needs of labour.

This was especially so in Bradford. Hurst has decidedly

grasped the wrong end of the stick in suggesting that organised labour in the town posed any threat to the Liberal establishment in the 1870s.[51] On the contrary, it has been shown in great detail how the union of labour and Radical middle-class Liberalism had nullified the official voice of labour.[52] Under the presiding genius of W.E. Forster, the accord between moderate Chartism and Liberalism emerged in the early 1850s, to be consolidated after 1857 by the most politically astute group within the northern employer class, the Dissenting Radicals led by 'Illingworth, Kell and Co.'. By the late 1860s these had raised Bright to the level of a popular demigod and class co-operation to the level of a political ideology. The Bradford Trades Council numberd many devout workingman Liberals among its leadership – especially those of the unrepentent Nonconformist-Temperance sort – and after a flurry of activity in the early 1870s it relapsed into political quietude until the late 1880s.[53]

This emphasis on the greater attraction Liberalism had for the labour interest should not devalue the considerable success the Conservative party had in appealing to the union activists. Certain Tories, like W.R. Callendar the Manchester leader, practised a kind of 'progressivism' no different from that of some Liberals at the end of the century. Callendar worked closely with the Tory leaders of the Manchester and Salford Trades Council, W.H. Wood and S.C. Nicholson, in order to promote the public acceptance of trade unionism.[54] This effort went hand in hand with the attack on *Manchestertum*, to which Conservative working-men joined their voices in denunciation of political economy and its free trade in the humanity of labour.[55] If the Tory politician was tarred with the brush of reaction, the Liberal was tarred with that of social and economic *laissez faire*. No matter how much the rigours of political economy had been moderated, something of the charge stuck, and the Tories did their best to see that it stuck. Summing up the 1874 election in the factory North Frederic Harrison noted the liability that the 'Radical Economist' could still be, especially when the Tories recalled their earlier role in the Factory Acts agitation:

The hard and fast man of the straightest sect of Liberalism or Radicalism who could say his economic catechism without stumbling ... has been wont to smile at the vision of a Conservative working man. Perhaps he smiles no longer. He has had a good deal to do with the making of the Conservative working man, who in all the measures which directly affect himself has found the Radical economist his stiffest opponent. Throughout the manufacturing districts it seems clear that the Conservative condidates, rather more often and distinctly than the Liberal candidates, have supported the measures desired by the workmen. In Lancashire and Yorkshire the old tradition was that the Conservative, and not the Liberal, was the workman's friend, and the Nine Hours Bill and the Masters' Federation have done much to revive the tradition.[56]

The receptivity of the national leadership to the moods and wishes of labour, reflected in the record of the Disraeli administration of 1874–80, was in large measure a product of the close links between the centre and two particularly important groups of regional leaders in Lancashire–Callendar, succeeded by W.H. Houldsworth in Manchester, and the Liverpool centre of Graves, Sandon and R.A. Cross, Disraeli's Home Secretary.[57] This very flexibility has long fostered the myth of Tory Democracy. Tory Democracy in the North of England had more to do with the Toryism of the democracy than any democracy in Toryism. Despite the genuine sympathy of some individuals, the history of Toryism and social reform makes this plain. The national leaders, and the vast majority of the regional ones, were set fair on the course of bourgeois, business Conservatism that led from Palmerston, *via* Disraeli, to the modern party.[58] It was with this kind of party that the labour interest had to deal.

Tory working men were Tory for reasons that usually had little to do with trade union matters. Tory Democracy in the localities was no different from Tory Democracy in the nation. In Blackburn it owed more to the audacity of the brewer George Whiteley – 'the idol of the many-headed' and the 'Lord Randolph of the local arena' as the Liberals dubbed him – than it owed to any real accommodation with labour.[59] W.H. Mills knew the tactical nature of Tory support on labour issues, noting what Tory Democracy amounted to in flag-waving, peer-respecting Stalybridge: ' . . . nor was there any part of the country in which Lord Randolph Churchill's half-defined and nebulous programme of Tory Democracy, which was understood to mean . . . a better time for the masses, always, however, within the established order of Church and State, met with a readier response.'[60]

Though the Conservative party drew handsomely on the support of union activists who were concerned with labour matters, fewer of the Tory than the Liberal-inclined labour interest put these matters to the forefront of their politics. The kind of party the Tory was set limits to the possibilities of any alliance. Yet there were exceptions. For these the dislike of Liberalism was so intense that the past record, and present opportunism, of the Conservative party were sufficient to obscure the business Conservatism that was at the heart of the local party establishments. Despite the difficulties, these men exhibited the same kind of independent-mindedness as marked those inclined to the Liberal alliance.

Even within the monolith of Blackburn Conservatism the dissenting voice could be heard. In the town a small group of self-made men gave leadership to workingmen who believed that the voice of labour should not be drowned in the party political chorus. This maverick strain was prepared to rock the party boat over both the stipendiary magistrate issue and the Hours cause.[61] The Tory populism of some of the south-east towns also transmitted to the present a measure of the independence of former days. Though, in the hands of Tory employers, politicians and clerics, this politics usually led away from the priority of labour's interests, the groups of workingmen who surrounded Stephens in Ashton and Stalybridge and J.M. Cobbett in Oldham fitted even more uneasily into the Conservative party's scheme of things than was the case in Blackburn.[62]

Popular Conservatism in the West Riding was always weaker than in Lancashire, cut off as it was from the sustenance of employer patronage and the presence of a large Irish minority. Nonetheless, the Tory Radical heritage was strong, especially in Huddersfield the centre of Oastler's Factory Acts agitation. In Huddersfield, Bradford and Keighley, though less so in Halifax, Tory-Anglican employers and clerics gave their support to Oastler's cause.[63] In Bradford, at least, this alliance had much to do with the antagonism between early-established Anglican-Tory business, with its landed links, and *nouveau riche* radical Nonconformity. That this juncture of interests was not purely tactical however, and in fact was probably less so than in Lancashire, is suggested by the intimate involvement of some of the Bradford employers with Oastler. Though a number, such as William Rand,[64] managed to combine support for the Factory Acts and Free Trade, the dislike of *laissez faire* was so intense in others as to make them Protectionists.

This small but vocal element was to maintain its support for the Hours cause in the 1850s and 60s, some of the sons of this generation inheriting the popularity of their fathers: M.W. Thompson the brewer, the son of Mathew Thompson the first of the Bradford worsted aristocracy, is a case in point. With the death or departure of the old school (William Wood withdrew from Bradford industry in the 1850s), and the appropriation of Oastler's memory by Liberal-Nonconformist employers,[65] the Factory Acts issue lost much of the urgency of personal experience that had earlier invested it. As in Lancashire, it became part of the Tory electoral mythology: Bradford Conservatism in the 1860s and 70s was more notable for its fear of 'Illingworth, Kell and Co.', and their alliance with organised labour, than for any attempt to reach such an accommodation itself.[66]

Whatever the attitude of the new Tory leadership, the memory of Oastler and of the Factory Acts and anti-Poor Law days was sufficiently close in the third quarter of the century to carry an element of class feeling into party politics. That the room for manoeuvre within the Tory alliance was, however, strictly limited is suggested by the fate of a number of the old radicals who had sided with the Tories. Joshua Hobson and John Hanson of Huddersfield were leading Chartists and lieutenants of Oastler, and Squire Auty a leading Bradford Hours campaigner. Auty blossomed into one of the most fervent Orangemen of his day,[67] and the other two became cogs in the Tory party machine of the the 1860s and 70s. Other Oastlerite Chartists found solace at the political hearth of organised Toryism, the moral hearth of Spiritualism, or else with the eccentric Russophobia of Urquart's Foreign Affairs Committees. John Hanson, an Owenite atheist in his prime, ended his days as an Anglican Sunday school teacher.[68]

Summary

Discussion here opens with a consideration of the relationship between industrial structure and politics in the North. The reality of popular adherence to the two parties, and of the lack of trade union involvement in party politics was paramount. Nonetheless, the potential for a qualified independence in politics was often realised among factory trade union activists, but especially among the non-factory trades, the sectors most effectively insulated from cultural politics. The skilled and craft workers' retention of a measure of autonomy in work was the source both of class independence and party political collaboration. Because of the intermittent and incomplete nature of the threat to work autonomy outside the factory the capacity to combine political and economic forms of organisation was often limited. This broad perspective, arising from the occupational community, is then related to the character of popular radicalism, particularly the Chartist legacy. As essentially an ideology of the artisanate adrift in the new social order of factory industry it is the limits of post-Chartist theory and rhetoric that are stressed. The failure to evolve an economic critique of this order, a failure arising from the social position of the craft worker, meant that radicalism and Liberalism coalesced at sufficiently numerous points to make Liberalism a sufficiently workable vehicle for radicalism. If Liberalism, as the classless union of individuals struggling not against industrial capital but against Privilege, had much in common with popular radicalism, the two were however not the same. It is indeed the contradictions rather than the compromises existing between the two that are most striking.

These considerations are taken up in the body of the chapter, which comprises a detailed account of local politics. The Liberal attachment of the bulk of the labour and radical interest is seen in terms of the political history of Blackburn especially. The quality of uneasy and ambiguous compromise is traced through the post-Chartist years and through the later history of the Liberal alliance. Variations in militance and independence, in part consequent upon the disposition of the party leadership groups in the localities, are traced within Lancashire, and particularly by means of the Yorkshire comparison. The greater resilience of Yorkshire popular radicalism, a product of the very different progress of the factory system in the region, is traced in terms of continuities between the mid-century years and the coming of socialism towards the end of the century. Nonetheless, the face of compromise was apparent here as elsewhere.

Popular Liberalism was not the only seat of independent-mindedness in those years, and this section closes with an account of the powerful current of radicalism in popular Toryism. However, the democracy were Tory for reasons other than democratic participation and social reform. Set fair on the road of Disraelian, bourgeois Conservatism, the party left little room for manoeuvre among radically-minded working men. This, however, did not prevent a number choosing the Tory party as the vehicle for their dislike of the Liberal, *laissez faire* platform. As in the Liberal alliance, radical Conservatism bore something of the freight of independence from the early part of the century to the later.

Notes

1. *Cotton Factory Times*, quoted in P.F. Clarke, *Lancashire and the New Liberalism* (Cambridge 1971), pp. 85, 87; see also *Cotton Factory Times*, 10 July 1885, 12 Jan., 12 Oct. 1900.
2. *Blackburn Times*, 7 Mar. 1868, 18 May, 19 Oct. 1889; *Blackburn Standard*, 17 Oct. 1885 (letters).
3. *Blackburn Times*, 31 Jan., 7 Feb. 1885; *Blackburn Standard*, 14, 21

Mar. 1885 (inc. letters); see also *Bb. Weekly Telegraph*, 5 June 1912; *Bb. Times*, 13 June 1912 and Clarke, *op. cit.* p. 331.

4. *Ashton Reporter*, 2 June 1877, 30 Apr. 1880.
5. Bishopsgate Institute, London: on Preston, Warrington, Macclesfield esp.
6. See above, pp. 290–2.
7. See above, pp. 52–3, 55–8, 61.
8. R.Q. Gray, *The Labour Aristocracy in Victorian Edinburgh* (Oxford 1976); T.R. Tholfsen, *Working Class Radicalism in Mid-Victorian Britain* (1976).
9. See above, pp. 61–3.
10. G. Stedman Jones, 'The limits of proletarian theory in England before 1850'; pre-publication draft.
11. See above, pp. 61–4.
12. *Preston Guardian*, 31 Jan., 7 Feb.; *Preston Herald*, 4, 14 Feb. 1874.
13. For these meetings, *Blackburn Times*, 10, 17, 24 Oct., 14 Nov. 1868.
14. J. Foster, *Class Struggle and the Industrial Revolution* (1974), pp. 205–14, also 238–54.
15. *Blackburn Standard*, 3 July 1852.
16. *Ibid.*, 2, 29, 31 July, 4 Aug. 1847; *Preston Guardian*, 2 June 1847.
17. For 1859 see Blackburn press for April, also *Blackburn Standard*, 4 May; *Blackburn Times*, 19 Mar.; *Blackburn Weekly Telegraph*, 29 Jan.
18. *Blackburn Times*, 7 Jan. 1865 (leader).
19. *Oldham Chronicle*, 14 Jan. 1868 (letters); H.A. Taylor, 'Politics in famine-stricken Preston', *Trans. Lancs. and Cheshire Historical Society*, **107**, 1955; Reform League reports, Macclesfield.
20. See above, pp. 270–2, 284.
21. J. Vincent, *The Formation of the Liberal Party 1857–1868* (1966); T.J. Nossiter, *Influence, Opinion and Political Idioms in Reform England: Case Studies from the North-East 1832–1874* (Hassocks 1975), ch. 9.
22. G. Roby, *The Disease of the Liberal Party* (Manchester, n.d., 1874).
23. W.A. Abram, *Blackburn Characters of a Past Generation* (Blackburn 1894), for Billington and Baker.
24. *Blackburn Times*, 13, 20 Feb. 1875 (obituary).
25. For Abram, *Bb. Standard and Weekly Express*, 5 May 1894; C.C. Miller, *Blackburn Worthies of Yesterday* (Blackburn 1959).
26. P. Joyce, 'Popular Toryism in Lancashire 1860–1890' (Oxford Univ. D. Phil. 1975), pp. 408–9.
27. *Ibid.* pp. 410–12 for further details.
28. *Blackburn Times*, 5, 26 Oct. 1861; 31 Aug. 1864 (Police).
29. The campaign can be followed in the Blackburn press May–Dec. 1885 (esp. letters and leaders); see also *Cotton Factory Times*, Nov. 1885. For an account, Joyce, *op. cit.* pp. 417–20.
30. *Blackburn Standard*, 16 May (leader), 4 Apr., 15 Aug. 1885.
31. See above, p. 293.
32. *Blackburn Standard*, 6 Nov. 1872.

33. See above, pp. 55–6.

34. *Blackburn Times*, 3 Feb. 1874.

35. On Bolton see P.A. Harris, 'Class conflict, the Trade Unions and working-class politics in Bolton, 1875–1896' (Lancaster Univ. M.A. 1971), and G. Evans, 'Social leadership and social control, Bolton 1870–1898' (Lancaster Univ. M.A. 1974). See also J.T. Fielding, *Speech on Foreign Competition in the Cotton Trade* (Bolton 1879), and above, ch. 2, note 59.

36. See above, pp. 62, 72–3.

37. R. Smith, 'A history of the Lancashire cotton industry between the years 1873 and 1896' (Ph.D. Birmingham 1954), p. 610.

38. For Burnley politics and unionism, J. Hill, 'Working-class politics in Lancashire 1885–1906; a regional study in the origins of the Labour Party' (Keele Univ. Ph.D. 1969), and R.P. Cook, 'Political élites and electoral politics in late nineteenth-century Burnley' (Lancaster Univ. M.A. 1974).

39. See above, pp. 63–4.

40. B. Turner, *Short History of the General Union of Textile Workers* (Heckmondwike 1920), chs XI, XVI.

41. W. Cudworth, *Rambles Round Horton* (Bradford 1886), pp. 223–4; D.G. Wright, 'Politics and opinion in 19th-century Bradford, 1832–1880' (Leeds Univ. Ph.D. 1966), ch. 5.

42. *Bradford Review*, 4 Nov. 1868.

43. B. Wilson, *The Struggles of an Old Chartist* (Halifax 1887).

44. E.P. Thompson, 'Homage to Tom Maguire', in A. Briggs and J. Saville, Eds, *Essays in Labour History* (1967).

45. K. Tiller, 'Working-class attitudes and organisation in three industrial towns' (Birmingham Univ. Ph.D. 1975), chs III, IV.

46. *Ibid.* ch. vii, and Thompson, *loc. cit.*, Wilson, *op. cit.*

47. Wright, *op. cit.*; Tiller, *op. cit.*, and R. Harrison, *Before the Socialists* (1965), pp. 282–3.

48. *Bradford Review*, 6, 13, Oct.; 29 Sept. and *Manchester Weekly Examiner and Times*, 29 Sept. 1866 (Manchester); *Bradford Review*, 20, 25, 27 Apr. 1867.

49. See above, pp. 212–3.

50. Tiller, *op. cit.* ch. VII.

51. M. Hurst, 'Liberal versus Liberal: the general election of 1874 in Bradford and Sheffield', *Historical Journal*, 15, 4 (1972). See also ch. 1, n. 138 above.

52. Wright, *op. cit.*, for a full account of Bradford politics in the period.

53. M. Ashraf, *Bradford Trades Council, 1872–1972* (Bradford T.C. 1972).

54. H.J. Hanham, *Elections and Party Management* (1959), pp. 316–17; *Manchester Guardian*, 30 Jan. 1874.

55. *Manchester Courier*, 14 Feb. 1874; *Ashton Standard*, 10 Dec. 1870.

56. F. Harrison, 'The Conservative reaction', *Fortnightly Review*, Mar. 1874, pp. 303–4.

57. For all these figures see E.J. Feuchtwanger, *Disraeli, Democracy and*

the *Tory Party* (Oxford 1968), pp. 9–10, 45–6; and P. Smith, *Disraelian Conservatism and Social Reform* (1967), *passim*.

58. Clarke, *op. cit.* pp. 30–3, 39–45.
59. *Blackburn Weekly Telegraph*, 7 Oct. 1899 (biographical note on Whiteley).
60. W.H. Mills, *Sir Charles Macara, Bart. A study of modern lancashire* (Manchester, 1917), pp. 65–6. On what the Tories usually meant by a labour candidate see the report of the candidacy of Thomas Knowles in Wigan. Knowles was a selfmade local coalowner who set himself up as the 'real' labour candidate against the miners' nominee. Knowles won handsomely at the polls, *Wigan Examiner*, 31 Jan. 1874.
61. For an account, Joyce, *op. cit.* pp. 433–5.
62. See above, p. 255, also Joyce, *op. cit.* pp. 435–8.
63. J.T. Ward, 'Some industrial reformers' and 'Two pioneers of industrial reform', *Bradford Textile Society Journal*, 1962–63; 1964. See also C. Driver, *Tory Radical, The life of Richard Oastler* (New York 1946), and on the Ferrands of Bingley, M. Speight, *Chronicles and Stories* of *Old Binglay* (1898), pp. 231–8.
64. *Bradford Review*, 11 Nov. 1868 (letters).
65. See account of inauguration of Oastler monument in Bradford, *Bradford Observer*, 20 May 1869.
66. Wright, *op. cit.*
67. S. Auty, *The Blue Book of the British Manufacturers; Or the Money-Mongers True Picture* (1848).
68. Ward, 'Some industrial reformers . . . '

EPILOGUE:THE PASSING OF THE OLD ORDER

BECAUSE of their different industrial structures and political histories the transition to class-based Labour party politics, and the outcome of that transition, were to differ considerably between Lancashire and the West Riding. Because each region began this process from differing levels in the formation of mass class consciousness, the nature of the outcome – the character of the new politics – was to reflect the initial difference strongly. To recapitulate our argument: later and less complete mechanisation, and thus the more primitive organisation of industry and of industrial relations, meant that the culture of the factory cut less deeply to the east of the Pennines, employer paternalism and the operatives' answering response less effectively sealing the society off from class antagonism. A major consequence of these differences was that in the West Riding working-class political organisation took precedence over trade union organisation, the Chartist political inheritance continuing as a vital presence in a radical tradition which reached more deeply into popular life than was the case in Lancashire.

Because it grew from a more powerful sense of class, because of the priority of the political tradition, and because of the radical nature of that tradition, the transition to independent labour politics in the West Riding was swifter, smoother and more complete than in Lancashire. The Bradford-born I.L.P. and its precursors capitalised on the primacy of the political over the industrial, fusing the influence of socialism and trade unionism, and so permeating society more deeply with a socialist outlook.[1] Unlike Lancashire, the trade union had not developed as the uniquely representative working-class institution, so that the acceleration of textile unionism and the development of the New Unionism were political events in themselves. In Lancashire the New Unionism was an event of little political significance.

For many among the politically active labour interest in Lancashire the politics of the Labour party were the culmination of the tradition of independence the course of which we have traced. Fully-fledged independence did represent a widening of horizons for the labour interest, but the continuities between the old politics and the new were more striking than the differences: the politics of the Labour party represented little more than a continuation of traditional trade union demands by other means. The centrality of the trade union in Lancashire life meant the Labour party there was the least ideological in the nation. The Lancashire unions, and especially the textile ones, fought to keep socialism out of union affairs and political initiatives, the I.L.P. succeeding in the region only on the union's terms.[2]

The creation of what can be called a labourist consciousness in the mass of Lancashire working people was however a real and momentous change. The transition from cultural to class politics involved a change of consciousness because the old politics had rested on social foundations in which the lives of successive generations had been rooted. Change came when these foundations were shaken: at the close of this discussion the underlying social changes that finally sundered the old order will be considered. For the moment, a recognition that a real change in consciousness did occur involves some further consideration of the nature of late-Victorian and Edwardian politics.

Lancashire has been a principal source of evidence for the contention that Edwardian Liberalism was in no fatal decline and Labour in no irresistible ascent before the First World War.[3] From the Lancashire example Peter Clarke has not been afraid to extrapolate to the nation at large.[4] These claims for progressive Liberalism in important measure rest on the assumption that after 1872 politics was a matter of political consciousness, and of whichever reference group was dominant in a political context. In this argument what happened in the early twentieth century was merely that religion ceded primacy to class, and the advent of class politics involved a political and not a class or structural change. It will be clear that the weight of evidence so far assembled concerning factory workers does not support this contention. Because the old politics was *not* a matter of political consciousness, but of community, deference and influence, the new politics of the Labour party involved a leap from one kind of consciousness to another. The Labour party was in large degree a product of that leap, which was in turn a product of changes which fatally weakened the old social order upon which politics had rested.

However limited was this new political consciousness it represented a basic social change, and a dissatisfaction with and departure from the established parties. Because the hold of the old order was so tenacious the effort needed to break free, and so travel even part of the road taken in the West Riding, was considerable. But limited these new political feelings were.

For the Lancashire rank-and-file, as for the labour activists, the central role history had assigned to the trade union in working-class life meant that labourism represented the horizon of political vision. There were of course exceptions, though these were less numerous than across the Pennines. In the same manner, the legacy of attitudes bequeathed from generations of experience within the social order of the factory was to be a powerful one in years to come. The nature of the past, the primacy of the trade union and the force of the culture of the factory, was to express itself in the political moderation and social conservatism of the twentieth century. The experience of the two regions was to differ then just as it had differed in the previous century.

The Blackburn labour candidacy of 1885 was typical of the widespread stirring of the labour interest from that decade onwards. Most activity was directed towards securing local representation, whether on Town Councils, School Boards, Boards of Guardians, or such as Technical School Committees.[5] This emphasis on the local was important, for it was in the immediate culture that the mass of workers were tied to the old order, and there that the erosion of support for the established parties had to begin. Electoral success was limited in the 1880s and 90s, however, and the Trades Councils who organised most of this activity were stoutly opposed to socialist incursions on their territory. The socialist share of the parliamentary and municipal vote was meagre until after 1900.[6]

The decline of the old order stemmed from gradual social change, and the hold of the past was profound. Socialist campaingers in 1890s Blackburn saw how the working class mistrusted itself, refusing to support its own kind but happy to defer to the gentlemen.[7] The poorer people were the happier they were to be represented by their superiors.[8] As late as 1907 the Blackburn Trades Council could report that though the cotton masters, brewers and lawyers who had ruled Blackburn for so long were frightened and on the run, trade unionists in droves still clung loyally to the 'enemies' of the two main parties.[9] The habits of more than one lifetime were difficult to break: in 1895 a Wigan miner testified to the difficulty of tearing himself free of the loyalty formed 'in the bosom of a Conservative family'.[10] We have seen already how little the cotton workers of the 1880s and 90s thought of independent political representation.[11]

The renewed activism of the labour interest in the 1880s was one beginning of the slow change. It was a renewal and not a new departure. Clarke has described the events of the early years of

the new century which led from 'status' to class politics: the onset
of the legal and economic attack on labour, the disillusion of the
cotton unions, in particular with the Conservative government's
response, and the alliance of the new Labour party with elements
within Liberalism in the cause of social reform.[12] These events
have to be understood in the context of what had preceded them,
and an important part of this context was the long history of
scepticism and distrust that existed between labour and Liberalism. What seems to have happened in the 1880s was a marked
accentuation of this legacy of distrust, and the further separation
of the two sides, a separation that as we have seen was already
considerable in both the ideological and organisational spheres.
It was this further breach that in part explains the renewed
militance of these years. No doubt C.P. Scott and progressive
Manchester Liberalism were beacons of foresight in troubled
seas, but whether the light that was emitted was sufficient to lead
Labour back to Liberalism seems doubtful. Too much had
happened by 1900.

However timid were the labour politics of the 1880s and 90s
they sufficed to scare many middle-class Liberals: so much is
apparent from the size of the 'straight' vote for the sole Liberal
candidate in the Blackburn election of 1885.[13] As one of the labour
candidates' committee explained, by the vote of 1885 would they
know their friends, and it was clear that neither William Briggs
the Liberal ('a subtle and dangerous opponent' as the labour
man called him) nor many of his middle-class supporters were
among them.[14] Independent Labour representation on Blackburn
Town Council encountered Liberal as well as Tory opposition
from the late 1880s onwards.[15] Events were confirming what
had long been felt in the region at large just as in Blackburn.
There is considerable evidence that progressivism was a voice
in the wilderness of the obtuse, parochial and exclusive
local Liberalism of the last two decades of the century. The
work of Challinor on the miners in politics, Hill on organised
labour in general, and Baxendale on Liberal party affairs, shows
how wide was the gulf between Liberalism and Labour by 1900.[16]
The case for the 'New Liberalism' in the West Riding is weaker
still.

As for the Tories, even the rhetoric of Tory Democracy was
becoming inappropriate to the kind of party the Conservative
party had become by the late nineteenth century. Though its
effects can be overestimated, 1886 did accelerate the movement
of property to the Right. The late nineteenth-century Conservative party was incapable of offering an alternative to labour.

As the years passed and the old generations died the party found it increasingly difficult to live off the fat of its traditional support for the Factory Acts cause. In the new political climate of the late nineteenth century denominational and ethnic issues were also losing their old potency.

This climate was profoundly altered by the coming of socialism in the 1880s. It was not that socialist ideology had a direct influence on the labour activists or on the mass of workers in Lancashire. Rather, it can be suggested that the existence of the socialist critique of capitalism acted as a spur to the labour interest, and was in part responsible for the renewed activism of the 1880s. The way in which it did this changed not only the perception of the few, but ultimately that of the many as well. For what socialism did was dare to suggest that the emperor had no clothes. Socialism may most effectively have worked not as a received body of ideology but as a force breaching the understandings of decades on which paternalism and deference had subsisted. It broke in on the employers' mastery of the situation – what was earlier called their 'social hegemony' – penetrating the closed immediacy of the factory community. It was upon this capacity to define the boundaries of people's outlook that paternalism in large measure depended. Distanced, external and appraising, socialism threatened this capacity, shaking the employers' powerful version of a community of interests. Something of this process has already been seen at work in Keighley and in South Wales.[17] As both cause and effect, socialism worked with the grain of powerful social changes opening out and so destroying the old culture of factory neighbourhood community.

In interpreting the relationship between labour process and politics as it concerned those outside the textile factory workforces, the importance of the socialist influence must again be stressed. For it was in a vastly different climate from the 1840s and 50s that what may be termed the second great wave in the consolidation of modern factory industry took effect. The creation of a textile factory proletariat took place in the ideological context of Chartism, a politics whose social critique owed more to the experience of the artisan than to the factory worker. Though the process whereby craft control of the labour process and craft-mindedness became subject to the organisation of modern factory production was of long duration, discontinuous, and greatly different in different trades,[18] the second half of the century was to see the gradual convergence in many trades on an end result of which the employers' renewed attack on the attenuated elements of craft status in engineering is only the most well-known example.[19] This attack was met not in the ideological limbo of Chartism, but in an environment in which the social relations of modern factory production were politically comprehended.

Thus the limitation to trade union as opposed to political ends that had been a consequence of the first great wave of modernity around mid-century was not to be duplicated in the later period, protest taking both political and industrial directions in the Labour party. It is in this framework of interpretation, rather than in that of the 'labour aristocracy', that the rise of the Labour party can perhaps be most fruitfully considered. As with textile workers in the 1830s and 40s, the potential for unifying political and industrial action was uppermost when control over the labour process was most threatened, and the whole way of life of the worker came under attack.[20]

It is in the light of this threat that the role of many craft workers in the formation of the Labour party can be interpreted: before this time, as was suggested,[21] the intermittent and partial nature of the threat led to a corresponding lack of urgency in combining political and industrial forms of organisation and protest, and thus to the history of alliance and compromise with the established parties, especially the Liberals. Of course, it was not only in a changed ideological climate that the new confrontation was played out. Opinion among the governing classes, and especially the employers, was different: paternalism was giving way to a more instrumental attitude to labour. Above all, the character of urban, industrial society, itself giving form to opinion and ideology, had changed profoundly. Industry by the end of the nineteenth century was rapidly approaching its modern condition of advanced centralisation and integration, sophisticated technology and managerial organisation, and increased size. The conditions of modern urban life began to obtain at the same time as those of modern industry. Momentous changes in the nature of the town itself, and in the character of popular culture, were transforming urban society into the rigidly class-based system we know today. These changes in turn led to a new history of labour's conflicts and alliances with the state, with industry and with the parties; a history that begins as this one ends.

Our present concern, however, is with the relationship between social change and the textile industry, the most highly developed of all forms of factory production. In the West Riding the double-engine of trade union advance and socialist influence was fuelled by the experience of economic depression in the 1880s. In Lancashire there was no effect comparable to that in worsted and woollens, and the old order was rooted more firmly. The culture of the factory was not, however, without considerable power in many parts of the West Riding. Some of the changes eroding this effect were described earlier: the increased work loads and falling wages, and the attacks on the status of certain textile trades, all of which economic depression brought about, as well as the declining number of adult males in West Riding textiles towards the end of the century, together being of particular importance.[22]

These developments, as well as the employers' bitter opposition to the renewed union activity of the 1880s, served to unmask claims to paternalism that usually had less foundation than in Lancashire. The Huddersfield strike of 1883 and the epic battle at S.C. Lister's Bradford Manningham mills in 1891 served to cement the relatively novel experience of solidarity among textile workers, and to reveal the indifference of the employers, an indifference that in the Bradford case extended to the Town Council as well.[23] By the mid-1890s the German observer Schulze-Gaevernitz could report that 'the old patriarchal domination' of the big Bradford worsted firms had at last been seen through.[24] Nevertheless, Bradford was never the region writ large. In 1907 the historian of West Riding textiles was clear that the old patriarchal *status quo* was still strong in many of the large and old-established mills, especially in the more rural areas.[25]

The decline of cultural politics in Lancashire involved the waning of the religious influence in popular life. In a town more pious than most, Beatrice Webb noted in the Bacup of the 1880s how the young and active were moving away from both religious adherence in general and the chapel as a centre of society, towards a new secularism that found its social focus in the co-ops.[26] This powerful undercurrent, as yet hardly charted by historians, was of national moment; Thomas Jones, describing the advent of class politics among the South Wales miners, remarked: 'They achieved power with very little preparation and at a time when they were deserting the culture of the Bible and the chapel.'[27] Secularism was only one aspect of a loosening of the bonds that had kept the old communities of the factory and the sect intact.

What was happening around the turn of the century was that the scope of people's lives grew larger, expanding as the towns and cities themselves grew larger. The loosening hold of the employers as the factory towns grew out of their reach has already been noted.[28] Employer housing, and the factory-dominated neighbourhoods, were slowly swamped by the tide of urban growth. As part of this process, developments in transport towards the end of the century were crucial in separating home and workplace,[29] and in liberating factory people from the known and the immediate. Suburbanisation also meant the separation of master and man. Charles Rowley of Ancoats, looking back on the old days from the vantage of 1899, regarded the leading employers of the district as 'chums': 'Our ignorance of each other grows worse as the railway separates us more and more.'[30]

In the factory towns proper, the tram and the bicycle were more important than the railway in this. Considering late nineteenth-century Ashton, W.H. Mills regarded it as still an isolated, inturned community despite the railway: the real change came only with the tram.[31] The bicycle club was perhaps more important than the socialist club in the mental life of Northern working people. Like the tram, the bicycle provided access to the countryside, and a new yardstick by which to measure the experience of urban, industrial life. The growth of bicycle clubs in the 1880s and 90s was but one reflection of a widespread expansion in the range of leisure activities.

The stabilization of urban life in the period gradually brought with it the organisation and commercialisation of the townsman's pursuits. Developments such as the success of the mass circulation popular press, the rise of Blackpool, and the organisation of football and rugby league, worked together with changes in public and private transport to shatter the social mould of a ritual life upon which the communities of work and sect had deeply drawn for sustenance.[32] The old order had flowered in a culture marked by the concrete particular, the local view, and personal participation.[33] The new culture slowly coming into being widened if it did not always deepen men's view of the world: the expansion of leisure competed with and finally triumphed over the hold on people's social life which political and denominational organisation and work had exercised for so long. In this process the expansion of a trade union social life towards the end of the century played its part.[34]

It was however from the work situation that the crucial, precipitating changes emerged. The role of authority in underpinning the old factory order has been considered in detail, especially the role of the Lancashire cotton overlooker.[35] It is especially revealing how, just as with the institution of commission weaving the overlooker became the direct agent of the employer's authority in the 1840s, so around 1900 distinctions between overlookers and production workers were being rapidly blurred as the overlookers moved closer to the attitudes and organisation of the latter. Also in terms of the link between labour process and larger historical change, a concentration on the fundamental importance of the family reveals that while in weaving in the 1840s tenting developed as a means of reconstituting the family unit and paternal authority in the workplace, again around the turn of the century fourloom weavers were dispensing with the services of a tenter as the powerloom became ever more technologically sophisticated.[36] In spinning too industrial reorganisation was altering the old balances: the growth of exlusively female ring and throstle spinning meant that though the absolute number of adult male mule spinners did not diminish, the adult male spinner held a declining proportionate share in the make-up of twentieth-century industry.

These developments were probably felt by women most of all, for it was in the early years of the new century that the acceleration of women's textile trade unionism in the 1880s and 90s combined with their involvement in the agitation for the vote to bring women workers into the mainstream of public life in the North.[37] This disturbance of the *status quo* of paternal family authority, on which so much of the mentality that sustained the wider authority relations of the old industrial order had depended, was of great importance in ushering in the new system of class relations, and the new politics that was based upon it.

Of probably the greatest significance in bringing about the new situation was the loss of the old bond between master and man, and here once again the chronology of change matches failrly closely the chronology of class voting in the parliamentary elections of the first decade of the new century. The coming of the limited company and the decay of private ownership transformed the industrial face of Lancashire. Reactions to the passing of the family company in Bolton have been described,[38] a town where industrial peace and class harmony owed much to Bolton's history as a bastion of private ownership. This regret was widely echoed in the Lancashire of the time. An officer of the Steam Engine Makers mourned the passing of the private firm in the 1890s,[39] and 'the old familiar friends' of the private companies received the blessing of the Iron Moulders' General Secretary.[40] The dislike of an anonymous managerial class was further echoed by the *Wigan Comet*, a labour journal of the 1890s, which spoke of the limiteds as 'a curse to the collier': the old, involved master knew what a fair day's work and a fair day's wage were.[41]

It was however in cotton that the greatest change occurred. One contemporary observer was a little precipitate in signalling the decline of the cottonocracy in 1892:

Great capitalists there yet are in the business, but they are few, become fewer every year; and such as remain, do so, they avow, not because they can make it pay, but from attachment to concerns founded by their fathers and grandfathers, or from a sense of obligation to the corps of working people whom they have employed so long, and who still trustfully look to them for work to earn the means of living.[42]

Nonetheless, the cotton industry was indeed transformed between about 1870 and the coming of the First World War. Though the process was slower in weaving than in spinning, the coming of the limiteds in the weaving North was greatly accelerated in the first decade of the twentieth century.[43] Above all in Oldham, but also in Rochdale and Darwen, the limiteds were well established in the 1880s. By 1900 in Stockport, Bury, Ashton and Staly-bridge the proportion of limiteds to the total size of local industry was around 50 per cent. The proportion in smaller centres like Heywood and Leigh was similar, and the later Bolton increase ran from around 25 per cent to 40 per cent between 1900 and 1910. The limiteds broke the back of personal patternalism, for it was the family dimension to the culture of the factory that was its primary source of stability. In place of this the limiteds brought in their train innovations of technology and work method that pointed forward to the rationality of industrial organisation in the twentieth century. The history of industrial relations in the limiteds was a history of bitterness and suspicion.[44]

The sense of industrial commitment in the private company was part of a wider sense of obligation to the town and to the workpeople. With the passing of the family firm, and especially in the years leading up to the First World War, the great employers bowed out of local life to reap the fruits of their labour in the sunnier South. With their passing ended a distinct culture, and a unique chapter in the history of industrial civilisation. Their presence had left an indelible mark on the history of class in England.

Afterword

This look at the decline and fall of the old industrial and political order draws together many of the strands interwoven in the previous narrative and analysis. The first area in which late nineteenth-century change is considered is the political, and questions raised in the previous chapter are viewed in a wider social setting, as well as related to the historiography of the rise of Labour and the decline of Liberalism. Differences in the industrial structure of the West Riding meant that the transition to a fully-independent class politics was quicker and more complete than in Lancashire. Nonetheless, this shift did occur in Lancashire, though in order for it to happen a profound change in the social awareness of the mass of Lancashire labour had to be brought about.

A recognition that social change did produce this new awareness must serve to qualify the notion that progressive Liberalism could have provided the medium for labour's needs before the First World War, a notion that in turn depends upon the contention that politics before this time were a matter merely of political consciousness. They were not, but in becoming this under the influence of late nineteenth-century changes in the nature of society, it is clear that the Labour party – itself the very product of these changes – was the natural resort of the new class-directed political awareness. In breaking out of the old order the Lancashire proletariat broke with the trappings of that order. The Liberal party was one of these trappings.

In terms of articulate labour politics and politicians, the breach between Liberalism and labour may have reached the proportions of a disaster as early as the 1880s. This breach represented but an accentuation of the legacy of distrust that had always characterised the Liberal alliance. On the other side of the party divide, the Tory party was rapidly losing what hold on labour it had as the century neared its end. These changes at the political level were powerfully accelerated by the coming of socialism, which acted as a spur to the labour interest from the 1880s onwards. Its primary, indirect effect lay, however, in breaching the mythology of paternalism and penetrating the closed worlds upon which employer hegemony had so long subsisted.

In considering the non-factory trades, the years around 1900 seem to have seen the culmination of the long, slow and discontinuous advance of mechanisation, an advance now coming to an issue in the spread of the factory system to trades that had hitherto been little touched by it. Proletarianisation, in the sense of the loss of still-powerful residues of control over the labour process, at this time took place not in the context of the ideological limbo of Chartism but in an environment in which the economic and social relations of capitalist industry were comprehended by the socialist economic critique. Political and industrial forms of organisation were now united in the Labour

342 *Work, Society and Politics*

party. But for craft and skilled workers, as well as for factory ones, it was not only, or mainly, the political or ideological climate that had changed. Both industry and the town were by the end of the nineteenth century rapidly taking on their modern forms, forms marked by the mutual ignorance and antagonism of the classes that we know today.

It is to a consideration of these momentous changes that we turn at the close of this work. Again, the discussion of change in the factory districts focuses many of the issues previously raised. The changing ecology of the factory town, and the increased degree of organisation and commercialisation in popular culture combined to enlarge the scope of people's lives, and break the hold of the old communities of work, religion and politics on their daily affairs. The waning of religion was both cause and effect in this transformation. The major developments in this liberation from the confines of the local took place in the sphere of work. The hold of authority in work was loosened, and the *status quo* of patriarchy in work was disrupted. The coming of the limited company was of fundamental importance. It sundered the old bond of master and man, replacing the paternalism of the private, family firm with a new anonymity and rationality in work organisation and method. The passing of the private firm meant the end of the local involvement of the patrician employers, and with it the end of the old order.

Notes

1. E.P. Thompson, 'Homage to Tom Maguire', in A. Briggs and J. Saville, eds, *Essays in Labour History* (1967).
2. J. Hill, 'Working-class politics in Lancashire 1885–1906; a regional study in the origins of the Labour Party' (Keele Univ. Ph.D. 1969).
3. P.F. Clarke, *Lancashire and the New Liberalism* (Cambridge 1971).
4. P.F. Clarke, 'Electoral sociology of Modern Britain', *History*, **52**, 189, Feb. 1972.
5. For T.U. and Trades Council political activity in late nineteenth-century Blackburn, G.N. Trodd, 'The local élite of Blackburn and the response of the working class to its social control, 1880–1900' (Lancaster Univ. M.A. 1974).
6. Hill, *op. cit.*
7. *Blackburn Times*, 13 May 1893, 23 Jan. 1897.
8. *Blackburn Weekly Telegraph*, 6 Oct. 1900.
9. Blackburn Trades Council Annual Report, 1907.
10. *Wigan Observer*, 6 July 1895.
11. See above, pp. 311–2.
12. Clarke, *Lancashire and the New Liberalism*, chs 4, 12.

13. See above, pp. 318–9.
14. *Cotton Factory Times*, Nov. 1885.
15. *Blackburn Times*, 26 Oct., 2 Nov. 1889. See obituary of Thomas Fenton, *ibid.*, 7 Nov. 1891.
16. R. Challinor, *The Lancashire and Cheshire Miners* (Newcastle upon Tyne 1972); Hill, *op. cit.* ; J.D. Baxendale, 'The Liberal Party in England with special reference to the North West, 1886–1900' (Oxford Univ. D. Phil. 1971).
17. See above, pp. 164–5, 228–30.
18. See above, pp. 52, 56, 60–2.
19. For the attack on the engineers' status see J.B. Jeffereys, *The Story of the Engineers* (1946), Pt III, ch. VI ; J. Swift of the A.S.E., 'Engineering' in F.W. Galton, ed., *Workers on their Industries* (1893); for the situation in Lancashire, C.S. Davies, *North Country Bred* (1963), pp. 103–4. For the widespread nature of the late nineteenth-century attack on craft status, see R.Q. Gray, *The Labour Aristocracy in Victorian Edinburgh* (Oxford 1976), ch. 9.
20. See above, pp. 55–6, 61–4.
21. See above, pp. 312–4.
22. See above, pp. 76–7.
23. Thompson, *loc. cit.* ; K. Laybourne, 'The attitude of the Yorkshire trade unions to the economic and social problems of the Great Depression, 1873–1896' (Lancaster Univ. Ph. D. 1972).
24. G. Von Schulze-Gaevernitz, *The Cotton Trade in England and on the Continent* (1895), pp. 206–7.
25. J.H. Clapham, *The Woollen and Worsted Industries* (1907), p. 207.
26. B. Webb, *My Apprenticeship* (Penguin edns, 1971), pp. 177, 180.
27. T. Jones, 'The life of the people' in *Fifty Years. Memories and Contrasts 1882–1932* (1932), p. 185, foreword by G.M. Trevelyan.
28. See above, p. 122.
29. See above, pp. 118–9.
30. G. Rowley, *Fifty Years of Ancoats, Loss and Gain* (1899), pp. 11–12. On the life of the working-class Manchester suburb in the 1890s, itself a kind of liberation, see Davies, *op. cit.* pp. 97–111, 124–5.
31. W.H. Mills, *Grey Pastures* (1924), p. 56.
32. R. Williams, *Communications* (1966), ch. 2.
33. See above, pp. 272–6, and ch. 5.
34. See above, p. 292.
35. See above, pp. 100–1.
36. See above, p. 58.
37. See above, pp. 115–16.
38. See above, p. 69.
39. *P.P.* 1893–4, XXXII (6894–vii), p. 220.
40. H.J. Fyrth and H.J. Collins, *The Foundry Workers* (Manchester, 1958), p. 41.
41. Challinor, *op. cit.* pp. 263–4; for the wider effects of the changeover to anonymous capital and management see W.L. Werner and

J. Low, *The Social System of the Modern Factory* (Yankee City Series no. 4, 1947).

42. W.A. Abram, 'The prospective decline of Lancashire', *Blackwood's Magazine*, **152**, July 1892, p. 5.

43. Cf. Clarke, *Lancashire and the New Liberalism*, pp. 78–9: Clarke overestimates the degree of change in the North, working as he does from the number of firms taken from local directories. The present figures are based on spindle/loom figures taken from *Worrall's Cotton Spinners' and Manufacturers' and Engineers' and Machine Makers' Advertiser* (Oldham), published annually.

44. On industrial relations in the Oldham of the 80s, the worst in all Lancashire, see R. Smith, 'A history of the Lancashire cotton industry between the years 1873 and 1896 (Birmingham Univ. Ph.D. 1954), ch. VII, and pp. 137, 414.

Firm amalgamation around the turn of the century also added to the loss of personal interest and control; see P.L. Payne, 'The emergence of the large-scale company in Great Britain 1870–1914', *Economic History Review*, **20**, no. 3, 1967.

Appendix: Occupational composition of the Bury electorate, 1868[1]

(A) Cotton	Liberal	Conservative
supervisory	35	52
(inc. overlookers	26	43
managers	3	7)
'skilled'[2]	94	112
(inc. spinners	27	36
sizers	13	7
cotton and loom jobbers	8	12
warehousemen	6	16)
'unskilled'	75	63
(inc. weavers	46	32
labourers	3	10
'cotton operatives'	12	7)

(B) Engineering and Iron	Liberal	Conservative
supervisory[3]	9	7
(inc. foremen	6	2)
'skilled'[4]	150	95
(inc. moulders	43	16
grinders	8	0
fitters	44	23)
'unskilled'[5]	128	60
(inc. labourers	53	25
semi-skilled: iron planers, slotters, drillers, dressers, stretchers, twiners, sliders, machinists, turners	59	23)
others[6]	66	47
(makers: roller, spindle, fly, shuttle, tools, bolts, boilers, machine; also iron founders	30	22

345

millwrights	11	8
mechanics	25	27)

(C) *Wool*	*Liberal*	*Conservative*
(no difference between grades, sorters, spinners or weavers	109	72)

(D) *Other factory workers*	*Liberal*	*Conservative*
paper	12	4
bleaching	9	14
dyeing	20	5
(E) *Crafts and skilled workers*[7]	339	227

(inc. building workers	87	71
blacksmiths	25	16
shoe and clogmakers	51	20
tailors	33	10
hatters	20	6
small masters[8]	58	46)
(F) *Retailers and dealers*	219	135

(inc. pubs	10	14
beerhouses	22	14
grocers	54	20
butchers	10	14
drapers and travelling drapers	25	13)
(G) *Labourers*	237	192

inc. Irish	36		5
agricultural labs.	30	(7 Irish)	16
railway labs.	22		15
carters	25		29
'labourers'	51	(9 Irish)	33
'outdoor labourers'	15		13
gardeners, coachmen, servants	10		23
colliers	15		15)
(H) *Others*	86		99

(inc. white collar[9]	40	30
farmers (mostly small)	7	14
respectables and employers	39	55)

Notes

The election result was as follows: R.N. Philips (Lib.) 2830
Viscount Chelsea (Cons.) 2264

1. From 1868 Bury pollbook, 1871 census enumerators' schedules; the individual polling district vote given in *Bury Times*, 21 Nov. 1868.

2. In addition to Blackburn trades includes a small number of calico printers and dressers, cotton finishers, makers-up, and fustian workers.

3. Includes book-keepers, managers, draughtsmen.

4. Includes 'engineers', glazers, pattern makers, core makers, mechanic turners, brass finishers, blacksmiths, painters, joiners, engine drivers.

5. Includes strikers, tenters, firemen.

6. Difficult to classify: many would have been small masters or journeymen. There is no indication in the census if they were factory-based.

7. Includes tinplateworkers, brushmakers, ropemakers, curriers, cabinet makers, wheelwrights, saddlers, sawyers, cordwainers, hairdressers, coopers, workers in leather, watchmaking, etc.

8. Includes master cloggers (7 L.–0C.), hat manufacturers (4 L.–1 C.), also masters-masons, bricksetters, cabinet-makers, plasterers, tailors, painters, etc. ; and cotton-waste dealers (10 C. – 9 L.), and contractors.

9. Includes municipal workers, travellers, surveyors, miscellaneous clerks, schoolmasters, sextons, unspecified managers.

INDEX

348